Contents

QA
76.575
G 528
2009
WEB

Accelerated Silverlight 3

Ashish Ghoda and Jeff Scanlon

Apress®

Accelerated Silverlight 3

Copyright © 2009 by Ashish Ghoda and Jeff Scanlon

All rights reserved. No part of this work may be reproduced or transmitted in any form or by any means, electronic or mechanical, including photocopying, recording, or by any information storage or retrieval system, without the prior written permission of the copyright owner and the publisher.

ISBN-13 (pbk): 978-1-4302-2429-7

ISBN-13 (electronic): 978-1-4302-2430-3

Printed and bound in the United States of America 9 8 7 6 5 4 3 2 1

Trademarked names may appear in this book. Rather than use a trademark symbol with every occurrence of a trademarked name, we use the names only in an editorial fashion and to the benefit of the trademark owner, with no intention of infringement of the trademark.

Lead Editor: Jonathan Hassell
Technical Reviewers: Stefan Turalski, James McFetridge
Editorial Board: Clay Andres, Steve Anglin, Mark Beckner, Ewan Buckingham, Tony Campbell, Gary Cornell, Jonathan Gennick, Michelle Lowman, Matthew Moodie, Jeffrey Pepper, Frank Pohlmann, Ben Renow-Clarke, Dominic Shakeshaft, Matt Wade, Tom Welsh
Project Manager: Richard Dal Porto
Copy Editors: Kim Wimpsett, April Eddy
Associate Production Director: Kari Brooks-Copony
Production Editor: Kelly Winquist
Compositor: Susan Glinert Stevens
Proofreader: Lisa Hamilton
Indexer: BIM Indexing & Proofreading Services
Artist: Kinetic Publishing Services, LLC
Cover Designer: Kurt Krames
Manufacturing Director: Tom Debolski

Distributed to the book trade worldwide by Springer-Verlag New York, Inc., 233 Spring Street, 6th Floor, New York, NY 10013. Phone 1-800-SPRINGER, fax 201-348-4505, e-mail orders-ny@springer-sbm.com, or visit http://www.springeronline.com.

For information on translations, please contact Apress directly at 2855 Telegraph Avenue, Suite 600, Berkeley, CA 94705. Phone 510-549-5930, fax 510-549-5939, e-mail info@apress.com, or visit http://www.apress.com.

Apress and friends of ED books may be purchased in bulk for academic, corporate, or promotional use. eBook versions and licenses are also available for most titles. For more information, reference our Special Bulk Sales–eBook Licensing web page at http://www.apress.com/info/bulksales.

The information in this book is distributed on an "as is" basis, without warranty. Although every precaution has been taken in the preparation of this work, neither the author(s) nor Apress shall have any liability to any person or entity with respect to any loss or damage caused or alleged to be caused directly or indirectly by the information contained in this work.

The source code for this book is available to readers at http://www.apress.com.

I dedicate this book to my grandparents (Nayansukhray and Kumud Ghoda, Mahavir and Sarla Majmudar), parents (Jitendra and Varsha Ghoda), sister (Kruti Vaishnav), and lovely family (Pratixa, Gyan, and Anand Ghoda) whose blessings, sacrifice, continuous support, and encouragement enabled me to achieve this dream.
—Ashish Ghoda

Contents at a Glance

About the Authors

ASHISH GHODA is a customer-focused and business values–driven senior IT executive with more than 12 years of IT leadership, technical and financial management, and enterprise architect experience.

He is the founder and president of Technology Opinion LLC, a unique collaborative venture striving for strategic excellence by providing partnerships with different organizations and the IT community. He is also the associate director at a Big Four accounting firm.

Ashish actively contributes to the IT community. He provides strategic advice to achieve IT goals and to define the product and technology road maps of organizations, he provides training in and speaks on IT leadership areas and Microsoft technologies, and he architects and develops customer-centric software services. In addition, he is the author of *Pro Silverlight for the Enterprise* from Apress and several articles on Microsoft technologies and IT management areas for *MSDN Magazine*, TechnologyOpinion.com, and advice.cio.com. He is also the technical reviewer of *Silverlight 3 Recipes*, a forthcoming book from Apress. Ashish reviews research papers submitted for the Innovative and Collaborative Business and E-Business Tracks of the European Conference on Information System (ECIS).

He has a master's degree in information systems from the New Jersey Institute of Technology (NJIT) and has the Microsoft Certified Professional (MCP) and Microsoft Certified Application Developer (MCAD) certifications in .NET.

JEFF SCANLON is an independent Microsoft consultant with extensive experience developing software using a variety of technologies. He designs and implements software across all layers with a focus on web-based applications. Jeff has led developer training sessions on software engineering practices and introductions to new technologies at nearly every company he has worked. His current work includes prototyping applications using technologies such as Silverlight, Windows Communication Foundation, and ASP.NET. His writing includes *Professional Java JDK 6 Edition* and its updated edition and he has written articles on .NET in *Software Development* magazine. He has several Microsoft certifications and a bachelor's degree in computer science.

About the Technical Reviewers

JAMES MCFETRIDGE is a Microsoft Certified Solutions Developer (MCSD) .NET and a software development professional with more than 12 years of application development experience. He has a bachelor's degree in computer engineering from Penn State, and he lives and works in the Raleigh, North Carolina, area as a C# software developer and information technology consultant. Jim actively participates in the events of the Triangle .NET User Group (www.trinug.org) and enjoys various outdoor activities. Currently he is working on additional certifications for Microsoft .NET.

STEFAN TURALSKI is a nice chap who is capable of performing both magic and trivial things, with a little help of code, libraries, tools, APIs, servers, and the like.

Wearing many hats, he has experienced almost all aspects of the software life cycle and is especially skilled in business analysis, design, implementation, testing, and QA, as well as team management.

His main area of interest is quite wide and could be summarized as emerging technologies, with a recent focus on RIAs (Silverlight, AIR), cloud computing, functional programming, and software engineering at large.

Before he realized that he enjoys criticizing other people's work more, Stefan published several technical articles, mainly about .NET technology, SOA, software engineering, and mobile development.

For the past 10+ years, he has been building solutions ranging from Perl scripts to integrations of SQLite to web sites to highly scalable .NET and COM+ enterprise-class systems.

Feel free contact him at stefan.turalski@gmail.com.

Acknowledgments

I would like to thank Jonathan Hassell and Ewan Buckingham—chief editors of Apress—for giving me another opportunity and remaining confidant that I could finish one of the first few books on Silverlight 3 at a highly accelerated speed.

The schedule was really aggressive, and positive support from Richard Dal Porto (project manager), Stefan Turalski and James McFetridge (technical reviewers), April Eddy and Kim Wimpsett (copy editors), Kelly Winquist (production editor), and other Apress team members enabled me to achieve this task successfully. They deserve special thanks for their through review and quick turnarounds, which helped me to produce quality content in the given challenging timeline.

Jeff Scanlon, coauthor, did the fantastic job of providing a sound foundation with the first edition, *Accelerated Silverlight 2*.

Jay Nanavaty, a senior consultant of Technology Opinion, dedicated long hours to helping me develop many examples of this book. Without his excellent work and thorough knowledge of Silverlight and .NET, it would have been challenging for me to finish the book.

With blessings from God and encouragement from my grandparents, parents, and in-laws, I was able to accomplish this task successfully. My wife, Pratixa, and two little sons, Gyan (5 years old) and Anand (1 year old), have continued their positive support to finish my second consecutive book. I thank my family for their unbelievable cooperation and encouragement and for keeping their faith in me during this aggressive endeavor.

Ashish Ghoda
Founder and President, Technology Opinion LLC

Introduction

Microsoft Silverlight is a cross-browser, cross-platform, and cross-device plug-in for delivering the next generation of .NET-based media experiences and rich Internet applications (RIAs) for the Web.

Silverlight 3 features many eye-catching enhancements to develop enterprise-level and high-performing RIAs within a secured environment. The following are some of them:

- Enriched media integration capabilities including live HD (720p+) streaming capabilities using IIS Media Services, true HD playback in full-screen using GPU acceleration, support for H.264/Advanced Audit Coding (AAC) audio, and enhanced content protection

- Enhanced visual effects capabilities with support for perspective 3D graphics, pixel shader effects, bitmap caching, a new bitmap API, and styling and templates

- Enterprise-level RIA development capabilities such as the Out of Browser feature, the navigation framework, deep linking, search engine optimization, the Save File dialog box, and the Child Window template

- Improved data integration capabilities such as element-to-element binding and data validation, an enhanced DataGrid control, and new controls such as DataForm and DataPager

- Extended networking capabilities such as cross-application communication and support for binary XML for better data communication

This book covers all aspects of Silverlight 3 with numerous examples providing you hands-on experience. Starting by covering Silverlight and its different versions, we will provide a detailed understanding of WPF, XAML, styling and templates, and Silverlight user controls (including new controls introduced in Silverlight 3) so you can build the effective presentation layer for your Silverlight applications. We will also cover the data integration capabilities and related user controls to show how to integrate with the different data sources using WCF services and LINQ. Seamless media integration and animations capabilities are key enhancements in Silverlight 3, so we will dive into the details of those capabilities. In addition, we will cover some advanced features such as the navigation framework, Out of Browser functionality, and the networking and security capabilities of Silverlight 3. This book will also give you details on how to unit test Silverlight applications and the best way to build and deploy these applications.

Accelerated Silverlight 3 aims to get you up to speed as quickly and efficiently as possible on Silverlight 3, and we hope you find what you're looking for within its pages.

Who This Book Is For

This book is for IT professionals and anyone in the .NET developer community who wants to get accelerated training on developing RIAs using Silverlight 3. The goal of this book is to get you up to speed on Silverlight as quickly and efficiently as possible.

This book assumes you have a reasonable degree of familiarity with .NET, such as understanding what assemblies are and how to develop applications on the .NET platform using C#. Although Windows Presentation Foundation (WPF) also uses XAML (which you'll learn about in Chapter 2, in case you're unfamiliar with this term), you do not need to be familiar with WPF.

How This Book Is Structured

This book covers a significant amount of Silverlight, from the new Extensible Application Markup Language (XAML) support to creating user interfaces to demonstrating enterprise-level capabilities for building real-world RIAs. The following sections more specifically detail what is covered in each chapter.

Chapter 1, "Introducing Silverlight"

This chapter discusses some of the background of cross-platform applications to help you understand where Silverlight fits into the overall technological picture. It also compares different versions of Silverlight and highlights key enhancements of Silverlight 3. This chapter concludes by showing how to use Visual Studio 2008 and Expression Blend to create your first Silverlight application using Silverlight 3.

Chapter 2, "Getting to Know XAML"

XAML is a declarative language at the base of WPF. It provides an easy way to create and configure object hierarchies and relationships in markup. This chapter introduces important concepts, such as markup extensions to support handling resources and data binding, type converters for interpreting property values, dependency properties, attached properties, events, code-behind managed code integration, and other important aspects of XAML and Silverlight.

Chapter 3, "Creating User Interfaces"

Silverlight provides important controls for organizing user interfaces, displaying information, and receiving user input. After discussing the important aspects of the Silverlight object hierarchy, we get right into creating user interfaces. The major layout controls are explored—the Canvas for absolute positioning, the StackPanel for organizing controls horizontally or vertically, and the Grid for placing controls in HTML-like tables. Next, all the standard user interface controls are covered, including those for creating text entry boxes, check boxes, radio buttons, content controls, password boxes, and list boxes. The chapter ends with the introduction of the navigation framework of Silverlight.

Chapter 4, "Network Communication"

An online application that does not talk to other systems (or even back to its hosting server) is a rare case, so Silverlight must provide ways to interact with other systems. The three main communication mechanisms Silverlight provides are services (via WCF), direct HTTP communication (via the `HttpWebRequest` and `WebClient` classes), and raw communication using sockets. In addition to the significant changes to WCF, including improved security and a binary binding, Silverlight 3 introduces the networking and offline APIs and cross-application communication. This chapter covers all these networking capabilities for Silverlight 3 applications.

Chapter 5, "Working with Data"

Communicating over the network is important for getting data, but once you have data, what do you do with it? This chapter details how to connect data from a data source to the user interface using Silverlight controls such as the DataGrid, DataForm, and DataPager and the data binding architecture. Data can be stored in a collection in the code-behind or in XML. Silverlight provides the ability to use LINQ expressions (introduced in .NET 3.5—but don't worry, Silverlight is still completely separate from the .NET Framework) in the code-behind; it also supports both reading and writing XML files and serialization to and from objects. This chapter concludes with a look at how to save state on the client, mainly through the use of isolated storage—a private, secure area on disk for Silverlight applications.

Chapter 6, "Working with Media"

Silverlight makes it easy to create rich user interfaces involving images, audio, and video. This chapter details how to access and utilize these media elements. Silverlight can be used to create sites that manage video such as YouTube (`www.youtube.com/`) or sophisticated image-browsing sites such as Hard Rock Memorabilia (`http://memorabilia.hardrock.com/`). Silverlight 3 introduces more capabilities to handle images with the use of the bitmap API and to develop high-performing applications by enabling GPU acceleration and bitmap caching for Silverlight applications. The chapter also covers the enhanced media management capabilities Silverlight offers by supporting new media formats such as H.264/Advanced Audit Coding (AAC)/MP4. Silverlight 3 introduces the new RAW audio/video pipeline that supports third-party codecs and enables live, on-demand, high-quality, and high-definition media streaming in a secure environment. This chapter details the various media controls, including Image, MediaElement, and MultiScaleImage (also known as Deep Zoom, which is the MultiScaleImage control used to create the Hard Rock Memorabilia site). The chapter concludes with a look at Silverlight Streaming, a service Microsoft provides to host both Silverlight applications and videos for streaming.

Chapter 7, "Extending the User Interface"

Although Chapter 2 detailed many controls useful for building Silverlight applications, it showed only one aspect of Silverlight's support for building user interfaces. This chapter returns to building user interfaces. Silverlight has support for 2D graphics, such as lines, ellipses, and even complex geometrical shapes. Almost anything that can be drawn on a user interface (such as 2D graphics or controls) can be transformed (for example, rotated or scaled down). These transforms are discussed along with performing custom transformations by using a transformation matrix. Silverlight 3 also supports 3D effects using perspective transforms. Along with the new pixel shader capabilities, we will look at the various brushes provided by Silverlight; brushes are useful for painting colors, images, video, or even color gradients onto the foregrounds or backgrounds of elements in a user interface. Finally, we will conclude this chapter with some new user controls introduced in Silverlight 3 such as the Save File dialog box, the Accordion control, and the Child Window template to develop extended user interface.

Chapter 8, "Styling and Templating"

Silverlight provides the ability to centrally manage styles that control the appearance of elements on a user interface, such as those for font face, font size, and color. It also supports the ability to completely replace the visual representation of controls using control templates. Both of these mechanisms are explored in this chapter.

Chapter 9, "Animation"

Animation provides the ability to change the properties of user interface elements over time. This chapter discusses the support Silverlight provides for animation (along with the newly introduced 3D animation capability), beginning with an explanation of a timeline and continuing with an exploration of storyboards and the different ways to animate elements of a user interface. The chapter concludes with a look at animating using Expression Blend, an invaluable tool for easily developing and previewing animation.

Chapter 10, "Dynamic Languages and the Browser"

A big aspect of Silverlight that is currently not officially available in .NET on Windows is the Dynamic Language Runtime (DLR). This enables the smooth execution of dynamic languages such as IronPython, IronRuby, and Managed JScript within Silverlight. After showing how to utilize dynamic languages in Silverlight applications with the use of Silverlight Dynamic Language (SDL) SDK, this chapter switches gears to the support Silverlight provides for interoperating with the browser. Silverlight provides the ability to send and receive data from the hosting browser, including invoking JScript and accessing the DOM.

Chapter 11, "Security"

Silverlight can interact with the host operating system; for example, isolated storage ultimately writes files to disk. This direct access is impossible from your application code because all application code is considered unsafe. This forms the core of the security model for executable code in Silverlight. Beyond the security of executable code, there are other aspects at an application level that contribute to sound security in Silverlight applications. These aspects include using authentication/authorization to control access, communicating over SSL, and using cryptography to protect sensitive data. This chapter explores all of these, along with how to design a Silverlight application with security in mind.

Chapter 12, "Testing and Debugging"

Applications must be tested to prove, as best as possible, that they are bug free and work as designed. This chapter primarily focuses on unit testing—testing Silverlight applications from the perspective of a developer using the Silverlight unit testing framework. A strong set of unit tests can prove a useful part of the build and verification process. When bugs are found, during development or from testing, the root cause must be discovered. This is where debugging proves useful. Debugging is more than simply attaching a debugger to a Silverlight application and tracing execution. Both proactive and reactive debugging measures are discussed.

Chapter 13, "Packaging and Deploying Silverlight Applications"

Silverlight is a client-side technology. A Silverlight application can be placed on any web server (e.g., IIS, Apache, and so on); however, there are some benefits to deploying Silverlight on IIS 7 (primarily in the handling of video). This chapter will discuss how Silverlight applications are packaged (with the in-package and on-demand files), how applications are deployed on web servers, how applications can be hosted by embedding in HTML/ASPX pages, and also what is necessary to support building Silverlight applications using MSBuild.

Chapter 14, "Advanced Silverlight 3 Features"

Key features missing in Silverlight 2 RIAs were the capabilities of deep linking and search engine optimization. Now with Silverlight 3, you can have browser history enabled to your application. In addition to these features, Silverlight 3 has introduced enterprise-level application development capabilities by introducing the navigation framework, which can help organizations implement reusability and standardization features as well as integrate with .NET RIA services to develop service-oriented applications in an agile mode. This chapter also covers two new advanced features. The first is the Out of Browser functionality, with which you can develop a truly rich Internet application that supports connected and disconnected modes and the integration between them. The second is the client-side local messaging capabilities across the Silverlight applications within the page, across browser tabs, across browsers, and in Out of Browser mode in a same-domain or cross-domain deployment scenario.

Chapter 15, "Threading in Silverlight"

One of the most frustrating things for users of an application is a frozen user interface. Long-running operations should never occur on the user interface thread, and you should be well aware of this if you've done any Windows Forms development. Silverlight supports several techniques to improve responsiveness of user interfaces, including asynchronous communication and threading. The final chapter of the book explores techniques to create responsive user interfaces by looking at both explicit and implicit ways of leveraging multiple threads. Silverlight also provides several timer-related classes useful for certain periodic tasks, such as providing a time signature for a video that is playing.

Prerequisites

This book provides many hands-on examples to give you Silverlight 3 application development practice. You can develop the examples using the following tools:

- Microsoft .NET Framework 3.5 SP1

- Microsoft Silverlight 3

- Microsoft Visual Studio 2008 SP1

- Microsoft Silverlight 3 Tools for Visual Studio 2008 SP1

- Silverlight Toolkit

- Microsoft Expression Blend 3

- Microsoft Deep Zoom Composer

- Silverlight Dynamic Languages SDK

- Silverlight Unit Testing Framework

Downloading the Code

The source code for this book is available to readers at www.apress.com by clicking the Source Code link on this book's page. Please feel free to visit the Apress web site and download all the code there. You can also check for errata and find related titles from Apress.

Contacting the Authors

Microsoft kept the excitement by delivering more promising features with the Silverlight 3 version. I really enjoyed writing this book and actually learned a lot.

I appreciate your continuous comments and feedback. You can send them to me, as well as any questions, via e-mail at AskAshish@TechnologyOpinion.com.

You can also visit my web sites, http://www.TechnologyOpinion.com and http://www.SilverlightStuff.net, to access my latest articles, instructor-led online training information, my blog, and news on different IT areas including Silverlight.

CHAPTER 1

■ ■ ■

Introducing Silverlight

Silverlight is a Microsoft .NET Framework–based technology platform that enables IT professionals to develop next-generation, media-rich, interactive Rich Internet Applications (RIAs) in an agile and cost-effective way, providing maximum customer satisfaction and helping organizations return the maximum Return on Investment (ROI). Silverlight provides a platform to develop cross-browser, cross-platform, and cross-device RIAs. All versions of Silverlight are a subset of Windows Presentation Foundation (WPF), providing a strong, abstracted presentation framework for defining interactive user interfaces that can be integrated seamlessly with media (audio, video, and images). At the core of the Silverlight presentation framework is the XML-based declarative Extensible Application Markup Language (XAML, pronounced *zammel*). XAML enables designers and developers to define externalized and decoupled user interfaces and related style sheets. Thus, Silverlight is a natural extension to technologies that are already in existence, specifically .NET and WPF. In other words, if you strip out the parts of .NET that just aren't needed or that don't easily work across platforms (such as interoperating with COM), add in an implementation of XAML that is the core of WPF, and mix in a few new things such as browser interoperability and the ability to execute dynamic languages such as Python (IronPython, as the .NET implementation is called), you are in the world of Silverlight—a platform-agnostic, next-generation, web development platform.

Developing applications that work on multiple platforms is a difficult problem. What constitutes a platform is an important question, and for the purposes of this book, it is any unique host environment that provides an execution environment for code. If you give it some thought, it is easy to categorize Windows XP, Windows Vista, OS X, and Linux as platforms; but Firefox, Internet Explorer 6, Internet Explorer 7, Opera, and so on also count as platforms. If you've done any web development targeting multiple browsers, you're familiar with the inherent headaches in getting a web site to render and operate in the same way on Internet Explorer as it does on Firefox and others. Technically, this web site is a cross-platform application. The goal of Silverlight is to create a consistent execution environment across different browsers and operating systems.

There is no magical reason why a cross-platform application is automatically "good." Any responsible software engineering starts with a careful examination of the business reasons for a project. If all users are on a single platform, such as Windows, there is no reason to spend extra development time ensuring that the software also works on other platforms. Also, a significant amount of software that enables business applications (data and business logic layers) has no need to work on multiple platforms (though it can potentially be *consumed* by different platforms), and in fact benefits from platform-specific optimizations.

However, cross-platform applications are definitely important—as is best evidenced by web sites that are usable, generally, on any browser. The ability to develop cross-platform applications is of the most importance when the potential users for an application are on multiple platforms. This is a rather obvious statement, but it is important to note that development of a cross-platform application offers no inherent benefits if all users are on a single platform; that is, unless the cross-platform aspect is free or nearly free (therefore helping to future-proof the application if the user base changes). This concept of "free or nearly free" is important—software engineering is already a challenging endeavor, and if making software cross-platform is difficult to implement, it requires either significantly more development time for a single code base, or a second code base for a different platform that replicates the functionality of the first (not to mention a third or fourth code base if other platforms must be supported). Without question, this means more time, more money, and more development resources are needed. Optimally, we want a relatively easy way to create cross-platform applications. Fortunately, a number of frameworks have attempted to make the creation of cross-platform applications free or nearly free.

Cross-Platform Frameworks

Frameworks for developing cross-platform applications are not new. Even the C language is arguably cross-platform, since the source can be written once and compiled on each target platform, thus enabling portability of projects written in C. While arguments over what truly constitutes cross-platform can be interesting, they aren't of much practical use for us here, so let's take a brief look at the serious contenders for developing cross-platform applications.

Qt

Qt (pronounced *cute*) is a cross-platform application development toolkit mainly for C++; however, it has support for other languages such as Java. The significant benefit to Qt is that programs execute natively after compilation (i.e., no new virtual machine is needed). The cross-platform nature of Qt is provided at the source level, as long as developers utilize Qt's platform-agnostic API. The major downsides to Qt are the learning curve for developers and the degree to which applications might become intertwined with Qt (though this might be acceptable to many organizations). Visit `www.trolltech.com/products/qt` for more information.

The Java Platform

The Java platform (mainly Java Applet and JavaFX) is possibly the closest comparison to Silverlight on the market. Much like the .NET Framework, the Java-based platform is a managed environment. Until Silverlight, though, .NET was mainly available on Windows. Both platforms provide the ability to compile a program and immediately execute it on multiple platforms. The Java platform and Silverlight approach this similarly: an execution environment (known as a virtual machine) is developed for each platform where programs might be run. Java source code is compiled to Java bytecode, which is then executed by the Java virtual machine. The downsides to this approach are the plethora of virtual machines that can be created, each with potential quirks that sometimes affect existing applications, and the time cost of starting up a Java virtual machine on a web site (you've no doubt seen the gray rectangle and the loading symbol on web pages). Sun also has a more direct competitor to Silverlight called JavaFX, a framework that includes a scripting language to more easily create Java applications. This framework makes the most sense for institutions and developers who are already used to working in the Java environment or need to extend their existing Java applications. Visit `http://java.sun.com/javafx/` if you are curious about learning more.

Adobe Flash/Flex/AIR

Adobe Flash is, by far, the most popular comparison to Silverlight. A browser plug-in that enables execution of rich content for the Web—doesn't that sound familiar? This comparison is made even more explicit with Adobe releasing Flex, an environment for executing rich applications in the browser and on the desktop. Adobe Flex provides a rich user interface component library and uses MXML, a declarative XML-based language, to develop rich, interactive user interfaces. While there are some feature differences between Flex and Silverlight that can make one more appealing than the other, Flex is a viable alternative to Silverlight; however, it caters to a different set of developers than Silverlight does. Flex capitalizes on the languages people already know, including JavaScript, HTML, CSS, and ActionScript. Silverlight, however, provides a brand-new markup language, but is an incredibly natural platform to develop on if you're already a .NET developer. Visit `www.adobe.com/products/flex/` if you want to learn more about Flex.

In addition to Adobe Flash and Adobe Flex, in February 2008, Adobe introduced Adobe AIR for developing desktop applications that you can extend as RIAs. Visit `http://www.adobe.com/products/air/` to get more information about Adobe AIR.

Microsoft ASP.NET AJAX

Microsoft ASP.NET AJAX, a set of JavaScript libraries built into ASP.NET 3.5, is available as a separate download for ASP.NET 2.0. Being an integral part of ASP.NET 3.5 and the AJAX Controls Toolkit for ASP.NET 3.5, now ASP.NET AJAX client- and server-side libraries are more integrated with Visual Studio 2008. The client-side library allows you to implement client-level processing such as processing and validating information entered by the end user, refreshing a portion of the web page, and developing rich, interactive user interfaces. You can also efficiently integrate the client-side library components with the server-side ASP.NET controls library in asynchronous mode. The key technology driver of ASP.NET AJAX is scripting. In general, script-based web applications face several challenges due to different browser settings (e.g., JavaScript is not enabled by default) on PCs and mobile devices. As a result, scripting is often not always the best strategy for enterprises to use to develop secured and scalable RIAs. ASP.NET AJAX also supports limited features of RIAs and does not support effective multimedia integration, managed code-behind integration, or metadata and information management. Microsoft ASP.NET AJAX is a widely accepted model for building RIAs, but it is very likely that, having Silverlight as an option, .NET developers will migrate ASP.NET AJAX applications to Silverlight RIAs. Visit `www.asp.net/ajax/` if you want to learn more about Microsoft ASP.NET AJAX.

Microsoft Silverlight

This section brings us to the subject of this book: Microsoft Silverlight. .NET Framework 3.0 included the first release of WPF, along with other key technologies. With WPF came XAML, essentially a way to create applications in markup (there is an almost one-to-one correspondence between XAML constructs and code). While XAML is not necessarily tied to presentation logic, the two most visible uses of it are in WPF and Silverlight. Microsoft Silverlight is a subset of WPF, which is part of .NET Framework 3.5. Silverlight is integrated with the broad range of Microsoft tools and services like Microsoft Visual Studio 2008, Microsoft Expression Blend, Microsoft Deep Zoom Composer, and Microsoft Silverlight Streaming by Windows Live for the easy development and deployment of Silverlight-based multimedia cross-browser, cross-platform, and cross-device RIAs. While Silverlight does contain a Common Language Runtime (CLR), it has absolutely no dependence on any of the .NET Framework versions. The free and small size (to be precise, the Silverlight 2 runtime is 4.68MB for Windows and 7.38MB for Mac) of the Silverlight runtime plug-in brings with it CLR and base class library components all its own. If a user does not have the Silverlight runtime plug-in installed, he will be automatically prompted to install it upon browsing the Silverlight application.

■**Note** Silverlight 3 is in the beta version and is available to developers only. As a result, the Silverlight 3 runtime is also available only to developers. The Silverlight 3 Beta Developers runtime is 6.23MB for Windows and 12.3MB for Mac. You can get them by visiting `http://silverlight.net/getstarted/silverlight3/default.aspx`.

If you are already a .NET developer, you will be in familiar territory after learning XAML and its features. The correspondence of XAML to classes in .NET is a major strength, and tool support built around XAML for designers and developers is strong and continuously growing.

The History of Silverlight

Three versions of Microsoft Silverlight are available to date: Silverlight 1, Silverlight 2, and Silverlight 3 (Beta).

Silverlight 1

Before the MIX07 conference in March 2007, Silverlight was known by the relatively boring but descriptive name WPF/E, which stands for Windows Presentation Foundation/Everywhere. While the details were sparse at the time, the rough goal of the technology was clear: a browser-hosted version of WPF. Silverlight 1 was unveiled at the conference and would no longer be known as WPF/E. This initial release of Silverlight 1 did not have CLR or anywhere close to the capabilities provided by Silverlight 2. What it did have, though, is support for a small subset of XAML and a variety of capabilities that foreshadowed the future of Silverlight. Possibly the most obvious aspect of Silverlight 1 is that applications are written either completely in XAML or in a mix of XAML and JavaScript with a Document Object Model (DOM) to manipulate the user interface. Since there is no CLR, there is no compilation step, and the JavaScript is interpreted on the client. The major features supported by Silverlight 1 follow:

Core architecture: This includes `DependencyObject` at the root and `UIElement` forming the base of the user interface classes (but no `FrameworkElement` class).

Basic layout: The Canvas is the only layout component, so user interface elements can only be placed using absolute positions.

Basic controls: The TextBlock and Run controls are provided to display text. In terms of handling user input, nothing specialized is provided. This limitation extended to Silverlight 1, and the full control architecture debuted when Silverlight 2 was first released in beta.

2D graphics: `Geometry`-based classes (which are flexible but can't be directly placed on a user interface) and `Shape`-based classes (which can be directly placed on a user interface) provide the ability to draw 2D shapes.

Media: Many early Silverlight applications showcased the image and video support provided by Silverlight. Also included is support for easily downloading media such as images, so that bandwidth can be utilized more effectively. The Silverlight Media Player controls support the WMA, WMV, and MP3 media file formats.

Animation: The `Storyboard` class from WPF became part of the XAML implementation in this first release of Silverlight, providing the ability to animate different user interface elements in a variety of ways.

Brushes and transforms: Brushes such as the image brush, video brush, and color brushes (solid colors and gradients) have been in Silverlight since this initial release.

Silverlight 1 does require a plug-in on the client side, and in the spirit of Microsoft's commitment to backward compatibility, Silverlight 1 applications still work on Silverlight 2. Two of the most important parts of Silverlight 2 not present in Silverlight 1 are a rich set of controls and performance advantages due to compiled code.

Silverlight 2

Soon after Silverlight 1 was released, the next version of Silverlight was released in preview form. This preview release was known as Silverlight 1.1, the most significant aspect of which is the cross-platform CLR. While Silverlight 1 could be used to develop some impressive and rich media-based applications, the possibilities greatly expanded with the ability to target the .NET platform and know that the application would run on multiple host platforms. The biggest missing feature from Silverlight 1.1 was a set of standard controls. This made developing useful user interfaces difficult. Handling input events was also difficult since events could only be captured on the root container. You then had to manually propagate the events to child objects. Input focus was also tricky.

After several months, as it got closer to the MIX08 conference in March 2008, Microsoft revealed that Silverlight 1.1 would actually be released as Silverlight 2 since the feature set grew so much. It was a big leap from the first basic version to version 2.

The following are key features of Silverlight 2:

- Provides a platform to develop cross-browser (Microsoft Internet Explorer, Mozilla Firefox, Apple Safari, and Google Chrome), cross-platform (Microsoft Windows, Apple Mac, Linux), and cross-device (desktop, laptop) RIAs.

- Silverlight 2 is based on Microsoft .NET Framework 3.5.

  - As a subset of WPF, the Silverlight user interface framework is based on .NET Framework 3.5, WPF, and XAML. Visual Studio and the Silverlight toolkit contain more than a hundred XAML-based user controls in the areas of layout management (e.g., Canvas, StackPanel, and Grid), form controls (e.g., TextBox, CheckBox), data manipulation (e.g., DataGrid, ListBox), functional controls (e.g., Calendar, DatePicker, ScrollViewer), and media controls (e.g., MediaElement) to develop rich, interactive applications.

  - Support for the CLR and the availability of .NET Base Class Libraries (BCL) components enable the integration of Microsoft .NET managed code-behind using default Microsoft .NET class libraries in Silverlight 2 projects.

  - Asynchronous loosely coupled data integration capabilities enable development of complex, media-rich, SOA-based enterprise RIAs.

  - Integration with WCF and Web Services via REST, WS*/SOAP, POX, RSS, and standard HTTP enables the application to perform various data transactions with external data sources (e.g., XML, relational databases) and feeds (e.g., RSS).

  - ADO.NET data services, LINQ, LINQ to XML, and XLinq can be used for data transformation.

  - Local data caching with isolated data storage capabilities support client-side data processing.

  - Dynamic Language Runtime (DLR) supports dynamic compilation and execution of scripting languages like JavaScript and IronPython to develop Silverlight-based applications.

- Silverlight 2 provides effective media management, supporting secured multimedia streaming.

  - Adaptive media streaming helps to improve synchronization of media by automatically adjusting bit rates based on the network bandwidth.

  - Digital rights management (DRM) for media streaming enables protected distribution of digital media.

- Silverlight 2 supports rich graphics and animation.

  - 2D vector graphics are supported.

  - Deep Zoom provides an effective and easy-to-implement zoom-in and zoom-out feature.

  - With the use of the Deep Zoom Composer, professionals can smoothly enable navigation of large amounts of visual information, regardless of the size of the data, and optimize the bandwidth available to download it.

- Object animation and embedded code-based animation provide high-performing graphics and animation support.

- Seamless integration with Microsoft Expression Blend allows the development of compelling graphics with minimal effort.

- Silverlight 2 provides networking support.

  - Silverlight is capable of background threading and asynchronous communication.

  - JSON-based services integration is supported. LINQ to JSON support enables querying, filtering, and mapping JSON results to .NET objects within a Silverlight application.

  - Policy-based application development and deployment can occur with cross-domain networking using HTTP and sockets.

- Support for different deployment options (in-package and on-demand) and cross-domain deployment capabilities enable users to access Silverlight RIAs in a high-performing and secure environment.

- Silverlight 2 supports the open source and cross-platform Eclipse development platform by providing Eclipse Tools for Microsoft Silverlight (eclipse4SL, see http:// www.eclipse4SL.org).

- The Silverlight XAML schema vocabulary specification (MS-SLXV) released under the Open Specification Promise (OSP) improves interoperability.

- End users need to have the Silverlight runtime installed to be able to create a sandbox environment to run Silverlight RIAs. No licensing is required for the Silverlight 2 runtime; it is free and a very small file for distribution and installation. The Silverlight 2 runtime is 4.68MB for Windows and 7.38MB for Mac. Silverlight 2 does not support Mac PowerPC.

Along with Silverlight 2, you can download the following supporting development tools from http://silverlight.net/GetStarted/:

- *Microsoft Silverlight Tools for Visual Studio 2008 SP1* enables you to develop Silverlight 2.0–based applications using the Visual Studio 2008 SP1 IDE.

- *Microsoft Expression Blend 2 SP1* is tightly integrated with Visual Studio 2008 SP1, and allows artists and designers to create rich XAML-based user interfaces for Silverlight applications.

- *Deep Zoom Composer* allows professionals to create and prepare images to implement the Deep Zoom feature within Silverlight applications.

- *Microsoft Expression Encoder 2* contains Silverlight Media Player templates used to author, manage, and publish media for Silverlight applications. Visit http://www.microsoft.com/expression and look for the Microsoft Expression Encoder within the Express product suit.

- *Eclipse Tools for Microsoft Silverlight (eclipse4SL)* enables development of Silverlight applications using the Eclipse open source and cross-platform development platform. You can install this tool set by visiting http://www.eclipse4sl.org/download/link.

Silverlight 3

Microsoft kept the trend of releasing new versions of Silverlight at the MIX conference by releasing the Silverlight 3 Beta version during MIX09 in March 2009. Silverlight 3 Beta is an extension to Silverlight 2 and mainly provides improvements in graphics capabilities, media management, application development areas (additional controls, enhanced binding support, and out-of-browser functionality), and integration in the designers' Expression Blend 3 tools.

In addition to the features mentioned in the Silverlight 2 section, the following are the key enhanced features in Silverlight 3 Beta:

- Improved graphics capabilities to support a richer and more interactive user interface.

  - *Support for 3D graphics* enables designers to apply 2D content to a 3D plane with Perspective transforms. You can simulate live content rotation in the 3D space by applying the Perspective transform to the proper XAML elements. To achieve this functionality, developers do not need to write a single line of code. You can get this feature by using Expression Blend only.

  - *Animation easing* allows users to generate impressive animation effects using the different animation easing functions available by default, such as BounceEase, ElasticEase, CircleEase, BackEase, ExponentialEase, and SineEase. You can also create your own custom, complicated, mathematical-formula-based animation effects.

  - *Pixel Shaders* drive the visual behavior of the graphical content. By default, Silverlight 3 supports drop-down and blur effects. You can create custom effects using Microsoft's High-Level Shading Language (HLSL) and DirectX Software Development Kit (SDK).

  - *Theme application support* allows you to apply theme-based styles at runtime to Silverlight 3 RIAs. Developers can cascade styles by basing them on each other.

  - *Enhanced control-skinning* capabilities enable developers to define a common set of controls external to application, allowing the reuse of styles and control skins across applications. This enhancement helps organizations to apply, maintain, and control a consistent look and feel for applications.

  - *Improved text rendering* enables efficient rendering and rapid animation of text. The use of *local fonts* improves overall application performance. *Bitmap caching* allows Vector graphics, text, and controls to be cached as bitmaps in the background, improving overall application-rendering performance.

  - *Bitmap APIs* enable dynamic generation of bitmaps by reading and writing pixels in the bitmap. The capability to render visual elements to a bitmap makes it possible to edit images at runtime and develop different types of effects.

- Enhanced media management supporting high-quality and secured multimedia streaming.

  - *Support for new media formats*, such as H.264/Advanced Audio Coding (AAC)/MP4, and *the new RAW audio/video pipeline*, which supports third-party codecs, brings opportunities to develop a broad range of media formats that support RIAs and broadens the overall industry-wide acceptance of Silverlight as a main web-development technology platform.

  - *IIS Media Services* (an integrated HTTP media delivery platform) enable high-performing and smooth, live and on-demand, high-quality and high-definition (HD) (720p+) media streaming. Silverlight 3 also leverages Graphics Processor Unit (GPU) hardware acceleration to deliver a true HD media experience in both in-browser and full-screen modes.

  - *Silverlight DRM for media streaming* enables Advanced Encryption Standard (AES)–based encryption or Windows Media DRM of media files and allows the protected distribution of digital media.

- Empowers developers to develop data-rich and media-rich interactive RIAs.

  - *New networking APIs* (to detect the connected, disconnected, and changed state) and the *new offline APIs Out-of-Browser functionality* allow Silverlight applications to run in disconnected mode as a rich client application in the sandbox environment. This feature lets organizations develop true RIAs that can support application functionalities in connected and disconnected mode.

  - *Silverlight 3 SDK* provides additional controls to develop rich and controlled applications in a rapid application development mode. The following bullet items outline some examples from Layout Management, Forms, and Data Manipulation.

  - *New LayoutXAML controls*, including DockPanel, WrapPanel, and TabPanel, help to control the application layout effectively.

  - *New FormsXAML controls*, including PasswordBox, AutoCompleteBox, SaveFileDialog, and the Save-As File dialog box, make it easier to write operation implementations and additional invalid Visual State Manager (VSM) states to the TextBox, CheckBox, RadioButton, ComboBox, and ListBox controls.

  - *New DataManipulationXAML controls*, including a multiselect ListBox control; a DataPager control to display data in multiple pages; and a DataForm control to support dynamic fields generation, fields layout, validation, and data paging. An enhanced DataGrid control supports grouping and validation, and new data validation controls such as DescriptionViewer, ErrorSummary, and FieldLabel allow automatic validity checking of user input.

- *New ContentXAML controls* such as ChildWindow and ViewBox help to manage the content display more effectively in Silverlight applications.

- *Other user interface framework improvements*, including the *Element-to-Element Binding* feature that uses ElementName to bind two controls properties to each other's value/state/position; BasedOn styling to enable changing the control's style at runtime dynamically; CaretBrush and access to SystemColors, which support high-contrast situations; and DeepLinking, which enables users to bookmark a page within an RIA.

- *Search Engine Optimization (SEO):* in Silverlight 3 resolves one of the key challenges of RIAs, the existence of the application in the search engine. With the use of business objects and ASP.NET controls and site maps on the server side, users can automatically mirror database-driven RIA content into HTML that can be easily indexed by the leading search engines.

Creating Your Silverlight 3-Based Application

Since Visual Studio 2008 SP1 supports .NET 3.5, WPF application support is already built in. However, since the release of Visual Studio 2008 preceded Silverlight 3, Silverlight support is not provided out of the box. To support Silverlight 3 development with Visual Studio 2008 SP1, you need to install Silverlight 3 Beta Tools for Visual Studio, which include the Silverlight 3 Beta Developers runtime, the Silverlight 3 SDK, and the Silverlight 3 Tools for Visual Studio 2008 SP1. You can also use Visual Web Developer 2008 Express SP1 instead of Visual Studio 2008 SP1. Visit www.silverlight.net/GetStarted/silverlight3/default.aspx to download and install Microsoft Silverlight 3 Beta Tools for Visual Studio 2008 SP1.

▪**Note** Visual Studio 2010 includes fully integrated Silverlight development support with interactive designer and debugging capabilities. Visit www.microsoft.com/visualstudio/en-us/products/2010/default.mspx to get more information on Visual Studio 2010.

After you install the Silverlight 3 Beta Tools for Visual Studio, Visual Studio 2008 SP1 gains support for building Silverlight 3 projects with Visual Basic and C# project templates, and adds a design surface and appropriate IntelliSense in the XAML editor. While Visual Studio is an established tool targeted to developers, tool support for WPF and Silverlight for both designers and developers is necessary. This need is satisfied by the Expression suite of products from Microsoft.

Including the Silverlight 3 Beta documentation, three more tools/services are available: Microsoft Expression Blend 3 Preview, the Silverlight Toolkit, and .NET RIA Services.

The Expression Blend 3 Preview release enables Silverlight 3 Beta application user interface design and development. Expression Blend 3 Preview also includes enhancements such as SketchFlow, used to develop dynamic user interfaces for developing rich and interactive prototypes; integration with Adobe Photoshop and Illustrator to import files directly; sample data integration during the design and development phases, used to understand the visual and functional behavior of the application without connecting to the live data in the development mode; and support for rich, graphics-based user interface development (e.g., 3D support, enhanced VSM). Download Expression Blend 3 Preview at `www.silverlight.net/GetStarted/silverlight3/default.aspx` to work on the examples covered in this book.

The new version of the Silverlight Toolkit includes updated Silverlight 2 controls, new Silverlight 3 Beta controls, and a new theme gallery. Download and install the Silverlight Toolkit at `www.silverlight.net/GetStarted/silverlight3/default.aspx`.

Finally, install the Deep Zoom Composer by visiting `www.silverlight.net/GetStarted/`. If you have seen the Hard Rock Memorabilia (`http://memorabilia.hardrock.com/`) site, you have seen a product of the Deep Zoom Composer. This technology will be discussed when we take a closer look at media support in Silverlight in Chapter 5.

When you edit a XAML file in a WPF application using Visual Studio, you have access to a toolbox of controls, a design surface onto which you can drag and drop controls, and a text editor view of the XAML code. When you edit a XAML file in a Silverlight application, you still have these three elements, but the design surface is read-only. This is probably a result of the Silverlight package being an add-on to Visual Studio. One thing you can do, though, is drag and drop controls from the toolbox onto the text editor. This can help a lot when you want to work with XAML exclusively in Visual Studio.

You can use Expression Blend if you want a full drag-and-drop user interface construction tool for Silverlight. It's possible to use Expression Blend simultaneously with Visual Studio. Modifications to both XAML files and the `Project/Solution` file are fine, since when you switch from one tool to the other, the tool will reload the updated files.

You can start creating a Silverlight project using Visual Studio or Expression Blend. Here we will start by loading Visual Studio 2008 and creating a new project (see Figure 1-1).

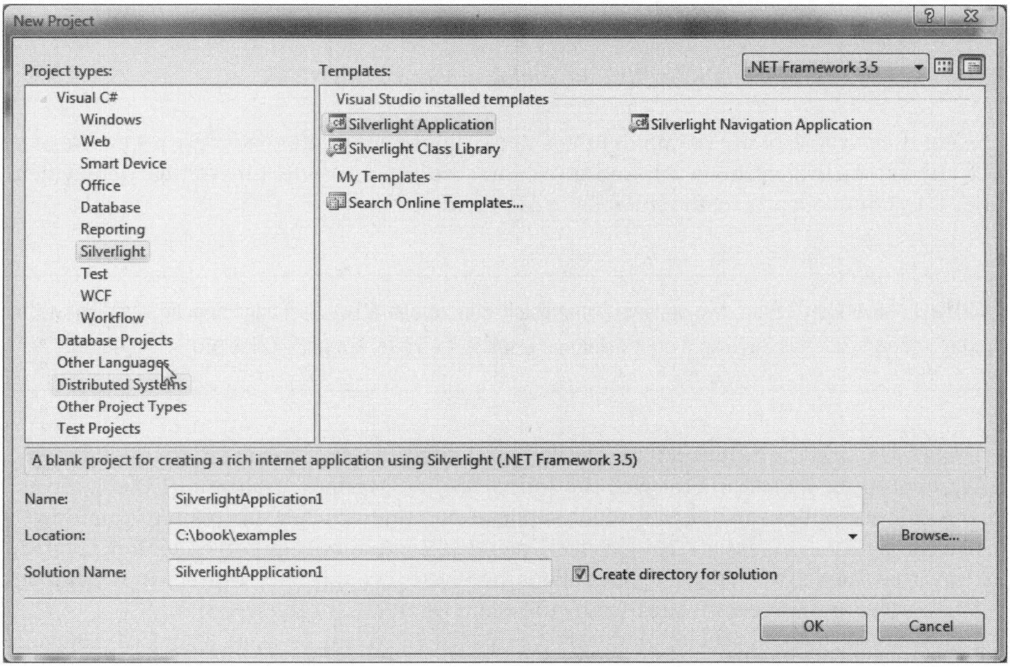

Figure 1-1. *The New Project dialog in Visual Studio 2008*

■**Note** As you see in Figure 1-1, a new project template, *Silverlight Navigation Application*, is available in Silverlight 3 Beta to create pre-built, framework-based RIAs with a predefined theme. We will cover this topic in more depth in Chapter 14.

After you click OK, the next dialog allows you to create a new ASP.NET web site/web application project that hosts the Silverlight application (see Figure 1-2).

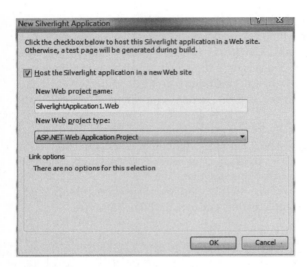

Figure 1-2. *The New Silverlight Application dialog in Visual Studio 2008*

For the purpose of the examples in this book, it does not matter if you use a web site or a web application project; however, web application projects are better for eventual deployment since they contain a project file suitable for MS Build.

■**Note** In Silverlight 3 Beta, two options, Dynamically generate an HTML test page to host Silverlight within this project and Link this Silverlight control into an existing Web site, are not available.

Click OK, and the Solution Explorer will show two projects: the Silverlight application (SilverlightApplication1) and the web site supporting it (SilverlightApplication1.Web). If you now build the application, the Silverlight application is built to a XAP file (with the naming convention `<SilverlightApplicationName>.xap`) that is automatically copied to the `ClientBin` folder within the web site. This XAP file contains the Silverlight application with startup assemblies and resources and will be downloaded by the client when it visits the web site.

If you now start the development server in Visual Studio (by pressing F5 or Ctrl+F5), you will see the Silverlight application start. If, however, you create a new web site in IIS, point the document root to SilverlightApplication1.Web, and navigate to this site, you will get a 404 error when trying to load the Silverlight application in your browser. What's going on? IIS 6 must know about the new file extension `.xap`. You accomplish this by adding a new MIME type to either the root of IIS or to the specific web site you created. The file extension is `.xap` and the MIME type is `application/x-silverlight-app`.

Note If you are using IIS 7, the XAP Silverlight package file type is already related to the `application/x-silverlight-app` MIME type. No additional steps are required.

Now let's take a look at Expression Blend 3 Preview, a tool used to lay out user interface controls and create animations in WPF and Silverlight. Without closing Visual Studio, start Expression Blend, and from the Projects tab window, choose Open Project or go to File ➤ Open Project/Solution, and navigate to the solution file created in Visual Studio (in `C:\book\examples\SilverlightApplication1` if you used the same directory structure).

The panes on the left in Expression Blend are devoted to managing project files (like the Solution Explorer in Visual Studio), triggers and events, and the visual states of the UserControl or control template. The panes on the right in Expression Blend are devoted to properties for various user interface elements; resources, which include style templates; animation storyboards stored in XAML; and the Data pane, which supports sample data integration to view the application with sample data (without connecting to the live data) while you are in development mode.

Note The Sample Data Integration feature, a new addition in Expression Blend 3 Preview, is used to integrate with Silverlight 3 applications.

Double-click MainPage.xaml from the Projects tab (see Figure 1-3) to open this XAML page in the designer.

Note In Silverlight 3, the `Page` class `Page.xaml` file and the `Page.xaml.cs` code -behind file— representing the main application user interface—are renamed to `MainPage.xaml` and `MainPage.xaml.cs`, respectively.

Along the left side of the Expression Blend screen is the toolbox. This provides access to both layout and input controls, and several tools used to modify the user interface, such as a paint bucket and a transform tool for brushes. Hold down the left mouse button when you select any icon with a white triangle in the lower-right corner, or right-click, and more tools will expand from it. Figure 1-4 shows an example of what clicking the Button icon (which looks like a mouse cursor hovering over a rounded rectangle) produces.

Figure 1-3. *The Projects tab in Expression Blend*

Figure 1-4. *The control toolbox in Expression Blend*

The Objects and Timeline area to the immediate right of the toolbox provides a place to create and manage animation storyboards, but more importantly for us right now, it shows the object hierarchy in XAML. After creating our application, we see [UserControl] and LayoutRoot. Click [UserControl] to highlight it and then click Properties in the top-right portion of the screen. The control with the gray highlight is the control that shows up in the Properties pane (see Figure 1-5).

Go to the Layout section of the Properties pane and set the Width and Height properties of the UserControl to 900 and 100, respectively, as shown in Figure 1-6.

Figure 1-5. *The Objects and Timeline pane in Expression Blend*

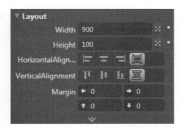

Figure 1-6. *Defining Width and Height properties for a control in Expression Blend*

You can also click XAML or Split along the right side of the design surface and view and edit the XAML directly. However, as interfaces get more complex, Expression Blend becomes an invaluable design tool for working with XAML indirectly. Hand-editing XAML should generally be used for tweaking some XAML instead of creating full-blown user interfaces.

Next, right-click LayoutRoot in the Objects and Timeline pane, and select Delete. This removes the default Grid layout control. While you can go to the toolbox and select the Canvas control (it's in the group four controls up from the bottom), let's view the XAML and create a Canvas control by hand. Click Split alongside the design surface to see the design surface simultaneously with the XAML. Edit the XAML to look like the following:

```
<UserControl
    xmlns="http://schemas.microsoft.com/client/2007"
    xmlns:x="http://schemas.microsoft.com/winfx/2006/xaml"
    x:Class="SilverlightApplication1.Page"
    Width="900" Height="100">
    <Canvas Height="Auto" Width="Auto" Background="White"/>
</UserControl>
```

Now go to the toolbox and select the TextBlock control, as shown in Figure 1-7.

Figure 1-7. *Choosing the TextBlock control from the toolbox*

This control is used to place text on a user interface, much like a label in Windows Forms or ASP.NET. Click the design surface and hold the mouse button down, and then drag right and down to create a rectangle describing the area for the TextBlock. Now the TextBlock control should appear as a child of Canvas in the Objects and Timeline pane. Make sure TextBlock is selected, and go to Properties.

If you've read even just one other programming book, you know what's coming next. We will make it a bit spicier though in context to Silverlight 3. Scroll down the properties until you see the Common Properties area, and set the Text property to "Hello World – It's Time to Light up the Web with Silverlight 3!", as shown in Figure 1-8.

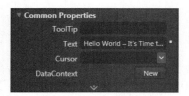

Figure 1-8. *Setting the Text property of a TextBlock in Expression Blend*

Similarly, go to the Text section of the Properties pane and change the FontFamily property to Arial and the FontSize to 30, as shown in Figure 1-9.

Figure 1-9. *Defining font styles*

If you now switch back to Visual Studio, it will ask you to reload MainPage.xaml. Go ahead and reload. Press F6 to build the application and then Ctrl+F5 to start the application without debugging. You should see something similar to Figure 1-10 in your browser.

Figure 1-10. *The Hello World application as viewed in Internet Explorer 7*

Now let's make it a bit spicier without a single line of code and see the power of Silverlight 3. Go back to Expression Blend, select the TextBlock control, and then go to the Miscellaneous section of the Properties pane. Add a new text effect by clicking New Effect, as shown in Figure 1-11.

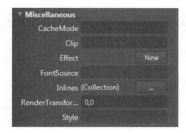

Figure 1-11. *Adding a new text effect to the TextBlock control*

The Select Object window that pops up lets you set up the text effect. Select the DropShadowEffect option, and click OK. Expression Blend will add the Text Effect and set the appropriate properties, as shown in Figure 1-12.

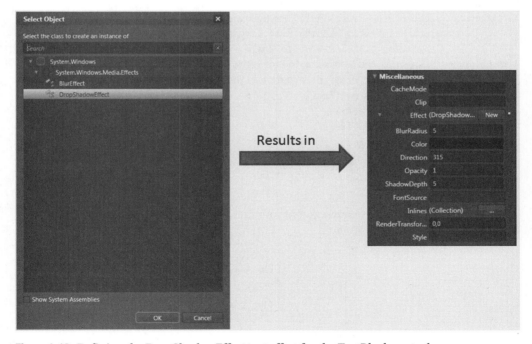

Figure 1-12. *Defining the DropShadowEffect text effect for the TextBlock control*

Now if you switch back again to Visual Studio, you will be asked to reload MainPage.xaml. Go ahead and reload. Press F6 to build the application, and then Ctrl+F5 to start the application without debugging. You should see something similar to Figure 1-13 in your browser.

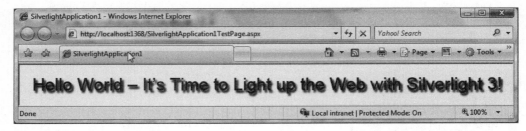

Figure 1-13. *The Hello World application with a text effect, as viewed in Internet Explorer 7*

The following is the complete XAML code for our Hello World Silverlight 3 application:

```
<UserControl
    xmlns="http://schemas.microsoft.com/winfx/2006/xaml/presentation"
    xmlns:x="http://schemas.microsoft.com/winfx/2006/xaml"
    xmlns:d=http://schemas.microsoft.com/expression/blend/2008
    xmlns:mc="http://schemas.openxmlformats.org/markup-
     compatibility/2006" x:Class="SilverlightApplication1.MainPage"
     Width="900" Height="100" mc:Ignorable="d">
    <Canvas Height="Auto" Width="Auto" Background="White">
        <TextBlock Height="49" Width="814" Canvas.Left="22"
            Canvas.Top="18" Text="Hello World – It's Time to
              Light up the Web with Silverlight 3!"
            TextWrapping="Wrap" d:LayoutOverrides="Height"
            FontSize="30" FontFamily="Arial">
            <TextBlock.Effect>
                <DropShadowEffect/>
            </TextBlock.Effect>
        </TextBlock>
    </Canvas>
</UserControl>
```

Congratulations, you have now created your first Silverlight 3 application using both Expression Blend and Visual Studio!

Summary

This chapter began with a discussion of Silverlight and its major competitors. We also learned the key differences between different versions of Silverlight. Next, we covered how to create a new Silverlight 3 application in Visual Studio with a supporting web site, how to modify the user interface in Expression Blend, and finally, how to build and execute an application in Visual Studio. While we built the application, I highlighted the key development aspect changes in Silverlight 3 compared to Silverlight 2. This should help if you are familiar with Silverlight 2 and would like to learn how to migrate Silverlight 2 applications to Silverlight 3.

The next stop on our journey through practical Silverlight development takes us to understand XAML. Many of the core concepts needed to understand how Silverlight works are covered in the next chapter, including markup extensions, dependency properties, and previews of features such as data binding and styling applications.

CHAPTER 2

■ ■ ■

Getting to Know XAML

Now you understand what Silverlight is and where it fits into the general technology landscape. You also have installed the tools necessary to develop in Silverlight and created your first Silverlight application. So, it is time to peel back the layers. This chapter will start by properly introducing Extensible Application Markup Language (XAML) and exploring its many features, such as the new property and event systems needed to support data binding, animation, and other key parts of Silverlight. The chapter will wrap up with more information on Silverlight applications, such as looking at the project structure and connecting XAML to events in the code-behind.

Introducing XAML

Let's jump right in and look at a simple Silverlight application. This application will display a basic login screen with a text entry area (for a username and password) and a button. There is no logic behind this screen—we will look only at the markup for now. Figure 2-1 shows the login screen displayed on Internet Explorer 7 and Windows Vista.

Figure 2-1. *A simple login screen as shown in Internet Explorer 7 on Windows Vista*

Being that Silverlight is a cross-platform technology platform, if you view the login screen on a Mac with a Safari or Mozilla browser, the application will look the same, which reinforces that Silverlight provides a viable cross-platform framework.

Now let's look at the XAML that describes the login section of the application. If you create a new Silverlight application, you can paste this code into `MainPage.xaml` (make sure the project is named XAMLTour, or change the namespace in the `x:Class` attribute to match the project name). Also, we'll discuss many aspects of this code in detail in later chapters, such as how the Grid and Canvas layout controls work.

```
<UserControl x:Class="XAMLTour.MainPage"
    xmlns="http://schemas.microsoft.com/winfx/2006/xaml/presentation"
    xmlns:x="http://schemas.microsoft.com/winfx/2006/xaml"
    Width="400" Height="300">
  <Canvas Background="White">
    <Grid Height="140" Width="250" Canvas.Left="25" Canvas.Top="15">
      <Grid.RowDefinitions>
        <RowDefinition/>
        <RowDefinition/>
        <RowDefinition/>
        <RowDefinition/>
      </Grid.RowDefinitions>
      <Grid.ColumnDefinitions>
        <ColumnDefinition Width="Auto"/>
         <ColumnDefinition/>
      </Grid.ColumnDefinitions>
      <TextBlock HorizontalAlignment="Center"
                 Text="Please enter your information"
                 Grid.Column="0" Grid.Row="0" Grid.ColumnSpan="2"/>
      <TextBlock Text="Username:" VerticalAlignment="Top"
                 HorizontalAlignment="Right"
                 Grid.Column="0" Grid.Row="1"/>
      <TextBox VerticalAlignment="Top" Grid.Column="1" Grid.Row="1"/>
      <TextBlock HorizontalAlignment="Right" VerticalAlignment="Top"
                 Grid.Column="0" Grid.Row="2">
        Password:
      </TextBlock>
      <!--If developing in Silverlight 3, you can use the
            PasswordBox control also -->
      <TextBox VerticalAlignment="Top" Grid.Column="1" Grid.Row="2"/>
      <Button Content="Login" Grid.Row="3" Width="100" Grid.Column="1"
              HorizontalAlignment="Left"/>
    </Grid>
  </Canvas>
</UserControl>
```

XAML is a markup language that provides mechanisms for constructing and configuring object hierarchies that are traditionally done in code, such as C#. With the use of C#, you can generate similar XAML code instead of writing directly in XAML, as shown here:

```
Canvas canvas = new Canvas { Background = new
    SolidColorBrush(Color.FromArgb(255, 255, 255, 255))};
Grid grid = new Grid(Height=140, Width=250);
grid.SetValue(Canvas.LeftProperty, 25d);
grid.SetValue(Canvas.TopProperty, 15d);
```

```
grid.RowDefinitions.Add(new RowDefinition());
grid.RowDefinitions.Add(new RowDefinition());
grid.RowDefinitions.Add(new RowDefinition());
grid.RowDefinitions.Add(new RowDefinition());
ColumnDefinition cd = new ColumnDefinition();
cd.Width = new GridLength(0, GridUnitType.Auto);
grid.ColumnDefinitions.Add(cd);
grid.ColumnDefinitions.Add(new ColumnDefinition());

TextBlock headerText = new
        TextBlock(HorizontalAlignment=HorizontalAlignment.Center);
headerText.Text = "Please enter your information";
headerText.SetValue(Grid.ColumnProperty, 0);
headerText.SetValue(Grid.ColumnSpanProperty, 2);
headerText.SetValue(Grid.RowProperty, 0);

TextBlock usernameText = new
        TextBlock(HorizontalAlignment=HorizontalAlignment.Right);
usernameText.Text = "Username:";
usernameText.SetValue(Grid.ColumnProperty, 0);
usernameText.SetValue(Grid.RowProperty, 1);

TextBox usernameInput = new TextBox(VerticalAlignment = VerticalAlignment.Top);
usernameInput.SetValue(Grid.ColumnProperty, 1);
usernameInput.SetValue(Grid.RowProperty, 1);

TextBlock passwordText = new
        TextBlock(HorizontalAlignment = HorizontalAlignment.Right);
passwordText.Text = "Password:";
passwordText.SetValue(Grid.ColumnProperty, 0);
passwordText.SetValue(Grid.RowProperty, 2);

//Note: Silverlight 3 also introduces PasswordBox control for the
//password input
TextBox passwordInput = new TextBox();
passwordInput.VerticalAlignment = VerticalAlignment.Top;
passwordInput.SetValue(Grid.ColumnProperty, 1);
passwordInput.SetValue(Grid.RowProperty, 2);

Button loginButton = new Button();
loginButton.Content = "Login";
loginButton.SetValue(Grid.ColumnProperty, 1);
loginButton.SetValue(Grid.RowProperty, 3);
loginButton.HorizontalAlignment = HorizontalAlignment.Left;
loginButton.Width = 100;
```

```
grid.Children.Add(headerText);
grid.Children.Add(usernameText);
grid.Children.Add(usernameInput);
grid.Children.Add(passwordText);
grid.Children.Add(passwordInput);
grid.Children.Add(loginButton);

this.Content = canvas;
canvas.Children.Add(grid);
```

The C# code is more verbose and thus more difficult to read and maintain than the XAML.
Both the C# code and the XAML files require a compilation step: C# for obvious reasons and
XAML files since they have the code-behind and must be packaged as part of a XAP file. C# also
requires a software developer to create the user interface, either by hand or by using a designer,
as with Windows Forms. XAML provides a way to create user interfaces such as the login screen
in a straightforward and (relatively) easy-to-maintain fashion. Markup is easier to read (at least
in small doses—complex user interfaces are a different story) and has far better tool support for
creating and maintaining. XAML isn't just another markup language—its strength lies in its
ability to model object hierarchies and easily configure object state via attributes or child
elements. Each element name (e.g., UserControl, Canvas, etc.) directly corresponds to a Silverlight object of the same name.

Let's look closer at the XAML. The root element is UserControl, a container for other controls.
A UserControl on its own has no visual representation—layout controls such as Canvas and
Grid combined with standard controls such as text input boxes and buttons create the visual
representation. User controls provide a way to compose controls into a reusable "master"
control, not unlike user controls in ASP.NET. The next chapter will take a closer look at what
goes into user controls in Silverlight.

Silverlight has rich support for composing what is ultimately viewed onscreen. Many
controls can contain arbitrary content, such as a ListBox containing Buttons as items or even
other ListBoxes! This makes composing a custom user interface possible using nothing other
than markup. Since XAML is a dialect of XML, elements describing content are nested in a tree
hierarchy. From the perspective of XAML, this tree is known as a *logical tree*.

■**Caution** XAML is case sensitive. Since XAML is a dialect of XML, it possesses all of the characteristics of
XML. Most importantly, all element names, property names, and so on, are case sensitive. Button is *not* the
same as button. However, this does not necessarily apply to property values, which are handled by Silverlight's XAML parser.

By reading this XAML code closely, you can see that it describes a UserControl that contains
a Canvas that contains a Grid that contains the various visual elements of the login screen. You
can view the logical tree of these elements in Visual Studio by right-clicking the design surface
and choosing Document Outline or, alternately, going to the View menu and choosing Other
Windows ➤ Document Outline. This displays a window showing the logical tree of elements
describing what's currently on the design surface. Figure 2-2 shows the document outline for
the login screen. This view of the logical tree is slightly different from a similar logical tree in

Windows Presentation Foundation (WPF), because the document outline focuses on what is explicitly found in the XAML. For example, if a ListBoxItem contains a Content attribute, the type-converted string is not shown. However, creating a Button as a child of a ListBoxItem will cause the Button to show up in the document outline.

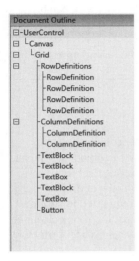

Figure 2-2. *The document outline describing the login screen*

Namespaces

We'll now elaborate on the XAML file structure. Two important namespaces appear in the root element of each XAML file. (Expression Blend adds a couple others, but we'll look at the two most important here.) The first is the default namespace, specified by `xmlns="http://schemas.microsoft.com/winfx/2006/xaml/presentation"`. This namespace contains the various elements that correspond to objects in Silverlight, such as UserControl, Canvas, and Grid. If you remove this declaration from a XAML file in Visual Studio, blue squiggly lines will show just how much is defined in this namespace.

The other namespace declaration contains Silverlight-specific extensions. Elements in this namespace are assigned to the x scope. While this is a convention, it is one that Silverlight and all Silverlight documentation follow. Table 2-1 describes the most important aspects of this namespace.

Table 2-1. *Features of the x: Namespace*

Feature	Description
x:Class	Joins different pieces of a partial class together. Valid syntax for this is x:Class="namespace.classname" and x:Class="namespace.classname;assembly=assemblyname". The XAML page generates code to a piece of the class that combines with the code-behind.
x:Key	Provides a unique identifier to resources defined in XAML, vital for referencing resources via a markup extension. Identifiers must begin with a letter or an underscore and can contain only letters, digits, and the underscore.

Table 2-1. *Features of the x: Namespace (Continued)*

Feature	Description
x:Name	Provides a way to give an identifier to an object element in XAML for accessing via the code-behind. This is not appropriate for use with resources (instead use x:Key). Many elements have a Name property, and while Name and x:Name can be used interchangeably, only one should be set. Identifiers must begin with a letter or an underscore and can contain only letters, digits, and the underscore.
x:Null	Corresponds to null in C# (or Nothing in VB .NET). Can be used via a markup extension ({x:Null}) or through a property element (<x:Null/>).

Dependency Property System

The dependency property system is a significant aspect of Silverlight. It provides a way for multiple discrete sources, such as animation and data binding, to gain access to object properties. Silverlight contains approximately classes that directly relate to constructing user interfaces. You can see the top classes in this hierarchy in Figure 2-3. Notice that the root of the hierarchy is DependencyObject. This root object provides much of the infrastructure needed to support the dependency property system, though it has only a few public methods. Let's look closer at what dependency properties are and then highlight a few aspects of DependencyObject that will make more sense in light of dependency properties.

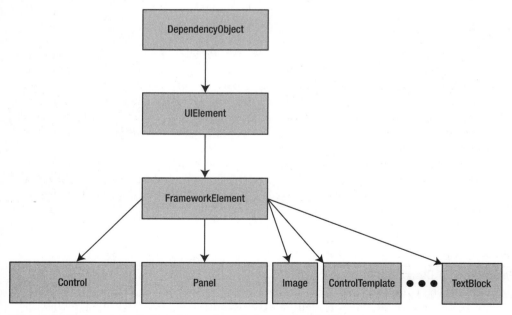

Figure 2-3. *Top portion of object hierarchy relating to visual elements*

Dependency Properties

A *dependency* property is a special type of property that backs a .NET property. The importance of dependency properties lies in the fact that the value depends on multiple sources (which is why it's called *dependency property*), and therefore, a standard .NET property is not enough. The value of a dependency property might come from data binding, animation, template resources specified in the XAML, styles, or local values. Figure 2-4 shows the precedence of these sources.

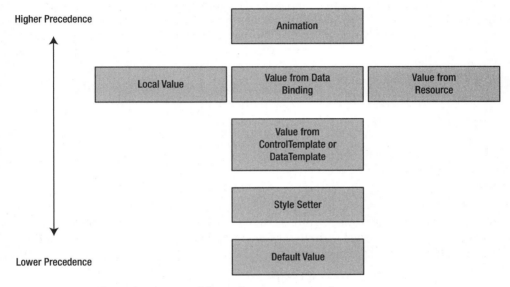

Figure 2-4. *Precedence for sources of dependency property values*

Animation has the highest precedence. Property values influenced by animation must be the values that take effect, or the user will never see the animation, since a different source would trump the animation values. Local values are those set via an attribute or property element. Local values can also be set via data binding or a static resource, so these are effectively local values—thus, at equal precedence. Next lowest are values from a data template or a control template, which take effect if a local value does not override them. Styles defined in the page/application are next lowest, and if absolutely nothing is set, the dependency property takes on its default value.

■**Caution** The base value for a property is not the same as its default value. A property's base value is determined by applying the sources in the preceding precedence chart but stopping before getting to anima-tion. A property's default value is its value when no other sources provide a value (e.g., a layout container's constructor may establish a default value for a size property, and if this is not modified anywhere else, its value remains untouched).

Let's examine an actual dependency property, one that you have already used. The Width property, defined in the FrameworkElement class, is first defined as a dependency property and then wrapped by a .NET property. This provides all the capability of a dependency property while providing a traditional approach to getting and setting its value. Let's examine how this particular dependency property is defined:

```
public static readonly DependencyProperty WidthProperty;
```

By convention, dependency properties end with the word Property, and this is adhered to throughout Silverlight. Notice that it is marked public—while this is also a convention, there is no compelling reason to not expose it publicly. The dependency property should be just as visible as the .NET property wrapper. The .NET property provides a shortcut, hiding the fact that there is an underlying dependency property, since it wraps the calls to GetValue and SetValue.

```
public double Width
{
   get {
      return (double) this.GetValue(WidthProperty);
   }
   set {
      base.SetValue(WidthProperty, value);
   }
}
```

Simply declaring the dependency property is not enough—it must be registered with the dependency property system using the DependencyProperty.Register static method. The Register method takes the following parameters:

```
public static DependencyProperty Register(
    string name,
    Type propertyType,
    Type ownerType,
    PropertyMetadata typeMetadata
```

Although you won't do much with it for now, let's create a new dependency property named TextSize in the MainPage.xaml.cs file. Add the following code to the class:

```
public static readonly DependencyProperty TextSizeProperty =
    DependencyProperty.Register("TextSize",
                              typeof(double),
                              typeof(MainPage),
                              new PropertyMetadata(new
                              PropertyChangedCallback(onTextSizeChanged)));
    public double TextSize
    {
        get { return ((double)this.GetValue(TextSizeProperty)); }
        set { this.SetValue(TextSizeProperty, value); }
    }
```

The name of the dependency property (passed as the first parameter to `Register`) does not need to have `Property` appended to it—this convention only holds for the actual field name in the class. Now you have a new dependency property that can be used for data binding or any of the other various sources that can modify dependency property values.

There is one other useful aspect to dependency properties: property change notifications. This ability to capture property changes is vital for validating a property value at the last possible moment. This is useful for scenarios such as a progress bar, where there is a clear minimum and maximum value, and values greater than or less than these values should be constrained to their respective endpoints. The final parameter to the `Register` method is where you specify a handler for the property change notification. Here's a handler for constraining `TextSizeProperty` to no larger than 36:

```
private static void onTextSizeChanged(DependencyObject source,
                                      DependencyPropertyChangedEventArgs e)
{
    if (((double)source.GetValue(e.Property)) > 36)
    {
        source.SetValue(e.Property, 36.0);
    }
}
```

■**Note** A callback for property changes is the perfect place to validate and constrain dependency property values. It is also a great place to hold logic for modifying dependent properties, so when one changes, it affects other dependency property values of the `DependencyObject` that contains the properties.

The first parameter is the instance of `DependencyObject`—this is what you use to retrieve and set the value for the property. The `Property` member of the `EventArgs` class for this handler is then used as a parameter to `GetValue` and `SetValue`. If you try setting the value of the `TextSize` property to higher than 36 and then display its value, you will see it goes no higher than 36.

Attached Properties

An *attached* property is a special type of dependency property. Attached properties provide a way to assign values to properties on objects that do not actually have the property—the attached property values are generally used by parent objects in the element hierarchy. You have already seen several attached properties. Let's look again at the XAML code used to create header text for the login screen:

```
<TextBlock HorizontalAlignment="Center"
           Text="Please enter your information"
           Grid.Column="0" Grid.Row="0" Grid.ColumnSpan="2"/>
```

The `Grid` class defines several attached properties, including `Column`, `Row`, and `ColumnSpan`, which are used by the `TextBlock` object. If you look up the `TextBlock` object on MSDN, you won't find anything close to `Grid.Row` or `Grid.Column` properties. This is because `Column`, `Row`, and `ColumnSpan` are defined as attached properties on the `Grid` class. The `Grid` class defines a total of four attached properties: Column, Row, ColumnSpan, and RowSpan. The dotted syntax is used to specify the class that *does* provide these dependency properties. By using this syntax, it is possible to attach arbitrary properties to objects that do not have them. The attached properties for the Grid layout control provide a way for child elements to specify where they should be located in the grid. You can identify the attached properties by looking for an "Attached Properties" section in the MSDN documentation for a particular class. If you attempt to use a random dependency property as an attached property, the parser will throw an exception. Registering an attached property is accomplished in a similar fashion to normal dependency properties but uses RegisterAttached instead of Register.

Dependency properties are important to many aspects of Silverlight and will be used often, generally transparently, throughout the rest of this book.

The Root of Visual Elements: DependencyObject

Any class inheriting from DependencyObject, directly or indirectly, gains the ability to interact with dependency properties. You have already seen the GetValue and SetValue methods, probably the two most important methods of DependencyObject. This root object also provides the ability to obtain the value of the property (its base value) as if no animation occurred.

Type Converters

XAML introduces type converters in order to easily support setting of complicated property values. A *type converter* simply converts a string representation of an object to the actual object but allows for complex handling, such as wrapping a value in several objects. While not explicitly tied to Silverlight (or WPF or XAML), type converters are heavily used when parsing XAML. Let's take a look at the definition of the Canvas layout control in the login screen's XAML:

```
<Canvas Background="White">
```

The Background property is type-converted from a string to its actual type. If you were to create this Canvas in C#, the code would look like the following:

```
Canvas canvas = new Canvas { Background = new
    SolidColorBrush(Color.FromArgb(255, 255, 255, 255))};
```

If you had to guess, you might think that the Background property is backed by the Color type; however, it is actually backed by a Brush. Using a Brush for the background provides the ability to easily display solid colors, gradients, and other fancy backgrounds, thus providing much more flexibility for creating backgrounds. Brushes will be discussed in more detail in Chapter 7. Specifying the Canvas control's background as an attribute in XAML is the quickest way to provide a background and is known as *property attribute* syntax. XAML also supports *property element* syntax, which makes the fact that the Background is a Brush explicit.

```
<Canvas>
    <Canvas.Background>
        <SolidColorBrush Color="White"/>
    </Canvas.Background>
</Canvas>
```

When the property appears as an element, it must take the form of object name, followed by a dot and then the property name, as in the case of Canvas.Background.

In many cases, content can also be provided via an attribute or inside an element's opening tag. Each approach is illustrated in the text labels for the username and password entry boxes. The username label uses the content attribute Text:

```
<TextBlock Text="Username:" VerticalAlignment="Top"
           HorizontalAlignment="Right"
           Grid.Column="0" Grid.Row="1"/>
```

The password label, however, is specified as a child of the TextBlock element:

```
<TextBlock HorizontalAlignment="Right" VerticalAlignment="Top"
        Grid.Column="0" Grid.Row="2">
        Password:
    </TextBlock>
```

The content attribute syntax, much like the property attribute syntax, is a useful shorthand, both in markup and when working with the code-behind. The content element syntax, however, is required when specifying more complex content than what can be captured by a simple attribute. Also note that content might be restricted based on which control you use—for example, a TextBox cannot contain a Button as content.

Markup Extensions

A *markup extension* is a special syntax used to specify property values that require interpretation. This interpretation is based on which markup extension is used. A markup extension takes the format of {, followed by the markup extension name, optionally followed by parameters to the markup extension, and ending with }. These are required to support some of the key features of Silverlight, including resources, data binding, and template binding. We'll briefly discuss each of these features here to highlight the syntax and usage of markup extensions.

■**Note** What's with the funny syntax? Markup extensions may seem strange at first and might leave you wondering why context can't dictate how a property value is interpreted (e.g., by utilizing a type converter). Markup extensions provide a mechanism to specify more than a simple value—they stand in for more complicated processing, such as completely changing the appearance of a user interface element via a style. If you want to explicitly show something in curly braces, such as a label, you must escape it by placing an empty set of curly braces in front—for example, {}{text here}.

Resource Dictionaries and Referencing Static Resources

Applications must maintain consistency throughout in order to give users a predictable experience, including using the same colors, fonts and font sizes, styles, and templates (used to control how items in controls are rendered or to change the appearance of the default controls). The customization used to create this application consistency needs to reside in a place where multiple controls, and even multiple XAML pages, will have easy access to it. That way, when you need to change any details, such as colors, you need to go to only a single place.

The place where you can store these customizations is called a *resource dictionary*. Resource dictionaries associate a value with a key, much like you'd do in a `Dictionary<string,object>` instance. In XAML, the key is set via the `x:Key` property. Any object that contains a `Resources` member can contain resources. This includes the layout containers (that you will encounter in the next chapter), and the `App.xaml` file provides resources for the entire application.

Let's revise the login screen to use a resource dictionary to specify font style information. This screen will look slightly different from the earlier example since the fonts are configured with different values. You can see the result in Figure 2-5. The resource dictionary makes it easy to change the appearance of the header and labels.

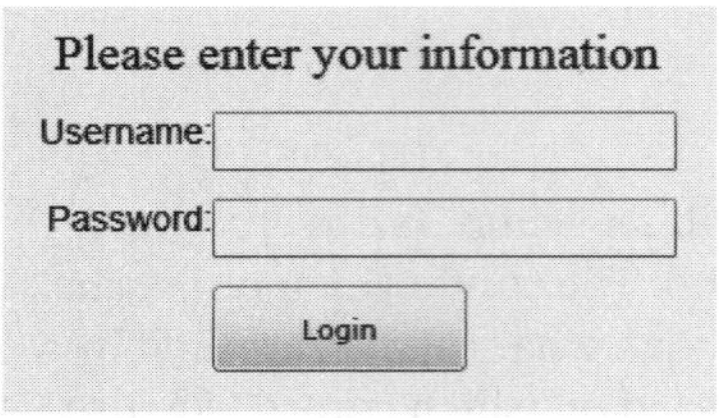

Figure 2-5. *The login screen with font properties specified by a style resource*

The revised XAML code for the login screen is shown here with the new additions in bold:

```xaml
<Canvas Width="300" Height="Auto" x:Name="canvasTag">
        <Canvas.Resources>
            <Style x:Key="LoginHeaderFontStyle" TargetType="TextBlock">
                <Setter Property="FontFamily" Value="Times New Roman"/>
                <Setter Property="FontSize" Value="20"/>
            </Style>
            <Style x:Key="LoginLabelFontStyle" TargetType="TextBlock">
                <Setter Property="FontFamily" Value="Arial"/>
                <Setter Property="FontSize" Value="14"/>
            </Style>
        </Canvas.Resources>

        <Grid Height="140" Width="250" Canvas.Left="25" Canvas.Top="15">
            <Grid.RowDefinitions>
                <RowDefinition/>
                <RowDefinition/>
                <RowDefinition/>
                <RowDefinition/>
            </Grid.RowDefinitions>
            <Grid.ColumnDefinitions>
                <ColumnDefinition Width="Auto"/>
                <ColumnDefinition/>
```

```
        </Grid.ColumnDefinitions>
        <TextBlock HorizontalAlignment="Center"
        Text="Please enter your information"
        Grid.Column="0" Grid.Row="0" Grid.ColumnSpan="2"
                Style="{StaticResource LoginHeaderFontStyle}" />
        <TextBlock Text="Username:" VerticalAlignment="Top"
        HorizontalAlignment="Right"
        Grid.Column="0" Grid.Row="1"
                Style="{StaticResource LoginLabelFontStyle}"/>
        <TextBox VerticalAlignment="Top" Grid.Column="1" Grid.Row="1"/>
        <TextBlock HorizontalAlignment="Right" VerticalAlignment="Top"
        Grid.Column="0" Grid.Row="2" Text="Password:"
                Style="{StaticResource LoginLabelFontStyle}">
        </TextBlock>
        <TextBox VerticalAlignment="Top" Grid.Column="1" Grid.Row="2"/>
        <Button Content="Login" Grid.Row="3"
                Width="100" Grid.Column="1" HorizontalAlignment="Left"/>
    </Grid>
</Canvas>
```

To reference static resources, you need a way to tell the XAML parser that you want to use a resource and which resource to use. The markup extension name for referencing a static resource is simply `StaticResource`, and it appears after the open curly brace. The `StaticResource` markup extension takes a single parameter: the name of the resource to reference.

The `x:Key` property is used to give each style a name for referencing in the markup extension. While we will discuss styles in detail in Chapter 8, what's going on here isn't a big mystery. The `TargetType` property of the `Style` element is used to specify the object type the style is meant for, and the `Setter` elements are used to specify values for properties on this target type. In this case, we are defining two styles: one for the header text (the "Please enter your information" text) and the other for the labels next to the text input boxes. By changing the `LoginLabelFontStyle`, you affect both the username and the password labels at the same time. This is good—it makes styling applications significantly easier both because the style information is stored in a central place and because the specific styles need only a single definition to affect potentially many elements of a user interface.

■**Note** Although you can use `{StaticResource}` from a resource dictionary to reference other resources within the dictionary, you can reference only those resources that appear before the reference.

Silverlight 3 provides further capability to the resource dictionaries via merged resource dictionaries. This makes it so you can reference resource dictionaries stored in content files within the XAP file, possibly even within another assembly within the XAP. The external resource dictionaries are referenced via the `Source` property of the `ResourceDictionary` class. The previous example used two styles, one for the header and one for the labels. Let's put each of these styles in a separate, external XAML file. The style for the header goes into a resource dictionary defined in `ExternalResources1.xaml`.

```xml
<?xml version="1.0" encoding="utf-8" ?>
<ResourceDictionary
    xmlns="http://schemas.microsoft.com/winfx/2006/xaml/presentation"
    xmlns:x="http://schemas.microsoft.com/winfx/2006/xaml" >
    <Style x:Key="LoginHeaderStyle_External" TargetType="TextBlock">
        <Setter Property="FontFamily" Value="Times New Roman"/>
        <Setter Property="FontSize" Value="20"/>
    </Style>
</ResourceDictionary>
```

The style for the labels goes into a similar XAML file named `ExternalResources2.xaml`. The key for these two styles was changed in order to distinguish the code from the previous example. These files are added to the Visual Studio project as regular XML files (but with the extension XAML), and their build action is changed from `Page` to `Content`. This ensures these files are simply placed in the XAP file as flat files. The Canvas no longer contains these styles, instead using the `MergedDictionaries` property to specify which external resource dictionaries to import and merge together.

```xml
<Canvas.Resources>
    <ResourceDictionary>
        <ResourceDictionary.MergedDictionaries>
            <ResourceDictionary Source="/ExternalResources1.xaml"/>
            <ResourceDictionary Source="/ExternalResources2.xaml"/>
        </ResourceDictionary.MergedDictionaries>
    </ResourceDictionary>
</Canvas.Resources>
```

The `Source` property is a URI specifying in which file the external resource dictionary is located. Resource dictionaries imported using the `Source` property cannot then define more resources.

We will revisit the Merged Resource Dictionary feature in Chapter 8 in the context of styles.

Data Binding

Data binding is a way to connect data between the user interface and a data source. It is possible to transfer data from a data source to the user interface once or each time the data changes, as well as to constantly keep the data source synchronized with the user interface. The markup extension controlling data binding is named `Binding` and has four possible syntaxes. Let's imagine the login screen authorizes access to an online bank. After customers log in, they're able to select one of their accounts to manage (and also instantly see their balance for each account), as shown in Figure 2-6.

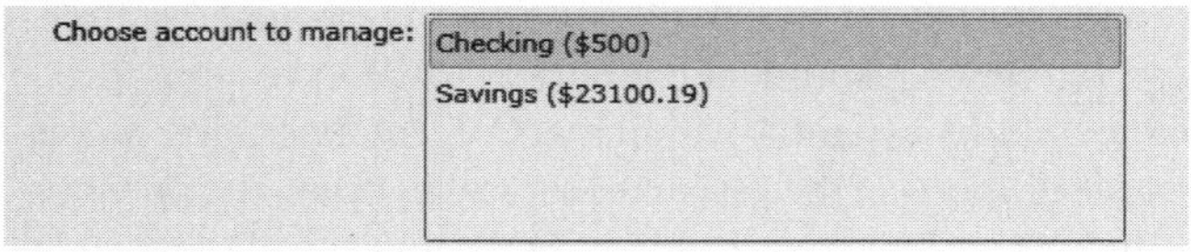

Figure 2-6. *Results of data binding Account objects to a ListBox*

Here's what a simplistic business object for account information looks like:

```
public class Account
{
    public string AccountName { get; set; }
    public double AccountBalance { get; set; }
    public Account(string n, double b)
    {
        this.AccountName = n;
        this.AccountBalance = b;
    }
}
```

Let's create a new UserControl in Visual Studio and call it ChooseAccount. You can do this by right-clicking the project in the top right and clicking Add ➤ New Item ➤ Silverlight User Control. Give it the name ChooseAccount.xaml and click OK. Edit the ChooseAccount.xaml.cs file, create a generic List containing the account type, and add a couple accounts. This will serve as a data source for the data binding.

```
private List<Account> accountList;
public ChooseAccount()
{
    // Required to initialize variables
    InitializeComponent();
    accountList = new List<Account>();
    accountList.Add(new Account("Checking", 500.00));
    accountList.Add(new Account("Savings", 23100.19));
    accountListBox.DataContext = accountList;
}
```

Notice the final line in the constructor—this is where the data source (accountList) is connected to the ListBox. The ListBox, named accountListBox, is our display control that we add to the XAML shown here. The markup extensions for data binding are in bold. (Here you will also notice that the Grid layout control is replaced by the StackPanel layout control.)

```
<UserControl
    xmlns=http://schemas.microsoft.com/winfx/2006/xaml/presentation
    xmlns:x="http://schemas.microsoft.com/winfx/2006/xaml"
    x:Class="XAMLTour.ChooseAccount">
    <StackPanel Orientation="Horizontal" Margin="30 30 0 0">
        <TextBlock Text="Choose account to manage: "></TextBlock>
        <ListBox x:Name="accountListBox" Height="100" Width="300"
                    VerticalAlignment="Top" ItemsSource="{Binding Mode=OneWay}">
            <ListBox.ItemTemplate>
                <DataTemplate>
```

```
            <StackPanel Orientation="Horizontal">
                <TextBlock Text="{Binding AccountName}" />
                <TextBlock Text=" ($"></TextBlock>
                <TextBlock Text="{Binding AccountBalance}" />
                <TextBlock Text=")"></TextBlock>
            </StackPanel>
        </DataTemplate>
    </ListBox.ItemTemplate>
  </ListBox>
 </StackPanel>
</UserControl>
```

The Binding markup extension used in the ItemsSource property specifies that the items in the ListBox are data bound, and here you can specify how the data binding works (in this case, OneWay, which causes data to flow only from the data source to the user interface). A DataTemplate is used to format the data coming from the data source, in this case by using the Binding markup extension to access properties on the data source (accountList). The Binding markup extensions used to bind to AccountName and AccountBalance treat the parent object (Account) implicitly. This is described in Table 2-2.

Table 2-2. *Data Binding Markup Extensions*

Syntax	Description
{Binding}	This signals data binding, configured with default properties (such as OneWay for Mode). See Chapter 5 for specific property values.
{Binding *path*}	This is used to specify specific object properties to pull data from. A dotted syntax is valid here, allowing you to drill down inside the objects from the data source.
{Binding *properties*}	This is used to set properties affecting data binding, following a *name=value* syntax. Specific properties affecting data binding will be discussed later.
{Binding *path, properties*}	The properties affect the data specified by the path. For example, a converter might be used to format data. The path must come first.

RelativeSource Markup Extension

The RelativeSource property of the Binding markup extension specifies that the binding source is relative to the location of the binding target. The RelativeSource markup extension is used to specify the value of the RelativeSource property of the Binding markup extension. It comes in the following two forms:

{RelativeSource TemplatedParent}: The source for the data binding is the control that has a ControlTemplate defined.

{RelativeSource Self}: The source for the data binding is the control in which this appears. This is useful for binding to another property on the control itself that is data bound.

The `TemplatedParent` is useful for properties in control templates that want to bind to properties of controls that are using the control template. For example, the `TemplateBinding` can be altered to retrieve the label from the `Tag` property of the Button.

```
<Style x:Key="ButtonStyle" TargetType="Button">
    <Setter Property="Template">
        <Setter.Value>
            <ControlTemplate TargetType="Button">
                <StackPanel Orientation="Horizontal"
                            Background="Gainsboro">
<TextBlock
Text="{Binding Tag, RelativeSource={RelativeSource TemplatedParent}}"
FontSize="16"/>
<ContentPresenter Content="{TemplateBinding Content}"/>
                </StackPanel>
            </ControlTemplate>
        </Setter.Value>
    </Setter>
</Style>
```

The text entered into the `Tag` property of a Button that uses this control template appears in the TextBlock via the `TemplatedParent` relative binding. The `Self` is even easier, because it simply provides a way to bind to a property within the control itself. The following TextBlock will show `Tahoma` since that is the value of the `FontFamily` property:

```
<TextBlock FontFamily="Tahoma" FontSize="24"
 Text="{Binding FontFamily, RelativeSource={RelativeSource Self}}"/>
```

We will delve deeper into data templates and data binding in Chapter 5.

Template Binding

Using something called a *control template* along with styles provides a mechanism to completely redefine how a control appears. This is one scenario where designers and developers can work independently—the designer fleshes out how the user interface looks, while the developer focuses on handling events and other logic related to the control. The `TemplateBinding` markup extension is used to connect the template to properties of the control that uses the template. Let's look at a brief example of utilizing control templates to enforce a consistent label on all buttons that use this template. Here's what the XAML looks like:

```
<UserControl
  xmlns=http://schemas.microsoft.com/winfx/2006/xaml/presentation
  xmlns:x="http://schemas.microsoft.com/winfx/2006/xaml"
  x:Class="XAMLTour.TemplateBindingExample">
  <Canvas Background="White">
    <Canvas.Resources>
      <Style x:Key="ButtonStyle" TargetType="Button">
```

```xml
                  <Setter Property="Template">
                     <Setter.Value>
                        <ControlTemplate TargetType="Button">
                            <StackPanel Orientation="Horizontal"
                                              Background="Gainsboro">
                               <TextBlock Text="Label from Template: "
                                              FontSize="16"/>
                               <ContentPresenter
                                      Content="{TemplateBinding Content}"/>
                           </StackPanel>
                        </ControlTemplate>
                     </Setter.Value>
                  </Setter>
            </Style>
         </Canvas.Resources>
         <Button Style="{StaticResource ButtonStyle}" Content="I'm a Button"/>
   </Canvas>
</UserControl>
```

The template is created as a style that the button references using the StaticResource markup extension. The first TextBlock contains the label that never changes, and the ContentPresenter is used to display any content the button specifies. In this case, the content is a simple string. The TemplateBinding is used to connect a property of a control in the template to a property on the control utilizing the template. Figure 2-7 shows the resulting user interface for this XAML.

Figure 2-7. *What a Button looks like when using the ControlTemplate*

The bad news about this approach is also the good news: the Button's visual implementation is completely overridden, so if you try to click it, nothing will happen visually. Using a control template, though, provides a way to create any visual representation you want for when the mouse hovers over the button and when the mouse clicks the button. The button is still a button—it can just look drastically different from the default Silverlight button through the control template mechanism, which will be covered in Chapter 8.

More About Silverlight Applications

Now that you should be comfortable with many of the new concepts Silverlight introduces, let's take a closer look at the Silverlight application that gets created. If you reveal the referenced assemblies in the Solution Explorer, you will see seven assemblies listed. These assemblies provide the majority of what you need when writing applications. Briefly, here are the important namespaces/classes in each assembly:

mscorlib: This is the CRL for Silverlight and thus provides the core functionality you always need, including collections, input/output, reflection, security, host interoperability, and threading. The important root namespace here is System, which includes System.Collections, System.Security, System.IO, and so on.

system: This supplements classes provided by mscorlib, such as by providing Queue and Stack classes in the System.Collections.Generic namespace.

System.Core: This contains LINQ support (in the System.Linq namespace) and cryptography support (System.Security.Cryptography).

System.Windows: This provides the bulk of what Silverlight uses, such as input-related classes in System.Windows.Input (mouse/keyboard event classes and stylus-related classes), image/video/animation-related classes in System.Windows.Media, the XAML parser in System.Windows.Markup, control classes in System.Windows.Controls, and many others. Chances are high that if you're looking for something, it's in this assembly.

System.Windows.Browser: This provides support classes for obtaining information about and communicating with the browser (via classes in the System.Windows.Browser namespace) and the managed host environment (via classes in System.Windows.Hosting).

System.Xml: This provides all XML-related classes (e.g., for an XML reader/writer/parser).

System.Net: This provides a simple programming interface for many of the network protocols such as HttpWebRequest, HttpWebResponse, and WebClient. The WebClient class provides common methods for sending data to and receiving data from a resource identified by a URI.

So far, you have seen several user interfaces created in XAML. Each XAML file has a corresponding code-behind file; however, there is a third file that we have not yet discussed explicitly. If you open the XAMLTour project in Visual Studio, open the MainPage.xaml.cs file, right-click the InitializeComponent method call, and choose Go to Definition, you will be taken to the MainPage.g.cs file. This is a generated file based on the XAML. Any objects in the XAML that have an x:Name will cause a class member to get placed in this generated file. Partial classes in C# make this assemblage of different pieces easy, as illustrated in Figure 2-8.

■**Note** The Name property on objects can be set only in XAML. This is most likely because the object is either created in XAML (in which case it needs a corresponding member on the class for manipulation in the code-behind) or created in code (in which case you have a reference to it that you can name and store however you like).

When you create a new Silverlight application in Visual Studio or Expression Blend, you might notice an App.xaml file along with an App.xaml.cs file. The application is based on the System.Windows.Application class—it supports centralization of resources for the application, it supports several important events, and it provides a direct connection to the browser/host environment.

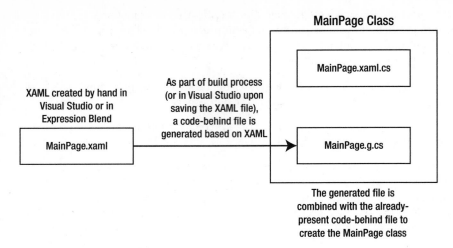

Figure 2-8. *How the full class implementation for XAML comes together*

The code placed in the initial project includes App.xaml and App.xaml.cs files. The App. xaml file doesn't have much in it, but there is one important feature to observe:

```
<Application xmlns="http://schemas.microsoft.com/winfx/2006/xaml/presentation"
             xmlns:x="http://schemas.microsoft.com/winfx/2006/xaml"
             x:Class="XAMLTour.App">
  <Application.Resources>
  </Application.Resources>
</Application>
```

The Application class contains a Resources element. Any resources specified in the Application class can be referenced throughout a Silverlight application. This is the perfect place to put style and template resources that are available to the entire application. The User-Control is actually turned into the main user interface for the application in the code-behind file, App.xaml.cs, as follows:

```
public partial class App : Application
{
  public App()
  {
    this.Startup += this.Application_Startup;
    this.Exit += this.Application_Exit;
    this.UnhandledException += this.Application_UnhandledException;
    InitializeComponent();
  }
```

```
private void Application_Startup(object sender, StartupEventArgs e)
{
  // Load the main control
  this.RootVisual = new MainPage();
}
private void Application_Exit(object sender, EventArgs e)
{
}
private void Application_UnhandledException(object sender,
                          ApplicationUnhandledExceptionEventArgs e)
{
}
}
```

The RootVisual property on the Application class specifies what will be shown when the application starts. The generated App.xaml.cs file also registers itself for all application-level events. The Exit and UnhandledException events come already registered with empty handler methods. The Startup method comes registered with a method that establishes where the main user interface comes from (RootVisual). This Startup event handler is where the connection to the MainPage class was established in the project code for this chapter.

These application events are the first events you've seen in this chapter. Many of the objects in Silverlight support events that can be hooked up either in the code-behind, as in the App.xaml.cs code, or through XAML.

Events in Silverlight

When a user clicks a button, chooses an item in a list box, or uses the cursor keys, the application must be able to respond to these events. These events are *input events* and are actually forwarded to Silverlight by the browser hosting the Silverlight plug-in. Other events, such as the application events just shown, are defined within Silverlight itself.

Keyboard and mouse events are *routed events*. These events bubble up the tree of objects starting at the first control to receive the input event. Let's create a simple example and hook up MouseLeftButton down events.

■**Note** If you have any experience with WPF, you should be aware that there is a vital difference between WPF routed events and Silverlight routed events. Silverlight routed events *only* bubble; they do not "tunnel" as they can in WPF. This means that events are only passed up the tree (bubbling); they cannot be passed down the tree (tunneling).

```
<UserControl
    xmlns="http://schemas.microsoft.com/winfx/2006/xaml/presentation"
    xmlns:x="http://schemas.microsoft.com/winfx/2006/xaml"
    x:Class="chapter2.RoutedEventExample"
    Width="400" Height="300">
    <Grid Background="Gray" MouseLeftButtonDown="Grid_MouseLeftButtonDown"
            Width="350" Height="250" >
```

```
            <Canvas Height="200" Width="300" MouseLeftButtonDown=
                "Canvas_MouseLeftButtonDown" Background="Black"  Margin="25">
              <StackPanel Height="150" Width="250" MouseLeftButtonDown=
                 "StackPanel_MouseLeftButtonDown" Background="Yellow"
                 Canvas.Top="25" Canvas.Left="25">
                <TextBlock Text= "'MouseLeftButtonDown' bubble up order" />
                <TextBlock x:Name="eventOrder" />
              </StackPanel>
            </Canvas>
        </Grid>
</UserControl>
```

In the previous code snippet, we placed a Canvas control inside the main container Grid. Inside the Canvas control we placed a StackPanel control. To differentiate them, we have set their Background properties to Gray, Black, and Yellow, respectively. For these three controls, we also defined the MouseLeftButtonDown event handler in the code-behind. When the mouse button is pressed, the click event starts at the lowest control that is aware of the event. For example, when the StackPanel is clicked, the event starts there. Look at Figure 2-9 to visualize the mousedown event bubbling up the nested controls.

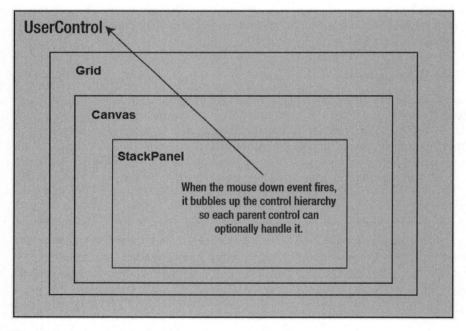

Figure 2-9. *An input event bubbling up nested controls*

The events are wired up to display which controls have received the mousedown event (which occurs when a StackPanel is clicked). The following is the code-behind showing the events handlers:

```
private void StackPanel_MouseLeftButtonDown(object sender, MouseButtonEventArgs e)
    {
        eventOrder.Text += " StackPanel";
    }

    private void Grid_MouseLeftButtonDown(object sender, MouseButtonEventArgs e)
    {
        eventOrder.Text += " Grid";
    }

    private void Canvas_MouseLeftButtonDown
      (object sender, MouseButtonEventArgs e)
    {
        eventOrder.Text += " Canvas";
    }
```

If you click StackPanel, the event originates at the StackPanel, gets sent up the tree to the enclosing Canvas control, and then gets sent up again to the enclosing Grid control. You can see the results of this in Figure 2-10. The controls receiving the event are shown in order of the TextBlock eventOrder just beneath the message "MouseLeftButtonDown' bubble up order".

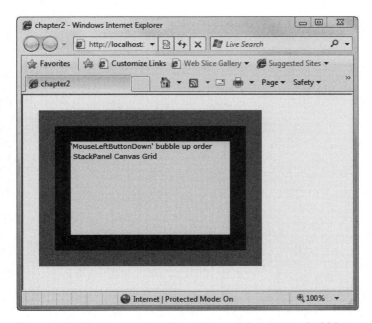

Figure 2-10. *Clicking the StackPanel causes the event to bubble up to the control's parents.*

Summary

This chapter covered the foundations of Silverlight. Before we can explore in detail more advanced topics such as theming, animation, handling media, and data binding, it is important to understand how these core features support the rest of Silverlight. Any exploration of Silverlight starts at understanding XAML and its many features, such as dependency properties, markup extensions, and resources. This chapter also showed how a Silverlight application is structured and how routed events work in Silverlight. You are now prepared to learn more about Silverlight. The next chapter explores creating user interfaces by using the layout controls and other standard controls, some of which you have already briefly seen.

CHAPTER 3

■ ■ ■

Creating User Interfaces

Now that you've seen what XAML is all about, let's look at the basic user interface controls that Silverlight provides. Silverlight supplies *standard controls* such as text boxes for display and for user input, list boxes, check boxes, radio buttons, and others. While a standard set of controls is important for building user interfaces, even more important is how these controls are placed on a user interface. This is handled by Silverlight's *layout controls*: one that enables absolute positioning and others that allow more intelligent layouts of controls. This chapter will conclude with an exploration of the new navigation framework that was introduced in Silverlight 3.

Building Blocks

Silverlight provides many useful controls for displaying information and handling data input. Before we get to the specifics of each control, it's important to understand the base functionality of all controls available for Silverlight. Figure 3-1 shows an abbreviated class diagram with a subset of Silverlight's controls and panels (used for positioning objects). While there is a `Control` class, not all elements of a user interface are controls, as you can see in Figure 3-1. This chapter will cover some of the key user interface controls and classes.

The `DependencyObject` class provides the functionality for interacting with the dependency property system. The next class, `UIElement`, is the sign that a class has a visual appearance. The `FrameworkElement` class provides some interesting behavior such as data binding, but the only requirement for a visual appearance is that a class must inherit (directly or indirectly) from `UIElement`. Chapter 7 will detail some classes that inherit from `UIElement` but not `FrameworkElement`. Let's start at the top of this class hierarchy so you can see just what functionality is provided by each class before getting to panels and controls.

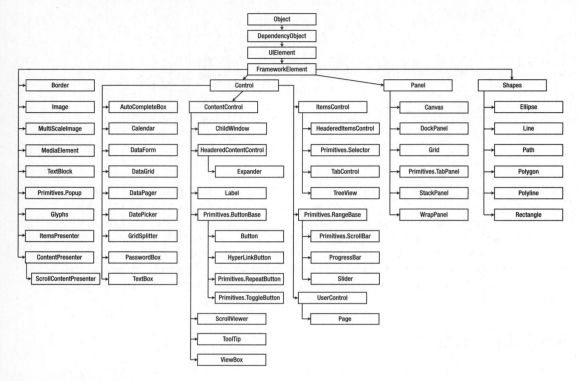

Figure 3-1. *Silverlight 3 user interface class hierarchy*

DependencyObject

The DependencyObject class is arguably the most important class in Silverlight. This object enables the dependency property system. In the previous chapter, you saw what dependency properties are and how to create them. The piece left out, however, is what enables the setting and reading of these properties. Any class that inherits directly or indirectly from DependencyObject can participate in Silverlight's dependency property system. Its most important features are the methods it provides, shown in Table 3-1.

Table 3-1. *Methods of the System.Windows.DependencyObject Class*

Method	Description
CheckAccess	Returns true if the calling thread has access to this object.
ClearValue	Removes the local value of the specified dependency property. The property might take on its default value or a value from another source.
GetAnimationBaseValue	Gets the value of the specified dependency property as if no animation were applied.

Table 3-1. *Methods of the System.Windows.DependencyObject Class*

Method	Description
GetValue	Returns the current effective value of the specified dependency property. The effective value is the result of the property system having evaluated all the possible inputs (such as property-changed callbacks, data binding, styles and templates, and animation) that participate in the property system value precedence.
ReadLocalValue	Returns the local value of the specified dependency property or UnsetValue if the property does not have a local value.
SetValue	Sets the value of the specified dependency property.

THREADING AND THE USER INTERFACE

Silverlight is a multithreaded environment. You can't modify elements of a user interface from a nonuser interface thread since it can lead to a number of problems. The proper way to modify a user interface from a different thread is by using a dispatcher. The DependencyObject class provides a single property, Dispatcher, which holds a reference to the associated dispatcher. If you want to set the value of a text block from a different thread, you must use Dispatcher.BeginInvoke to queue the modification on the main thread's work items queue ike this:

```
Dispatcher.BeginInvoke(delegate() { textBlock.Text = "changed"; });
```

You'll get a closer look at threading in Silverlight in Chapter 15.

UIElement

The UIElement class is the next class you encounter as you walk down the inheritance hierarchy. This class forms the base for all classes that have the ability to draw themselves on a user interface, including input handling, focus support, and basic layout support. Table 3-2 lists key methods of this class.

Table 3-2. *Key Methods of the System.Windows.UIElement Class*

Method	Description
Arrange	Positions objects contained by this visual element and determines size for the UIElement. Invoked by the layout system.
CaptureMouse	Sends mouse input to the object even when the mouse pointer is not within its bounding box. Useful for drag-and-drop scenarios. Only one UIElement can have the mouse captured at a time.
InvalidateArrange	Causes UIElement to update its layout.
Measure	Sets the DesiredSize property for layout purposes. Invoked by the layout system.

Table 3-2. *Key Methods of the System.Windows.UIElement Class (Continued)*

Method	Description
OnCreateAutomationPeer	Implemented by inheritors that participate in the automation system. Returns an AutomationPeer object.
ReleaseMouseCapture	Removes the mouse capture obtained via CaptureMouse.
TransformToVisual	Returns a GeneralTransform that is used to transform coordinates from this UIElement to the object passed in.
UpdateLayout	Ensures all child objects are updated for layout. Invoked by the layout system.
AddHandler	Adds a routed event handler for a specified routed event by adding the handler to the handler collection on the current element.
RemoveHandler	Removes the specified routed event handler from the UIElement.

Table 3-3 lists key properties of the UIElement class.

Table 3-3. *Key Properties of the System.Windows.UIElement Class*

Property	Type	Description
CacheMode	CacheMode	Indicates that the render content should be cached when possible.
Clip	Geometry	Defines a clipping region for the UIElement.
DesiredSize	Size	Indicates the size of the UIElement as determined by the measure pass, which is important for layout. RenderSize provides the actual size of the UIElement.
Effect	Effect	Defines the pixel shader effect to use for rendering the UIElement.
IsHitTestVisible	bool	Gets or sets whether UIElement can participate in hit testing.
Opacity	double	Specifies the opacity/transparency of the UIElement. The default value is 1.0, corresponding to full opacity. Setting this to 0.0 causes the UIElement to disappear visually, but it can still respond to hit testing.
OpacityMask	Brush	Uses a brush to apply opacity to the UIElement. This uses only the alpha component of a brush. Do not use a video brush for this property because of the lack of an alpha component.
Project	Projection	Defines the perspective projection (3D effect) to apply when rendering the UIElement.
RenderSize	Size	Indicates the actual size of the UIElement after it has passed through the layout system.
RenderTransform	Transform	Applies a transform to the rendering position of this UIElement. The default rendering offset is (0,0)—the top left of the UIElement.

Table 3-3. *Key Properties of the System.Windows.UIElement Class*

Property	Type	Description
RenderTransformOrigin	Point	Gets or sets the render transform origin. Defaults to (0,0) if not specified. This can be used to translate the UIElement.
UseLayoutRounding	Boolean	Determines whether rendering for the object and its subtree should use rounding behavior that aligns rendering to whole pixels.
Visibility	Visibility	Gets or sets the visibility state of the UIElement. Set this to Visibility.Collapsed to hide the UIElement (it does not participate in layout, is removed from the tab order, and is not hit testable). Set this to Visibility.Visible to restore the UIElement's position in its container.

UIElement also defines several important events, shown in Table 3-4.

Table 3-4. *Events of the System.Windows.UIElement Class*

Event	Description
GotFocus	Fires when the UIElement gains focus, if it doesn't already have it. Event args class: RoutedEventHandler.
KeyDown	Fires when a key is pressed. This event will bubble up to the root container. Event args class: KeyEventHandler.
KeyUp	Fires when a key is released. This event also bubbles. Event args class: KeyEventHandler.
LostFocus	Fires when the UIElement loses focus. This event bubbles. Event args class: RoutedEventHandler.
LostMouseCapture	Fires when the object loses mouse (or stylus) capture.
MouseEnter	Fires if the mouse pointer is in motion and enters the UIElement's bounding box. A parent UIElement, if it also handles this event, will receive the event before any children. Event args class: MouseEventHandler.
MouseLeave	Fires when the mouse pointer leaves the UIElement's bounding box. Event args class: MouseEventHandler; however, the information provided in the event args is without meaning since the mouse has left the UIElement's bounds.
MouseLeftButtonDown	Fires when the mouse's left button is pressed down while the mouse pointer is within the bounds of the UIElement. Event args class: MouseButtonEventHandler.
MouseLeftButtonUp	Fires when the mouse's left button is released while the mouse pointer is within the bounds of the UIElement. Event args class: MouseButtonEventHandler.
MouseMove	Fires each time the mouse pointer moves within the bounds of the UIElement. This event bubbles. Event args class: MouseEventHandler.

FrameworkElement

The next class, FrameworkElement, adds to the support introduced by UIElement. This class extends the layout support, introduces object lifetime events (such as when a FrameworkElement is loaded), and provides data binding support. This class forms the direct base of Panel and Control, the base classes for object positioning support and most controls such as Border, ContentPresenter, Image, MultiscaleImage, MediaElement, Primitives.Popup, and Shape. Table 3-5 lists key methods of this class.

Table 3-5. *Key Methods of the System.Windows.FrameworkElement Class*

Method	Description
GetBindingExpression	Retrieves the BindingExpression for a dependency property where a binding is established.
FindName	Searches the object tree, both up and down relative to the current FrameworkElement, for the object with the specified name (x:Name in XAML). Returns null if the object is not found.
OnApplyTemplate	When overridden in a derived class, is invoked whenever application code or internal processes (such as a rebuilding layout pass) call the ApplyTemplate method.
SetBinding	Binds a specified dependency property to a System.Windows.Data.Binding instance.

Table 3-6 shows the key properties of FrameworkElement's properties.

Table 3-6. *Key Properties of the System.Windows.FrameworkElement Class*

Property	Type	Description
ActualWidth	double	Indicates the width of the FrameworkElement after rendering.
ActualHeight	double	Indicates the height of the FrameworkElement after rendering.
Cursor	System.Windows.Input.Cursor	Gets/sets the cursor that is shown when the mouse hovers over this element. Possible values (from the Cursors type): Arrow, Eraser, Hand, IBeam, None (invisible cursor), SizeNS, SizeWE, Stylus, Wait. Set to null to revert to default behavior.
DataContext	Object	Defines context (source of data) used in data binding.
Height	double	Indicates the asked-for height of the FrameworkElement.

Table 3-6. *Key Properties of the System.Windows.FrameworkElement Class*

Property	Type	Description
HorizontalAlignment	HorizontalAlignment	Gets/sets the horizontal alignment. Behavior of this property is deferred to the layout control hosting this FrameworkElement. Possible values: Left, Center, Right, Stretch (default: fills the entire layout slot).
Language	System.Windows.Markup.XmlLanguage	Specifies localization/globalization language used by this FrameworkElement. Consult the XmlLanguage class documentation and RFC 3066 for details.
Margin	Thickness	Gets/sets the outer margin of this FrameworkElement.
Name	String	Gets the name of the FrameworkElement. When set in XAML, corresponds to the name of the variable automatically generated.
Resources	ResourceDictionary	Returns the resource dictionary defined on this FrameworkElement.
Style	Style	Gets/sets the style applied during rendering of this FrameworkElement.
Tag	Object	Places arbitrary information on a FrameworkElement. Restricted to the string type, although defined as an object.
VerticalAlignment	VerticalAlignment	Gets/sets the vertical alignment. Behavior is subject to the container that has this control. Possible values: Top, Center, Bottom, Stretch (default).
Width	double	Indicates the asked-for width of the FrameworkElement.

Table 3-7 shows the key events of FrameworkElement.

Table 3-7. *Key Events of the System.Windows.FrameworkElement Class*

Event	Description
BindingValidationError	Fires when a data validation error occurs as part of data binding. Event args class: ValidationErrorEventArgs.
LayoutUpdated	Fires when the layout of the FrameworkElement is updated. Event args type: EventArgs (this is a CLR event).
Loaded	Fires when the layout is complete and the element is ready for interaction. Event args type: RoutedEventHandler.
SizeChanged	Fires when the ActualWidth or ActualHeight properties are updated by the layout system. Event args type: SizeChangedEventHandler.

Positioning Objects Onscreen

Having a variety of controls and other visual objects gives us the raw material for user interfaces, but in order to form a full user interface, these objects must be positioned onscreen. This is accomplished via the Panel class—the base class of layout containers.

A layout container is used to contain controls and to oversee positioning of these controls on a user interface. In ASP.NET, layout of controls on a web page results from the application of styles to HTML tags that contain ASP.NET controls. In Windows Forms, layout is accomplished via absolute positioning, and there is no layout control; instead, controls specify their position and size. Silverlight strikes a balance between these two approaches, providing layout controls that work in conjunction with properties of its children controls (such as size properties). Silverlight provides many layout controls: Canvas, Grid, StackPanel, DockPanel, WrapPanel, and Primitives (as a base class of many complex controls). The Canvas control provides the ability to absolutely position child elements, much like in Windows Forms. The Grid control provides support for laying out controls in a tabular configuration with rows and columns. The StackPanel control displays its child controls one next to the other, either in a horizontal orientation or in a vertical orientation. The DockPanel control is useful for easily placing controls at the edges of a container, similar to the behavior of the Dock property in WinForms controls. The WrapPanel control is similar to the StackPanel, but when the edge of the container is reached, new content is placed in the next row or column. The Primitives control contains many classes and controls for more complex controls. Some examples of Primitives classes are RangeBase, TabPanel, ScrollBar, and so on. Layout controls can be nested, so by combining multiple controls you can assemble some sophisticated user interfaces.

Canvas

The Canvas provides the ability to absolutely position elements. Controls that are added directly to a Canvas can use the Canvas.Left and Canvas.Top attached properties to specify where they should appear on the canvas. Figure 3-2 depicts several controls placed on a canvas, including a nested canvas.

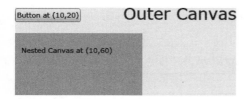

Figure 3-2. *The Canvas panel*

The XAML for this screen looks like this:

```
<UserControl x:Class="chapter3.CanvasDemo"
    xmlns="http://schemas.microsoft.com/winfx/2006/xaml/presentation"
    xmlns:x="http://schemas.microsoft.com/winfx/2006/xaml"
    Width="400" Height="300">
    <Canvas x:Name="LayoutRoot" Background="White">
        <Button Canvas.Left="10" Canvas.Top="20" Content="Button at (10,20)"/>
```

```
    <TextBlock Text="Outer Canvas" Canvas.Left="180" Canvas.Top="10"
        FontSize="26"/>
    <Canvas Canvas.Top="60" Canvas.Left="10" Background="LightSkyBlue"
                Width="200" Height="100">
        <TextBlock Text="Nested Canvas" Canvas.Left="10" Canvas.Top="20"/>
    </Canvas>
  </Canvas>
</UserControl>
```

StackPanel

A StackPanel stacks visual objects next to each other, either horizontally or vertically. The Orientation property of the StackPanel can be set to Vertical (the default) or Horizontal. Figure 3-3 shows stacking a label next to a text entry box in a horizontal orientation.

Figure 3-3. *The StackPanel*

Here's the XAML for this control:

```
<StackPanel x:Name="LayoutRoot" Background="White" Orientation="Horizontal">
    <TextBlock Text="Enter user id: "/>
    <TextBox Width="200" Height="20" VerticalAlignment="Top"/>
</StackPanel>
```

Grid

The Grid is the most complicated (relatively) and most capable layout container. It consists of one or more rows and one or more columns. Let's look at the XAML for a simple grid consisting of two rows and two columns:

```
<Grid x:Name="LayoutRoot" Background="White">
    <Grid.ColumnDefinitions>
        <ColumnDefinition/>
        <ColumnDefinition/>
    </Grid.ColumnDefinitions>
    <Grid.RowDefinitions>
        <RowDefinition/>
        <RowDefinition/>
    </Grid.RowDefinitions>
</Grid>
```

Four attached properties control where in the grid content is placed. Table 3-8 explains these attached properties.

Placing content within a grid is a simple matter of creating content and then setting values for the various attached properties. Figure 3-4 shows the result of placing content in each column of the first row and then using RowSpan to cause the content to fill the second row.

Table 3-8. *Properties of the System.Windows.Controls.Control Class*

Property	Type	Description
Grid.Row	Int32	The row of the grid where content is placed. The first row is index 0. The default value is 0.
Grid.Column	Int32	The column of the grid where content is placed. The first column is 0. The default value is 0.
Grid.RowSpan	Int32	The number of rows the content will occupy. The default value is 1.
Grid.ColumnSpan	Int32	The number of columns the content will occupy. The default value is 1.

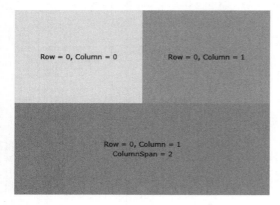

Figure 3-4. *The Grid panel*

■**Note** There is an attribute called ShowGridLines that you can set to true on the Grid element to visibly see where the columns and rows are. This is incredibly useful when designing the grid; however, the grid lines aren't especially pretty. You should use this only for designing/debugging grids. If you want grid lines, look to the Border control.

Here's what the XAML looks like to create what's shown in Figure 3-4.

```
<Border Grid.Row="0" Grid.Column="0" Background="Beige">
    <TextBlock HorizontalAlignment="Center" VerticalAlignment="Center"
                    Text="Row = 0, Column = 0"/>
</Border>
<Border Grid.Row="0" Grid.Column="1" Background="BurlyWood">
    <TextBlock HorizontalAlignment="Center" VerticalAlignment="Center"
                    Text="Row = 0, Column = 1"/>
</Border>
```

```
<Border Grid.Row="1" Grid.Column="0" Grid.ColumnSpan="2" Background="DarkKhaki">
    <StackPanel HorizontalAlignment="Center" VerticalAlignment="Center" >
        <TextBlock Text="Row = 0, Column = 1"/>
        <TextBlock HorizontalAlignment="Center" Text="ColumnSpan = 2"/>
    </StackPanel>
</Border>
```

The ColumnDefinition class has a property named Width that allows you to set the width of the column. Likewise, the RowDefinition class has a property named Height. These properties are of type GridLength, a special class that provides capabilities beyond a simple double value representing size. In XAML, the Width and Height properties can be set to the special value Auto. The Auto value causes the row/column to size automatically to the largest piece of content. More sophisticated control over space is provided by something known as *star sizing*.

The Width and Height properties can be set to the special value *, or a *star*, with a number in front, such as 2* or 3*. This syntax gives a proportional amount of the available space to a row or a column. Figure 3-5 shows a grid with a single row and two columns given the star sizes * and 2*.

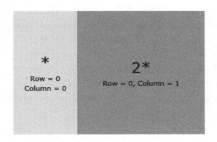

Figure 3-5. *Using star sizing with a grid*

The XAML to create this grid looks like this:

```
<UserControl x:Class="chapter3.StarSizingDemo"
    xmlns="http://schemas.microsoft.com/winfx/2006/xaml/presentation"
    xmlns:x="http://schemas.microsoft.com/winfx/2006/xaml"
    Width="300" Height="200">
    <Grid x:Name="LayoutRoot" Background="White">
        <Grid.ColumnDefinitions>
            <ColumnDefinition Width="*"/>
            <ColumnDefinition Width="2*"/>
        </Grid.ColumnDefinitions>
        <Grid.RowDefinitions>
            <RowDefinition/>
        </Grid.RowDefinitions>
        <Border Grid.Row="0" Grid.Column="0" Background="Beige">
            <StackPanel HorizontalAlignment="Center" VerticalAlignment="Center">
                <TextBlock HorizontalAlignment="Center" Text="Row = 0"/>
                <TextBlock HorizontalAlignment="Center" Text="Column = 0"/>
            </StackPanel>
        </Border>
```

```
    <Border Grid.Row="0" Grid.Column="1" Background="BurlyWood">
        <TextBlock HorizontalAlignment="Center"
                    VerticalAlignment="Center" Text="Row = 0, Column = 1"/>
    </Border>
  </Grid>
</UserControl>
```

The total width of the grid is 300. The second column is twice as big as the first, specified by the 2* property value for the width. If no number is specified before the star, it is treated the same as if the value were 1*. In this case, the first column is 100 since the second column is twice as big, and 200 added to 100 gives the total width of the grid, 300. If you combine the other sizing methods with star sizing, the value of 1* will equal whatever space is available.

DockPanel

The DockPanel is one of the new layout containers introduced in Silverlight 3. It is designed to place content around the edge of the panel. The Dock dependency property (which can be set to Left, Right, Top, or Bottom) defines the location of the child element. As its name suggests, the LastChildFill property, if set to true (which is the default value), will allow the last added child element to cover the remaining size of the panel only if the added child element is allowed to resize. Otherwise, the element will appear with the specified size in the middle of the remaining space. Figure 3-6 shows two example configurations of the DockPanel, along with the order that content was added to the DockPanel. The LastChildFill property is set to its default value of true, meaning the last child added to the DockPanel control will completely fill the remaining space.

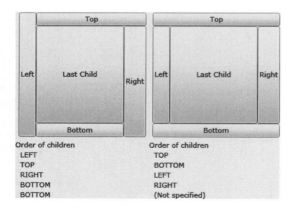

Figure 3-6. *The DockPanel*

The XAML for the first configuration in Figure 3-6 sets the Dock property on all the child content, as shown here:

```
<c:DockPanel Height="200" Width="200" Grid.Column="0" Grid.Row="1">
    <Button c:DockPanel.Dock="Left" Content="Left"/>
    <Button c:DockPanel.Dock="Top" Content="Top"/>
    <Button c:DockPanel.Dock="Right" Content="Right"/>
    <Button c:DockPanel.Dock="Bottom" Content="Bottom"/>
    <Button c:DockPanel.Dock="Bottom" Content="Last Child"/>
</c:DockPanel>
```

The XAML for the second configuration in Figure 3-6 leaves the Dock property unspecified for the last child, as shown here:

```
<c:DockPanel Height="200" Width="200" Grid.Column="1" Grid.Row="1">
    <Button c:DockPanel.Dock="Top" Content="Top"/>
    <Button c:DockPanel.Dock="Bottom" Content="Bottom"/>
    <Button c:DockPanel.Dock="Left" Content="Left"/>
    <Button c:DockPanel.Dock="Right" Content="Right"/>
    <Button Content="Last Child"/>
</c:DockPanel>
```

The order in which child content is added is important. Content added to the left and right sides will completely fill the vertical space available to them. Content added to the top and bottom will completely fill the horizontal space available to them. You can observe this in Figure 3-6 since the left content was added first to the first configuration and the top content was added first to the second configuration. When LastChildFill is true, the Dock property of the last child doesn't matter, as you can see in the second configuration where the Dock property had no value. The picture changes, however, when the LastChildFill property is set to false, as shown here:

```
<c:DockPanel Height="200" Width="200"
             Grid.Column="2" Grid.Row="1"
             LastChildFill="False">
    <Button c:DockPanel.Dock="Top" Content="Top"/>
    <Button c:DockPanel.Dock="Bottom" Content="Bottom"/>
    <Button c:DockPanel.Dock="Left" Content="Left"/>
    <Button c:DockPanel.Dock="Right" Content="Right"/>
    <Button c:DockPanel.Dock="Bottom" Content="Inner Bottom"/>
    <Button c:DockPanel.Dock="Top" Content="Inner Top"/>
</c:DockPanel>
```

Figure 3-7 shows what the inner nesting of controls looks like.

By preventing the last child from filling the space, it's possible to place more content around the edges of the container. The unfortunate consequence of this is that now the leftover space won't automatically be used by the last child added. One way to fill up the remaining space is by setting the width/height on the last child so that it fills up the space. Another technique is to nest a DockPanel within a DockPanel, giving you the ability to create the same interface as shown in Figure 3-7 without losing the fill behavior of the last child.

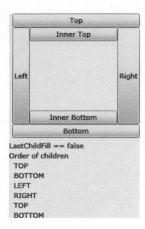

Figure 3-7. *The DockPanel with inner nesting of controls*

WrapPanel

The WrapPanel is the other new layout container in Silverlight 3. Its behavior is similar to the StackPanel in that you can automatically place content adjacent to each other (left to right or top to bottom), but it adds the behavior of wrapping content to the next row or column of an invisible grid when the content reaches the end of its available space. Figure 3-8 and Figure 3-9 show the behavior of the WrapPanel in the horizontal and vertical configurations.

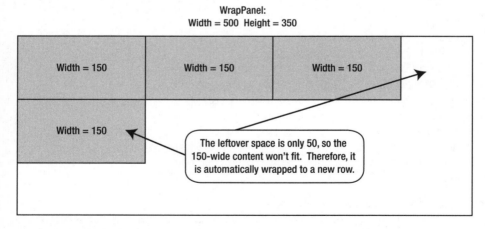

Figure 3-8. *Horizontal behavior of the WrapPanel*

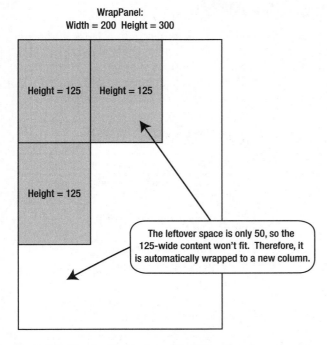

Figure 3-9. *Vertical behavior of the WrapPanel*

The WrapPanel exposes three new properties, as shown in Table 3-9, all of which are also dependency properties. The Orientation property controls whether child content is stacked horizontally (wrapping to the next row) or vertically (wrapping to the next column).

Table 3-9. *Key Properties of the System.Windows.Controls.WrapPanel Class*

Property	Type	Description
ItemHeight	Double	Specifies the height of each item. Can be set to Auto or a quali-fied value using the suffix px for device independent pixels, in for inches, cm for centimeters, or pt for points. The default is pixels.
ItemWidth	Double	Specifies the width of each item. Can be set to Auto or a qualified value using a suffix.
Orientation	Orientation	Specifies whether child content is stacked horizontally (wrapping to the next row) or vertically (wrapping to the next column). Can be set to Horizontal or Vertical.

Customizing Silverlight Controls

The System.Windows.Controls.Control class forms the base of many controls in the complete Silverlight control set and uses ControlTemplate to define the appearance of the control. This class provides properties for setting the background and foreground of a control, configuring the appearance of text within the control, and enabling control templating (something we will look at in Chapter 8). Table 3-10 describes the key properties the Control class introduces.

Table 3-10. *Key Properties of the System.Windows.Controls.Control Class*

Property	Type	Description
Background	Brush	Gets/sets the current brush used to paint the background of the control.
BorderBrush	Brush	Gets/sets the brush used to draw the border of the control.
BorderThickness	Thickness	Gets/sets the thickness of the control's border.
FontFamily	FontFamily	Indicates the font used for the text shown in the control.
FontSize	double	Gets/sets font size of the text shown in control. Defaults to 11 pt.
FontStretch	FontStretch	Gets/sets font compression/expansion for fonts that support it.
FontStyle	FontStyle	Gets/sets the font style. Possible values: Normal (default) and Italic.
FontWeight	FontWeight	Gets/sets thickness of font. Possible values range from Thin (100) to ExtraBlack (950). The default is Normal (400).
Foreground	Brush	Gets/sets the brush used to draw the foreground of the control.
IsTabStop	bool	Gets/sets whether the control participates in tab order.
IsEnabled	bool	Defines whether the user can interact with the control.
Padding	Thickness	Gets/sets the space between the content of the control and its border or margin (if no border).
TabIndex	Int32	Gets/sets the position of the control in the tab order. Lower numbers are encountered first in the tab order.
TabNavigation	KeyboardNavigationMode	Controls how tabbing with this control works. Possible values: Local (default), None, Cycle.
Template	Template	Gets/sets the control template used for the visual appearance of this control.

Border

The Border control is used to surround content with a border. It also provides the ability to easily add a background to a smaller part of a user interface. Table 3-11 describes its key properties.

Table 3-11. *Key Properties of the System.Windows.Controls.Border Class*

Property	Type	Description
Background	Brush	Gets/sets the brush used to paint the background.
BorderBrush	Brush	Gets/sets the brush used to paint the border.
BorderThickness	Thickness	Gets/sets the thickness of the border.
Child	UIElement	Indicates the single child that the border is drawn around.
CornerRadius	CornerRadius	Gets/sets the degree of rounding used for each corner. Can be set to a single value to apply a uniform rounding for all corners.
Padding	Thickness	Defines the space between the child content and the border.

Figure 3-10 shows the Border control used in various ways.

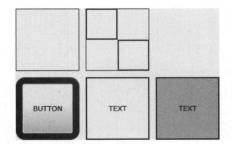

Figure 3-10. *The Border control*

The fanciest border uses a gradient brush and contains a button. We'll take a closer look at brushes in Chapter 7. Here's what the XAML looks like. The Border control can contain a single child element that forms the child content of the control, and in this case it is the first button, as shown here:

```
<Border BorderThickness="10" Width="100" Height="100" CornerRadius="10">
    <Border.BorderBrush>
        <LinearGradientBrush StartPoint="0,1" EndPoint="1,0">
            <GradientStop Color="#FF000000" Offset="0"/>
            <GradientStop Color="#FFFFF0000" Offset="1"/>
        </LinearGradientBrush>
    </Border.BorderBrush>
    <Button Content="BUTTON"></Button>
</Border>
```

The Button Controls

Many specialized versions of buttons exist, all inheriting directly or indirectly from the `ButtonBase` class (in the `System.Windows.Controls.Primitives` namespace). The `ButtonBase` class provides the basic pressing behavior that is common to all buttons. Table 3-12 describes its key properties.

Table 3-12. *Key Properties of the System.Windows.Controls.Primitives.ButtonBase Class*

Property	Type	Description
ClickMode	ClickMode	Controls how the mouse triggers the `Click` event. Possible values: `Hover` (when the mouse moves over the button); `Press` (the left mouse button is pressed down); `Release` (the left mouse button is released while over the button). Defaults to `Release`.
IsFocused	bool	True if this button has focus, `false` otherwise.
IsMouseOver	bool	True if the mouse pointer is hovering over this button, `false` otherwise.
IsPressed	bool	True if the button is in a pressed state, `false` otherwise.

The `ButtonBase` class provides a single event, `Click` (event args class: `RoutedEventHandler`). Figure 3-11 shows what various buttons look like by default.

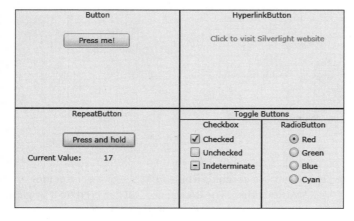

Figure 3-11. *Collection of different button controls*

Button

The Button control provides basic button functionality. Its implementation is completely supplied by the base class, `BaseButton`. Here's a basic button in XAML where the content is set to text:

```
<Button Canvas.Left="74" Canvas.Top="20" Width="100"
        Content="Press me!" x:Name="button"
        Click="Button_Click" />
```

In the previous code snippet, the `Click` event of the Button control calls the code-behind `Button_Click`, as shown here:

```
private void Button_Click(object sender, RoutedEventArgs e)
{
    //Put your custom code here
}
```

HyperlinkButton

The HyperlinkButton control introduces the capability to cause the browser to navigate to a specific web site when it is clicked. Table 3-13 describes the new properties provided by the `HyperlinkButton` class.

Table 3-13. *New Properties of the System.Windows.Controls.HyperlinkButton Class*

Property	Type	Description
NavigateUri	Uri	Gets/sets the URI to navigate to
TargetName	String	Gets/sets the name of target window/frame where navigation happens

Here's the XAML for the hyperlink button shown in Figure 3-11:

```
<HyperlinkButton x:Name="hyperlinkButton"
       Canvas.Left="45" Canvas.Top="20" Width="200"
       Content="Click to visit Silverlight website"
       NavigateUri="http://www.silverlight.net"
       TargetName="_blank/>
```

RepeatButton

The functionality introduced by a RepeatButton is the repeated firing of the `Click` event for as long as the button is clicked. You can set several properties to control how the `Click` event fires; Table 3-14 lists them.

Table 3-14. *Properties of the System.Windows.Controls.Primitives.RepeatButton Class*

Property	Type	Description
Delay	Int32	Number of milliseconds before the click action repeats, after the button is initially pressed. The default is 250.
Interval	Int32	Number of milliseconds between repeated `Click` events, after repeating starts. The default is 250.

Here's the XAML for the repeat button shown in Figure 3-11:

```
<RepeatButton Canvas.Left="73" Canvas.Top="20" Width="110"
                        Content="Press and hold" Click="RepeatButton_Click"/>
```

An event handler shows the current value increment as the button is held down:

```
private int currentValue = 0;
private void RepeatButton_Click(object sender, RoutedEventArgs e)
{
    currentValue++;
    repeatButtonValue.Text = currentValue.ToString();
}
```

Toggle Buttons: CheckBox and RadioButton

The ToggleButton provides the base functionality for both radio buttons and check boxes, which are controls that can switch states. Table 3-15 shows its key properties.

Table 3-15. *Key Properties of the System.Windows.Controls.Primitives.ToggleButton Class*

Property	Type	Description
IsChecked	Nullable<bool>	Indicates true if checked, false if not, and null if in an indeterminate state. If IsThreeState is set to true, the user can cause this property's value to cycle between true/false/null.
IsThreeState	bool	Gets/sets whether the control supports three states. If false, the button supports only two states.

The ToggleButton class introduces three new events: Checked, Unchecked, and Indeterminate. These events use RoutedEventArgs as the event argument type and capture the various states a ToggleButton can switch into. The two classes that inherit from ToggleButton are CheckBox and RadioButton. The main distinguishing factor between check boxes and radio buttons is that radio buttons can be grouped, so only one specific radio button within a group can be selected at any given moment. Table 3-16 describes the key properties of RadioButton. If no group is specified, all ungrouped radio buttons within a single parent control become part of the same group.

Table 3-16. *Key Properties of the System.Windows.Controls.RadioButton Class*

Property	Type	Description
GroupName	string	Gets/sets the name of the group to which this radio button belongs

Here's the XAML for the check boxes shown in Figure 3-11:

```
<CheckBox x:Name="checkBox" Canvas.Left="25" Canvas.Top="20"
                    IsChecked="True" Content="Checked"/>
```

```
<CheckBox x:Name="checkBox2" Canvas.Left="25" Canvas.Top="40"
                   IsChecked="False"  Content="Unchecked"/>
<CheckBox x:Name="checkBox3" Canvas.Left="25" Canvas.Top="60"
                   IsChecked="" IsThreeState="True" Content="Indeterminate"/>
```

The radio buttons are given unique names, but they share the group name to ensure the mutual exclusion functionality.

```
<RadioButton x:Name="radioButton1" GroupName="group1"
                   Canvas.Left="40" Canvas.Top="20" Content="Red"/>
<RadioButton x:Name="radioButton2" GroupName="group1"
                   Canvas.Left="40" Canvas.Top="40" Content="Green"/>
<RadioButton x:Name="radioButton3" GroupName="group1"
                   Canvas.Left="40" Canvas.Top="60" Content="Blue"/>
<RadioButton x:Name="radioButton4" GroupName="group1"
                   Canvas.Left="40" Canvas.Top="80" Content="Cyan"/>
```

GridSplitter

The GridSplitter control, which is inherited from the Control class, is used to provide the user with the capability of changing sizes of rows and columns in a grid. It exposes three key properties, as described in Table 3-17.

Table 3-17. *Key Properties of the System.Windows.Controls.GridSplitter Class*

Property	Type	Description
IsEnabled	bool	Gets/sets whether the grid splitter responds to user interaction
PreviewStyle	Style	Gets/sets the style used for previewing changes
ShowsPreview	bool	Gets/sets whether the preview is shown before changes from the grid splitter are applied

Figure 3-12 shows a checkerboard pattern with a grid splitter between the first and second column, spanning all three rows.

The XAML for this GridSplitter looks like this:

```
<Grid x:Name="LayoutRoot" Background="White">
    <!-- 3 rows, 3 columns -->
    <!-- Border controls to draw a different
         background in each cell -->
    <c:GridSplitter Grid.Row="0" Grid.Column="1"
                   Width="10" Grid.RowSpan="3"
                   HorizontalAlignment="Left"
                   VerticalAlignment="Stretch"/>
</Grid>
```

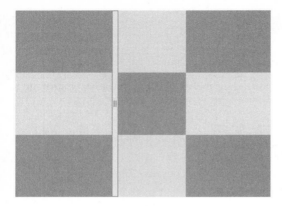

Figure 3-12. *The GridSplitter control*

TextBlock

The TextBlock control is used to display text on a user interface. This directly compares to the label controls in both Windows Forms and ASP.NET. Table 3-18 describes its properties.

Table 3-18. *Properties of the System.Windows.Controls.TextBlock Class*

Property	Type	Description
FontFamily	FontFamily	Gets/sets the set of font families. Each specified after the first is a fallback font in case a previous font is not available. Defaults to `Portable User Interface`, which encompasses several fonts in order to render the range of international language possibilities.
FontSize	double	Gets/sets the desired font size in pixels. Defaults to `14.666` (11 pt).
FontSource	FontSource	Gets/sets the font used to render text.
FontStretch	FontStretch	Gets/sets the degree to which a font is stretched. Possible values are from the `usWidthClass` definition in the OpenType specification.
FontStyle	FontStyle	Gets/sets the font style used for rendering text. Possible values: `Normal` (default) and `Italic`.
FontWeight	FontWeight	Gets/sets the desired font weight. Possible values are from the `usWeightClass` definition in the OpenType specification.
Foreground	Brush	Gets/sets the brush to apply to the text.
Inlines	InlineCollection	Gets/sets the collection of inline elements, such as `Run` and `LineBreak`, to render.

Table 3-18. *Properties of the System.Windows.Controls.TextBlock Class*

Property	Type	Description
LineHeight	double	Specifies the height of a line of text in pixels. This property is used only when the LineStackingStrategy is set to BlockLineHeight.
LineStackingStrategy	LineStackingStrategy	Specifies how each line of text is stacked. Possible values: MaxHeight (maximum height of an element within the line dictates height of line) and BlockLineHeight (maximum height controlled by the LineHeight property).
Padding	Thickness	Gets/sets the amount of space between the border of the content area and the text.
Text	string	Gets/sets the text to display.
TextAlignment	TextAlignment	Gets/sets horizontal alignment of text. Possible values: Left, Center, Right.
TextDecorations	TextDecorationCollection	Gets/sets the set of decorations to apply to the text. Currently the only decoration available is Underline.
TextWrapping	TextWrapping	Controls how text wraps when it reaches the edge of its content area. Possible values: Wrap and NoWrap.

The TextBlock control can contain inline elements, providing an alternative way to piece text together. This approach is most useful when you want to apply specific font styles, such as different colors or sizes, to elements of a larger set of text. Figure 3-13 shows several uses of the TextBlock control.

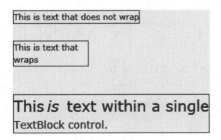

Figure 3-13. *The TextBlock control*

Here's the XAML used for each of the TextBlock controls shown in Figure 3-13, including one where the TextBlock contains multiple inline elements:

```
<Border BorderBrush="Black" BorderThickness="1" Canvas.Left="20" Canvas.Top="20">
    <TextBlock Text="This is text that does not wrap"/>
</Border>
```

```
<Border BorderBrush="Black" BorderThickness="1" Canvas.Left="20" Canvas.Top="60">
    <TextBlock Text="This is text that wraps" TextWrapping="Wrap" Width="100"/>
</Border>
<Border BorderBrush="Black" BorderThickness="1" Canvas.Left="20" Canvas.Top="130">
    <TextBlock>
        <Run FontSize="20" Text="This"/>
        <Run FontSize="20" FontStyle="Italic" Text="is "/>
        <Run FontSize="20" Text="text within a single"/>
        <LineBreak/>
        <Run Foreground="Red" FontSize="14" Text="TextBlock control."/>
    </TextBlock>
</Border>
```

TextBox

The TextBox control is used to get free-form text-based information from a user. It provides single-line and multiline input and the ability to let the user select text. Table 3-19 describes its key properties.

Table 3-19. *Key Properties of the System.Windows.Controls.TextBox Class*

Property	Type	Description
AcceptsReturn	bool	Indicates true if the text box accepts/interprets newline characters. False otherwise.
FontSource	FontSource	Defines the font used for text within the text box.
HorizontalScrollBarVisibility	ScrollBarVisibility	Controls how/when the horizontal scrollbar is displayed. Possible values: Disabled (scrollbar never appears); Auto (scrollbar appears when content cannot fully be displayed within the bounds); Hidden (like Disabled, but the dimension of the content is not set to the viewport's size); and Visible (scrollbar is always visible).
IsReadOnly	bool	Indicates no edits from the user are allowed if true. Defaults to false.
MaxLength	Int32	Defines the maximum number of characters that can be entered into a text box. The default is 0 (no restriction).
SelectedText	string	Gets the currently highlighted text. If set, the highlighted text is replaced with the new string. Any change (including programmatic) causes the SelectionChanged event to fire.
SelectionBackground	Brush	Specifies the brush used to paint the background of selected text.

Table 3-19. *Key Properties of the System.Windows.Controls.TextBox Class*

Property	Type	Description
SelectionForeground	Brush	Specifies the brush used to paint the text within the selection.
SelectionLength	Int32	Defines the number of characters currently selected, or zero if there is no selection.
SelectionStart	Int32	Specifies the index where the selected text begins within the text of the text box.
Text	string	Defines the text currently stored in the text box.
TextAlignment	TextAlignment	Gets/sets alignment of text within a text box. Possible values: Left, Center, Right.
TextWrapping	TextWrapping	Controls whether text wraps when it reaches the edge of the text box. Possible values: Wrap, NoWrap.
VerticalScrollBarVisibility	ScrollBarVisibility	Controls how/when a vertical scrollbar is displayed. See HorizontalScrollBarVisibility for possible values.

Figure 3-14 shows a single-line TextBox control and a multiline TextBox control with scrollbars. Note that for scrollbars to appear on a TextBox, the AcceptsReturn property must be set to true.

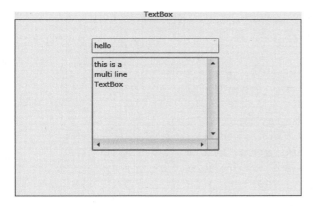

Figure 3-14. *The TextBox control*

Here's the corresponding XAML:

```
<TextBox Canvas.Top="30" Canvas.Left="120" Width="200"/>
<TextBox Canvas.Top="60" Canvas.Left="120" Height="150" Width="200"
          AcceptsReturn="True" HorizontalScrollBarVisibility="Visible"
          VerticalScrollBarVisibility="Visible"/>
```

PasswordBox

The newly introduced PasswordBox control is designed to facilitate password entry. It provides a single line or nonwrapping multiple lines for a user to enter their password. Each entered character is displayed as a defined password character based on the defined `PasswordChar` property value. Table 3-20 describes PasswordBox's key properties.

Table 3-20. *Key Properties of the System.Windows.Controls.PasswordBox Class*

Property	Type	Description
PasswordChar	Char	Defines the password-masking character
Password	String	Gets or sets the password held by the PasswordBox control
MaxLength	Integer	Defines maximum length (characters) that can be entered in the PasswordBox control

Figure 3-15 shows the use of the PasswordBox (with the masking character set to *) and the use of the `PasswordChanged` event to display the text entered in the PasswordBox control in a TextBox control.

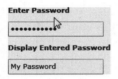

Figure 3-15. *The PasswordBox control*

Here's the corresponding XAML:

```
<StackPanel x:Name="LayoutRoot" Background="White">
<TextBlock Margin="30,10,0,0" Text="Enter Password"
    FontWeight="bold"/>
<PasswordBox x:Name="EnterPassword" Margin="30,10,0,0"
    PasswordChanged="EnterPassword_PasswordChanged" MaxLength="11"
    Height="25" Width="150" HorizontalAlignment="Left" />
<TextBlock Text="Display Entered Password" Margin="30,10,0,0"
    FontWeight="bold"/>
<TextBox x:Name="DisplayPassword" Margin="30,10,0,0"
    HorizontalAlignment="Left" IsReadOnly="True" Height="25"
    Width="150" />
</StackPanel>
```

And here's the code-behind for the `PasswordChanged` event:

```
private void EnterPassword_PasswordChanged(object sender,
    RoutedEventArgs e)
{
    DisplayPassword.Text = EnterPassword.Password;
}
```

ItemsControl

Certain controls provide the ability to present a set of content as individual items. These controls are Primitives.Selector.ListBox, Primitives.Selector.ComboBox, TabControl, TreeView, and HeaderedItemsControl. The base class that provides the item handling behavior is `ItemsControl`. Table 3-21 describes its key properties.

Table 3-21. *Key Properties of the System.Windows.Controls.ItemsControl Class*

Property	Type	Description
DisplayMemberPath	string	Gets/sets the path to the property on the source object to display.
Items	ItemCollection	Defines a collection of items to display if this is non-null.
ItemsPanel	ItemsPanelTemplate	Specifies the panel to use for displaying items. Defaults to an `ItemsPanelTemplate` that uses a StackPanel.
ItemsSource	IEnumerable	Similar to `Items`, provides the set of items to display, but provides more flexibility since any `IEnumerable` can be used.
ItemTemplate	DataTemplate	Specifies the data template used to display items. Used with data binding.

ListBox

The ListBox control is derived from the `Systems.Windows.Controls.Primitives.Selector` class and allows users to select an item from a collection of items. The ListBox provides a way to display one or more items and allows the user to select among them. Table 3-22 describes its properties.

Table 3-22. *Properties of the System.Windows.Controls.ListBox Class*

Property	Type	Description
ItemContainerStyle	Style	Gets/sets the style applied to the container for the list box's items.
SelectedIndex	Int32	Indicates the index of first selected item, or -1 if no items are selected (inherited from the `Selector` class).

Table 3-22. *Properties of the System.Windows.Controls.ListBox Class (Continued)*

Property	Type	Description
SelectedItem	Object	Indicates the first selected item, or null if no items are selected (inherited from the Selector class).
SelectedItems	IList	Defines the list of selected items for the ListBox controls.
SelectionMode	SelectionMode	Defines the way the user selects items in the ListBox control. If set to Single, then the user can select only one item at a time. If set to Multiple, then the user can select multiple items with a mouse. If set to Extended, then the user can select multiple items by pressing a modifier key, such as Ctrl or Shift.

It exposes one event, called SelectionChanged event args: SelectionChangedEventArgs), which is inherited from the Selector class.

The ListBoxItem class represents a ListBox's individual item. This class inherits from ContentControl and so can contain a wide variety of content. It exposes a single property of type bool, IsSelected, that is true when the item is selected. The appearance of the list box items can be controlled by setting the ItemTemplate property of the ListBox control. As implied by the properties shown in Table 3-22, the ListBox control supports only single selection. You can include a check box in the content for each item or create a custom list control (which can inherit from ListBox, or you can combine a ScrollViewer with a StackPanel).

Figure 3-16 shows a ListBox containing several simple items (text blocks).

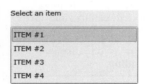

Figure 3-16. *The ListBox control*

The corresponding XAML looks like this:

```
<ListBox Canvas.Top="50" Canvas.Left="40" Width="200">
    <ListBox.Items>
        <ListBoxItem>
            <TextBlock Text="ITEM #1"/>
        </ListBoxItem>
        <ListBoxItem>
            <TextBlock Text="ITEM #2"/>
        </ListBoxItem>
        <ListBoxItem>
            <TextBlock Text="ITEM #3"/>
        </ListBoxItem>
```

```
        <ListBoxItem>
            <TextBlock Text="ITEM #4"/>
        </ListBoxItem>
    </ListBox.Items>
</ListBox>
```

We'll take a look at displaying more complex items in a ListBox by using data templates in Chapter 5.

TabControl

The TabControl is used to host content within a set of pages, with each page accessible via a tab. Table 3-23 describes its key properties.

Table 3-23. *Key Properties of the System.Windows.Controls.TabControl Class*

Property	Type	Description
SelectedContent	Object	Specifies the content of the currently active TabItem.
SelectedIndex	Int32	Gets/sets the index of the currently active TabItem, or -1 if no TabItem is active.
SelectedItem	Object	Specifies the currently active TabItem, or null if no TabItem is active.
TabStripPlacement	Dock	Gets/sets how TabItem headers align relative to the TabItem content and thus define the place where tabs are displayed within the TabControl. The Dock inumeration has four possible values specifying the behavior of the TabControl. They are Left, Top (default), Right, and Bottom.

The TabControl provides one event, SelectionChanged (event args class: SelectionChangedEventArgs). The TabControl consists of TabItems, each with a Header property that is used to set the tab label and a Content property used to set the contents of the specific tab page. Figure 3-17 shows a TabControl with three tabs.

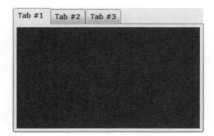

Figure 3-17. *The TabControl*

Here's the XAML for this control:

```xaml
<Canvas x:Name="LayoutRoot" Background="White">
    <c:TabControl Canvas.Left="20" Canvas.Top="40"
                  Width="300" Height="200">
        <c:TabItem Header="Tab #1">
            <Canvas Background="Red"></Canvas>
        </c:TabItem>
        <c:TabItem Header="Tab #2">
            <Canvas Background="Green"></Canvas>
        </c:TabItem>
        <c:TabItem Header="Tab #3">
            <Canvas Background="Blue"></Canvas>
        </c:TabItem>
    </c:TabControl>
</Canvas>
```

TreeView

The TreeView control implements a tree display where items can be nested within each other, such as you'd see in Windows Explorer with its directory tree. Since this control inherits from ItemsControl, its behavior is much like you'd expect, only the organization of items is different. Figure 3-18 shows what the TreeView looks like with a few of the chapter examples listed from the following XAML:

```xaml
<c:TreeView>
    <c:TreeView.Items>
        <c:TreeViewItem Header="Layout Panel Demonstrations"
                        IsExpanded="True">
            <c:TreeViewItem Header="Canvas" IsSelected="True"/>
            <c:TreeViewItem Header="WrapPanel"/>
            <c:TreeViewItem Header="DockPanel"/>
            <c:TreeViewItem Header="Grid"/>
            <c:TreeViewItem Header="StackPanel"/>
        </c:TreeViewItem>
    </c:TreeView.Items>
</c:TreeView>
```

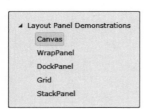

Figure 3-18. *The TreeView control*

Table 3-24 defines the key properties of the TreeView control. Only one event is new to the TreeView class, the SelectedItemChanged event.

Table 3-24. *Properties of the System.Windows.Controls.TreeView Class*

Property	Type	Description
ItemContainerGenerator	ItemContainerGenerator	Accesses the mappings between items and their containers.
ItemContainerStyle	Style	Specifies the container around each item. See Chapter 8 for details about styles.
SelectedItem	Object	Specifies the currently selected item, or null if no item is selected. This cannot be set because of a private setter.
SelectedValue	Object	Specifies the value of the SelectedItem property, or null if no item is selected. The SelectedValuePath specifies which property of SelectedItem to return.
SelectedValuePath	String	Specifies the property path used for the SelectedValue property.

The TreeViewItem Class

The most interesting functionality for the TreeView is provided by the TreeViewItem class. This class inherits from HeaderedItemsControl, so it has the ability to store a header and content separately. Table 3-25 describes its properties, and Table 3-26 describes its events.

Table 3-25. *Properties of the System.Windows.Controls.TreeViewItem Class*

Property	Type	Description
HasItems	bool	Returns true if this TreeViewItem has items, and false otherwise
IsExpanded	bool	Returns true if this TreeViewItem is expanded, and false otherwise
IsSelected	bool	Returns true if this TreeViewItem is selected, and false otherwise
IsSelectionActive	bool	Returns true if this TreeViewItem has focus, and false otherwise

Table 3-26. *Events of the System.Windows.Controls.TreeViewItem Class*

Event	Description
Collapsed	Occurs when the value of IsExpanded is changed from true to false
Expanded	Occurs when the value of IsExpanded is changed from false to true
Selected	Occurs when the value of IsSelected is changed from false to true
Unselected	Occurs when the value of IsSelected is changed from true to false

HeaderedItemsControl

The HeaderedItemsControl provides a straightforward way to display a list of items with a header area. Figure 3-19 shows what this control looks like when displaying a few color names from a string array (via data binding, which we'll look at in Chapter 5). No selection is supported with this control (combine a ListBox with a HeaderedContentControl to accomplish selection).

Figure 3-19. *The HeaderedItemsControl*

Table 3-27 defines the key properties of the HeaderedItemsControl class.

Table 3-27. *Key Properties of the System.Windows.Controls.HeaderedItemsControl Class*

Property	Type	Description
Header	object	Specifies what is used as content for the header.
HeaderTemplate	DataTemplate	Specifies the date template used to dynamically supply data for the header. See Chapter 5 for details.
ItemContainerGenerator	ItemContainerGenerator	Accesses the mappings between items and their containers.
ItemContainerStyle	Style	Specifies the style of the container around each item. See Chapter 8 for details about styles.

The XAML used to render the HeaderedItemsControl in Figure 3-19 provides a static header, and the items are supplied in the code-behind:

```
<Grid x:Name="LayoutRoot" Background="White">
    <c:HeaderedItemsControl x:Name="headeredItems">
        <c:HeaderedItemsControl.Header>
            <TextBlock FontSize="22" Text="Colors"
                        TextDecorations="Underline"/>
        </c:HeaderedItemsControl.Header>

        <c:HeaderedItemsControl.ItemTemplate>
            <DataTemplate>
                <TextBlock Text="{Binding}"/>
            </DataTemplate>
        </c:HeaderedItemsControl.ItemTemplate>
    </c:HeaderedItemsControl>
</Grid>
```

The data binding simply points the ItemsSource property in the direction of a string array:

```
string[] colors = { "Red", "Green", "Blue", "Cyan" };

headeredItems.ItemsSource = colors;
```

ContentControl

Many controls can define their content by using other controls. This provides an amazing degree of flexibility over how you construct user interfaces. One place where this is useful is in the ListBox control, where the items of the list box can be anything you can construct in XAML using controls. The controls that support this capability inherit from System.Windows.Controls. ContentControl. You can tell immediately that a specific control inherits from the ContentControl class by noticing it has a Content property in the IntelliSense window. Table 3-28 describes the key properties of ContentControl.

Table 3-28. *Key Properties of the System.Windows.Controls.ContentControl Class*

Property	Type	Description
Content	Object	Defines the value of the ContentControl dependency property
ContentTemplate	DataTemplate	Gets/sets the data template for this content control, used for data binding
IsEnabled	Boolean	Defines whether the user can interact with the control
Language	XmlLanguage	Defines localization/globalization language information that applies to FrameworkElement, from which it is inherited

The controls that inherit from ContentControl are ChildWindow, Frame, HeaderedContentControl, Label, ListBoxItem, Primitives.ButtonBase, Primitives.ScrollViewer, DataGridCell, Primitives.DataGridColumnHeader, Primitives.DataGridRowHeader, TabItem, ToolTip, and ViewBox.

HeaderedContentControl

The HeaderedContentControl provides an easy way to display a header above arbitrary content. This control is much more flexible than HeaderedItemsControl since there's no requirement for the nature of the content. The following XAML creates the same list of colors as the HeaderedItemsControl example, using a StackPanel to display the colors vertically:

```
<c:HeaderedContentControl>
    <c:HeaderedContentControl.Header>
        <TextBlock FontSize="22" Text="Colors"
                TextDecorations="Underline"/>
    </c:HeaderedContentControl.Header>
```

```
    <c:HeaderedContentControl.Content>
        <StackPanel Orientation="Vertical">
            <TextBlock Text="Red"/>
            <TextBlock Text="Green"/>
            <TextBlock Text="Blue"/>
            <TextBlock Text="Cyan"/>
        </StackPanel>
    </c:HeaderedContentControl.Content>
</c:HeaderedContentControl>
```

Table 3-29 defines the key properties of the HeaderedContentControl class.

Table 3-29. *Key Properties of the System.Windows.Controls.HeaderedContentControl Class*

Property	Type	Description
Header	object	Specifies what is used as content for the header.
HeaderTemplate	DataTemplate	Specifies the date template used to dynamically supply data for the header. See Chapter 5 for details.

AutoCompleteBox

The AutoCompleteBox provides the ability to automatically show a drop-down of items that match the partial input into a text box by a user. For example, if the AutoCompleteBox contains the items Blue, Red, Green, and Black and the user types **B**, a drop-down box will appear displaying Blue and Black. It is also possible to perform custom filtering on the AutoCompleteBox, making this control quite flexible. Although this control contains items (the data for the autocompletion), it is technically not an ItemsControl. Creating a simple AutoCompleteBox in your user interface is a matter of placing the control in the XAML and specifying the data source used for the autocompletion possibilities, like so:

```
<navigation:Page
     xmlns:input=
        "clr-namespace:System.Windows.Controls;
         assembly=System.Windows.Controls.Input"
     x:Class="chapter3.AutoCompleteBoxDemo"
  xmlns="http://schemas.microsoft.com/winfx/2006/xaml/presentation"
  xmlns:x="http://schemas.microsoft.com/winfx/2006/xaml"
  xmlns:navigation="clr-namespace:System.Windows.Controls;
                    assembly=System.Windows.Controls.Navigation"
  Title="AutoCompleteBox Demonstration">
    <StackPanel x:Name="LayoutRoot" Background="White">
        <TextBlock Text="Choose a state"/>
        <input:AutoCompleteBox x:Name="stateSelection" Width="175">
        </input:AutoCompleteBox>
    </StackPanel>

</navigation:Page>
```

Notice that this control is in a different assembly than the other controls in this chapter: System.Windows.Controls.Input. The constructor for this page creates a List<string> that is used to supply a list of states in the United States to the autocompletion box:

```
List<string> stateList = new List<string>();
stateList.Add("Alabama");
stateList.Add("Alaska");
// ...
stateList.Add("Wisconsin");
stateList.Add("Wyoming");

stateSelection.ItemsSource = stateList;
```

Figure 3-20 shows this control in action after the user types **A**.

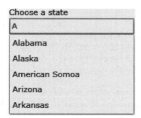

Figure 3-20. *The AutoCompleteBox control*

Table 3-30 shows the key properties of the AutoCompleteBox control, and Table 3-31 describes its key events.

Table 3-30. *Key Properties of the System.Windows.Controls.AutoCompleteBox Class*

Property	Type	Description
IsDropDownOpen	bool	Returns true if the drop-down box is open, false otherwise. Setting this to true will open the drop-down.
IsEditable	bool	Returns true, signifying the user can edit text in the text box. This is a read-only property and will always return true, unless this class is derived and this property is overridden.
IsTextCompletionEnabled	bool	When set to true, the first match found during the filtering process will appear in the text box. Defaults to false.
ItemFilter	AutoCompleteSearchPredicate<Object>	Specifies the custom method to use for item filtering. When set, the SearchMode property is automatically set to Custom.

Table 3-30. *Key Properties of the System.Windows.Controls.AutoCompleteBox Class (Continued)*

Property	Type	Description
ItemsSource	IEnumerable	Specifies an IEnumerable data source used to populate the drop-down list.
ItemTemplate	DateTemplate	Specifies how items are displayed in the drop-down box.
MinimumPopulateDelay	Int32	Specifies the time, in milliseconds, before the drop-down box starts populating after a user starts to type in the text box. Note that if the population of the drop-down box is a lengthy operation, the drop-down box won't appear immediately after the time specified in this property.
MinimumPrefixLength	Int32	Specifies the minimum number of characters the user has to type into the text box before the drop-down box will appear.
SearchMode	AutoCompleteSearchMode	Specifies the search mode used to filter items for display in the drop-down box. See Table 3-31 for a complete list.
SearchText	String	Specifies the text entered into the text box by the user and used for searching the list of items. This property is set after the TextChanged event and before the Populating event, so although it usually coincides with the Text property, it may not always.
Text	String	Specifies the text entered in the text box of this control.
TextBoxStyle	Style	Specifies the style to apply to the text box of this control.
TextFilter	AutoCompleteSearchPredicate<String>	Specifies the custom method to use for filtering of items based on the text in the text box. When set, SearchMode is automatically set to Custom.
ValueMemberBinding	Binding	Converts objects to strings so items shown in the drop-down box can be custom converted to a form suitable for the text box.

Table 3-31. *Key Events of the System.Windows.Controls.AutoCompleteBox Class*

Event	Description
DropDownClosed	Occurs when the IsDropDownOpen property is set to true and changes to false when the drop-down opens.
DropDownClosing	Occurs when the IsDropDownOpen property is set to true and changes to false.
DropDownOpened	Occurs when the IsDropDownOpen property is set to false and changes to true when the drop-down opens.
DropDownOpening	Occurs when the IsDropDownOpen property is set to false and changes to true.
Populated	Occurs after the drop-down is finished populating.
Populating	Occurs right before the drop-down starts populating.
SelectionChanged	Occurs when the selection in the drop-down changes.
TextChanged	Occurs when the text in the text box portion of the control changes.

Table 3-32 defines the possible values of SearchMode.

Table 3-32. *Possible Values of SearchMode (from AutoCompleteSearchMode Enumeration)*

SearchMode	Description
None	No filter; all items are returned.
StartsWith	Filters items that start with the text entered. Culture sensitive. Case insensitive.
StartsWithCaseSensitive	Filters items that start with the text entered. Culture sensitive. Case sensitive.
StartsWithOrdinal	Ordinal, case-insensitive filter based on items that start with the text entered.
StartsWithOrdinalCaseSensitive	Ordinal, case-sensitive filter based on items that start with the text entered.
Contains	Filters items that contain the text entered. Culture sensitive, case insensitive.
ContainsCaseSensitive	Filters items that contain the text entered. Culture sensitive, case sensitive.
ContainsOrdinal	Ordinal, case insensitive filter based on items that contain the text entered.
ContainsOrdinalCaseSensitive	Ordinal, case-sensitive filter based on items that contain the text entered.
Equals	Filters items that equal the text entered. Culture sensitive, case insensitive.

Table 3-32. *Possible Values of SearchMode (from AutoCompleteSearchMode Enumeration) (Continued)*

SearchMode	Description
EqualsCaseSensitive	Filters items that equal the text entered. Culture sensitive, case sensitive.
EqualsOrdinal	Filters items that equal the text entered. Ordinal, case insensitive.
EqualsOrdinalCaseSensitive	Filters items that equal the text entered. Ordinal, case sensitive.
Custom	Indicates a custom filtering is used, as specified by TextFilter or ItemFilter.

Popup

The Popup control is used to display content over the existing user interface, for example, showing a tool tip. Table 3-33 describes its properties.

Table 3-33. *Properties of the System.Windows.Controls.Primitives.Popup Class*

Property	Type	Description
Child	UIElement	Gets/sets the content to display.
HorizontalOffset	double	Defines the horizontal offset used in displaying the pop-up. Defaults to 0 (left side).
IsOpen	bool	Gets/sets whether the pop-up is open.
VerticalOffset	double	Vertical offset used in displaying the pop-up. Defaults to 0 (top).

The Popup class provides two events: Opened and Closed. These events fire when the pop-up is opened or closed via setting of the IsOpen property. Figure 3-21 shows a button and the pop-up that opens when the button is clicked.

Figure 3-21. *The Popup control*

The XAML for the pop-up looks like this:

```
<Popup x:Name="xamlPopup" VerticalOffset="40"
            HorizontalOffset="270" IsOpen="False">
    <Border BorderBrush="Black" BorderThickness="5" CornerRadius="3">
        <Button Content="Click to close" Click="button_Click"/>
    </Border>
</Popup>
```

The showing and hiding of the pop-up is done programmatically by simply setting the IsOpen property of the Popup control to the correct value to show or hide the pop-up.

```
void button_Click(object sender, RoutedEventArgs e)
{
    xamlPopup.IsOpen = false;
}
private void showPopup_Click(object sender, RoutedEventArgs e)
{
    xamlPopup.IsOpen = true;
}
```

ToolTipService

The ToolTipService class is used to programmatically associate a UIElement describing content of the tool tip with the control. It provides an attached property (ToolTip) that is used in the XAML to create a tool tip without having to go to the code-behind. Figure 3-22 shows two buttons, the first with a tool tip already attached (displayed in Figure 3-21) and the second that gets a tool tip after the first button is clicked.

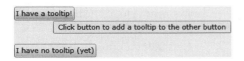

Figure 3-22. *The tool tip control*

The XAML for the first button looks like this:

```
<Button Canvas.Left="20" Canvas.Top="40"
        ToolTipService.ToolTip="Click button to add a tooltip to the other button"
        Content="I have a tooltip!"   Click="Button_Click"/>
```

The click handler programmatically adds the second button's tool tip via the SetTooltip method.

```
private void Button_Click(object sender, RoutedEventArgs e)
{
    Border b = new Border();
    b.BorderBrush = new SolidColorBrush(Color.FromArgb(255, 128, 128, 128));
    b.BorderThickness = new Thickness(5);
    TextBlock t = new TextBlock();
    t.Margin = new Thickness(5);
    t.Text = "I am another tool tip";
    b.Child = t;
    ToolTipService.SetToolTip(secondButton, b);
}
```

ScrollViewer

The ScrollViewer control is used to display content that is possibly larger than the allotted space, so scrollbars are used to let the user scroll to different sections of the content. It exposes a large set of properties that control the presentation of content, shown in Table 3-34.

Table 3-34. *Key Properties of the System.Windows.Controls.ScrollViewer Class*

Property	Type	Description
ComputedHorizontalScrollBarVisibility	Visibility	Gets/sets whether the horizontal scrollbar is currently visible
ComputedVerticalScrollBarVisibility	Visibility	Gets/sets whether the vertical scrollbar is currently visible
HorizontalOffset	double	Gets/sets the current horizontal offset of the content
HorizontalScrollBarVisibility	Visibility	Gets/sets whether the horizontal scrollbar should be displayed
ScrollableHeight	double	Defines the total vertical size of the content
ScrollableWidth	double	Defines the total horizontal size of the content
VerticalOffset	double	Gets/sets the current vertical offset of the content
VerticalScrollBarVisibility	Visibility	Gets/sets whether the vertical scrollbar should be displayed
ViewportHeight	double	Gets/sets the height of the viewport (the window into the content that is onscreen)
ViewportWidth	double	Gets/sets the width of the viewport

Figure 3-23 shows a grid with a checkerboard pattern contained in a ScrollView control. The content is too large to display completely, so the vertical scrollbar is added automatically (the horizontal scrollbar is added automatically but must be set to Auto first).

Here's the XAML to create the grid inside the scroll viewer:

```
<Canvas x:Name="LayoutRoot" Background="White">
    <ScrollViewer Canvas.Left="60" Canvas.Top="70" Width="250"
                Height="200" HorizontalScrollBarVisibility="Auto">
        <Grid Background="White" Height="300" Width="400">
            <!-- 3 rows, 3 columns -->
            <!-- Border controls to draw a different background in each cell -->
        </Grid>
    </ScrollViewer>
</Canvas>
```

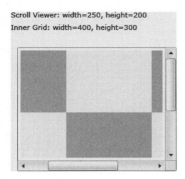

Figure 3-23. *The ScrollViewer control*

The RangeBase Class

The RangeBase class provides behavior to handle a range of values and a selected value within this range. It is the base class of the ScrollBar, Slider, and ProgressBar controls. The RangeBase class uses value coercion in order to ensure the current value is within the range. An ArgumentException will be raised if any of the properties defining the end points of the range are set to a value that does not make sense, such as setting Minimum to NaN or SmallChange to a value less than zero. Table 3-35 shows the properties of RangeBase.

Table 3-35. *Properties of the System.Windows.Controls.Primitives.RangeBase Class*

Property	Type	Description
LargeChange	double	Specifies the value to add/subtract from the current value. Defaults to 1. Exact behavior is specified by the inheritor.
Maximum	double	Defines the highest value possible for this range.
Minimum	double	Defines the lowest value possible for this range.
SmallChange	double	Specifies the value to add/subtract from the current value. Defaults to 0.1. Exact behavior is specified by the inheritor.
Value	double	Gets/sets the current value. This property is subjected to value coercion to ensure it stays within range.

The RangeBase provides one event: ValueChanged.

ScrollBar

The ScrollBar class is visually represented by two RepeatButton controls and a Thumb control that corresponds to the currently selected value within the range. You can see what a horizontal and vertical scrollbar on their own look like in Figure 3-24.

Figure 3-24. *ScrollBar controls*

Table 3-36 describes ScrollBar's properties.

Table 3-36. *Key Properties of the System.Windows.Controls.Primitives.ScrollBar Class*

Property	Type	Description
Orientation	Orientation	Gets/sets the orientation of the scrollbar. Possible values: Horizontal, Vertical.
ViewportSize	double	Specifies the amount of content that is currently visible according to the position of the thumb within the scrollbar. Defaults to 0.

The ScrollBar class provides one event: Scroll (event args class: ScrollEventArgs). This event fires only when the user changes the position of the thumb, not when the Value property is changed in the code-behind.

The XAML for the scrollbars shown in Figure 3-24 looks like this:

```
<Canvas x:Name="LayoutRoot" Background="White">
    <TextBlock Text="Horizontal Scroll Bar" Canvas.Left="20" Canvas.Top="40"/>
    <ScrollBar Orientation="Horizontal" Canvas.Left="20" Canvas.Top="70" Width="200"
                   Minimum="0" Maximum="100"
                   SmallChange="1" LargeChange="10" Value="50"/>
    <TextBlock Text="Vertical Scroll Bar" Canvas.Left="20" Canvas.Top="100"/>
    <ScrollBar Orientation="Vertical" Canvas.Left="150" Canvas.Top="100"
        Width="25"/>
</Canvas>
```

Slider

The Slider control is essentially a scrollbar, but it provides the capability to select a value from within a range. It inherits from RangeBase. Table 3-37 shows its properties.

Table 3-37. *Properties of the System.Windows.Controls.Slider Class*

Property	Type	Description
IsDirectionReversed	bool	Reverses the direction of increasing values if true: down for vertical sliders and left for horizontal sliders.
IsFocused	bool	Returns true if the slider currently has input focus.
Orientation	Orientation	Gets/sets the orientation of slider. Possible values: Vertical, Horizontal.

Figure 3-25 shows what a horizontal and vertical slider look like.

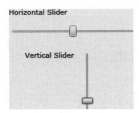

Figure 3-25. *Slider controls*

Here's the XAML used to create those sliders:

```
<Canvas x:Name="LayoutRoot" Background="White">
    <TextBlock Text="Horizontal Slider" Canvas.Left="20" Canvas.Top="40"/>
    <Slider Orientation="Horizontal" Canvas.Left="20" Canvas.Top="70" Width="200"
            Minimum="0" Maximum="100" SmallChange="1" LargeChange="10"
            Value="50"/>
    <TextBlock Text="Vertical Slider" Canvas.Left="20" Canvas.Top="100"/>
    <Slider Orientation="Vertical" Canvas.Left="130" Canvas.Top="100"
            Width="25" Height="100"/>
</Canvas>
```

ProgressBar

The ProgressBar control represents the advancement of the defined operation. It also inherits from RangeBase. You can define the following two visual styles for the ProgressBar control using the IsIndeterminate property:

- You can have a progress bar with a repeating pattern. You need to set the IsIndeterminate property to true.

- You can have a progress bar that gets filled based on the value. You need to set the IsIndeterminate property to false and define the range by setting the Minimum and Maximum properties and by setting the value using the Value property.

Table 3-38 shows its key property.

Table 3-38. *Key Property of the System.Windows.Controls.ProgressBar Class*

Property	Type	Description
IsIndeterminate	bool	Defines the progress bar's visual style as a repeating pattern or filling bar based on the value.

Figure 3-26 shows the progress bar with a repeating pattern and with a filled style.

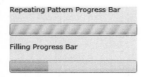

Figure 3-26. *ProgressBar control in two different styles*

Here's the XAML used to create the different styles of the progress bar:

```
<Canvas x:Name="LayoutRoot" Background="White">
    <TextBlock Text="Repeating Pattern Progress Bar"
        Canvas.Left="20" Canvas.Top="40"/>
    <ProgressBar Height="20" Width="200" IsIndeterminate="True"
        Canvas.Left="20" Canvas.Top="70"/>
    <TextBlock Text="Filling Progress Bar"
        Canvas.Left="20" Canvas.Top="100"/>
    <ProgressBar Height="20" Width="200" IsIndeterminate="False"
        Minimum="0" Maximum="100" Value="30"
        Canvas.Left="20" Canvas.Top="130"/>
</Canvas>
```

Calendar and DatePicker

The Calendar control provides a full calendar onscreen that the user can use to navigate to a month and select a date. It supports forbidding certain dates from being selected and constraining itself to a given date range. Table 3-39 shows the key properties for the Calendar control.

Table 3-39. *Key Properties of the System.Windows.Controls.Calendar Class*

Property	Type	Description
BlackoutDates	CalendarDateRangeCollection	Contains a set of dates that are blacked out and thus cannot be selected by a user.
CalendarButtonStyle	Style	Defines Style related to the control's internal CalendarButton object.
CalendarItemStyle	Style	Defines Style related to the control's internal CalendarItem object.
DisplayDate	DateTime	Specifies the date to display in the calendar.
DisplayDateStart	Nullable<DateTime>	Specifies the first date to display.
DisplayDateEnd	Nullable<DateTime>	Specifies the last date to display.
DisplayMode	CalendarMode	Controls how the calendar presents itself. Possible values: Month (displays a full month at a time), Year (displays a full year at a time), and Decade (displays a decade at a time).
FirstDayOfWeek	DayOfWeek	Specifies the day that marks the beginning of the week. Defaults to DayOfWeek.Sunday.
IsTodayHighlighted	bool	Returns true if today's date is selected in the calendar.
SelectedDate	Nullable<DateTime>	Indicates null if no date is selected, otherwise the selected date.
SelectedDates	SelectedDatesCollection	Contains one or more selected dates, unless selection mode is None.
SelectionMode	CalendarSelectionMode	Gets/sets how the selection works in the calendar. The CalendarSelection-Mode enum members are None (no selections are allowed), SingleDate (only one date can be selected), SingleRange (only one consecutive range of dates can be selected), MultipleRange (different, disconnected ranges of dates can be selected).

The Calendar control provides three events: DisplayDateChanged, DisplayModeChanged, and SelectedDatesChanged.

There is another control, the `DatePicker`, which allows selecting a date. It consists of a TextBox, a Button, and a Calendar control. The user can enter a date in the TextBox control or click the Button and select a date. The Calendar control appears only when the button is clicked. The DatePicker control contains many properties similar to the Calender control. If the user types a date in the TextBox, the date can be retrieved using the Text property. If the entered value is not a valid date, then a DateValidationError event will be raised, unless the `ThrowException` property is set to `false`.

Figure 3-27 shows what the Calendar and DatePicker controls look like.

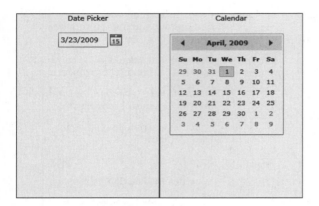

Figure 3-27. *The Calendar and DatePicker controls*

The XAML for these controls looks like this:

```
<Border Grid.Column="0" Grid.Row="0" Grid.RowSpan="2"
            BorderBrush="Black" BorderThickness="1">
    <Canvas>
        <swcx:DatePicker x:Name="datePicker" Canvas.Top="30" Canvas.Left="65"/>
    </Canvas>
</Border>
<Border Grid.Column="1" Grid.Row="0" Grid.RowSpan="2"
            BorderBrush="Black" BorderThickness="1">
    <Canvas>
        <swcx:Calendar x:Name="calendar" Canvas.Top="30" Canvas.Left="15"
                                SelectionMode="SingleRange"/>
    </Canvas>
</Border>
```

Creating Application Navigation

Silverlight provides a `UserControl` class and a `Page` class, both of which you can use to construct user interface screens, since both can contain arbitrary content. In general, you should use the user controls for reusable pieces of user interfaces, such as combining a country, state, and postal code selection so they can be used in different parts of an application (such as for shipping, billing, and contact information). The `Page` class is a larger, more enveloping type of container that is meant to contain different screens in an application that a user will interact with since it's aware of the navigation capabilities of the application. Silverlight 3 introduces a navigation framework to connect different XAML pages together to form a complete application. While *navigation* brings with it the connotation of moving forward/backward like we are used to in web browsers, navigation is really a broader concept that encompasses how separate XAML pages can be brought together to form an application.

Implementing Custom Navigation

Before we take a look at the navigation support in Silverlight 3, let's look at one approach for implementing your own navigation. This custom navigation was necessary in Silverlight 2. In Silverlight 3, custom navigation can still prove useful in certain scenarios, even if it isn't mandated any longer. In the previous edition of this book, a user control called XAML_Viewer was used throughout to demonstrate XAML pages from each chapter. (Please note that the XAML_Viewer is included with the code only for this particular chapter.) Figure 3-28 shows what this looks like.

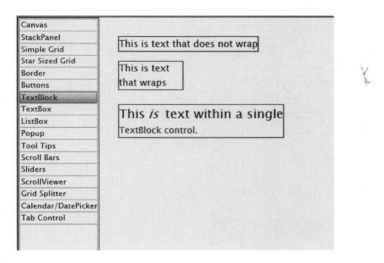

Figure 3-28. *The XAML_Viewer*

The XAML for XAML_Viewer simply holds an empty ListBox within a Grid container:

```
<UserControl x:Class="chapter3.XAML_Viewer"
    xmlns="http://schemas.microsoft.com/winfx/2006/xaml/presentation"
    xmlns:x="http://schemas.microsoft.com/winfx/2006/xaml">
    <Grid x:Name="LayoutRoot" Background="White">
        <Grid.ColumnDefinitions>
            <ColumnDefinition Width="Auto"/>
            <ColumnDefinition Width="Auto"/>
        </Grid.ColumnDefinitions>

        <Grid.RowDefinitions>
            <RowDefinition/>
```

```
        </Grid.RowDefinitions>

        <ListBox x:Name="xamlPageList"
                SelectionChanged=
                    "xamlPageList_SelectionChanged">
        </ListBox>
    </Grid>
</UserControl>
```

The specific demonstrations were added via an addXamlPage method invoked from the App.xaml.cs code (on application startup, each chapter's startup handler will add the demonstrations):

```
public void addXamlPage(string friendlyName,
                        UserControl xamlPage)
{
    xamlPageList.Items.Add(friendlyName);
    pageDictionary.Add(friendlyName, xamlPage);

    LayoutRoot.Children.Add(xamlPage);

    xamlPage.SetValue(Grid.ColumnProperty, 1);
    xamlPage.SetValue(Grid.RowProperty, 0);
    xamlPage.VerticalAlignment = VerticalAlignment.Top;
    xamlPage.Visibility = Visibility.Collapsed;

    if (xamlPageList.Items.Count == 1)
    {
        // Automatically make first page visible
        currentPage = xamlPage;
        currentPage.Visibility = Visibility.Visible;
    }
}
```

This method adds each demonstration to a Dictionary<string, UserControl> that maps the name of the demonstration as shown in the ListBox control to the instance of the user control for the demonstration. It does the extra work of making sure each demonstration is located in the proper place in the Grid container and of making sure the first added demonstration is automatically visible. All demonstrations after the first one are left in the Collapsed state, meaning they aren't visible (though they are still instantiated and present in the visual tree).

If you look back at the XAML code, you'll notice that the SelectionChanged event is wired up. This is how you expose the control of the navigation to the user. The event handler hides the currently displayed demonstration and makes the one the user clicked visible.

```
private void xamlPageList_SelectionChanged(object sender,
                              SelectionChangedEventArgs e)
{
    if (currentPage != null)
    {
        currentPage.Visibility = Visibility.Collapsed;
    }

    UserControl page =
        pageDictionary[(string)xamlPageList.SelectedItem];

    if (page != null)
    {
        currentPage = page;
        currentPage.Visibility = Visibility.Visible;
        currentPage.Focus();
    }
}
```

The only extra work this event handler does is to set the focus to the newly displayed demonstration. This is an effective way to manually handle navigation, though it has one ramification that must be considered before using it. Since the user controls are still present in the visual tree, they can receive events that propagate from a higher source. If multiple user controls are handling some of these events (for example, contacting the server when the application detects it is online), any state you rely on might change without your immediate notice. If you want to avoid this, then the class that implements the custom navigation (XAML_Viewer, in this case) can disconnect user controls from the visual tree and then re-connect them as the user navigates via the selection list. This disconnection and re-connection is done via LayoutRoot.Children.Add and LayoutRoot.Children.Remove. The revised addXamlPage and selection event handler ensure only one demonstration user control is ever located in the Children collection.

```
public void addXamlPage(string friendlyName, UserControl page)
{
    xamlPageList.Items.Add(friendlyName);
    pageDictionary.Add(friendlyName, page);

    if (xamlPageList.Items.Count == 1)
    {
        // Automatically make first page visible
        LayoutRoot.Children.Add(page);

        showPage(page);
    }
}
```

```
private void xamlPageList_SelectionChanged(object sender,
                            SelectionChangedEventArgs e)
{
    UserControl page =
        pageDictionary[(string)xamlPageList.SelectedItem];

    showPage(page);
}
```

The showPage method does the dirty work for you:

```
private void showPage(UserControl page)
{
    if (currentPage != null)
    {
        LayoutRoot.Children.Remove(currentPage);
    }

    currentPage = page;

    LayoutRoot.Children.Add(page);

    page.SetValue(Grid.ColumnProperty, 1);
    page.SetValue(Grid.RowProperty, 0);
    page.VerticalAlignment = VerticalAlignment.Top;
    page.Visibility = Visibility.Visible;
    page.Focus();
}
```

That is basically all there is to implementing a manual navigation scheme. The first approach simply hides and shows the proper user controls to implement navigation from one user interface screen to another, and the latter approach ensures controls not being used are disconnected from the visual tree. Since Silverlight applications can live in the browser, you might be wondering whether it's possible to integrate with the browser's back and forward buttons. This is possible in Silverlight 3 using its navigation framework, but it's also possible to implement this manually.

We'll expand on adding this functionality to the manual navigation in Chapter 10 when we look at invoking browser functionality from Silverlight. Let's now look closer at the navigation functionality in Silverlight 3 since it will likely be what most developers use for navigation. Another quick sample using the navigation framework is also provided in Chapter 15.

Using the Navigation Framework

There are several important pieces to the navigation framework, including the new Frame class that is in charge of the navigation, the Page class that subjects itself to navigation, the URI mapping for simplifying page references, a journal, and, of course, integration with the host browser's forward and back buttons. We'll explore the navigation framework by taking the XAML_Viewer example and turning it into DemoPresenter, a new user interface that acts as a container for the chapter demonstrations. The navigation framework is located in the System. Windows.Navigation namespace, with supporting controls in the System.Windows.Controls and

System.Windows.Controls.Navigation namespaces. These namespaces are located in the System.Windows.Controls.Navigation assembly (this is automatically added as a reference in new Silverlight 3 applications and also is added as part of the project upgrade process in Visual Studio 2008).

The Frame Class

The Frame class is responsible for displaying the page (actually any user control, because the Page class inherits from UserControl) that is the target of the navigation. Tables 3-40, 3-41, and 3-42 show the properties, methods, and events of the Frame class.

Table 3-40. *Properties of the System.Windows.Controls.Frame Class*

Property	Type	Description
CanGoBack	bool	Returns true if there are entries in the navigation journal previous to the currently active entry.
CanGoForward	bool	Returns true if there are entries in the navigation journal after the currently active entry.
CurrentSource	Uri	Stores the URI corresponding to the last navigation. This property is updated only after the navigation has completed.
JournalOwnership	JournalOwnership	Controls the behavior of the journal. Possible values are Automatic (top-level frames integrate with browser journal; otherwise, frame uses its own journal); OwnsJournal (the frame uses its own journal); and UsesParentJournal (integrates with browser's journal; if set on a non-top-level frame, an exception is thrown).
Source	Uri	Stores the URI of the next navigation. This is distinct from CurrentSource because its value is set at the beginning of the navigation. After navigation is complete, the value of Source and CurrentSource will be the same.

Table 3-41. *Methods of the System.Windows.Controls.Frame Class*

Method	Description
GoBack	Navigates to the previous journal entry if there is a journal entry previous to the currently active entry.
GoForward	Navigates to the next journal entry if there is a journal entry after the currently active entry.
Navigate	Navigates to the specified URI. The URI can be an absolute path to XAML within the application or a URI specified in an URI mapping.
OnApplyTemplate	Overrides the FrameworkElement.OnApplyTemplate and is called when the template generation for the visual tree is created.
StopLoading	Stops the navigation request, most useful when the navigation request triggers downloading of content or lengthy creation of the XAML that is the target of the navigation.

Table 3-42. *Events of the System.Windows.Controls.Frame Class*

Event	Description
FragmentNavigation	Occurs at the beginning of a navigation request
Navigated	Occurs after a navigation completes
Navigating	Occurs at the beginning of a navigation request
NavigationFailed	Occurs after an error during a navigation attempt
NavigationStopped	Occurs after StopLoading is invoked or the current navigation is aborted via a new navigation request

The Page Class

The Page class inherits from UserControl, so it inherits a large chunk of functionality. The reason the Page class exists is to have a navigation-aware user control. It provides event handlers that you can override to conduct custom processing based on navigation. It also exposes a Title property that you can use to show some meaningful text in the navigation history and a couple properties that give you access to the navigation service. Tables 3-43 and 3-44 show the properties and methods of the Page class.

Table 3-43. *Properties of the System.Windows.Controls.Page Class*

Property	Type	Description
NavigationContext	NavigationContext	Provides access to the Uri and the QueryString data.
NavigationService	NavigationService	Provides access to the NavigationService instance that the Frame is using. Exposes same properties as Frame except for JournalOwnership. It also exposes the same events as Frame. A navigation request can be initiated from a Page via this object.
Title	String	The text of the Title property gets displayed in the navigation history and the browser's title bar. If this is not set, the title bar and navigation history show the URI.

Table 3-44. *Key Methods of the System.Windows.Controls.Page Class*

Method	Description
OnFragmentNavigation	Called when navigation to a fragment starts
OnNavigatedFrom	Called when a page is no longer active (navigation to another page has started)
OnNavigatedTo	Called when the page is made the active page via navigation
OnNavigatingFrom	Called before the page is no longer active (navigation to another page has started)

Between the Frame class and the Page class, there are a lot of events that provide opportunities to step into the navigation process and perform custom work. Figure 3-29 shows the order these events fire.

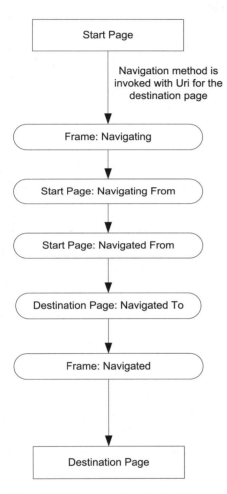

Figure 3-29. *Events order during the navigation process*

Developing the Demonstration Presenter

The user interface for DemoPresenter adds extra space and also uses Expander controls for categorizing demonstrations (we won't be looking at the categorization piece here, but it's in the code for you to explore). You can see what DemoPresenter looks like in Figure 3-30.

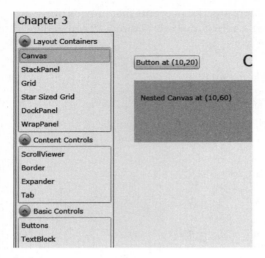

Figure 3-30. *The DemoPresenter*

Here's the XAML for DemoPresenter:

```
<navigation:Page
    xmlns:controls="clr-namespace:System.Windows.Controls;
                    assembly=System.Windows.Controls"
    x:Class="chapter3.DemoPresenter"
    xmlns=
      "http://schemas.microsoft.com/winfx/2006/xaml/presentation"
    xmlns:x=
      "http://schemas.microsoft.com/winfx/2006/xaml"
    xmlns:navigation=
      "clr-namespace:System.Windows.Controls;
       assembly=System.Windows.Controls.Navigation"
    Title="DemoPresenter Page">
    <Grid x:Name="LayoutRoot" Background="White">
        <Grid.ColumnDefinitions>
            <ColumnDefinition Width="Auto"/>
            <ColumnDefinition Width="Auto"/>
        </Grid.ColumnDefinitions>

        <Grid.RowDefinitions>
            <RowDefinition Height="Auto"/>
            <RowDefinition Height="Auto"/>
        </Grid.RowDefinitions>
```

```
<TextBlock x:Name="demoTitle"
           Grid.Row="0" Grid.Column="0"
           FontFamily="Tahoma" FontSize="16"
           Margin="5">Chapter 3</TextBlock>

<ListBox x:Name="demoList"
     SelectionChanged="demoList_SelectionChanged"
     Grid.Row="1" Grid.Column="0">
</ListBox>

<navigation:Frame x:Name="MainFrame"
     HorizontalContentAlignment="Left"
     VerticalContentAlignment="Top"
     Grid.Row="1" Grid.Column="1">
</navigation:Frame>
    </Grid>

</navigation:Page>
```

The first significant item of note about this XAML is the new namespace declaration, xmlns:navigation. This imports the namespace to expose the controls you need, specifically Frame and Page. The Page class is a user control that provides some extra functionality, such as a title property that will automatically show in the browser's title bar. The next item of note is the placement of the Frame control. The Frame class acts as a container for content, so you can place it anywhere you'd like within an existing user interface. Provided it is the top-level frame (that is, it isn't a frame embedded within another frame), it can integrate with the browser's navigation journal (and will do so automatically, unless specified otherwise via the JournalOwnership property). The ListBox control again contains the list of demonstrations; however, the Dictionary<> object in the code-behind no longer holds instances to the XAML pages.

```
private Dictionary<string, string> demos;

internal void addDemo(string title, string uri)
{
    demos.Add(title, uri);
    demoList.Items.Add(title);
}
```

The Dictionary<> instead associates the friendly name of a demonstration (what's shown in the list box) with its URI (in string form). The selection changed event of the ListBox control is significantly shorter than it is in the XAML_Viewer. Since the URIs of the XAML pages are readily available, all it takes is a single call to Navigate to change which demonstration is currently on display.

```
private void demoList_SelectionChanged(object sender,
                            SelectionChangedEventArgs e)
{
    MainFrame.Navigate(new Uri(demos[(string)demoList.SelectedItem],
                            UriKind.Relative));
}
```

When `Navigate` is called, the URI is a relative URI since the location of the XAML page is relative to the root of the Silverlight application. If you were to explore this chapter's XAML pages via the code just provided, you'd see the URL and title bar in your browser, as shown in Figure 3-31.

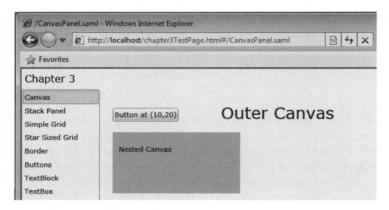

Figure 3-31. *The URI revealed in the browser's title bar*

The text after the hash mark (the # symbol) in the browser URL is called a *fragment*. In this case, the fragment is the path to the XAML page, which is referred to as *deep linking*. In the past, pages within Silverlight applications could be bookmarked only using custom code. If a user bookmarked the page that a Silverlight application was hosted in, the application would always start at the same place for all users. Deep linking enables the bookmarking of pages within a Silverlight application, so a user can easily return to a specific part of the application.

There are two main problems with directly using the URIs of XAML pages within the application. First, when the frame is using the browser's navigation journal, the title bar will display the fragment as opposed to something more user-friendly. Second, it ties the paths and names of XAML pages directly to the navigational organization of the application. To address these issues, you can use a *URI mapper* to map arbitrary URIs that you define to the actual URIs of the XAML pages within the application. You can place the URI mappings within any resource dictionary. Here's what the XAML looks like if you were to add the URI mapper to the application-level resource dictionary:

```
<Application
  xmlns="http://schemas.microsoft.com/winfx/2006/xaml/presentation"
  xmlns:x="http://schemas.microsoft.com/winfx/2006/xaml"
  x:Class="chapter3.App"
  xmlns:nav=
```

```
"clr-namespace:System.Windows.Navigation;
  assembly=System.Windows.Controls.Navigation">
<Application.Resources>
    <nav:UriMapper x:Key="uriMapper">
        <nav:UriMapping Uri="Canvas"
                    MappedUri="/CanvasPanel.xaml"/>
        <nav:UriMapping Uri="Stack Panel"
                    MappedUri="/StackPanelExample.xaml"/>
    </nav:UriMapper>
</Application.Resources>
</Application>
```

If you define the URI mapper in a XAML page, you must also import the System.Windows.
Navigation namespace. This is done via the xmlns:nav declaration. This gives you access to
UriMapper and UriMapping. The Uri property contains the user-friendly URI that might be displayed
in the browser's title bar (page titles override the URI for display purposes). Spaces are allowed,
but remember that they will be encoded to %20 in the browser's URL, as will other special characters. The MappedUri property contains the actual URI that the navigation will use. It's too
much work to track two lists of the demonstration XAML pages for each chapter (one in App.
xaml.cs and one in App.xaml for the URI mappings), so, instead, we'll dynamically create these
URI mappings in the DemoPresenter example's code-behind. The revised addDemo method
creates the UriMapper instance (if it doesn't already exist) in the frame's resource dictionary
and then adds the new UriMapping instance:

```
internal void addDemo(string title, string uri)
{
    demoList.Items.Add(title);

    UriMapper mapper =
        (UriMapper)MainFrame.Resources["uriMapper"];

    if (mapper == null)
    {
        mapper = new UriMapper();
        MainFrame.Resources.Add("uriMapper", mapper);
    }

    UriMapping mapping = new UriMapping();
    mapping.Uri = new Uri(title, UriKind.Relative);
    mapping.MappedUri = new Uri(uri, UriKind.Relative);

    mapper.UriMappings.Add(mapping);
}
```

One nice side effect of using the UriMapping is that it eliminates the need to manually track
the user-friendly names of the XAML pages with their URIs in the Dictionary<string,string>.

■**Note** If the URI passed to the Navigate method is not found in the URI mappings, it is treated as a URI to a page within the application. If the page is also not found within the application, only then does the navigation fail.

■**Caution** You're likely familiar with using public interfaces in class design. Any public interface used by external code now depends on that interface not going anywhere. If you were to get rid of the interface, any external code with that dependency will now be broken. The picture is exactly the same when it comes to deep linking, only it is users and not developers that now depend on their links working. This is one benefit of URI mapping, because you can change the underlying page (such as reorganizing the application as it grows) without the bookmark changing, but you still must think carefully before removing any URI that users may have bookmarked.

Since the user-friendly name is stored in the list box, the selection changed event handler is a bit simpler:

```
private void demoList_SelectionChanged(object sender,
                              SelectionChangedEventArgs e)
{
    MainFrame.Navigate(new Uri((string)demoList.SelectedItem,
                         UriKind.Relative));
}
```

The text from the list box both is used as the URI for navigation and appears in the browser's title bar, as shown in Figure 3-32.

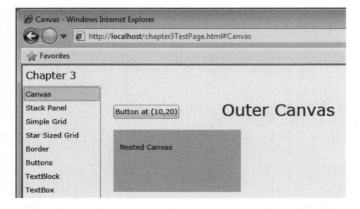

Figure 3-32. *The user-friendly URI now shown in the browser's title bar*

Handling Navigation Errors

Navigation can fail for a number of reasons. Some simple reasons include a user manually typing in an invalid fragment that your application attempts to navigate to, outdated fragments (because you changed the application and users still have it bookmarked), and interruption while loading a large amount of content (such as losing network connectivity), amongst many other possible reasons. If you don't perform any error handling at all, navigation to an invalid URI will manifest itself in the form of a JavaScript error in the browser that looks like this:

```
Message: Unhandled Error in Silverlight Application
Code: 4004
Category: ManagedRuntimeError
Message: System.InvalidOperationException: No XAML was found at the
location '/Fake.xaml'
   at System.Windows.Navigation.NavigationService.RaiseNavigationFailed
 (Uri uri, Exception exception)
   at System.Windows.Navigation.NavigationService.ContentLoader_BeginLoad_
 Callback(IAsyncResult result)
   at
System.Windows.Navigation.PageResourceContentLoader.BeginLoad_
 OnUIThread(AsyncCallback userCallback,
 PageResourceContentLoaderAsyncResult result)
   at
System.Windows.Navigation.PageResourceContentLoader.<>c__
   DisplayClass4.<BeginLoad>b__0(Object args)
```

Just like many web sites display a user-friendly page for 404 errors (the browser requesting a page that doesn't exist on the web server), you should do the same in your Silverlight applications. The way to go about this is handling the Frame's NavigationFailed event and navigating to an error page in the application. In the DemoPresenter class, the event is wired up in the constructor:

```
public DemoPresenter()
{
    InitializeComponent();

    MainFrame.NavigationFailed +=
       new NavigationFailedEventHandler(
                 MainFrame_NavigationFailed);
}
```

The event handler itself just performs the navigation to a XAML page that presents a pleasant error message to the user:

```
void MainFrame_NavigationFailed(object sender,
                        NavigationFailedEventArgs e)
{
    MainFrame.Navigate(new Uri("/Missing.xaml",
                        UriKind.Relative));
}
```

Summary

This chapter introduced the classes that enable the dependency property system and enable the visual dimension of Silverlight: `DependencyObject`, `UIElement`, and `FrameworkElement`. After going over these important classes, you were exposed to many of the controls that come with Silverlight 2 and some of the new ones introduced in Silverlight 3. This chapter concluded with a look at how to implement your own navigation support and the navigation framework built into Silverlight 3 that provides deep linking functionality. You will see another example of the simplified navigation framework with Silverlight 3 in Chapter 14. The next chapter focuses on the support of Silverlight for networking.

■ ■ ■

CHAPTER 4

Network Communication

So far, you've seen XAML and how to create user interfaces in Silverlight. The next major pieces of Silverlight relate to communicating with other systems and working with data (which we'll delve into in the next chapter). The three main communication mechanisms Silverlight provides are services via Windows Communication Foundation (WCF), direct HTTP communication via the `HttpWebRequest` and `WebClient` classes, and raw communication using sockets. Silverlight 3 introduces some significant enhancements to WCF, including improved security and a binary binding. Two other interesting aspects related to networking were also introduced in Silverlight 3. First, Silverlight is now aware of when the network is available. This gives you the ability to gracefully handle a loss of network connectivity, perhaps queuing up what the user requested for when the network comes back alive. The other new aspect is the functionality for one Silverlight application to talk directly with another Silverlight application. Before we get to the specifics of networking, though, it's important to understand cross-domain communication restrictions in Silverlight.

Enabling Cross-Domain Communication

Silverlight can communicate over the network via sockets or HTTP, but if a Silverlight application could communicate to any arbitrary host, then it could be leveraged for hacking into a network or participating in a denial-of-service attack. Therefore, network communication in Silverlight must be controlled. A simplistic approach is to restrict communication between a Silverlight application and the server that serves it (known as the application's site of origin), as shown in Figure 4-1.

Figure 4-1. *Communication with site of origin*

When Silverlight is communicating with its site of origin, such as contacting a web service, no restrictions are placed on the communication. Contacting any other server, however, is forbidden unless the server explicitly grants access. This permission is granted via a special property file that controls network access in specific ways. This property file is only downloaded when Silverlight determines that a network request is cross-domain. Three conditions must be met to identify a request as from the site of origin, and if any of these conditions aren't met, the request is viewed as cross-domain and triggers downloading of the cross-domain policy file. These conditions follow:

- The protocol must be the same. If the application was served over HTTP, it can only communicate over HTTP; likewise for HTTPS.

- The port must be the same. Again, the port must match the original URL the application was downloaded from.

- The domain and path in the URL must match exactly. If the Silverlight application was downloaded from `http://www.fabrikam.com/app` and the request is made to `http://fabrikam.com/app`, the domains don't match.

■**Caution** There are restrictions placed on what characters are considered valid in a request's URI to help prevent canonicalization attacks. The valid characters are all lowercase and uppercase letters (*A* through *Z* and *a* through *z*), all digits (0 through 9), the comma (,), the forward slash (/), the tilde (~), the semicolon (;), and the period (.), as long as there aren't two consecutive periods.

What if Silverlight determines that a particular request is cross-domain? Before deeming the request invalid, Silverlight checks permissions on the remote server. A server that wishes to provide cross-domain permissions to Silverlight applications hosts a cross-domain policy file. There are actually two cross-domain policy files usable by Silverlight: `crossdomain.xml`, introduced by Flash, and `clientaccesspolicy.xml`, introduced by Silverlight.

■**Note** During the lifetime of a Silverlight application, only a single request is made to a cross-domain policy file per server. This means it is safe (and suggested) to mark the cross-domain policy files as no-cache. This prevents the browser from caching the file while offering no performance penalty to Silverlight, since Silverlight will cache the file itself.

The `crossdomain.xml` file is the most straightforward since it is used to opt in the entire domain. No other capabilities from this file are supported by Silverlight.

```
<?xml version="1.0"?>
<!DOCTYPE cross-domain-policy
          SYSTEM
          "http://www.macromedia.com/xml/dtds/cross-domain-policy.dtd">
```

```
<cross-domain-policy>
   <allow-access-from domain="*"/>
</cross-domain-policy>
```

■**Caution** The cross-domain policy files must be located in the root of the server. If you are trying to enable cross-domain communication and it isn't working, ensure the file is located in the server root, not in a subpath such as www.fabrikam.com/services. You can use a tool such as Fiddler (www.fiddlertool.com), an HTTP traffic sniffer, to see the requests your Silverlight application is making. If this file is present and being downloaded successfully, check the contents of the cross-domain policy file.

If you want more granular control over the allowed domains, you must use the clientaccesspolicy.xml. This file provides the capability to restrict which domains are allowed and which paths on the server can be accessed. The domains correspond to where the Silverlight application is served, not any host information based on the client computer. Let's take a look at the structure of this clientaccesspolicy.xml file:

```
<?xml version="1.0" encoding="utf-8"?>
<access-policy>
   <cross-domain-access>
      <policy>
         <allow-from http-request-headers=" CustomHeader,Mail">
            <domain uri="http://www.fabrikam.com"/>
            <domain uri="https://www.fabrikam.com"/>
         </allow-from>
         <grant-to>
            <resource path="/services" include-subpaths="false"/>
         </grant-to>
      </policy>
   </cross-domain-access>
</access-policy>
```

The root element must only appear once; however, multiple cross-domain-access elements can be specified in order to link different sets of allowed domains with paths on the server.

The list of domains being granted access is located beneath the allow-from element. Access is granted to all Silverlight applications if you use the value * for the domain element. The http-request-headers attribute is optional, but must be specified in order to allow the sending of HTTP headers with requests from the client. It takes the form of a comma-separated list of header names. To allow all headers, set http-request-headers to *.

The grant-to element is the parent of resources (paths) local to the server that the set of domains are allowed to access. Each resource element has a path attribute used to specify the path (relative to the server root) to grant access to. The include-subpaths attribute is optional. Setting this to true is an easy way to grant access to an entire hierarchy of paths by specifying the base path in the path attribute. The default value for this attribute is false.

This file is also used to grant access to Silverlight applications communicating over sockets. The format is basically the same, but instead of using resource in the grant-to section, socket-resource is used.

```xml
<?xml version="1.0" encoding="utf-8"?>
<access-policy>
  <cross-domain-access>
    <policy>
      <allow-from>
        <domain uri="*"/>
      </allow-from>
      <grant-to>
        <socket-resource port="4502-4534" protocol="tcp"/>
      </grant-to>
    </policy>
  </cross-domain-access>
</access-policy>
```

The port attribute can be a range of ports or a single port. The only ports Silverlight can use are between 4502 and 4534, inclusive. Currently, the only supported protocol is TCP and thus the protocol attribute must be set to tcp.

The need for this policy file is placed on all communication, including client proxies generated for services, the System.Net.WebClient class, and the System.Net.HttpWebRequest class. Now that we've gone over the network security restrictions placed on communication in Silverlight, let's take a closer look at all the ways Silverlight can communicate with other systems.

Network-Aware Applications

Silverlight 3 introduces the capability for a Silverlight application to detect changes in the local network. This can prove especially useful for a Silverlight application deployed to the desktop. If it requires the network, such as invoking web services, a loss of network connectivity might trigger the queuing of work that will get done when the application detects the network is available again.

The System.Net.NetworkInformation namespace in the System.Net assembly provides two classes useful for detecting changes in the network. The first, NetworkChange, exposes the NetworkAddressChanged event. Since a loss of network connectivity has the effect of losing the IP address, this event fires.

```
NetworkChange.NetworkAddressChanged +=
        new NetworkAddressChangedEventHandler
          (NetworkChange_NetworkAddressChanged);
```

The other class, NetworkInterface, provides the GetIsNetworkAvailable static method that can be called in the network address–changed event handler.

```
void NetworkChange_NetworkAddressChanged(object sender, EventArgs e)
{
    if (NetworkInterface.GetIsNetworkAvailable())
    {
        statusEllipse.Fill = new SolidColorBrush(Colors.Green);
    }
    else
    {
        statusEllipse.Fill = new SolidColorBrush(Colors.Red);
    }
}
```

You can register for this event in the App.xaml.cs to control application logic based on the status of the network. We will cover this topic in more detail with a real example in Chapter 14.

Consuming Web Services with WCF

Windows Communication Foundation (WCF) is a communication stack introduced in .NET 3.0 that separates the implementation of a service from how it communicates. The details of the communication can be configured after deployment by modifying the application's configuration file. This makes it easy to change the service from HTTP to HTTPS or to change whether data is sent in a textual or a binary format. The fundamental aspects of WCF services are known as the ABCs. These letters stand for Address, Binding, and Contract. The address specifies the location of the service. Bindings are used to control the nature of the communication channel, such as encodings, transports and time-outs. Contracts specify the operations that a particular service implements. Together, these aspects combine to form an endpoint for a service. These endpoints are configured both on the service side and the client side in the configuration files.

Creating a WCF Service Consumable by Silverlight

Let's write a simple web service that will be used by a Silverlight application. This web service will retrieve book-related information.

First, create a Silverlight application project named chapter4, and add a BookInfo class under the web project. This class details the book profile and a list of chapters, as shown in the following code snippet:

```
public class BookInfo
{
    public string Title;
    public string Author;
    public string ISBN;
    public List<string> Chapters;
}
```

The service must use the basicHttpBinding as this is the only binding Silverlight can use. While you can create a WCF service and change the binding, you can shortcut this by creating a new "Silverlight-enabled WCF Service," as shown in Figure 4-2. You can add the Silverlight-enabled WCF service by selecting Add New Item to the Web project in the Solution Explorer.

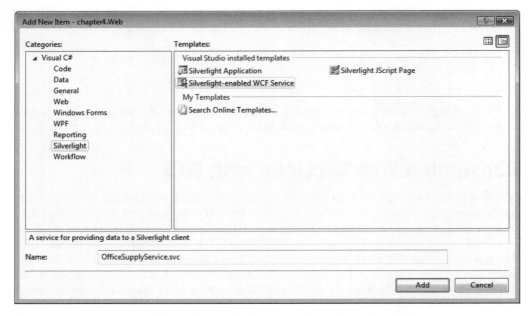

Figure 4-2. *Creating a new Silverlight-enabled WCF service in Visual Studio*

The service is located in the GetBookInfo.svc file. The code-behind contains only the service class, decorated with two attributes, ServiceContract and AspNetCompatibilityRequirements. We will add three simple methods—initBooks, GetByTitle, and GetAllTitle—to the code-behind file GetBookInfo.svc.cs. The initBooks method will initialize the sample BookInfo object array, and GetByTitle and GetAllTitle will query this BookInfo object array. The following code snippet is for GetBookInfo.svc.cs:

```
namespace chapter4.Web
{
[ServiceContract(Namespace = "")]
[AspNetCompatibilityRequirements(RequirementsMode =
    AspNetCompatibilityRequirementsMode.Allowed)]
public class GetBookInfo
{
    //Sample book data array
    private BookInfo[] books = new BookInfo[3];
```

```
//initialize the books object
private void initBooks()
{
if (books != null)
{
    books[0] = new BookInfo();
    books[0].Title = "Pro Silverlight for the Enterprise";
    books[0].Author = "Ashish Ghoda";
    books[0].Chapters = new List<string>
    { "Chapter 1- Understanding Silverlight",
    "Chapter 2-Developing a Simple Silverlight Application",
    "Chapter 3-Silverlight: An Enterprise-Ready Technology Platform",
    "Chapter 4-Silverlight and Service-Oriented Architecture",
    "Chapter 5-Developing a Service-Oriented Enterpise RIA"};
    books[0].ISBN = "978-1-4302-1867-8";

    books[1] = new BookInfo();
    books[1].Title = "Pro Silverlight 2 in C# 2008";
    books[1].Author = "Matthew MacDonald";
    books[1].Chapters = new List<string>
    { "Chapter 1-Introducing Silverlight",
    "Chapter 2-XAML",
    "Chapter 3-Layout",
    "Chapter 4-Dependency Properties and Routed Events",
    "Chapter 5-Elements"};
    books[1].ISBN = "978-1-59059-949-5";

    books[2] = new BookInfo();
    books[2].Title = "Silverlight 2 Visual Essentials";
    books[2].Author = "Matthew MacDonald";
    books[2].Chapters = new List<string>
    { "Chapter 1-Introducing Silverlight",
    "Chapter 2-Layout",
    "Chapter 3-Dependency Properties and Routed Events",
    "Chapter 4-Elements",
    "Chapter 5-The Application Model"};
    books[2].ISBN = "978-1-4302-1582-0";
    }

}

//Get books by title
[OperationContract]
public BookInfo GetByTitle(string Title)
{
```

```
            initBooks();
            foreach (var item in books)
            {
                if (item.Title.ToUpper() == Title.ToUpper())
                    return item;
            }
            return null;
        }
        //Get all book titles
        [OperationContract]
        public List<string> GetAllTitle()
        {
            initBooks();
            List<string> allTitles= new List<string>();
            foreach (var item in books)
            {
                    allTitles.Add(item.Title);
            }
            return allTitles;
        }
    }
}
```

While WCF services are generally separated into an interface (the contract) and the service implementation (that implements the interface), it's possible to use the ServiceContract attribute on the service implementation class. The OperationContract attribute specifies which methods form the operations of the service for the service contract.

Every WCF service must have a host. In classic ASMX web services, the host was ASP.NET itself. The way a client contacts ASP.NET for web pages is the same way a client invokes a web service. Using WCF, the host is outside the HTTP pipeline of ASP.NET. By using the AspNetCompatibilityRequirements attribute, you can ensure a service will be consumable by Silverlight. By setting the RequirementMode property of the attribute to AspNetCompatibilityRequirementsMode.Allowed you ensure that ASP.NET compatibility can be turned on in the application configuration file within the system.serviceModel section. Since this service is part of an ASP.NET web application, the configuration details are located in web.config in the system.serviceModel section. There are four significant elements in this section: behaviors, bindings, serviceHostingEnvironment, and services.

```
<system.serviceModel>
  <behaviors>
   <serviceBehaviors>
    <behavior name="chapter4.Web.GetBookInfoBehavior">
     <serviceMetadata httpGetEnabled="true" />
     <serviceDebug includeExceptionDetailInFaults="false" />
    </behavior>
   </serviceBehaviors>
  </behaviors>
  <bindings>
```

```
  <customBinding>
   <binding name="customBinding0">
    <binaryMessageEncoding />
    <httpTransport />
   </binding>
  </customBinding>
 </bindings>
 <serviceHostingEnvironment aspNetCompatibilityEnabled="true" />
 <services>
  <service behaviorConfiguration="chapter4.Web.GetBookInfoBehavior"
        name="chapter4.Web.GetBookInfo">
   <endpoint address="" binding="customBinding"
        bindingConfiguration="customBinding0"
        contract="chapter4.Web.GetBookInfo" />
   <endpoint address="mex" binding="mexHttpBinding"
        contract="IMetadataExchange" />
  </service>
 </services>
</system.serviceModel>
```

We must build the service now so it can be readily available to the other operations in our Silverlight project that will consume the service.

XAML to Consume Information

Next, define the `MainPage.xaml` UserControl to display the user-entered, title-based book information. Call the web service through the button-click event code-behind to get the book information related to the user-entered title. You bind the returned book data, based on the `BookInfo` class object, to UserControls. (We will learn more about data binding in the next chapter.) The following is the related XAML code:

```
<StackPanel x:Name="LayoutRoot" Background="White">
    <TextBlock Text="Insert Book Title"/>
    <TextBox x:Name="txtTitle"/>
    <Button x:Name="getDetail" Content="Get Book detail"
        Click="getDetail_Click" Width="150"/>
    <StackPanel x:Name="InfoPanel">
        <TextBlock x:Name="title" Text="{Binding Title}"/>
        <TextBlock x:Name="author" Text="{Binding Author}"/>
        <TextBlock x:Name="ISBN" Text="{Binding ISBN}"/>
        <ListBox x:Name="chapters" ItemsSource="{Binding Chapters}"/>
    </StackPanel>
</StackPanel>
```

Invoking Services from Silverlight

Before Silverlight can consume a web service, it must know what the available operations on the service are and also have relevant type information, such as the `BookInfo` type, as shown previously. There are two ways to generate this proxy. The first is using the Add Service Reference functionality in Visual Studio 2008, and the other is using a new Silverlight 3 tool, named SLsvcUtil.exe (Silverlight Service Utility).

Figure 4-3 shows what the Add Service Reference dialog looks like after contacting the GetBookInfo service.

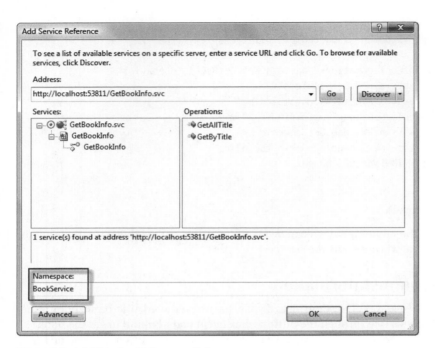

Figure 4-3. *Add Service Reference dialog*

After adding a service reference, the ServiceReferences.ClientConfig file gets created in the Silverlight project. The configuration file has a system.serviceModel section that's similar to the web.config file we discussed earlier, but now has a client element along with the bindings element. We will discuss each option of this file when we create a similar file using the new Silverlight Service Utility tool.

Silverlight Service Utility Tool

The Silverlight Service Utility tool, SLsvcUtil.exe, is part of the Silverlight 3 SDK and can be found under C:\Program Files\Microsoft SDKs\Silverlight\v3.0\Tools in a 32-bit environment; in a 64-bit environment, the tool can be found under C:\Program Files (x86)\Microsoft SDKs\Silverlight\v3.0\Tools.

This tool provides a large number of options. The default operation of the tool creates the client service configuration file (ServiceReferences.ClientConfig) and the necessary proxy code to contact the web service and handle any required types. Table 4-1 describes a number of the most useful options to this tool.

Table 4-1. *Command-Line Options for SLsvcUtil.exe*

Option	Description	Short Form
`/directory:<directory>`	Specifies the output directory	`/d`
`/config:<fileName>`	File name to use for the configuration file	
`/out:<fileName>`	File name for the generated code	`/o`
`/enableDataBinding`	Implements `INotifyPropertyChanged` on all data contract types for data binding	`/edb`
`/collectionType:<type>`	Fully qualified or assembly qualified name of the data type used for collections	`/ct`
`/reference:<path>`	Referenced types that contain types used by metadata	`/r`
`/noConfig`	No configuration file is generated	
`/mergeConfig`	Configuration file changes are merged into an existing file instead of being put into a new one	
`/serializer:<serializer>`	Specifies which serializer to use; possible values are `Auto`, `DataContractSerializer`, and `XmlSerializer`	

For demonstration purposes, we created the `GetBookInfo` service proxy using the Add Service Reference option. Delete the created `BookService` proxy and `ServiceReferences.ClientConfig`. Now let's create the `GetBookInfo` service proxy using `SLsvcUtil.exe`. Open a command prompt and navigate to `C:\Program Files\Microsoft SDKs\Silverlight\v3.0\Tools` for a 32-bit environment or `C:\Program Files (x86)\Microsoft SDKs\Silverlight\v3.0\Tools` for a 64-bit environment. As we are going to generate a proxy on the running service, make sure that the `GetBookInfo.svc` service is running. Then, issue the following command to generate the service proxy:

```
slsvcutil.exe http://localhost:53811/GetBookInfo.svc
```

Note that in the previous command, the port value may differ on your machine. If you are using an IIS server, there will not be a port value; in that case, replace/remove the port value as appropriate.

After the successful completion of the previous command, navigate to the directory where `SLsvcUtil.exe` resides. You will see the service proxy and the configuration files `ServiceReferences.ClientConfig` and `GetBookInfo.cs` created under that folder. Copy both files to the chapter4 Silverlight project. As mentioned earlier, the configuration file contains a `system.serviceModel` section that's similar to the `web.config` file, but now has a `client` element along with the `bindings` element.

```xml
<?xml version="1.0" encoding="utf-8"?>
<configuration>
    <system.serviceModel>
        <bindings>
            <customBinding>
```

```
            <binding name="CustomBinding_GetBookInfo">
                <binaryMessageEncoding />
                <httpTransport maxReceivedMessageSize="2147483647"
                        maxBufferSize="2147483647" />
            </binding>
        </customBinding>
    </bindings>
    <client>
        <endpoint address="http://localhost:53811/GetBookInfo.svc"
                binding="customBinding"
                bindingConfiguration="CustomBinding_GetBookInfo"
                contract="GetBookInfo"
                name="CustomBinding_GetBookInfo" />
    </client>
</system.serviceModel>
</configuration>
```

In the `ServiceReferences.ClientConfig` file, the address of the endpoint specifies where the service is located. Remember that if you are crossing a domain boundary, the cross-domain policy file must be located one directory above `chapter4.Web` on the server. The binding matches that of the service, specifically using HTTP and the binary message encoding. The default configuration file supplies values for the maximum buffer size and maximum received message size, two configuration options not specified in the `services` configuration section. The `GetBookInfo.cs` file contains the `BookInfo` class (as derived from the metadata of the service) and the `GetBookInfo` interface.

When you want to invoke the service, using the default constructor is the easiest approach. Other constructors on the service provide a way to specify the endpoint to use (provided multiple endpoints are specified in the configuration file) by creating a binding and an endpoint programmatically as follows. Note that for this approach, you need to add the namespace `System.ServiceModel`:

```
GetBookInfoClient GetBook = new
    GetBookInfoClient(new BasicHttpBinding(),
        new EndpointAddress("http://localhost:53811/GetBookInfo.svc"));
```

Asynchronous Communication

The proxy supports two asynchronous mechanisms to invoke the service. The first, slightly easier, method is to provide a `Completed` event handler along with the operations of the service, followed by `Async`. The other method uses `IAsyncResult` with `Begin`/`End` methods for each operation of the service. The key difference between these two is that the first approach is available directly on the client proxy and executes on the foreground thread, so it will block the user interface while contacting the service, but makes connecting the data to the user interface much easier. The second approach runs in the background thread and will not block the user interface while contacting the service.

Let's look at the first approach. The code for the `MainPage.xaml.cs` button-click event is as follows:

```
private void getDetail_Click(object sender, RoutedEventArgs e)
{
            GetBookInfoClient GetBook = new GetBookInfoClient();
            GetBook.GetByTitleCompleted += new
                EventHandler<GetByTitleCompletedEventArgs>
                (GetBook_GetByTitleCompleted);
            if (txtTitle.Text != string.Empty)
                 GetBook.GetByTitleAsync(txtTitle.Text);
            else
                //Call GetAllTitle using IAsyncResult
                //Detailed later in this section
}
```

A new instance of the GetBook proxy is created when you click the getDetail button with the default constructor, so the endpoint in ServiceReferences.ClientConfig is populated. Before invoking the GetByTitleAsync method, the corresponding Completed event is connected to an event handler. The event handler simply connects the result of the call to a StackPanel InfoPanel on the user interface via data binding.

```
void GetBook_GetByTitleCompleted(object sender,
  GetByTitleCompletedEventArgs e)
{
    InfoPanel.DataContext = e.Result;
}
```

If you run the project, enter **Pro Silverlight for the Enterprise** in the text box, and click the button, the result should be similar to what's shown in Figure 4-4 showing book details.

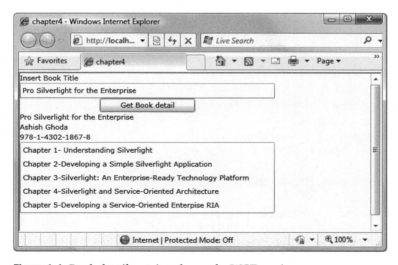

Figure 4-4. *Book details retrieved over the WCF service*

The EventArgs instances for these service calls always have a set of useful properties, which are described in Table 4-2.

Table 4-2. *Properties of Client Proxy Operation EventArgs classes*

Property	Type	Description
Cancelled	bool	True when the asynchronous operation was cancelled.
Error	Exception	The Exception instance if an exception happened during the operation.
Result	Varies, depending on the data	The data type corresponding to the data returned from the service operation.
UserState	object	The Async methods for the service operations include a second constructor, providing a way to pass arbitrary data from the call of the service operation to the completed event handler. If this parameter was used, UserState stores that data.

While we will take a closer look at data binding in Chapter 5, the data returned from the service operations is suitable for data binding. When non-array types are used, they are wrapped in an ObservableCollection and implement the INotifyPropertyChanged interface in order to support two-way data binding (that is, automatically updating when the underlying data source changes).

Now let's look at the second approach. In order to use the Begin/End methods for invoking service operations, the client proxy instance must be cast to its interface. The interface for the GetBookInfo service looks like the following in the GetBookInfo.cs file:

```
[System.CodeDom.Compiler.GeneratedCodeAttribute("System.ServiceModel", "3.0.0.0")]
[System.ServiceModel.ServiceContractAttribute(Namespace="", ConfigurationName=
"GetBookInfo")]
public interface GetBookInfo
{
    [System.ServiceModel.OperationContractAttribute
      (AsyncPattern=true, Action="urn:GetBookInfo/GetByTitle",
        ReplyAction="urn:GetBookInfo/GetByTitleResponse")]

    System.IAsyncResult BeginGetByTitle(string Title,
      System.AsyncCallback callback, object asyncState);

    chapter4.Web.BookInfo EndGetByTitle(System.IAsyncResult result);

    [System.ServiceModel.OperationContractAttribute
      (AsyncPattern=true, Action="urn:GetBookInfo/GetAllTitle",
        ReplyAction="urn:GetBookInfo/GetAllTitleResponse")]
    System.IAsyncResult BeginGetAllTitle
      (System.AsyncCallback callback, object asyncState);

    string[] EndGetAllTitle(System.IAsyncResult result);
}
```

If you've worked with the asynchronous programming model on .NET, these method signatures should be no surprise. This time, invocation of a service operation is slightly different since the Dispatcher must be used to update the user interface since the asynchronous callback happens on a background thread. To demonstrate, invoke GetAllTitle by calling BeginGetAllTitle within the getDetail_Click method else section, as follows:

```
else
{
   //Call GetAllTitle using IAsyncResult
   GetBookInfo GetBook1 = (GetBookInfo)GetBook;
   GetBook1.BeginGetAllTitle
     (new AsyncCallback(GetAllTitle_AsyncCallBack), GetBook1);
}
```

Next, the asynchronous callback method calls EndGetAllTitle to get the result of the operation and then binds it to the Chapters list box on the user interface.

```
void GetAllTitle_AsyncCallBack(IAsyncResult ar)
{
        string [] items =
                ((GetBookInfo)ar.AsyncState).EndGetAllTitle(ar);

        Dispatcher.BeginInvoke(delegate()
        {
            chapters.ItemsSource = items;
        });
}
```

Run the project. When you click the Get Book detail button, you should see the book titles displayed, as shown in Figure 4-5.

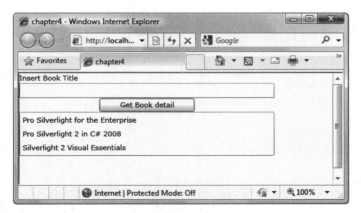

Figure 4-5. *Invoking GetAllTitle using Async Callback*

Handling Errors

If you use the previous approach to invoke a service and an exception happens in the service, Silverlight will only receive limited information about the exception. You can check for the exception in the Result property of the EventArgs class or by wrapping the End method in a try/catch block. If something goes wrong in the service, the browser will get an HTTP 500 error message from the server. Unfortunately, Silverlight can't access the details of the exception, so you must modify the WCF service by augmenting the endpoint to ensure the fault data is sent via an HTTP 200 error message, rather than an HTTP 500 error message. This is accomplished using a custom IDispatchMessageInspector method and a custom IEndpointBehavior method on the service side. The custom IDispatchMessageInspector method simply changes the HTTP status code to 200 (OK) when the message that passes through it is a fault.

```
public class SilverlightFaultProcessor : IDispatchMessageInspector
{
    #region IDispatchMessageInspector Members

    public object AfterReceiveRequest(
        ref System.ServiceModel.Channels.Message request,
        System.ServiceModel.IClientChannel channel,
        System.ServiceModel.InstanceContext instanceContext)
    {
        return (null);
    }

    public void BeforeSendReply(
      ref System.ServiceModel.Channels.Message reply,
      object correlationState)
    {
        if (reply.IsFault)
        {
            // If it's a fault, change the status code
            // to 200 so Silverlight can receive the
            // details of the fault

            HttpResponseMessageProperty responseProperty =
                new HttpResponseMessageProperty();

            responseProperty.StatusCode =
                    System.Net.HttpStatusCode.OK;

            reply.Properties[HttpResponseMessageProperty.Name]
                = responseProperty;
        }
    }

    #endregion
}
```

The custom IEndpointBehavior method also inherits from BehaviorExtensionElement so the behavior can be used in the configuration file. Methods from the interfaces that do not have implementations are not shown here in the interest of space.

```
public class SilverlightFaultBehavior : BehaviorExtensionElement,
                          IEndpointBehavior, IServiceBehavior
{
    public override Type BehaviorType
    {
        get { return (typeof(SilverlightFaultBehavior)); }
    }

    protected override object CreateBehavior()
    {
        return (new SilverlightFaultBehavior());
    }

    #region IEndpointBehavior Members

    public void ApplyDispatchBehavior(ServiceEndpoint endpoint,
            System.ServiceModel.Dispatcher.EndpointDispatcher
            endpointDispatcher)
    {
        SilverlightFaultProcessor processor =
            new SilverlightFaultProcessor();

        endpointDispatcher.DispatchRuntime.
            MessageInspectors.Add(processor);
    }
}
```

All that's left is to change the configuration file to add this behavior to the service's endpoint. This requires adding the behavior extension under a new element, extensions, and then using it in the behavior (the added/updated items are shown in bold in the following snippet):

```
<system.serviceModel>
  <extensions>
    <behaviorExtensions>
      <add name="silverlightFaults"
          type="SilverlightFaultBehavior, chapter4.Web,
                Version=1.0.0.0,
                Culture=neutral, PublicKeyToken=null"/>
    </behaviorExtensions>
  </extensions>
  <behaviors>
    <endpointBehaviors>
      <behavior name="SilverlightFaultBehavior">
        <silverlightFaults />
      </behavior>
```

```
    </endpointBehaviors>
    <serviceBehaviors>
  <behavior name="chapter4.Web.GetBookInfoBehavior">
    <serviceMetadata httpGetEnabled="true" />
    <serviceDebug includeExceptionDetailInFaults="false" />
  </behavior>
  </serviceBehaviors>
  </behaviors>
```

The revised service element includes the behaviorConfiguration attribute (shown in bold in the following snippet) in order to make the new Silverlight fault behavior work:

```
<services>
  <service behaviorConfiguration="chapter4.Web.GetBookInfoBehavior"
    name="chapter4.Web.GetBookInfo">
    <endpoint address="" binding="customBinding"
      behaviorConfiguration="SilverlightFaultBehavior"
      bindingConfiguration="customBinding0"
      contract="chapter4.Web.GetBookInfo" />
    <endpoint address="mex" binding="mexHttpBinding"
      contract="IMetadataExchange" />
  </service>
  </services>
```

Now the Silverlight application can receive faults from the service. Let's augment the GetByTitle operation with a fault contract. A *fault contract* states certain faults are expected by the application, such as placing an order for too many supplies.

```
[OperationContract]
[FaultContract(typeof(BookNotFound))]
public BookInfo GetByTitle(string Title)
{
    initBooks();
    …
    …
}
```

BookNotFound is a simple class that contains a custom message.

```
public class BookNotFound
    {
        public string NotFoundMessage { get; set; }
    }
```

There are two types of faults a service client might receive from the service. The first are unhandled faults, and the details of these faults should only be communicated back to the client in test/ debug scenarios. The second are violations of application logic and thus are expected and can be safely communicated back to the client (in this case, Silverlight) for graceful application operation. If you are developing a Silverlight application and want to configure the service to send the full details of the unhandled faults to Silverlight, you can set the `includeExceptionDetailInFaults` attribute to `true` in the `serviceDebug` element of a behavior.

```
<behavior name="chapter4.Web.GetBookInfoBehavior">
  <serviceMetadata httpGetEnabled="true" />
  <serviceDebug includeExceptionDetailInFaults="True" />
</behavior>
```

■**Note** Get more details on creating and handling faults in Silverlight by visiting the Microsoft MSDN web site at `http://msdn.microsoft.com/en-us/library/dd470096(VS.96).aspx`.

Communicating Directly over HTTP

Two classes are provided to support direct communication over HTTP: `System.Net.WebClient` and `System.Net.HttpWebRequest`. `WebClient` is simpler but only exposes simplified access to the GET and POST methods of HTTP. `WebClient` is most useful for easily downloading resources. The `HttpWebRequest` class provides greater control over HTTP communication.

The WebClient Class

The `WebClient` class provides simplified access to communicating over HTTP (it is located in the `System.Net` assembly). Its most important members are listed in Table 4-3.

Table 4-3. *Members of the System.Net.WebClient Class*

Name	Type	Description
DownloadStringAsync	Method	Asynchronously downloads data and returns it as a string.
DownloadStringCompleted	Event	Occurs when DownloadStringAsync is complete.
UploadStringAsync	Method	Uploads a string to a specified URI.
OpenReadAsync	Method	Asynchronously downloads data and returns it as a Stream.
OpenReadCompleted	Event	Occurs when OpenReadAsync is complete.
DownloadProgressChanged	Event	Occurs when some/all data is transferred. This is useful for building a status indicator such as a download progress bar.
CancelAsync	Method	Used to cancel an already issued asynchronous operation.
BaseAddress	Property (URI)	Gets/sets the base address. This is useful for using relative addresses in multiple operations with a single WebClient.
IsBusy	Property (bool)	Indicates whether an asynchronous operation is in progress.

One aspect of Silverlight that is really useful is its support of archived media. You can store images, audio, and video in a ZIP file, download it to the client via `WebClient`, and then use `MediaElement`'s or `BitmapImage`'s `SetSource` method to connect the visual element to the media content within the archive. Let's take a look at a simple Silverlight application to download and display images. We'll also implement the `DownloadProgressChanged` event for showing a simple progress indicator. We need a `System.Windows.Resources.StreamResourceInfo` object in the code-behind to store the result of the download (i.e., the archive of images).

```
private StreamResourceInfo imageArchive;
```

Next, we'll implement the click event on the button to initiate the download. We are using the `OpenReadAsync` method to download a stream of data and thus implement an `OpenReadCompleted` event handler to handle the data when it is finished downloading.

```
private void downloadButton_Click(object sender, RoutedEventArgs e)
{
    WebClient wc = new WebClient();
    wc.OpenReadCompleted +=
            new OpenReadCompletedEventHandler(wc_OpenReadCompleted);
    wc.DownloadProgressChanged +=
            new DownloadProgressChangedEventHandler(wc_DownloadProgressChanged);
    wc.OpenReadAsync(new Uri("/ImageBrowser/renaissance.zip", UriKind.Relative));
}
```

The `OpenReadCompleted` event handler is straightforward: we'll check for an error or a cancel and make our list box of image names visible (we're cheating here—the image names are hard-coded in a `String` type array). We could add a metadata file to the ZIP archive that the Silverlight application can access and then cache the downloaded image archive for later use (in our case it is `renaissance.zip`).

```
private void wc_OpenReadCompleted(object sender, OpenReadCompletedEventArgs e)
{
    if ((e.Error == null) && (e.Cancelled == false))
    {
        imageListBox.Visibility = Visibility.Visible;
        imageArchive = new StreamResourceInfo(e.Result, null);
    }
}
```

The download progress indicator is simply a percentage value displayed in a TextBlock. `DownloadProgressChangedEventArgs` contains several useful properties (listed in Table 4-4), including the percentage progress, so we don't have to calculate percentage completion.

```
private void wc_DownloadProgressChanged(object sender,
                                        DownloadProgressChangedEventArgs e)
{
    progressTextBox.Text = e.ProgressPercentage + "%";
}
```

Table 4-4. *Members of the DownloadProgressChangedEventArgs Class*

Name	Type	Description
Address	URI	The URI to the file currently downloading
BytesReceived	long	A count of the bytes received so far
ProgressPercentage	int	A number from 0 to 100 representing the percentage of bytes downloaded; equates to the formula (BytesReceived / TotalBytesToReceive) * 100
TotalBytesToReceive	long	Corresponds to the file size of the file requested
UserState	object	Corresponds to the optional data passed to the OpenReadAsync or DownloadStringAsync method

Now that we have the image archive cached in the class, we can access an image inside when the user selects a different image in the ListBox.

```
private void imageListBox_SelectionChanged(object sender,
SelectionChangedEventArgs e)
{
    BitmapImage bitmapImageSource = new BitmapImage();
    StreamResourceInfo imageResourceInfo =
        Application.GetResourceStream(imageArchive, new
            Uri(imageListBox.SelectedItem.ToString(),
                UriKind.Relative));
    bitmapImageSource.SetSource(imageResourceInfo.Stream);
    image.Source = bitmapImageSource;
}
```

First, we need to get access to the specific image inside the archive. We use the Application. GetResourceStream to access the specific image we want. GetResourceStream has two overloads: one to access resources stored in the application, and the other to access resources within an arbitrary ZIP stream. The resource to access is specified by a Uri object. The images in the ZIP archive are referenced relative to the path within the ZIP—the path to the Silverlight application has no relation to the paths of images inside the archive. The only other remarkable thing about this piece of code is that the BitmapImage class is needed to get a source for the Image object.

The DownloadStringAsync method works just like the OpenReadAsync method does. The only difference is that the Result property of the DownloadStringCompletedEventArgs class is of type String instead of Stream. This method makes it easy to download content such as XML documents for parsing by the XML classes. We will be utilizing DownloadStringAsync in the next chapter.

The WebClient class provides only basic communication support. Downloading files, either as a String or a Stream, is done via the GET method of HTTP. The HTTP POST method is supported via the UploadStringAsync method. There are three overloads of this method. One version takes a Uri and the string to upload. A second version takes the Uri, a string specifying the HTTP method (it defaults to POST if this parameter is null) to use, and the string to upload. The final variant includes a user token that is passed to the asynchronous response handler.

If we want to utilize HTTP in more complex ways, manipulate cookies, or communicate securely, we need something more powerful. This power is provided by the System.Net. HttpWebRequest class.

The HttpWebRequest Class

The HttpWebRequest is a specialization of the WebRequest class designed to communicate over the HTTP and HTTPS protocols. It also supports the POST method along with GET, whereas WebClient only supports GET. Generally, if the host browser can do it, the HttpWebRequest can do it too, since this class leverages the host browser's networking. To use this class, you must first add a reference to the System.Net assembly since Silverlight projects do not include this by default.

An instance of HttpWebRequest cannot be created directly. The WebRequest class contains a factory method named Create that returns an appropriate instance of a WebRequest inheritor, based on the protocol specified in the URI. Silverlight only supports the HTTP and HTTPS protocols, and both cause Create to return an instance of HttpWebRequest (actually, since HttpWebRequest is also abstract, a concrete implementation of HttpWebRequest is created; however, for all intents and purposes, it is an HttpWebRequest). For example:

```
Uri uri = new Uri("http://www.technologyopinion.com");
HttpWebRequest myHttpWebRequest1=
    (HttpWebRequest)WebRequest.Create(uri);
```

The HttpWebRequest class works in concert with HttpWebResponse to handle the data sent back from the server. The nature of communication using HttpWebRequest is also asynchronous; however, it utilizes the Begin*XXX*/End*XXX* pattern that you may be familiar with from .NET. Tables 4-5 and 4-6 describe the methods and properties of this class, respectively.

Table 4-5. *Methods of the System.Net.HttpWebRequest Class*

Name	Description
BeginGetRequestStream	Begins an asynchronous request to obtain a Stream to write data.
EndGetRequestStream	Returns a Stream. Use this in the asynchronous callback method passed to BeginGetRequestStream to get the Stream to write your request to.
BeginGetResponse	Begins an asynchronous request to communicate with a server.
EndGetResponse	Returns a WebResponse; provides access to a Stream containing the data downloaded from the server.
Abort	Cancels an executing asynchronous operation.

Table 4-6. *Properties of the System.Net.HttpWebRequest Class*

Name	Description
ContentType	Corresponds to the Content-Type HTTP header.
HaveResponse	true if a response has been received; false otherwise.
Headers	A collection containing the HTTP headers.
Method	Corresponds to the method used in the request. Currently, it can only be GET or POST.
RequestUri	The URI of the request.

The EndGetResponse of the HttpWebRequest class returns a WebResponse. Much like the WebRequest, the WebResponse is abstract and actually requires us to look one level deeper in the hierarchy, so let's take a look at the HttpWebResponse class.

The HttpWebResponse class provides access to the data sent by the server to Silverlight. Its most important method is GetResponseStream, inherited from the WebResponse class. This method gives you a Stream containing the data sent by the server. When you are done with the response, make sure you call its Close method since the connection to the server remains open in the meantime. Tables 4-7 and 4-8 describe the methods and properties of this class, respectively.

Table 4-7. *Methods of the System.Net.HttpWebResponse Class*

Name	Description
Close	Closes the stream and releases the connection to the server.
GetResponseStream	Returns a Stream. Use this to access the data sent by the server to Silverlight.

Table 4-8. *Properties of the System.Net.HttpWebResponse Class*

Name	Description
ContentLength	Length of the data sent to Silverlight
ContentType	MIME type of the content sent, if available
ResponseUri	URI of the server that sent the response

One way to use the HttpWebRequest class is to retrieve data from a server. In this case, we can go straight to using the BeginGetResponse method, since all we care about is retrieving data from a server, not sending data. This code uses an address we enter in a user interface to connect to, such as downloading an HTML file from our site of origin.

```
HttpWebRequest request = (HttpWebRequest)HttpWebRequest.Create(
                                            new Uri(addressTB.Text));
request.BeginGetResponse(new AsyncCallback(responseHandler), request);
```

The implementation of the response handler is where we read the response from the server.

```
void responseHandler(IAsyncResult asyncResult)
{
   try
   {
      HttpWebRequest request = (HttpWebRequest)asyncResult.AsyncState;
      HttpWebResponse response =
                        (HttpWebResponse)request.EndGetResponse(asyncResult);
      StreamReader reader = new StreamReader(response.GetResponseStream());
      string line;
      outputTB.Text = "";
      while ((line = reader.ReadLine()) != null)
      {
         outputTB.Text += line;
      }
   }
   catch (Exception ex)
   {
      outputTB.Text = ex.Message;
   }
}
```

In the response handler, we grab the request object via the AsyncState parameter, and then get the Stream from EndGetResponse. This is the equivalent of the HTTP GET method.

Sending data to a server is similar to initiating an asynchronous operation for retrieving the response. BeginGetRequestStream starts the operation, and then EndGetRequestStream gives us the Stream in the asynchronous callback method passed to BeginGetRequestStream. This is equivalent to the HTTP POST method.

Communicating via Sockets

While most applications will use either the service proxy or one of the classes for downloading via HTTP/HTTPS, some applications will need a raw communication channel. Performance is the chief reason for using sockets for communication, since less data is sent between the client and server, but there's also the potential for needing to interoperate with existing systems that communicate via sockets. Silverlight places severe restrictions on socket communication, and just like communicating over HTTP, a client access policy file must be obtained.

Controlling Client Access via Socket Policy Server

Since there is no web server that Silverlight can automatically obtain the client access policy from, this policy file must be supplied by some other means. This other means is a socket policy server listening on port 943, located on the same machine that the Silverlight application will use to communicate via sockets. The details of the socket policy server are straightforward. It listens on TCP port 943 and waits for a connection. If it receives the string <policy-file-request/> from the client, it sends the contents of the clientaccesspolicy.xml file back to the Silverlight application. The details of the client access policy were shown earlier in this chapter, but as a refresher, this file looks like the following for sockets:

```
<?xml version="1.0" encoding="utf-8"?>
<access-policy>
  <cross-domain-access>
    <policy>
      <allow-from>
        <domain uri="*"/>
      </allow-from>
      <grant-to>
        <socket-resource port="4502-4534" protocol="tcp"/>
      </grant-to>
    </policy>
  </cross-domain-access>
</access-policy>
```

As shown, Silverlight supports a full valid range (from 4502 to 4534) of ports with the use of the TCP protocol. Based on the settings of the domain element, the communication can be made between the same domains, all domains, or specific domains. Further details are provided in the "Enabling Cross-Domain Communication" section of this chapter.

The System.Net Namespace

The System.Net namespace provides a programming interface for the network communication using different protocols. Several key classes are used in the course of communicating over sockets. The System.Net.Socket class contains the core functionality for socket communication. The System.Net.SocketAsyncEventArgs class is used to pass parameters to a socket operation and also to handle the result of a socket operation, such as receiving data. The System.Net.DnsEndPoint class specifies an endpoint as a combination of a hostname and port number, while System.Net.IPEndPoint specifies the endpoint as an IP address and port number. An endpoint must be specified when executing a socket operation.

The Socket Class

The Socket class has three socket operations: connecting (ConnectAsync), sending data (SendAsync), and receiving data (ReceiveAsync). The socket must first connect to a remote endpoint, described by either the IPEndPoint or DnsEndPoint class. The former is used to connect to an IP address, and the latter is used to connect to a hostname. Tables 4-9 and 4-10 display the methods and properties of the Socket class, respectively. You should always call the Shutdown method before Close to ensure that data is finished sending/receiving on the open socket.

Table 4-9. *Methods of the System.Net.Socket Class*

Name	Description
ConnectAsync	Initiates a connection to a remote host. A nonstatic version takes only a SocketAsyncEventArgs, while a static version takes a SocketType, a ProtocolType, and a SocketAsyncEventArgs. It returns true if the operation is pending, and false if the operation has completed.
CancelConnectAsync	Used to cancel a pending connection. It must pass the SocketAsyncEventArgs used in the ConnectAsync method.
SendAsync	Sends data specified in a SocketAsyncEventArgs. It returns true if the operation is pending, and false if the operation has completed.
ReceiveAsync	Receives data from the open socket. It returns true if the operation is pending, and false if the operation has completed.
Shutdown	Shuts down sending, receiving, or both on the socket. It ensures that pending data is sent/received before shutting down a channel, so you should call this before you call Close.
Close	Closes the socket, releasing all resources.

Table 4-10. *Properties of the System.Net.Socket Class*

Name	Description
AddressFamily	Addressing scheme used to resolve addresses. Valid values from the AddressFamily enumeration are Unknown, Unspecified, InterNetwork (for IPv4), and InterNetworkV6 (for IPv6). AddressFamily is initially specified when a socket is created.
Connected	Used to cancel a pending connection. It must pass the SocketAsyncEventArgs used in the ConnectAsync method.
NoDelay	Sends data specified in a SocketAsyncEventArgs.
OSSupportsIPv4	Static property; indicates whether IPv4 addressing is supported or not.
OSSupportsIPv6	Static property; indicates whether IPv6 addressing is supported or not.
ReceiveBufferSize	The size of the socket's receive buffer.
RemoteEndPoint	The endpoint of the remote server.
SendBufferSize	The size of the socket's send buffer.
Ttl	The time-to-live value for IP packets.

The SocketAsyncEventArgs Class

The SocketAsyncEventArgs class is possibly the most important class for socket communication, since it is used as a way to both pass data/configuration to the three socket operation methods and pass access status information/data after an asynchronous call completes. Table 4-11 lists its members.

Table 4-11. *Members of the System.Net.SocketAsyncEventArgs Class*

Name	Type	Description
SetBuffer	Method	Initializes the data buffer for an asynchronous operation. One overload sets only the Count and Offset properties (Buffer is set to null) while the other also sets the Buffer property to an array of bytes.
Buffer	Property (byte[])	Accesses the data buffer. This property is read-only—use the SetBuffer method to initialize and possibly place data into this buffer.
BufferList	Property (IList<ArraySegment<byte>>)	Specifies an array of data buffers for use by ReceiveAsync and SendAsync. This property has precedence over the Buffer property.
BytesTransferred	Property (int)	Number of bytes transferred in socket operation. After a read operation, if this property is 0, it indicates that the remote service has closed the connection.
ConnectSocket	Property (Socket)	Socket related to this operation.
Count	Property (int)	Maximum number of bytes to send/receive. It is set via SetBuffer.
LastOperation	Property (SocketAsyncOperation)	Valid values from SocketAsyncOperation enumeration are None, Connect, Receive, and Send. This is set to None before one of the asynchronous methods is invoked, and then it is set to the value corresponding to the asynchronous operation.
Offset	Property (int)	The offset, in bytes, into the Buffer property. This is set via the SetBuffer method.
RemoteEndPoint	Property (EndPoint)	Specifies the remote endpoint used for the ConnectAsync method. This can be IPEndPoint or DNSEndPoint. It supports both IPv4 and IPv6 addressing.
SocketError	Property (SocketError)	Corresponds to a socket error from the most recent socket operation (Connect, Send, or Receive). There are a large number of error codes; however, SocketError.Success is the only code representing success. Check against this to ensure that the most recent operation succeeded.
UserToken	Property (object)	Arbitrary object used to pass data from the invocation of an asynchronous method to the Completed event handler.
Completed	Event	Used to specify an event handler that is invoked when the asynchronous operation is complete.

Building a Socket-based Sample Text Chat Application

On Windows, the best approach to implement this server is as a Windows service. An implementation of a socket policy server is included in the source code for this book. It is a standard Silverlight application project with the name chapter4Socket with two Windows Service projects (in C#) named PolicyServer and MessengerServer. The policy server's functionality resides in two key custom-created classes in this project. The first class, SocketPolicyServer, is responsible for waiting and listening for connections. When a connection is received, it's handed over to a new instance of the second class, SocketPolicyConnection, which then sends the policy file. This implementation of the policy server should fulfill the requirements for most policy servers, but if not, it offers a great base to start with. Figure 4-6 shows the sample text chat application project (chapter4Socket) solution structure in the Visual Studio Solution Explorer.

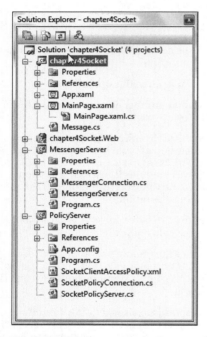

Figure 4-6. *Project structure for sample chapter4Socket solution enabling text chat*

In this chapter, we are not going to detail the full implementation of the text chat application project, so I will assume that you have gone through the provided source code of the chapter4Socket project. It is recommended that you open the project as a reference for the remainder of this chapter.

The PolicyServer Windows Service Project

The PolicyServer project includes two custom classes, SocketPolicyServer.cs and SocketPolicyConnection.cs, and a SocketClientAccessPolicy.xml file, as shown in Figure 4-6.

The SocketPolicyServer Class

The following is an overall skeleton of the SocketPolicyServer class:

```
//additional references
using System.IO;
using System.Net;
using System.Net.Sockets;

namespace PolicyServer
{
    class SocketPolicyServer
    {

        private TcpListener Listener;
        private byte[] Policy;

        // Path to an XML file containing the
         //socket policy as a parameter
        public SocketPolicyServer(string PathToPolicyFile)
        {

        }
        // This method gets called when we receive
         //a connection from a client
        public void OnConnection(IAsyncResult ar)
        {

        }

        //This method gets called upon shutting down
         //the policy server
        public void Close()
        {

        }
    }
}
```

The constructor of the SocketPolicyServer class of the PolicyServer Windows service contains a path to the cross-domain policy file as a parameter. The constructor reads the contents of the policy file (as specified in App.config in a custom configuration section) and caches it in a byte array. The implementation of the SocketPolicyServer class constructor is as follows:

```
// Path to an XML file containing the socket policy as a parameter
public SocketPolicyServer(string PathToPolicyFile)
{
  // Load the policy file in a FileStream object
  FileStream PStream = new
    FileStream(PathToPolicyFile, FileMode.Open);
  Policy = new byte[PStream.Length];
  PStream.Read(Policy, 0, Policy.Length);
  PStream.Close();

  // Port 943 is the default listener port in Silverlight
  Listener = new TcpListener(IPAddress.Any,943);
  Listener.Start();
  Listener.BeginAcceptTcpClient
    (new AsyncCallback(OnConnection), null);
}
```

As shown in the previous code snippet, the constructor invokes the OnConnection method with the callback. The OnConnection method reads the data sent from the client, converts the raw bytes to a string, and, if the string matches <policy-file-request/>, sends the data to the client.

```
// This method gets called when we receive a connection from a client
public void OnConnection(IAsyncResult ar)
{
  TcpClient Client = null;
  try
  {
    Client = Listener.EndAcceptTcpClient(ar);
  }
  catch (SocketException)
  {
    return;
  }
  // handle this policy request with a SocketPolicyConnection
  SocketPolicyConnection PCon = new
    SocketPolicyConnection(Client, Policy);

  // Then look for other connections
  Listener.BeginAcceptTcpClient
    (new AsyncCallback(OnConnection), null);
}
```

In the previous method, the SocketPolicyConnection class has a simple task. An instance of this class stores a reference to the policy file data. When the OnReceive method is called, the instance accesses the network stream for the new connection and attempts to read from it. If everything goes well, after reading the string containing the text <policy-file-request/>, the instance sends policy data to that client, and closes the connection. For the full implementation of this class, you need to look at the SocketPolicyConnection.cs file under the PolicyServer Windows service project. Notice that the end of the OnConnection method effectively loops back on itself, instructing the Listener instance to wait for another connection (this isn't recursion since the method isn't being invoked directly). This is essentially all there is to a socket policy server. Fortunately it's not tricky to implement.

Now that you can grant a Silverlight application permission to communicate via sockets, let's explore exactly how to do just that. There are several key classes used in the course of communicating over sockets. The Socket class contains the core functionality for socket communication. The SocketAsyncEventArgs class is used to pass parameters to a socket operation and also to handle the result of a socket operation, such as receiving data. The DnsEndPoint class specifies an endpoint as a combination of a hostname and port number, while IPEndPoint specifies the endpoint as an IP address and port number. An endpoint must be specified when executing a socket operation.

The SocketPolicyConnection Class

The following is an overall skeleton of the SocketPolicyConnection class:

```
//additional references
using System.Net.Sockets;

namespace PolicyServer
{
  class SocketPolicyConnection
  {
    private TcpClient Connection;

    // Buffer to receive client request
    private byte[] Buffer;
    private int Received;
    // The policy to return
    private byte[] Policy;

    //The request string that is expected from the client
    private static string PolicyRequestString =
      "<policy-file-request/>";

    public SocketPolicyConnection(TcpClient client, byte[] policy)
    {

    }

    // Called when we receive data from the client
    private void OnReceive(IAsyncResult res)
    {

    }
```

```
    // Called after sending the policy and
    //closes the connection
    public void OnSend(IAsyncResult ar)
    {

    }
  }
}
```

The SocketPolicyConnection class constructor stores a reference to the policy file data and starts receiving the request from the client. Then, the Async callback to the OnReceive method checks for the valid PolicyRequestString and sends back the policy file to the client. This method also makes a call to the OnSend method, which simply closes the connection upon successful delivery of the policy file.

```
public SocketPolicyConnection(TcpClient client, byte[] policy)
{
  Connection = client;
  Policy = policy;
  Buffer = new byte[PolicyRequestString.Length];
  Received = 0;
  try
  {
    // receive the request from the client
    Connection.Client.BeginReceive(Buffer, 0,
      PolicyRequestString.Length, SocketFlags.None,
      new AsyncCallback(OnReceive), null);
  }
  catch (SocketException)
  {
    Connection.Close();
  }
}
```

The OnReceive method checks for the valid PolicyRequestString and sends back the policy file to the client.

```
private void OnReceive(IAsyncResult res)
{
  try
  {
    Received += Connection.Client.EndReceive(res);
    // Make sure that we received a full request or
     //try to receive again
```

```
    if (Received < PolicyRequestString.Length)
    {
      Connection.Client.BeginReceive(Buffer, Received,
        PolicyRequestString.Length - Received,SocketFlags.None,
        new AsyncCallback(OnReceive), null);
      return;
    }
    // Make sure the request is valid by
    //comparing with PolicyRequestString
    string request = System.Text.Encoding.UTF8.
      GetString(Buffer, 0, Received);
    if (StringComparer.InvariantCultureIgnoreCase.
      Compare(request, PolicyRequestString) != 0)
    {
      Connection.Close();
      return;
    }
    // Now send the policy
    Console.Write("Sending the policy...\n");
    Connection.Client.BeginSend(Policy, 0, Policy.Length,
      SocketFlags.None,new AsyncCallback(OnSend), null);
  }
  catch (SocketException)
  {
    Connection.Close();
  }
}
```

The SocketClientAccessPolicy.xml Policy File

Add the following SocketClientAccessPolicy.xml policy file to allow access to all domains and define socket communication using port 4530 and the TCP protocol:

```xml
<?xml version="1.0" encoding="utf-8"?>
<access-policy>
  <cross-domain-access>
    <policy>
      <allow-from>
        <domain uri="*" />
      </allow-from>
      <grant-to>
        <socket-resource port="4530" protocol="tcp" />
      </grant-to>
    </policy>
  </cross-domain-access>
</access-policy>
```

The MessengerServer Windows Service Project

In the chapter4Socket solution, we have added MessengerServer as a separate Windows service project. Like the PolicyServer project, the MessengerServer project contains two classes: MessengerServer, which listens for requests and tracks clients, and MessengerConnection, which handles the interaction of a single client.

The MessengerServer Class

The following is an overall skeleton of the MessengerServer class:

```
//added
using System.Net.Sockets;
using System.Threading;
using System.Net;

namespace MessengerServer
{
  public class MessengerServer
  {
    private Socket Listener;
    private int ClientNo;
    private List<MessengerConnection> Clients = new
      List<MessengerConnection>();
    private bool isRunning;

    public void Start()
    {

    }

    private void OnConnection(IAsyncResult ar)
    {

    }

    public void Close()
    {

    }

    public void DeliverMessage(byte[] message, int bytesRead)
    {

    }
  }
}
```

As shown in the following code, the `Start` method of the `MessengerServer` class listens on port 4530 and invokes the `OnConnection` method with the callback:

```
public void Start()
{
    Listener = new Socket
     (AddressFamily.InterNetwork, SocketType.Stream,
        ProtocolType.Tcp);
    Listener.SetSocketOption(SocketOptionLevel.Tcp,
     (SocketOptionName)SocketOptionName.NoDelay, 0);
    // The allowed port range in Silverlight is 4502 to 4534.
    Listener.Bind(new IPEndPoint(IPAddress.Any, 4530));
    // Waiting on connection request
    Listener.Listen(10);
    Listener.BeginAccept
      (new AsyncCallback(OnConnection), null);
    isRunning = true;
}
```

When the `MessengerServer` receives a connection request, it performs two tasks. First, it creates an instance of a `MessengerConnection` class to handle the communication. Next, it adds the client to a collection so it can keep track of all the connected clients. This is the only way to achieve interaction between these clients. So the collection here performs the tracking, and we give each new client a different identifying number. The following is a code snippet of the `OnConnection` method:

```
private void OnConnection(IAsyncResult ar)
{
  if (isRunning==false)
    return;
  ClientNo++;
  // Look for other connections
  Listener.BeginAccept
   (new AsyncCallback(OnConnection), null);
  Console.WriteLine("Messenger client No: " +
   ClientNo.ToString() + " is connected.");
  Socket Client = Listener.EndAccept(ar);

  // Handle the current connection
  MessengerConnection NewClient = new
    MessengerConnection(Client, "Client " +
    ClientNo.ToString(), this);
  NewClient.Start();

  lock (Clients)
  {
    Clients.Add(NewClient);
  }
}
```

When the message is received, the MessengerConnection class' OnMsgReceived method calls the DeliverMessage method of the MessengerServer class to send the message to all clients that are currently connected with MessengerServer. The OnMsgReceived method also checks for disconnected clients and removes them from the tracking collection of connected clients to avoid future attempts to send a message.

```
public void DeliverMessage(byte[] message, int bytesRead)
{
  Console.WriteLine("Delivering the message...");
  // Duplication of connection to prevent cross-threading issues
  MessengerConnection[] ClientsConnected;
  lock (Clients)
  {
    ClientsConnected = Clients.ToArray();
  }

  foreach (MessengerConnection cnt in ClientsConnected)
  {
    try
    {
      cnt.ReceiveMessage(message, bytesRead);
    }
    catch
    {
      // Remove disconnected clients
      lock (Clients)
      {
        Clients.Remove(cnt);
      }
      cnt.Close();
    }
  }
}
```

The MessengerConnection Class

The following is an overall skeleton of the MessengerConnection class:

```
//added
using System.Net.Sockets;
using System.IO;

namespace MessengerServer
{
  public class MessengerConnection
  {
    private Socket Client;
    private string ID;
    private MessengerServer MServer;
```

```
    public MessengerConnection(Socket Client, string ID,
      MessengerServer server)
    {

    }

    private byte[] Message = new byte[1024];

    public void Start()
    {

    }

    public void OnMsgReceived(IAsyncResult ar)
    {

    }

    public void Close()
    {

    }

    public void ReceiveMessage(byte[] data, int bytesRead)
    {

    }
  }
}
```

The MessengerConnection class constructor sets the reference to the current client and MessengerServer server class.

```
public MessengerConnection(Socket Client, string ID,
  MessengerServer server)
{
  this.Client = Client;
  this.ID = ID;
  this.MServer = server;
}
```

The Start method prepares the connection to listen for messages. This method also makes an Async callback to the OnMsgReceived method, which delivers the message to all connected clients by utilizing the stored reference to MessengerServer, as shown in the following code snippet:

```
public void Start()
{
  try
  {
    // Listen for messages
    Client.BeginReceive(Message, 0, Message.Length, SocketFlags.None,
      new AsyncCallback(OnMsgReceived), null);
  }
  catch (SocketException se)
  {
    Console.WriteLine(se.Message);
  }
}
```

The OnMsgReceived method calls the DeliverMessage method of the MessengerServer class to send the message to all clients that are currently connected with MessengerServer by utilizing the stored reference to message server. After delivering the message, the OnMsgReceived method prepares the connection to listen for the next message, as shown in the following code snippet:

```
public void OnMsgReceived(IAsyncResult ar)
{
  try
  {
    int bytesRead = Client.EndReceive(ar);
    if (bytesRead > 0)
    {
      //Send message to all connected clients
      MServer.DeliverMessage(Message, bytesRead);

      // Listen for next message
      Client.BeginReceive(Message, 0, Message.Length,
        SocketFlags.None, new AsyncCallback(OnMsgReceived), null);
    }
  }
  catch (Exception err)
  {
    Console.WriteLine(err.Message);
  }
}
```

The ReceiveMessage method simply sends the message data to each of the connected clients.

```
public void ReceiveMessage(byte[] data, int bytesRead)
{
  Client.Send(data, 0, bytesRead,SocketFlags.None);
}
```

The MainPage.xaml File

Let's build a simple user interface for the Silverlight text chat application. First, put the following self-explanatory XAML in the `MainPage.xaml` file:

```
<UserControl x:Class="chapter4Socket.MainPage"
    xmlns="http://schemas.microsoft.com/winfx/2006/xaml/presentation"
    xmlns:x="http://schemas.microsoft.com/winfx/2006/xaml"
    Width="400" >
    <StackPanel x:Name="LayoutRoot" Background="White">
        <ScrollViewer  x:Name="Scroller" Height="200">
            <TextBlock x:Name="Messages" TextWrapping="Wrap"/>
        </ScrollViewer>
        <StackPanel Orientation="Horizontal">
            <TextBlock Text="Enter your name: "/>
            <TextBox x:Name="txtName" MaxLength="20" Width="200"/>
            <Button x:Name="btnConnect" Width="100"
                Content="Connect" Click="btnConnect_Click"/>
        </StackPanel>
        <StackPanel Orientation="Horizontal" Margin="0,10,0,0" >
            <TextBox x:Name="txtMessage" MaxLength="200"
              Height="100" Width="300"/>
            <Button x:Name="btnSend" Width="100"
              Click="btnSend_Click" Content="Send"/>
        </StackPanel>
    </StackPanel>
</UserControl>
```

Here we have wired up the `Click` event handler for the `btnConnect` button and the `btnSend` button controls. You will see the implementation of this event handler in the next section when we construct the code-behind.

The MainPage.xaml.cs Code-Behind File

Before we start anything, first you need to add the following four additional assembly references to the `MainPage` class:

```
using System.Net.Sockets;
using System.IO;
using System.Text;
using System.Xml.Serialization;
```

Next, declare the `Socket` object type variable at the `MainPage` class level to define the primary socket-based connection, as follows:

```
// The MSocket for the connection
private Socket MSocket;
```

Now let's implement the Click event for the btnConnect button control.

```
private void btnConnect_Click(object sender, RoutedEventArgs e)
{
  try
  {
    if ((MSocket != null) && (MSocket.Connected == true))
      MSocket.Close();
  }
  catch (Exception err)
  {
    AddMessage("ERROR: " + err.Message);
  }
  DnsEndPoint endPoint = new
    DnsEndPoint(Application.Current.Host.Source.DnsSafeHost, 4530);
  MSocket = new Socket(AddressFamily.InterNetwork,
    SocketType.Stream, ProtocolType.Tcp);
  SocketAsyncEventArgs SocketArgs = new SocketAsyncEventArgs();
  SocketArgs.UserToken = MSocket;
  SocketArgs.RemoteEndPoint = endPoint;
  SocketArgs.Completed += new
    EventHandler<SocketAsyncEventArgs>(SocketArgs_Completed);
  MSocket.ConnectAsync(SocketArgs);
}
```

The previous code snippet is self-explanatory. Before creating a new socket-based connection, first check if the socket is already open. If the socket is already open, close the connection. Then, an object of type DnsEndPoint is created to identify the location of the remote host. In this case, the location of the removed host is the web server that hosts the Silverlight page, and the port number is 4530. Finally, the code creates SocketAsyncEventArgs, and attaches the SocketArgs_Completed event to the Completed event. Note that the catch block calls the AddMessage method, as shown in the following code:

```
private void AddMessage(string message)
{
  //Separate thread
  Dispatcher.BeginInvoke(
    delegate()
    {
      Messages.Text += message + "\n";
      Scroller.ScrollToVerticalOffset(Scroller.ScrollableHeight);
    });
}
```

Here, to implement typical Windows chat message behavior, the Scroller ScrollViewer automatically scrolls to the bottom of each message and is added to the Messages TextBlock.

The send button performs the send and receive of the text message and then appends the response to the main text box that shows the chat conversation.

```
private void btnSend_Click(object sender, RoutedEventArgs e)
{
  SocketAsyncEventArgs Args = new SocketAsyncEventArgs();
  // Prepare the message.
  XmlSerializer serializer = new
    XmlSerializer(typeof(Message));
  MemoryStream ms = new MemoryStream();
  serializer.Serialize(ms, new
    Message(txtMessage.Text, txtName.Text));
  byte[] messageData = ms.ToArray();
  List<ArraySegment<byte>> bufferList = new
    List<ArraySegment<byte>>();
  bufferList.Add(new ArraySegment<byte>(messageData));
  Args.BufferList = bufferList;
  // Send the message.
  MSocket.SendAsync(Args);
  //clear the text box
  txtMessage.Text = string.Empty;
}
```

Executing the Text Chat Application

While you are in development mode, before you open the application, visit C:\book\examples\chapter4Socket\PolicyServer\bin\Debug to start the PolicyServer Windows service and double-click the PolicyServer.exe file to run it. Similarly, visit C:\book\examples\chapter4Socket\MessengerServer\bin\Debug to start the MessengerServer Windows service and double-click the MessengerServer.exe file to run it. (Note that these paths may differ, based on where you set up the application.) Two command shell windows should open, indicating that both services are running, as shown in Figure 4-7.

Now you are all set to run the project. Go to the Solution Explorer of the open chapter4Socket project in Visual Studio. Select chapter4SocketTestPage.html or chapter4SocketTestPage.aspx to open the project in the browser. You should see the socket client text chat application default user interface before connecting to a remote service, as shown in Figure 4-8.

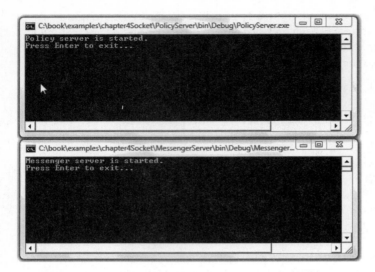

Figure 4-7. *PolicyServer and MessengerServer Windows services started*

Figure 4-8. *Socket client text chat application before connecting to a remote service*

As you can see, we need to provide a name and click on the Connect button to join the chat room. Upon successful connection to the server, the message "Connected to server" is appended to the message box. Figure 4-9 shows two chat clients connected to the MessengerServer using two different browser windows (i.e., Internet Explorer 7 and Mozilla Firefox 3), and the messages history between them is shown with the date and time appended after each message.

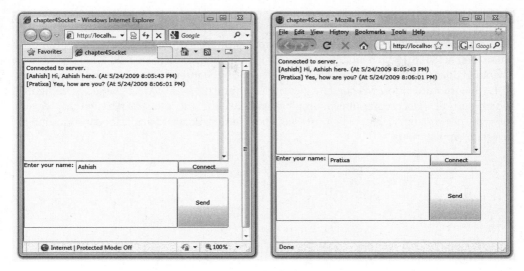

Figure 4-9. *Socket client example after connecting and sending data*

Considerations for Using Networking

So far, you have seen three ways to communicate over HTTP and one way to communicate over sockets in Silverlight. Great questions to ask at this point are "How do these approaches compare to each other?" and "When should I use which?"

Generating a client proxy for a service is the easiest from a development standpoint. It's also easy to use a different endpoint when constructing an instance of the client proxy. Using a generated proxy is the easiest, best way to call services exposed on the World Wide Web. If the service changes, you can simply update the proxy. If there are multiple endpoints exposed, you will see these in the ClientConfig and can choose which to use. It is also important to note that this approach uses SOAP 1.1 as a way to communicate with objects over HTTP.

The easiest way to download a resource from a site is to use the System.Net.WebClient class. The two biggest resources are files (e.g., the archived media in the example earlier in this chapter) and text files (such as syndication feeds in XML format). The WebClient class provides a way to download data via a Stream or as a String, making the access of resources quite easy.

Although the WebClient class provides both the HTTP GET and POST methods, it is impossible to send more complicated requests to a server. The System.Net.HttpWebRequest class supports both GET and POST, and also supports both the HTTP and HTTPS protocols. The other major benefit of the HttpWebRequest class is that capabilities provided by the browser, such as authentication and cookies, are supported.

Finally, the socket support exists to directly communicate with an exposed TCP service. Whereas HTTP is an application layer protocol, socket communication has no application layer protocol. A communication protocol must be previously agreed on between a service and the Silverlight application. The major benefit to socket communication is performance—a well-designed TCP service can have less overhead than communication directly over HTTP/SOAP.

Summary

Silverlight exists in a connected world. Its network support is primarily focused on communication over HTTP(S), which enables it to easily invoke services on the World Wide Web and download documents such as syndication feeds. In this chapter, you've seen the support for HTTP(S) communication provided by the `WebClient` and `HttpWebRequest` classes. Silverlight also supports raw socket communication, albeit with severe restrictions. The next two chapters will utilize the networking support built into Silverlight to retrieve data and media for consumption by Silverlight applications.

CHAPTER 5

■■■

Working with Data

Data can take many forms, from simple types passed back from web services to complex formats such as XML. In the previous chapter, you saw how to consume web services from Silverlight and connect to various servers, including ones that live outside your application's host domain and others that communicate over sockets. Once you have data, though, you must process it and/or display it to users. Silverlight 3 provides an enhanced DataGrid control, new DataForm and DataPager controls, a data binding architecture to connect data to user interface elements, and even item templates for controls like the ListBox to specifically define how each item should appear. On the data-processing side, Silverlight provides a number of classes for working with XML, including Language Integrated Query (LINQ), which was introduced in .NET 3.5 on Windows (but remember, while Silverlight is based on .NET 3.5, it has no dependence on .NET Framework 3.5!). Another important aspect to data is how to save data on the client. While you can use cookies, Silverlight provides something called *isolated storage* that provides file system semantics for saving and loading data. Let's dig into all this support Silverlight provides for working with data.

Displaying Data

In Chapter 3, you were introduced to a number of controls, including the ListBox. Data templates and the `Binding` markup extension were previewed in Chapter 2. Controls such as ListBox enable you to connect a user interface element to a data source and automatically display data. One control that wasn't discussed in Chapter 2 is DataGrid—a control specifically designed for displaying data in rows and columns. It provides a lot of flexibility for displaying the data and the column headers and footers. We'll take a brief look at this control in this section.

Data Binding

Data binding is the connection of a data source to a user interface element such as a TextBlock, TextBox, or ListBox. It is possible to do one-way data binding where data is simply displayed in the user interface, and two-way data binding where any changes a user makes within the user interface elements gets reflected in the underlying data source. Data sources in Silverlight are generally objects or collections of objects with properties that can be accessed.

Before we can take a closer look at data binding, we need to examine what makes it happen: the `Binding` markup extension. This can be used either in XAML or in the code-behind. It's not possible to bind directly to basic data types such as Int32 and string, so we need at least one containing class, such as AccountSettings shown here:

```
public class AccountSettings
{
    public string Name { get; set; }
    public string EmailAddress { get; set; }
    public string SignatureLine { get; set; }
    public bool HideEmailAddress { get; set; }
}
```

This class contains several properties that will be used in the data binding. If we have a TextBlock control and want to display the Name property, we first bind the Text property of the TextBlock control to the Name property.

```
<TextBlock x:Name="nameTextBlock" Text="{Binding Name}"/>
```

This gets us halfway there. The other step is to set the DataContext property of the Text-Block control to the AccountSettings object. This step is only necessary when it isn't possible to set the data context in XAML, and a simple object like this is one of those cases. The Binding markup extension provides support for three modes of operation: OneTime, OneWay, and TwoWay. These modes of operation control how data is bound and controls the flow between the data source and user interface elements. The following list describes each of these modes:

OneTime: The data binding happens exactly once, meaning that any changes to the data source after the initial binding will not be reflected in the user interface.

OneWay: The data flows only from the data source to the user interface. Any time the data source is updated, the user interface will reflect the changes. This is the default mode.

TwoWay: The data flows from the data source to the user interface and also from the user interface to the data source. Any changes on either side will automatically be reflected in the other side.

Table 5-1 displays the various valid XAML syntax for the Binding markup extension.

Table 5-1. *Valid Syntax for the Binding Markup Extension*

Syntax	Description
{Binding}	This signals data binding. The mode of operation is OneWay. This is most commonly used with item templates for controls such as ListBox.
{Binding *path*}	This signals data binding and specifies which property will supply the data. The path takes the form of object properties separated by dots, allowing you to drill down into an object.
{Binding *properties*}	This signals data binding but provides the ability to set data binding configuration properties using a *name=value* syntax.
{Binding *path*, *properties*}	This combines the previous two formats, allowing you to specify which object property supplies the data and also configure the data binding.

There are a number of properties that help control how data binding behaves, such as controlling how errors during data binding are handled. The full list of properties is shown in Table 5-2.

Table 5-2. *System.Windows.Data.Binding Properties*

Name	Type	Description
Converter	IValueConverter	This is used to easily perform a custom conversion of the data on its way to or from the data source. This is useful for changing how data appears in the user interface while still maintaining proper data format for the data source.
ConverterCulture	CultureInfo	This is used to specify the culture the converter uses.
ConverterParameter	object	This is a custom parameter for use in the converter.
ElementName	String	This specifies the name of the element to use as the binding source object.
Mode	BindingMode	The binding mode specifies how and where data flows between the data source and user interface. The valid modes are OneWay, OneTime, and TwoWay.
NotifyOnValidatonError	bool	When set to `true`, the data binding system will raise a `BindingValidationError` event if validation fails when committing changes to the data source in TwoWay data binding. If `false`, validation errors will be ignored.
Path	string	This specifies the target property path of the data binding source.
RelativeSource	RelativeSource	This specifies the binding source by specifying its location relative to the position of the binding target.
Source	object	This specifies the source object for data binding. This overrides the `DataContext` set on containing elements within the visual tree.
ValidatesOnExceptions	bool	When this and `NotifyOnValidationError` are `true`, any exceptions generated from the source object's setters or the binding engine's type converters will be reported by raising `BindingValidationError`. If this is `false`, or if it's `true` and `NotifyOnValidationError` is `false`, your application will not be aware of exceptions generated by the data binding system. This only applies in TwoWay binding when the data source is updated.

Now let's take a closer look at data binding an AccountSettings object. This will be a TwoWay data binding scenario, where changes done to the user interface will be reflected in the data source and vice versa. Figure 5-1 shows an interface where the same data is shown twice.

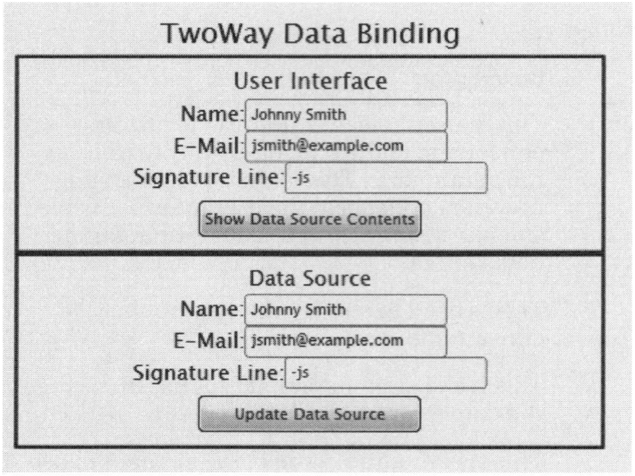

Figure 5-1. *TwoWay data binding example*

In the top half, the user interface elements (in this case, text boxes) are bound to the data source. Any changes made to these text boxes are reflected in the data source. You can verify this by clicking Show Data Source Contents after modifying a value. The lower half lets you change the data source directly. When you click Update Data Source, the values in the data source will be updated directly and the corresponding fields in the top half will automatically change. The following XAML shows how the upper half of the user interface is put together and how the Binding markup extension is used on several of the user interface elements:

```
<Border BorderBrush="Black" BorderThickness="2" Grid.Row="1">
    <StackPanel Orientation="Vertical">
        <TextBlock Text="User Interface" FontSize="16"
                        HorizontalAlignment="Center"/>
        <StackPanel Orientation="Horizontal" HorizontalAlignment="Center">
            <TextBlock Text=" Name:"/>
            <TextBox x:Name="nameTextBox"
                        Text="{Binding Name, Mode=TwoWay}" Width="140"/>
        </StackPanel>
        <StackPanel Orientation="Horizontal" HorizontalAlignment="Center">
            <TextBlock Text="E-Mail:"/>
            <TextBox x:Name="emailTextBox" Width="140"
                        Text="{Binding EmailAddress, Mode=TwoWay}"/>
        </StackPanel>
        <StackPanel Orientation="Horizontal" HorizontalAlignment="Center">
            <TextBlock Text="Signature Line:"/>
            <TextBox x:Name="signatureTextBox" Width="140" />
        </StackPanel>
```

```
    <Button x:Name="viewDataSourceButton" Margin="5" Width="155"
            Content="Show Data Source Contents"
            Click="viewDataSourceButton_Click"/>
  </StackPanel>
</Border>
```

The lower half of the user interface is similar but uses no data binding. An instance of AccountSettings is created in the constructor of this page and then connected when the page loads via the Loaded event handler.

```
private void UserControl_Loaded(object sender, RoutedEventArgs e)
{
    dsNameTextBox.Text = settings.Name;
    dsEmailTextBox.Text = settings.EmailAddress;
    dsSignatureTextBox.Text = settings.SignatureLine;
    nameTextBox.DataContext = settings;
    emailTextBox.DataContext = settings;
    Binding dataBinding = new Binding("SignatureLine");
    dataBinding.Source = settings;
    dataBinding.Mode = BindingMode.TwoWay;
    signatureTextBox.SetBinding(TextBox.TextProperty, dataBinding);
}
```

There are two things of note in this event handler. First, the DataContext property for two of the text boxes must be set. Between the DataContext and the Binding markup extension, the data source is fully linked to the user interface element. The second thing of note is how to create this linkage completely in the code-behind. If you look at the XAML again, you'll see that the SignatureLine doesn't use the Binding markup extension. Instead, the property name is set in the Binding constructor, the data source is linked, and then the data is bound by setting the TextProperty dependency property to the Binding instance. This is almost everything we need to completely enable TwoWay data binding.

Enabling Data Change Notification

If you assemble the code as is, you'll discover that direct changes to the data source are not reflected immediately in the user interface. This is because the data binding system isn't aware that the data source changed. In order to provide this notification, the object being used as the data source must implement the INotifyPropertyChanged interface. This interface defines a single event, PropertyChanged, that must be provided. Let's modify the AccountSettings class to implement this interface.

```
public class AccountSettings : INotifyPropertyChanged
{
    public event PropertyChangedEventHandler PropertyChanged;
    protected void OnPropertyChanged(string propertyName)
    {
        PropertyChangedEventHandler handler = PropertyChanged;
```

```
            if (handler != null)
            {
                handler(this, new PropertyChangedEventArgs(propertyName));
            }
        }
        private string _name;
        public string Name
        {
            get { return (_name); }
            set
            {
                _name = value;
                OnPropertyChanged("Name");
            }
        }
        // other properties; each setter must invoke OnPropertyChanged
}
```

Each time the Name property is updated, the PropertyChanged event will be raised and the data binding system will be notified. This is the mechanism that will cause the user interface elements (the top half of our demonstration interface) to change immediately after clicking the button to update the data source directly.

Next, let's take a look at using data binding to supply the items for a ListBox. This is accomplished by combining two concepts: item templates and data templates. *Item templates* are specifically related to various controls that can contain items, such as ListBox. They are used to define the appearance of each item within the control. *Data templates* define, using user interface elements, how a single data object within an item's control uses properties from each item stored in a data source such as a collection. Figure 5-2 shows a ListBox used to display a customer's bank accounts. A customer can have one or more bank accounts. These are stored within a collection and the collection is set as the data source for the ListBox.

Figure 5-2. *A data template used to connect data to items within a ListBox*

Let's use the following BankAccount class to hold details about a customer's bank account:

```
public class BankAccount
{
    public string AccountNumber { get; set; }
    public double Balance { get; set; }
    public string AccountName { get; set; }
}
```

Here's what the ListBox looks like in the XAML:

```
<ListBox Grid.Row="2" x:Name="accountsListBox">
    <ListBox.ItemTemplate>
        <DataTemplate>
            <StackPanel Orientation="Vertical">
                <StackPanel Orientation="Horizontal">
                    <TextBlock FontSize="16" Text="Account #"/>
                    <TextBlock FontSize="16" Text="{Binding AccountNumber}"/>
                </StackPanel>
                <StackPanel Orientation="Horizontal">
                    <TextBlock FontSize="12" Text="Account Type: "/>
                    <TextBlock FontSize="12" Text="{Binding AccountName}"/>
                </StackPanel>
                <StackPanel Orientation="Horizontal">
                    <TextBlock FontSize="12" Text="Current Balance: "/>
                    <TextBlock FontSize="12" Text="{Binding Balance}"/>
                </StackPanel>
            </StackPanel>
        </DataTemplate>
    </ListBox.ItemTemplate>
</ListBox>
```

In the code-behind, we create a List<BankAccount> collection to hold the bank accounts, create a couple dummy accounts, and then set the ItemsSource property of the ListBox to the collection.

```
List<BankAccount> accounts = new List<BankAccount>();
BankAccount ba1 = new BankAccount();
ba1.AccountName = "Checking";
ba1.AccountNumber = "9048120948109185";
ba1.Balance = 2300.17;
accounts.Add(ba1);
BankAccount ba2 = new BankAccount();
ba2.AccountName = "Savings";
ba2.AccountNumber = "9128059128590812";
ba2.Balance = 18964.00;
accounts.Add(ba2);
accountsListBox.ItemsSource = accounts;
```

The rest happens automatically. Between the item template and the data template, each item within the data source is queried for the property specified in the `Binding` markup extension in the XAML. This makes it easy to display a set of objects within a data source.

Type Converters

This is basically all there is to combining data binding with an item's control, such as a ListBox for displaying data from a data source. Actually, wouldn't it be nice to have better formatting for the balance amount than what is shown in Figure 5-2? Silverlight provides something called a type converter that can be used by the data binding system to conduct custom conversion as the data flows from the data source to the user interface or vice versa. A custom type converter implements the `IValueConverter` interface, providing the `Convert` and `ConvertBack` methods for handling the conversion. Here's the implementation of a type converter used for formatting the currency. Just in case this type converter is used in a TwoWay data binding scenario, the `ConvertBack` method is also implemented.

```
public class BalanceConverter : IValueConverter
{
    public object Convert(object value, Type targetType,
                          object parameter,
                          System.Globalization.CultureInfo culture)
    {
        return (String.Format("{0:C}", (double)value));
    }
    public object ConvertBack(object value, Type targetType,
                              object parameter,
                              System.Globalization.CultureInfo culture)
    {
        string balance = (string)value;
        return(System.Convert.ToDouble(balance.Replace("$", "").Replace(",", "")));
    }
}
```

The type converter must be registered as a resource and assigned an `x:Key` value before it can be used in the XAML. Here's what this registration looks like in the `BankAccountsPage.xaml` page:

```
<UserControl x:Class="chapter5.BankAccountsPage"
             xmlns="http://schemas.microsoft.com/winfx/2006/xaml/presentation"
             xmlns:x="http://schemas.microsoft.com/winfx/2006/xaml"
             xmlns:u="clr-namespace:chapter5"
             Width="400" Height="300" Margin="10">
    <UserControl.Resources>
        <u:BalanceConverter x:Key="BalanceConverter"/>
    </UserControl.Resources>
</UserControl.Resources>
```

Next, the TextBlock used to show the balance for an account is modified to include the type converter in the `Binding` markup extension:

```
<TextBlock FontSize="12"
           Text="{Binding Balance, Converter={StaticResource BalanceConverter}}"/>
```

Now this gives us a nicely formatted balance without having to exert too much effort. You can see the result in Figure 5-3.

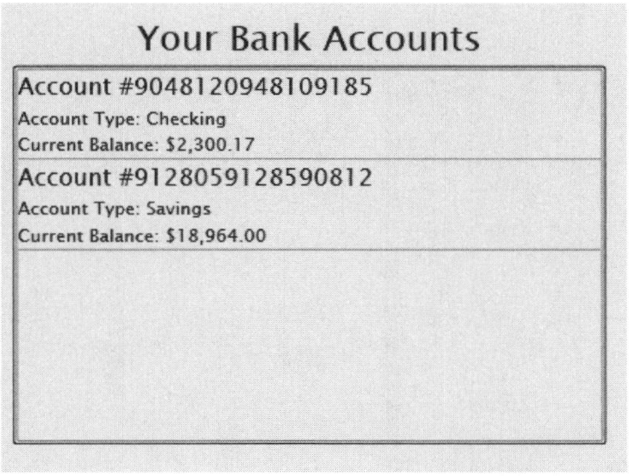

Figure 5-3. *Using a type converter to format data for the user interface*

XAML Element Data Binding / Element-to-Element Binding

In Silverlight 2, it is certainly possible to perform XAML-based element-to-element binding that allows two user interface components to integrate through properties for a WPF-based rich client application. However, Silverlight 2 developers spend time coding to achieve this feature. So for Silverlight 2 applications, if you want to set the Volume of a MediaElement using a Slider control, some code is needed to pull the value of the slider and change the volume according to the slider's value.

Silverlight 3 makes the developer community happy by introducing XAML element property data binding to Common Language Runtime (CLR) objects and other user interface components. This allows you to bind elements' properties to each other so the value/behavior of the bound element changes based on the element's changes. You can achieve element-to-element data binding by adding the ElementName property in the binding expression. The following example binds the TextBlock control's Text property to the mySlider control's Value property, as follows:

```
Text="{Binding Value, ElementName=mySlider}">
```

Now let's look at this example's complete code snippet.

```
<UserControl x:Class="chapter5.ElementBinding"
    xmlns="http://schemas.microsoft.com/winfx/2006/xaml/presentation"
    xmlns:x="http://schemas.microsoft.com/winfx/2006/xaml"
    Width="400" Height="300">
    <StackPanel x:Name="LayoutRoot" Background="White">
        <TextBlock x:Name="myValue" Height="32" Width="auto"
            FontSize="14" Text="{Binding Value, Mode=OneWay,
            ElementName=mySlider}"/>
        <Slider x:Name="mySlider" Maximum="100" Minimum="1" Value="5"/>
    </StackPanel>
</UserControl>
```

As shown in Figure 5-4, the text value is now set to the default value 5. This value will change as you move the mySlider control to the left or right. If you move the control to the right, the value will increase (the maximum value is set to 100); if you move the control to the left, the value will decrease (the minimum value is set to 1).

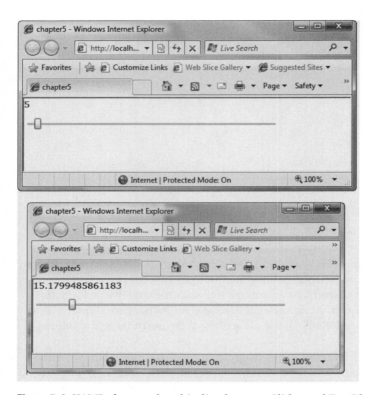

Figure 5-4. *XAML element data binding between Slider and TextBlock controls*

Introducing the DataGrid Control

The DataGrid control is useful for displaying data in tabular format with rows and columns. It isn't part of the core Silverlight installation, so you must download the Silverlight SDK and distribute the System.Windows.Controls.Data assembly with your application. In order to use DataGrid in XAML, you must make its namespace visible.

```
<UserControl x:Class="chapter5.DataGridDemo"
    xmlns="http://schemas.microsoft.com/winfx/2006/xaml/presentation"
    xmlns:x="http://schemas.microsoft.com/winfx/2006/xaml"
    xmlns:c="clr-namespace:System.Windows.Controls;
                assembly=System.Windows.Controls.Data"
    Width="400" Height="300" Margin="10">
    <Grid x:Name="LayoutRoot" Background="White">
        <c:DataGrid x:Name="accountsDataGrid"/>
    </Grid>
</UserControl>
```

You then connect the DataGrid to a data source using the `ItemsSource` property. By default, DataGrid automatically generates column headings. The appearance of the default DataGrid after connecting it to the collection of bank accounts used previously is shown in Figure 5-5.

Figure 5-5. *The default DataGrid control*

DataGrid provides a lot of functionality. You can change the style of rows, alternate rows, and column/row headers. DataGrid can be configured to permit or prevent the reordering of columns, enable row selection, and enable in-place editing of data. It also provides a number of events to give you plenty of opportunity to transform or otherwise handle data. In Silverlight 3, the DataGrid control is more enhanced, with features such as RowGrouping, additional events, and cell- and row-level data validation. Let's look at these features one by one.

RowGrouping

The Silverlight 3 DataGrid control includes the RowGrouping feature, which lets you group information by properties by adding `GroupDescriptions` to DataGrid. The following example includes an `Employee` class with some common employee-related properties, and we will define the XAML code to display these employees in a DataGrid control grouped by the `State` property.

The `Employee` class includes the `string` type properties `Name`, `Email`, `City`, `State`, and `Pincode`.

```
public class Employee
{
    public string Name { get; set; }
    public string Email { get; set; }
    public string City { get; set; }
    public string State { get; set; }
    public string Pincode { get; set; }
}
```

The XAML code includes two additional items: a namespace, `System.ComponentModel`, to enable access to `PropertyGroupDescription`, and `GroupDescriptions` for the property `State`. The following is the complete XAML code for the DataGrid population bound with the `Employee` class and grouped by the `State` property:

```
<UserControl xmlns:controls="clr-namespace:System.Windows.Controls;
   assembly=System.Windows.Controls"
   xmlns:data="clr-namespace:System.Windows.Controls;
     assembly=System.Windows.Controls.Data"
   x:Class="chapter5.DataGridRowGrouping"
   xmlns="http://schemas.microsoft.com/winfx/2006/xaml/presentation"
   xmlns:x="http://schemas.microsoft.com/winfx/2006/xaml"
   xmlns:cmpmd="clr-namespace:System.Windows.Data;
     assembly=System.ComponentModel"
   Width="500" Height="300">
   <Grid x:Name="LayoutRoot" Background="White">
      <data:DataGrid x:Name="myDataGrid" AutoGenerateColumns="False" >
         <data:DataGrid.Columns>
            <data:DataGridTextColumn Binding="{Binding Name}"
               Header="Name" />
            <data:DataGridTextColumn Binding="{Binding Email}"
               Header="Email"  />
            <data:DataGridTextColumn Binding="{Binding City}"
               Header="City"  />
            <data:DataGridTextColumn Binding="{Binding Pincode}"
               Header="Pin Code"  />
         </data:DataGrid.Columns>
         <data:DataGrid.GroupDescriptions>
            <cmpmd:PropertyGroupDescription PropertyName="State" />
         </data:DataGrid.GroupDescriptions>
      </data:DataGrid>
   </Grid>
</UserControl>
```

In the code-behind class, create the Employee class–related array, populate it, and bind it to the DataGrid control's ItemsSource property in the Loaded event of the class. The following is the code-behind class code snippet:

```
void DataGridRowGrouping_Loaded(object sender, RoutedEventArgs e)
{
   Employee[] emps = new Employee[10];

   emps[0] = new Employee ();
   emps[0].Name="Ashish Ghoda";
   emps[0].Email = "aghoda@TechnologyOpinion.com";
   emps[0].City="New Providence";
   emps[0].Pincode="07974";
   emps[0].State="New Jersey";

   emps[1] = new Employee();
   emps[1].Name = "Jay Nanavaty";
   emps[1].Email = "jnanavaty@TechnologyOpinion.com";
   emps[1].City = "Baroda";
```

```
    emps[1].Pincode = "390023";
    emps[1].State = "Gujarat";

    emps[2] = new Employee();
    emps[2].Name = "Kruti Vaishnav";
    emps[2].Email = "kvaishnav@TechnologyOpinion.com";
    emps[2].City = "Delhi";
    emps[2].Pincode = "350025";
    emps[2].State = "Delhi";

    emps[3] = new Employee();
    emps[3].Name = "Pratixa Ghoda";
    emps[3].Email = "pghoda@TechnologyOpinion.com";
    emps[3].City = "New Providence";
    emps[3].Pincode = "07974";
    emps[3].State = "New Jersey";

    myDataGrid.ItemsSource = emps;
}
```

Now if you run the project you should see all the added employee information displayed in the DataGrid control grouped by state, as shown in Figure 5-6.

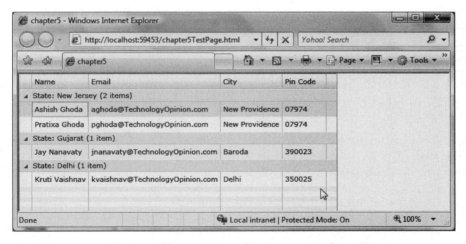

Figure 5-6. *DataGrid grouped by state viewed in Internet Explorer (IE) 7*

Just now you created one-level grouping by adding one property in GroupDescriptions. You can achieve multilevel grouping very easily: just add more than one property in GroupDescriptions. Using the previous example, let's group by the State and then the City property. The order of grouping is from top to bottom, according to the order in which properties are added under GroupDescriptions. So, to group by State and then by City, remove the City property from DataGrid.Columns and add it under GroupDescriptions as PropertyGroupDescription, as shown in the following code:

```
<data:DataGrid.GroupDescriptions>
    <cmpmd:PropertyGroupDescription PropertyName="State" />
    <cmpmd:PropertyGroupDescription PropertyName="City" />
</data:DataGrid.GroupDescriptions>
```

Figure 5-7 shows the DataGrid grouped by the State and then the City property.

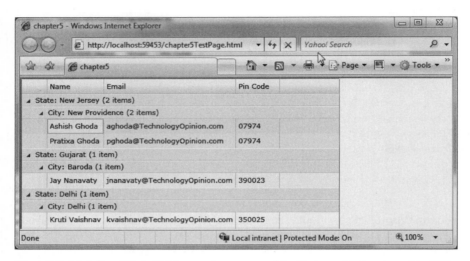

Figure 5-7. *Multilevel DataGrid grouping, grouped by State and City, viewed in IE 7*

DataGrid Editing Events

With support for explicit binding, Silverlight 3 supports the DataGrid editing events CellEditEnding, CellEditEnded, RowEditEnding, and RowEditEnded. With the use of these events, DataGrid can properly raise cancellable editing events and ended notifications, as in the following code snippet:

```
public event EventHandler<DataGridCellEditEndingEventArgs>
    CellEditEnding;
public event EventHandler<DataGridCellEditEndedEventArgs>
    CellEditEnded;
public event EventHandler<DataGridRowEditEndingEventArgs>
    RowEditEnding;
public event EventHandler<DataGridRowEditEndedEventArgs>
    RowEditEnded;
```

Cell-Level Data Validation

In Silverlight 3, the DataGrid control supports framework validation at the cell level by default. Developers do not have to write a single line of code or set any property to perform basic framework, data-level validation of each cell.

To demonstrate cell-level validation, I added an additional `int` type property, `Yearjoined`, to the `Employee` class and changed the XAML code appropriately to display it in the DataGrid. As you can see in Figure 5-8, I entered "Text" instead of any integer value for the Year Joined column, and automatically DataGrid raised a type conversion error at the time of binding the value. The message in the red box is displayed automatically, and the row background color changes to pink.

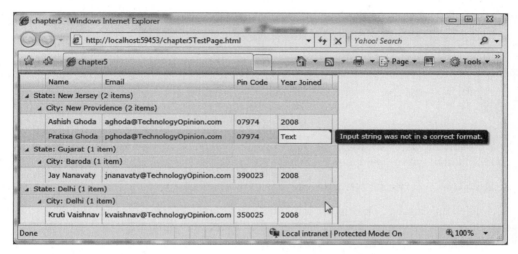

Figure 5-8. *Default cell validation in the Silverlight 3 DataGrid control*

Row-Level Data Validation

You saw how easy it is to implement cell-level validation; now, with some minor custom coding, let's implement row-level validation when you commit a particular row or entity in DataGrid.

Row-level validation uses the features of `System.ComponentModel.DataAnnotations`. You decorate the class with the `CustomValidation` attribute, specifying the validation class and the method to be used for validation. Row-level validation errors show at the bottom of the Data-Grid in an error ListBox. If you implement custom validation for more than one property and you have more than one error, all errors are displayed at the bottom of the DataGrid in the ListBox. If you click the error in the ListBox, focus goes to the cell where the error occurred. When the error is resolved, the error entry is removed from the ListBox automatically.

Using our previous example, let's implement row-level validation for the `Email` attribute. First, include a reference to the `ComponentModel` and `DataAnnotations` assemblies to the class, as shown in the following code:

```
using System.ComponentModel;
using System.ComponentModel.DataAnnotations;
```

Now let's implement the `ValidateEmployee` validation class to validate if the Email field in the DataGrid is empty. If the Email field is empty, a customized message is displayed.

```
public static class ValidateEmployee
{
   public static bool EmailNotNull(object employeeObject,
     ValidationContext context, out ValidationResult validationResult)
   {
     validationResult = null;
     Employee emp = employeeObject as Employee;
     string email= emp.Email;
     if (email== null)
     {
        validationResult = new ValidationResult("Email cannot be empty");
     }
     return !(email == null);
   }
}
```

Now add the CustomValidation attribute to define ValidateEmployee as the validation class and EmailNotNull as the validation method at the Employee class level.

```
[CustomValidation(typeof(ValidateEmployee), "EmailNotNull")]
```

Finally, the Employee class has to implement the INotifyPropertyChanged interface to get notified about property changes. For that, first modify the signature of the Employee class as follows:

```
public class Employee : INotifyPropertyChanged
```

As you implement the INotifyPropertyChanged, you must implement the PropertyChanged event.

```
public event PropertyChangedEventHandler PropertyChanged;
```

Now the NotifyPropertyChanged will raise the PropertyChanged event, passing the source property that is being changed, as follows:

```
private void NotifyPropertyChanged(String changedproperty)
{
   if (PropertyChanged != null)
   {
      PropertyChanged(this, new
        PropertyChangedEventArgs(changedproperty));
   }
}
```

In the end, you need to call NotifyPropertyChanged when the Email property is being changed by updating the code as follows:

```
[Required]
public string Email
{
get { return email; }
```

```
set
  {
    if (value != email)
    {
      email = value;
      NotifyPropertyChanged("email");
    }
  }
}
```

As you can see in Figure 5-9, if you keep the Email field empty, the message is displayed at the end of the DataGrid in the ListBox and the row background color changes to pink.

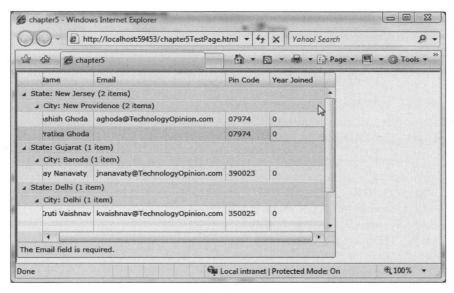

Figure 5-9. *Row custom validation in the Silverlight 3 DataGrid control*

Introducing the DataForm Control

The newly introduced DataForm control in Silverlight 3 empowers designers and developers to implement enterprise-level and data-driven form-based applications in an agile mode. The DataForm control can be bound to the data and allows you to present and perform data operations including data validation very easily. You can easily extend the integration of the DataForm control with Silverlight's code-behind capabilities, such as integration with LINQ and Windows Communication Foundation (WCF) services (discussed in Chapter 4), to develop enterprise-level, complex, data-driven, and service-oriented multitier applications. Let's jump into understanding the DataForm control without wasting further time.

For any DataForm control-based applications, you need to add the following four assemblies as a reference to the Silverlight project:

```
System.ComponentModel
System.ComponentModel.DataAnnotations
System.Windows.Controls.Data
System.Windows.Controls.Data.DataForm
```

There are two ways to bind the DataForm control. The first (discussed next) is by creating a resource to the current UserControl with a set of properties in the corresponding class, and the second (discussed in the "Introducing the DataPager Control" section) is by creating ObservableCollection.

For the first approach, create a simple Consultant class with the FirstName, LastName, Email, and Website properties of string type, as shown in the following code:

```
public class Consultant
{
    public string FirstName { get; set; }
    public string LastName { get; set; }
    public string Email { get; set; }
    public string Website { get; set; }
}
```

Now in the XAML code, define the DataForm XML namespace DF in the UserControl. This allows the DataForm control in the layout and local namespace to set a reference to the project itself so we can use the Consultant class, as in the following code:

```
<UserControl x:Class="chapter5.DataForm"
    xmlns="http://schemas.microsoft.com/winfx/2006/xaml/presentation"
     xmlns:x="http://schemas.microsoft.com/winfx/2006/xaml"
     xmlns:DF="clr-namespace:System.Windows.Controls;
         assembly=System.Windows.Controls.Data.DataForm"
     xmlns:local="clr-namespace:chapter5"
     Width="600" Height="300">
```

Next, define the local resource by adding UserControl.Resources and local:Consultant with the defined Key, as follows:

```
<UserControl.Resources>
    <local:Consultant x:Key="C1"
            FirstName="Ashish"
            LastName="Ghoda"
            Email="aghoda@TechnologyOpinion.com"
            Website="TechnologyOpinion.com" >
    </local:Consultant>
</UserControl.Resources>
```

Now you are all set to add the DataForm control to the project. Add the DataForm control instance, and use the ItemsSource property to bind to the local resource C1 (defined in the previous code snippet). Also, set the other properties, as follows:

```
<Grid x:Name="LayoutRoot" Background="White">
    <DF:DataForm  ItemsSource="{Binding C1}"
```

```
        Header="TechnologyOpinion.com –
            Strive for the Strategic Excellence"
        Background="Cyan"
        FieldLabelPosition="Auto">
    </DF:DataForm>
</Grid>
```

Now you are all set to run your first DataForm control project. Are you thrilled? I am! Run the project, and you should see a DataForm displaying the fields associated with the `Consultant` class properties populated by the local data resource, as shown in Figure 5-10.

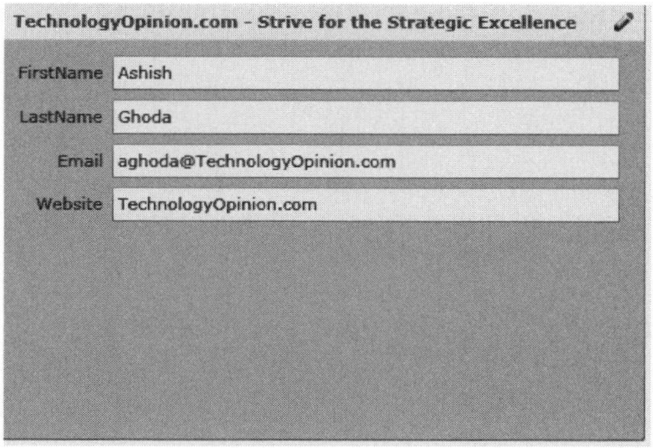

Figure 5-10. *The DataForm control in action*

Take a look at the top-right corner of Figure 5-10. The pencil symbol allows you to change the mode of the DataForm to Edit mode. The `Binding` markup extension set on the fields determines whether you can modify the fields. At present, we have not set up any `Binding` markup extension, so by default the `BindingDirection` is set to `TwoWay` for all fields. If you click the pencil symbol once, all fields become editable and the Save button becomes available, as shown in Figure 5-11.

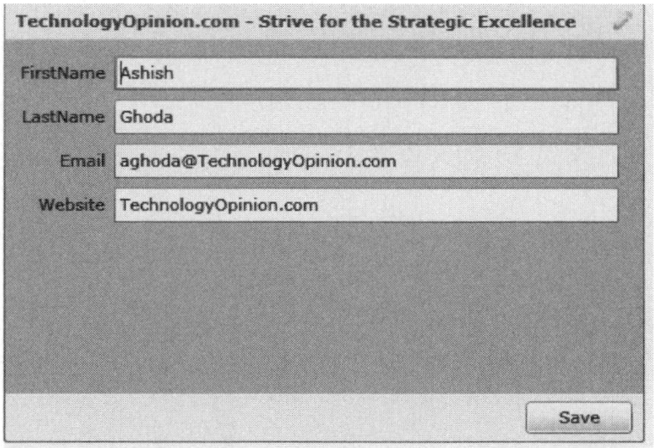

Figure 5-11. *DataForm in Edit mode*

Binding Modes

There are three possibilities to bind your attribute:

- [Bindable(false)] will not display the respective fields in the DataForm.

- [Bindable(true, BindingDirection.TwoWay)] allows the respective fields to be displayed and edited in the DataForm.

- [Bindable(true, BindingDirection.OneWay)] allows the respective fields to be displayed but read only in the DataForm.

You can bind class attributes at the class level, which is applicable to all attributes, or at the specific attribute level. If you set up binding at both levels, the attribute-level binding definition will be applicable to the DataForm control.

IEditableObject Interface Implementation

You can also apply the IEditableObject interface implementation to the Consultant class to get more custom control with the BeginEdit, CancelEdit, and EndEdit methods, as demonstrated in the following code:

```
public class Consultant : IEditableObject
{
   public string FirstName { get; set; }
   public string LastName { get; set; }
   public string Email { get; set; }
   public string Website { get; set; }

   public void BeginEdit()
   {
     //Implement code here
   }

   public void CancelEdit()
   {
     //Implement code here
   }

   public void EndEdit()
   {
     //Implement code here
   }
}
```

This implementation gives you more control over the DataForm. The key change is the availability of the Save and Cancel buttons in Edit mode.

Customized Display of DataForm Fields

You can customize an individual field's attributes, such as Name, Description, Order, GroupName, Prompt, ResourceType, ShortName, etc. The following code demonstrates the customized names, descriptions, and order of the Consultant class attributes:

```
public class Consultant
{
    [Display(Name = "First Name :",
            Description = "Enter Your First Name", Order = 1)]
    public string FirstName { get; set; }
    [Display(Name = "Last Name :",
            Description = "Enter Your Last Name", Order = 2)]
    public string LastName { get; set; }
    [Display(Name = "Email :", Description = "Enter Your Email", Order = 4)]
    public string Email { get; set; }
    [Display(Name = "Website :",
            Description = "Enter Your Website Url", Order = 3)]
    public string Website { get; set; }
}
```

Change the Binding attribute of the DataForm control in the XAML code to Consultants, as shown in the following code:

```
<DF:DataForm ItemsSource="{Binding Consultants}"
    Header="TechnologyOpinion.com –
        Strive for the Strategic Excellence"
    Background="Cyan"
    FieldLabelPosition="Auto">
</DF:DataForm>
```

Run the project, and you should see the customized names for the fields. Also, the Email and Website fields are reordered, and an information button is available for each field. Highlighting the information button displays the field description, as shown in Figure 5-12.

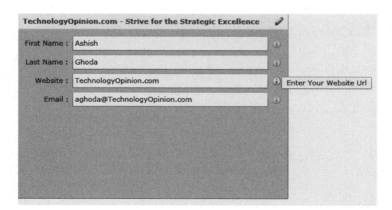

Figure 5-12. *Customized DataForm with display attributes applied to fields*

Field-Level Validation

You can use these different approaches based on field types to perform validation:

- Apply the [Required (ErrorMessage = "This field cannot be blank")] attribute to any attribute to force it to be a required field. If the user does not enter a value, the defined error message is displayed to the field upon validation.

- Apply different attributes for different types of validation:

  - For an int type field, use the [Range(1, 200, ErrorMessage="Over Value")] attribute.

  - For a string type field, use the [StringLength(40, ErrorMessage="Exceed number of characters")] attribute.

  - For other field types, use the RegularExpression attribute.

In our sample application, apply the Required attribute to the Email property and run the application. If you do not populate the Email field, you will get an error message at the bottom of the DataForm and the respective field will be highlighted in red, as shown in Figure 5-13.

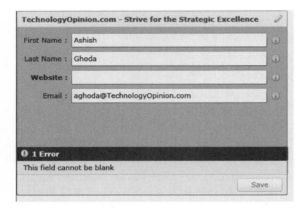

Figure 5-13. *Custom field validation in the DataForm control*

Introducing the DataPager Control

In order to support data paging, you need to have multiple records available. To accomplish this, first you need to bind the DataForm to ObservableCollection in the code-behind class, as shown in the following code:

```
public ObservableCollection<Consultant> Consultants
{
    get
    {
        if (consultants == null)
        {
            consultants = new ObservableCollection<Consultant>();
            consultants.Add(new Consultant()
```

```
                 {
                     FirstName = "Ashish",
                     LastName = "Ghoda",
                     Email = "aghoda@TechnologyOpinion.com",
                     Website = "www.TechnologyOpinion.com"
                 });
           consultants.Add(new Consultant()
                 {
                     FirstName = "Jay",
                     LastName = "Nanavaty",
                     Email = "jnanavaty@TechnologyOpinion.com",
                     Website = "www.TechnologyOpinion.com"
                 });
     }
     return (consultants);
   }
}
private ObservableCollection<Consultant> consultants;
```

In the Loaded event of the UserControl, set `DataContext` as follows:

```
this.DataContext = this;
```

And finally, change the DataForm control binding in the XAML code from the local source binding to `ObservableCollection` consultants, as follows:

```
</Grid>
  <DF:DataForm
    ItemsSource="{Binding Consultants}"
    Header="TechnologyOpinion.com –
        Strive for the Strategic Excellence"
    Background="Cyan">
  </DF:DataForm>
</Grid>
```

Upon running the project, you should see a DataPager navigation panel on the top-right corner of the DataForm, as shown in Figure 5-14. This navigation panel lets you go to the next, previous, first, and last records; add a new record; or delete any existing record.

■**Note** A good introductory video session on DataForm and DataPager by Mike Taulty is available on Silverlight.net. You can view the video by visiting `http://silverlight.net/learn/learnvideo.aspx?video=187317`.

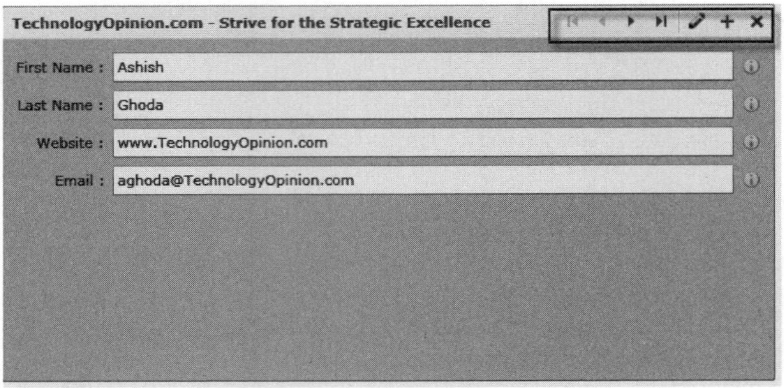

Figure 5-14. *The DataForm control with the DataPager control*

Processing Data

You've seen how to connect data directly to the user interface. This data can be retrieved in a number of ways, including directly downloading it via WebClient or HttpWebRequest/Response, and having it returned from a web service call. The sample code for this chapter has a simple implementation of a web search utilizing Microsoft's Live Search web service. The ListBox is configured with bindings to properties in the result set from Live Search.

```
<ListBox Grid.Row="3" x:Name="resultsListBox">
    <ListBox.ItemTemplate>
        <DataTemplate>
            <StackPanel Orientation="Vertical">
                <TextBlock FontFamily="Arial" Text="{Binding Title}"/>
                <TextBlock FontSize="10" Text="{Binding Url}"/>
                <TextBlock Text="{Binding Description}" FontSize="10" />
            </StackPanel>
        </DataTemplate>
    </ListBox.ItemTemplate>
</ListBox>
```

Invoking the web service is done according to the Live API documentation available on MSDN, the code for which is shown here:

```
MSNSearchPortTypeClient client = new MSNSearchPortTypeClient();
client.SearchCompleted += new
                EventHandler<SearchCompletedEventArgs>
                                (client_SearchCompleted);
SearchRequest req = new SearchRequest();
SourceRequest[] sourceReq = new SourceRequest[1];
sourceReq[0] = new SourceRequest();
sourceReq[0].Source = SourceType.Web;
req.Query = searchTerms.Text;
req.Requests = sourceReq;
```

```
req.AppID = /* enter your AppID here!! */
req.CultureInfo = "en-US";
client.SearchAsync(req);
```

The asynchronous callback simply sets `ItemsSource` to the data source, provided no error has occurred:

```
resultsListBox.ItemsSource = e.Result.Responses[0].Results;
```

This demonstrates how easy it can be to hook up data returned from web services to the user interface. The services infrastructure within Silverlight handles the serialization/deserialization of data for communication purposes, so your application can focus on the objects that can serve as data sources. Of course, sometimes you'll retrieve data directly; for example, by downloading XML data files specific to your application. Silverlight provides a rich set of XML classes for reading/writing/processing XML files. And since Silverlight is based on the .NET Framework 3.5, it also provides support for LINQ, a new technology that provides syntax roughly similar to SQL for working with data directly within C# or VB .NET.

Parsing XML

The `System.Xml.XmlReader` class provides the ability to parse XML documents from a variety of sources, such as a stream or a string. It also provides the ability to directly access an XML file contained in the XAP file. These various approaches to handling an XML file are accessed through the many overloads of the `XmlReader.Create` method. Let's use the `BankAccount` class again, this time stored in an XML file.

```
<?xml version="1.0" encoding="utf-8"?>
<ArrayOfBankAccount xmlns:xsi="http://www.w3.org/2001/XMLSchema-instance"
                            xmlns:xsd="http://www.w3.org/2001/XMLSchema">
  <BankAccount>
    <AccountNumber>8203598230958</AccountNumber>
    <Balance>1100.27</Balance>
    <AccountName>Checking</AccountName>
  </BankAccount>
  <BankAccount>
    <AccountNumber>8293852952359</AccountNumber>
    <Balance>91824.00</Balance>
    <AccountName>Savings</AccountName>
  </BankAccount>
</ArrayOfBankAccount>
```

You use `XmlReaderSettings` to configure the behavior of `XmlReader`. In this case, we'll instruct `XmlReader` to ignore whitespace. If we didn't do this, it would take more code to advance to the correct nodes within the XML file.

```
List<BankAccount> bankAccounts = new List<BankAccount>();
XmlReaderSettings settings = new XmlReaderSettings();
settings.IgnoreWhitespace = true;
XmlReader xmlReader = XmlReader.Create("BankAccountData.xml", settings);
```

```
while (xmlReader.ReadToFollowing("BankAccount"))
{
    BankAccount account = new BankAccount();
    xmlReader.ReadToDescendant("AccountNumber");
    account.AccountNumber =
                    xmlReader.ReadElementContentAsString("AccountNumber","");
    account.Balance = xmlReader.ReadElementContentAsDouble("Balance","");
    account.AccountName = xmlReader.ReadElementContentAsString("AccountName","");
    bankAccounts.Add(account);
}
```

Silverlight also provides an XmlWriter class that you can use to write data to isolated storage—essentially a secure, private file system for your Silverlight applications.

Serializing XML

Sometimes you'll need to use XmlReader to parse XML files directly, such as when you want to extract only certain details. If you're saving/loading business objects manually (i.e., not leveraging the automatic serialization provided by web services), then you can use serialization directly. The System.Xml.Serialization namespace provides the XmlSerializer class that you can use to easily save and load objects to any stream. XmlSerializer also supports working directly with XmlReader and TextReader.

After creating a couple more fake bank accounts, this is how you can serialize the List<BankAccount> collection to isolated storage. Using serialization with isolated storage is an easy way to save a collection of objects to a special permanent storage area on the client.

```
XmlSerializer ser = new XmlSerializer(typeof(List<BankAccount>));
using (IsolatedStorageFile rootStore =
                        IsolatedStorageFile.GetUserStoreForApplication())
{
    using (IsolatedStorageFileStream fs =
                    new IsolatedStorageFileStream("accounts.xml",
                                        FileMode.Create, rootStore))
    {
        ser.Serialize(writer, accounts);
    }
}
```

After serializing the list to isolated storage, you can verify that the file is created and even view its contents. When you want to turn the file within isolated storage back into objects, you follow a similar pattern, but invoke Deserialize.

```
List<BankAccount> bankAccounts = new List<BankAccount>();
XmlSerializer ser = new XmlSerializer(typeof(List<BankAccount>));
using (IsolatedStorageFile rootStore =
                        IsolatedStorageFile.GetUserStoreForApplication())
```

```
{
    using (IsolatedStorageFileStream fs =
                    new IsolatedStorageFileStream("accounts.xml",
                                         FileMode.Open, rootStore))
    {
        bankAccounts = (List<BankAccount>)ser.Deserialize(fs);
    }
}
```

Serialization is by far the easiest way to save business objects to XML files and load them from sources such as isolated storage, or download them via the Web using a class like WebClient.

Using LINQ

LINQ is a language-level technology that makes working with data such as collections of objects and XML documents much easier. While it looks like SQL in some regards, and uses relational model thinking, it has many differences. One similarity, though, is that you can use LINQ to query databases. Revisiting the bank accounts, this time we'll download the accounts.xml file (containing the bank account data) packaged in the XAP file. Then we can use LINQ to easily process the data and load it into an array.

```
void wc_DownloadStringCompleted(object sender, DownloadStringCompletedEventArgs e)
{
    XDocument xmlDocument = XDocument.Parse(e.Result);
    var bankAccountData = from b in xmlDocument.Descendants("BankAccount")
                          select new BankAccount
                          {
                              AccountName = b.Element("AccountName").Value,
                              AccountNumber = b.Element("AccountNumber").Value,
                              Balance = Convert.ToDouble(b.Element("Balance").Value)
                          };
    outputTextBox.Text = "";
    int count = 1;
    foreach (BankAccount ba in bankAccountData)
    {
        outputTextBox.Text += "Record #" + count + "\r\n";
        outputTextBox.Text += "----------\r\n";
        outputTextBox.Text += "Account Number: " + ba.AccountNumber + "\r\n";
        outputTextBox.Text += "Account Name: " + ba.AccountName + "\r\n";
        outputTextBox.Text += "Account Balance: " +
                                    string.Format("{0:C}", ba.Balance) +"\r\n";
        outputTextBox.Text += "\r\n";
        count++;
    }
}
```

The var keyword is a LINQ-ism that can be viewed as a way to hold a reference to an unknown type. It provides an easy way to obtain an IEnumerable from the LINQ query—in this case, the BankAccount objects. The var keyword here could easily be replaced with IEnumerable<BankAccount> since we know the query will return a collection of BankAccount objects. The call to Descendents is used to get a hold of all the BankAccount nodes. Next, new BankAccount is used to signal the creation of new BankAccount objects, which the data we "select" will fill. The compound statement specifies exactly where the properties of BankAccount get their values from—specifically the values of the three elements within each BankAccount element. Since the Value property is of type string, it must be converted to a double value, which is accomplished how it normally is in C#. LINQ is a huge topic that can't satisfactorily be covered in this chapter. If you want to learn more about LINQ, consult *Pro LINQ: Language Integrated Query in C# 2008* by Joseph C. Rattz, Jr. (Apress, 2007). If you want to learn more about the differences between LINQ in .NET 3.5 and Silverlight, consult the MSDN online documentation.

Saving State on the Client

There are two ways to store data on the client: through cookies and through isolated storage. The most direct method to save and access cookies is through the HtmlPage.Document class.

```
HtmlPage.Document.Cookies = "name=value; expires=Saturday, 1-Nov-2009 12:00:00 GMT";
```

I won't go into too much detail on working with cookies, since the important thing is how to access them from Silverlight. Isolated storage, however, is much more interesting. It is a mechanism provided by Silverlight to cache data or store user-specific data on the client. The isolated storage support in Silverlight is based on the isolated storage support in .NET, so you may already be familiar with this topic. Besides granting the ability to persist information on the client, the two biggest advantages to isolated storage are safety and ease of use. Each Silverlight application has its own dedicated storage area on disk, but the application isn't aware of the actual disk usage since it is managed by the runtime. This ensures safety because each application can only use its own dedicated storage area, and there is isolation between the application and the actual disk, mediated by the runtime. Different users on the same computer using the same Silverlight application will each have their own isolated store for the application, ensuring any data stored for one user is safe from other users since each user's store is private and isolated.

The other advantage is ease of use. While access to the underlying disk is prevented, nonetheless, file/directory semantics are used for saving and accessing data in isolated storage. The runtime transparently handles the translation of isolated storage paths to physical paths on the computer.

In Silverlight, the isolated storage area is linked to a Silverlight application via the application's address—including its full path. For example, if you use a Silverlight application at http://www.fabrikam.com/productbrowser, each time you visit this address, the application served will access the same isolated storage area. By default, each application is limited to 1MB of storage. This limit can be increased; however, it requires the user to explicitly grant permission. When a Silverlight application attempts to grow its reserved space in isolated storage, a pop-up like the one shown in Figure 5-15 will ask the user for permission.

Figure 5-15. *Confirmation dialog shown when application attempts to increase space*

The two significant classes used when working with isolated storage are IsolatedStorageFile and IsolatedStorageFileStream. These can be found in the mscorlib assembly in the System.IO.IsolatedStorage namespace. The IsolatedStorageFile class contains methods for working with directories and files, and querying and increasing allocated space. It has 2 properties (listed in Table 5-3) and 16 methods (listed in Table 5-4). All methods will throw an IsolatedStorageException if the store has been removed (through IsolatedStorageFile.Remove) or if there's an isolated storage–related error. They also will throw an ObjectDisposedException if you attempt an operation on an IsolatedStorageFile instance that has been disposed.

Table 5-3. *System.IO.IsolatedStorageFile Properties*

Name	Type	Description
AvailableFreeSpace	long	The free space, in bytes, for the current application; read-only
Quota	long	The maximum space allocated, in bytes, for the current application; read-only

Table 5-4. *System.IO.IsolatedStorageFile Methods*

Name	Description
CreateDirectory	Attempts to create a directory based on the string path passed in. It can create a tree of directories by passing in a path such as \root\data.
CreateFile	Attempts to create a file at the specified string path. If successful, it returns an instance of the IsolatedStorageFileStream class.
DeleteDirectory	Attempts to remove a directory from isolated storage. The directory must be empty for the delete to succeed.
DeleteFile	Attempts to delete a specific file from isolated storage.

Table 5-4. *System.IO.IsolatedStorageFile Methods (Continued)*

Name	Description
DirectoryExists	Returns true if the specified directory exists, and false otherwise.
FileExists	Returns true if the specified file exists, and false otherwise.
GetDirectoryNames	Overloaded. The parameterless version returns a string array of directory names from the root of the store. The overload accepts a string search expression to search subdirectories and also uses wildcards: the ? matches a single character and the * matches multiple characters. If no results are found, the Length property of the returned array will be 0.
GetFileNames	Overloaded. The parameterless version returns a string array of files in the root of the store. The overload accepts a string search expression to search subdirectories and also uses wildcards: the ? matches a single character and the * matches multiple characters. If no results are found, the Length property of the returned array will be 0.
GetUserStoreForApplication	Static method. Used to get a reference to the isolated storage for the current user and application.
OpenFile	Overloaded. Opens a specified file from the store using the requested FileMode and, optionally, FileAccess and FileShare options.
Remove	Removes all contents from the isolated storage and the store itself.
IncreaseQuotaTo	Enables an application to increase the quota to a certain size, specified in bytes. Expanding the size of an isolated store causes a confirmation dialog to appear for user confirmation. It returns true if the new quota is accepted by the user, and false otherwise.

The System.IO.FileMode enumeration contains the following options. This enumeration is the type for the only parameter used in all of the OpenFile overloads.

Append: Appends to an existing file or creates the file if it does not exist.

Create: Creates a file if one doesn't exist. If a file does exist, OpenFile will fail.

CreateNew: Creates a file if one doesn't exist, and re-creates it if it does exist (use with caution).

Open: Opens a file. Unless Append is specified, it also sets the file pointer at the beginning of the file.

OpenOrCreate: Opens the file if it exists, and creates it otherwise.

Truncate: Removes all contents from the file.

The System.IO.FileAccess enumeration contains the following options. This is used to specify the type of access requested to the file.

Read: Only allows reading from the file

ReadWrite: Allows reading from and writing to the file

Write: Only allows writing to the file

The System.IO.FileShare enumeration contains the following options. This is used to specify the type of access concurrently granted to other FileStream objects.

Delete: Allows the file to be deleted by others

Inheritable: Allows the file handle to be inherited by others

None: Disallows shared access

Read: Allows others to read from but not write to the file

ReadWrite: Allows others to read from and write to the file

Write: Allows others to write to the file but not read from it

The code for this chapter has an isolated storage explorer. It provides functionality to view contents of the store, create and delete files and directories, and expand the size of the store. Let's take a look at the code for these operations.

First, we need to get an IsolatedStorageFile object to work with isolated storage. This is accomplished using the IsolatedStorageFile.GetUserStoreForApplication static method. Following best practices in .NET, it's a good idea to always wrap this in a using statement so that Dispose is automatically called.

```
using (IsolatedStorageFile rootStore =
                 IsolatedStorageFile.GetUserStoreForApplication())
{
    // can now interact with isolated storage files/directories/etc.
}
```

The XmlReader example uses isolated storage to store an object in XML format. The IsolatedStorageFileStream inherits from System.IO.FileStream, so we can use it directly with the Serialize method since it can write to any Stream.

```
XmlSerializer ser = new XmlSerializer(typeof(List<BankAccount>));
using (IsolatedStorageFile rootStore =
                  IsolatedStorageFile.GetUserStoreForApplication())
{
    using (IsolatedStorageFileStream fs =
                new IsolatedStorageFileStream("accounts.xml",
                                 FileMode.Create, rootStore))
    {
        ser.Serialize(fs, accounts);
    }
}
```

Once we have an instance of IsolatedStorageFile to work with, we can do things like create files. We could use the CreateFile method of IsolatedStorageFileStream; however, the Stream class also offers the ability to create files. It has three constructors that mirror the parameters of IsolatedStorageFile's OpenFile method, but each constructor takes IsolatedStorageFile as a final parameter. Its public properties are listed in Table 5-5 and its public methods are listed in Table 5-6.

Table 5-5. *System.IO.IsolatedStorageFileStream Properties*

Name	Type	Description
CanRead	bool	Returns true if reading from the file is allowed, and false otherwise; read-only
CanSeek	bool	Returns true if the position of the file pointer can be changed, and false otherwise; read-only
CanWrite	bool	Returns true if writing is allowed, and false otherwise; read-only
Length	long	Specifies the length of the file in bytes; read-only
Position	long	Specifies the current position of the file pointer

Table 5-6. *System.IO.IsolatedStorageFileStream Methods*

Name	Description
BeginRead	Asynchronous method to begin a read operation. Accepts a byte array buffer along with an offset into the array to start writing to, and the maximum number of bytes to read.
BeginWrite	Asynchronous method to begin a write operation. Accepts a byte array buffer along with an offset into the array to start reading, and the number of bytes to write.
EndRead	Used when the read operation ends. Returns an int specifying the number of bytes read.
EndWrite	Used when the write operation ends.
Flush	Flushes any pending data from the internal buffer to disk.
Read	Synchronous read operation. Accepts a byte array buffer along with an offset into the array to start writing to, and the maximum number of bytes to read. Returns the number of bytes actually read.
ReadByte	Synchronously reads a single byte from the stream and returns it.
Seek	Moves the stream pointer to the specified offset, modified by the SeekOrigin option specified. SeekOrigin.Begin treats the offset as an absolute offset from the beginning of the file. SeekOrigin.Current treats the offset as a relative offset from the current position. SeekOrigin.End treats the offset as relative from the end of the file.
SetLength	Attempts to set the length of the file to the passed-in value.
Write	Synchronous write operation. Accepts a byte array buffer along with an offset into the array to start reading, and the number of bytes to write.
WriteByte	Synchronously writes a single byte to the stream.

Summary

This chapter discussed how Silverlight is getting into the main stream by providing data-driven RIAs. Connecting data to the user interface and synchronizing the interface with data sources is now easy to implement and very efficient, thanks to an enhanced DataGrid control, element-to-element data binding, new editing events, RowGrouping, row- and cell-level data validation capabilities, and new DataForm and DataPager controls introduced in Silverlight 3. It also covered support for working with XML documents, including the `System.Xml` classes and LINQ. We finished the chapter with a discussion of how to save state on the client using isolated storage.

The next chapter will demonstrate how to work with media, including images, video, and audio. You are now close to having all the pieces to start putting together sophisticated data-connected user interfaces in Silverlight.

CHAPTER 6

■ ■ ■

Working with Media

Now that you've seen the support Silverlight provides for communicating with other systems and retrieving, saving, displaying, and manipulating data, it's time to focus again on building user interfaces with Silverlight. Ever since the debut of Silverlight 1 under its code name WPF/E, Silverlight has provided support for working with images and video. A significant amount of Silverlight 1 applications featured video. Silverlight 2 and 3 provide the benefits of a managed and secured environment and bring with it rich support for working with images, audio, and video. As you've seen in previous chapters, it isn't too difficult to connect an Image control with an image file on a server. However, it's also possible to package images along with other media, including video files, and work with them on the client side. Microsoft has also introduced two interesting technologies to help enable rich Silverlight applications. The first, Silverlight Streaming, is an environment to host and stream video to Silverlight applications. The second, Deep Zoom, is a way to efficiently handle the presentation and network transfer of a large collection of high-quality images. I'll detail these technologies in this chapter.

Images

We have already utilized the Image control in several previous examples, but we haven't delved into the specifics. Silverlight currently supports only PNG and JPEG formats. There are restrictions placed on the PNG formats used, though. The only indexed color depths supported are 1 bit, 4 bits, and 8 bits per channel. The truecolor color depths supported are 24 and 32 bits per channel (for truecolor plus alpha). The simplest way to place an image on a user interface is by using the Image control and setting its `Source` property:

```
<Image Source="sunny.png"/>
```

The Image control inherits from `FrameworkElement`, so it inherits the bits from `FrameworkElement` and `UIElement`. The new properties and event introduced by the Image class are listed in Tables 6-1 and 6-2.

The specific image to display is set via the `Source` property. In XAML, you can specify the Source using a relative or an absolute address.

```
<Image Source="../Images/10062506.jpg"/>
```

Table 6-1. *Properties of the Image Class*

Property	Type	Description
DownloadProgress	double	Holds a value between 0 and 100 representing the percentage of the image downloaded.
Source	ImageSource	Gets or sets the image source. Currently, only the BitmapImage class can be an image source. From XAML, you can specify a relative or an absolute URI.
Stretch	Stretch	Gets or sets how the image is sized within the width/height set on the Image control.

Table 6-2. *Events of the Image Class*

Event	Description
ImageOpened	Fires when the image source is downloaded and decoded with no failure. You can use this event to determine the size of an image before rendering it. If the image-decode fails for any reason, this event does not fire. Once this event fires, the PixelHeight and PixelWidth properties are guaranteed to be valid.
ImageFailed	Fires if there's a problem downloading or rendering an image. Possible causes are the image not being found at the specified address and the image format not being supported. The EventArgs class is ExceptionRoutedEventArgs and provides ErrorException (the thrown Exception) and ErrorMessage properties.

The Source property is being type-converted to a BitmapImage that inherits from ImageSource. BitmapImage has two events, shown in Table 6-3. The specific image that BitmapImage represents can be a Uri set via a constructor or via the UriSource property after object creation.

■**Tip** Images (and media) can have their Build Action set to Resource within Visual Studio in order for them to be exposed via a relative path. If you can't or don't want to do this, you can make things easy on yourself by utilizing the Application.Current.Host.Source property to retrieve the path to where the Silverlight application is served. This can be useful when constructing image/media sources in the code-behind without needing to know the full path at compile time, such as when things change between development and production. If you specify a relative path in the XAML, however, it's relative to the XAP location, such as the ClientBin folder in this chapter's example code.

You can also download an image and pass the `Stream` object to the `SetSource` method. Currently, this is the only `ImageSource` inheritor, so this class handles both PNG and JPEG images.

Table 6-3. *Events of BitmapImage*

Event	Type
ImageOpened	Fires when the image source is downloaded and decoded with no failure. You can use this event to determine the size of an image before rendering it. If the image-decode fails for any reason, this event does not fire. Once this event fires, the `PixelHeight` and `PixelWidth` properties are guaranteed to be valid.
DownloadProgress	Reports the progress of the image download. The `EventArgs` class is `DownloadProgressEventArgs` and contains a `Progress` property that either reports a 0 (indicating that the image is possibly in the process of downloading) or 1 (indicating that the image has finished downloading).
ImageFailed	Fires when the image cannot be downloaded or the image format is invalid. The event handler is passed an `ExceptionRoutedEventArgs` instance, which has `ErrorException` (the thrown `Exception`) and `ErrorMessage` properties.

If you don't specify a width or height for an image, it will display without any modifications to the image's natural width and height. The Image control has a property named `Stretch` (it is also a dependency property) that controls how an image conforms to a container. The `Stretch` property can have one of the following four enum values:

`None`: The image maintains its original size.

`Fill`: The image completely fills the output area, both vertically and horizontally. The image might appear distorted because the aspect ratio is not preserved.

`Uniform`: The image fills the output area, both vertically and horizontally, but maintains its aspect ratio. This is the default value.

`UniformToFill`: The image is scaled to completely fill the output area, but its aspect ratio is maintained.

You can see the result of the various `Stretch` values in Figure 6-1. Reading left to right and top to bottom, `Stretch` takes on the values `None`, `Fill`, `Uniform`, and `UniformToFill`.

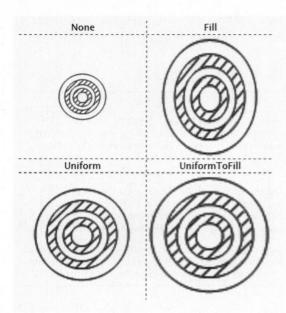

Figure 6-1. *A visual demonstration of each Stretch value*

The image is 100×80, so we can see how the image is treated in a 200×200 square area. The bounding box for the image is defined on the Image control.

```
<Image Source="target.png" Stretch="None" Height="200" Width="200"/>
```

The image is left completely unaltered when Stretch is set to None—it maintains its size of 100×80. When Stretch is set to Fill, the image appears distorted because it is taller than it is wide. For Uniform, the image now almost doubles in size. It doesn't quite fill its bounding box because it is maintaining its aspect ratio. Finally, UniformToFill is similar to Uniform but the image is scaled to the full size of the bounding box—while this specific image can still be completely seen, it is possible that the image will be cut off either horizontally or vertically in order to simultaneously fill its bounding box and maintain its aspect ratio.

You've seen some simple implementations of using images with list boxes in previous chapters. Let's take a closer look at an implementation of an image viewer. A ListBox will contain several ListBoxItem instances, each containing an image scaled down by setting its width/height (we're only using one source image, but for a serious image browser, you might want to store thumbnails separately due to image file size). When a specific image is clicked, the image is shown at full size. The resulting user interface is shown in Figure 6-2.

Figure 6-2. *User interface for an image browser using a ListBox*

```
<ListBox x:Name="thumbnailList" Width="100" Grid.Column="0"
        SelectionChanged="thumbnailList_SelectionChanged">
    <ListBox.Items>
        <ListBoxItem>
            <Image Source="/SpaceImages/10062506.jpg" Width="75" Height="50"/>
        </ListBoxItem>
        <ListBoxItem>
            <Image Source="/SpaceImages/10063680.jpg" Width="75" Height="50"/>
        </ListBoxItem>
    </ListBox.Items>
</ListBox>
```

The full-size image is represented by the following Image control in the XAML:

```
<Image Grid.Column="1" Width="250" x:Name="fullImage"/>
```

The following code is used to display the full-size image. Note that we can't set the source of the fullImage to the same source; it instead must reference a new BitmapImage instance.

```
private void thumbnailList_SelectionChanged(object sender,
                        SelectionChangedEventArgs e)
{
    ListBox lb = (ListBox)sender;
    ListBoxItem item = (ListBoxItem)lb.SelectedItem;
    Image img = (Image)item.Content;
    fullImage.Source = new BitmapImage(((BitmapImage)img.Source).UriSource);
}
```

Bitmap APIs

Silverlight 3 introduces a new Bitmap API based on the `WriteableBitmap` class. With the help of the Bitmap API you can achieve the following image-management features:

- Dynamic generation of bitmaps by reading/writing pixel by pixel

- Client-side manipulation of images loaded from the server or client machine

- Rendering a portion of the visual tree to a bitmap

- Creation of transforms that can be used to create reflections and similar kinds of effects

The `WriteableBitmap` class is found in the `System.Windows.Media.Imaging` namespace. Tables 6-4 and 6-5 define the key methods and properties of the `WriteableBitmap` class, respectively.

Table 6-4. *Methods of the WriteableBitmap Class*

Method	Type
Render	Renders an element within the bitmap. This can be used to create transforms like reflection, etc.
Lock	Reserves the back buffer for updates.
Unlock	Releases the back buffer to make it available for display. The object must be unlocked before it can be used for display in the Image control.
Invalidate	Requests a drawing of the entire bitmap. Call this method before `Unlock`.

Table 6-5. *Properties of the WriteableBitmap Class*

Property	Type
Dispatcher	Gets the `Dispatcher` associated with the object. Note that only the thread the `Dispatcher` was created on may access the object.
Item	Gets or sets a pixel within the pixels array.
PixelHeight	Gets the height of the bitmap in pixels. It is inherited from the `BitmapSource` class, which provides a source object for properties that use a bitmap.
PixelWidth	Gets the width of the bitmap in pixels. It is inherited from the `BitmapSource` class, which provides a source object for properties that use a bitmap.

The following example shows the use of the `WriteableBitmap` class to generate the reflection of the image. To create the reflection effect, first create a regular Silverlight 3 project using the Silverlight Application project template.

We are going to add a source image of the size 256×256. To create the same size reflection, the minimum height of the UserControl should be set to double the height of the source image (i.e., in our case, 512 pixels), and the minimum width of the UserControl should be the same as the image size (i.e., 256 pixels). Keep the default 400-pixel width, and change the Height property of the MainPage.xaml UserControl to 512 pixels. Next, remove the Grid layout control, and add the StackPanel control as the LayoutRoot control instead, as shown in the following code snippet:

```
<UserControl x:Class="Chapter6_Reflection.MainPage"
    xmlns="http://schemas.microsoft.com/winfx/2006/xaml/presentation"
    xmlns:x="http://schemas.microsoft.com/winfx/2006/xaml"
    Width="400" Height="512">
    <StackPanel x:Name="LayoutRoot" Background="Black" Orientation="Vertical" >
    </StackPanel>
</UserControl>
```

Now we want to add an image named Buddy.png. First, drag and drop the Buddy.png image to the Silverlight project to add it as a resource. Next, add the Buddy.png image using the Image control, and set the x:Name property to source, as shown in the following code. Note that the Height and Width properties of the image are set to 256.

```
<Image x:Name = "source" Source="Buddy.png"  Height="256" Width="256" ></Image>
```

Add another Image control named target to display the reflection of the source Image control. To start the reflection, at the bottom of the source Image control, set the Orientation of the LayoutRoot's StackPanel to Vertical. As we are going to create a reflection effect, we need to flip the image vertically. For this, set TranslateTransform for the y axis to -256 so the reflection of the source Image control starts right from the bottom of the image. Also, set ScaleTransform ScaleY to -1 to flip the scaled object but not change its vertical size. (You will learn more about the image transform in the next chapter.) To make the reflected image fade out at the bottom, set an OpacityMask for the target Image control and use a LinearGradientBrush with two GradientStops with the Color property set to White, as shown in the following code:

```
        <Image x:Name="target" Stretch="None" >
            <Image.RenderTransform>
                <TransformGroup>
                    <TranslateTransform Y="-256" />
                    <ScaleTransform ScaleY="-1" />
                </TransformGroup>
            </Image.RenderTransform>
            <Image.OpacityMask>
                <LinearGradientBrush EndPoint="0,1">
                    <GradientStop Color="White" Offset="1"/>
                    <GradientStop Offset="0"/>
                </LinearGradientBrush>
            </Image.OpacityMask>
        </Image>
```

Now generate the source for the target Image control in the Loaded event of the UserControl, as shown in the following code:

```
using System;
using System.Collections.Generic;
using System.Linq;
using System.Net;
using System.Windows;
using System.Windows.Controls;
using System.Windows.Documents;
using System.Windows.Input;
using System.Windows.Media;
using System.Windows.Media.Animation;
using System.Windows.Shapes;
//added namespace
using System.Windows.Media.Imaging;

namespace Chapter6_Reflection
{
    public partial class MainPage : UserControl
    {
        public MainPage()
        {
            InitializeComponent();
            this.Loaded += new RoutedEventHandler(MainPage_Loaded);
        }

        void MainPage_Loaded(object sender, RoutedEventArgs e)
        {
            WriteableBitmap bmp = new WriteableBitmap((int)source.Width,

            (int)source.Height, PixelFormats.Bgr32);

            bmp.Render(source, new TranslateTransform());

            target.Source = bmp;
        }
    }
}
```

In order to use the WriteableBitmap class, first add a reference to the System.Windows.Media.Imaging namespace. Now generate the source for the target Image control in the Loaded event of the UserControl. To generate the reflection effect, render the source Image control within the bitmap using the Render method of the WriteableBitmap class. Finally, set the target Image control's Source property to the rendered bitmap. Run the project, and you should see the reflection effect of the image, as shown in Figure 6-3.

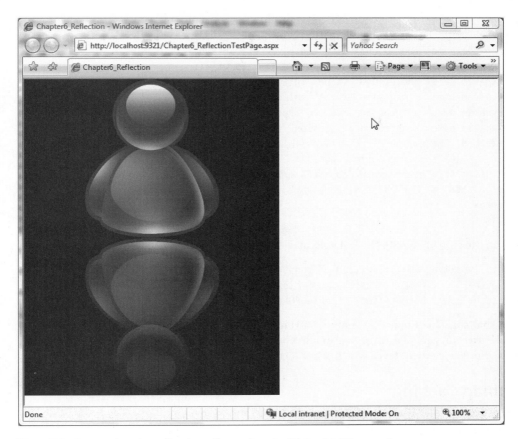

Figure 6-3. *Generating the reflection effect using the WriteableBitmap class*

GPU Hardware Acceleration

Silverlight 3 also leverages Graphics Processor Unit (GPU) hardware acceleration to deliver a true high-definition (HD) media experience in the in-browser and full-screen modes. In Silverlight 1 and 2, media rendering is performed by the software that makes the playback of animations and video files dependent on the capabilities of the CPU of the host PC. This can cause performance issues for complex media files. With Silverlight 3, we can now easily fix this performance problem by taking advantage of GPU hardware acceleration, if enabled, and provide a rich and smooth media experience to users. GPU hardware acceleration allows Silverlight to use the user's video card to render portions of the user interface, which can greatly improve performance. To take advantage of the video hardware, Silverlight uses DirectX for Windows-based and OpenGL for Mac-based devices.

GPU hardware acceleration is an opt-in feature on the Silverlight plug-in and thus is disabled by default. To explicitly enable GPU hardware acceleration in the case of an HTML page, set the newly introduced `EnableGPUAcceleration` parameter at the Silverlight `Object` tag level to `true`, as shown in the following code:

```
<object data="data:application/x-silverlight-2,"
   type="application/x-silverlight-2" width="100%" height="100%">➡
    <param name="source" value="ClientBin/chapter6.xap"/>
    <param name="onerror" value="onSilverlightError" />
    <param name="background" value="white" />
    <param name="minRuntimeVersion" value="3.0.40307.0" />
    <param name="autoUpgrade" value="true" />
    <param name="EnableGPUAcceleration" value="true" />
    <a href="http://go.microsoft.com/fwlink/?LinkID=141205" ➡
       style="text-decoration: none;">
     <img src="http://go.microsoft.com/fwlink/?LinkId=108181" ➡
       alt="Get Microsoft Silverlight" style="border-style: none"/>
    </a>
</object>
```

In the case of an ASP .NET Silverlight web control:

```
<asp:Silverlight ID="Silverlight1" runat="server"
   Source="~/ClientBin/chapter6.xap" MinimumVersion="3.0.40307.0" ➡
   Width="100%" Height="100%" EnableGPUAcceleration="True" />
```

That's it. This single line enables GPU hardware acceleration at the Silverlight plug-in level. Now you can take advantage of it in your application to enable bitmap caching at the user interface element level, which is our next topic.

Bitmap Caching

Along with GPU hardware acceleration, Silverlight 3 introduces a new technique to improve the rendering performance of applications by caching vector content, text, and controls into bitmaps. Bitmap caching can be a useful and high-performing tactic in scenarios where content needs to scale without changes being made to its internal appearance.

Bitmap caching is also an opt-in feature, and you need to explicitly enable it at the user interface element level. You can enable bitmap caching by setting the CacheMode attribute of the user interface element to BitmapCache. If enabled, the caching feature is applicable to that particular element and its children elements (if any). To take advantage of bitmap caching, GPU hardware acceleration must be enabled at the Silverlight plug-in level.

Once you enable GPU hardware acceleration, the following example shows bitmap caching enabled at the Grid control level:

```
<UserControl x:Class="chapter6.MainPage"
    xmlns="http://schemas.microsoft.com/winfx/2006/xaml/presentation"
    xmlns:x="http://schemas.microsoft.com/winfx/2006/xaml"
    Width="400" Height="300">
    <Grid CacheMode="BitmapCache" x:Name="LayoutRoot" Background="White">
        <!-- XAML Code -->
    </Grid>
</UserControl>
```

Along with bitmap caching, Silverlight 3 also offers cache visualization of user interface element(s). To achieve this in the case of an HTML page, set the newly introduced `EnableCacheVisualization` parameter at the Silverlight `Object` tag level to `true` (very similar to enabling GPU hardware acceleration), as shown following:

```
<param name="EnableCacheVisualization" value="true" />
```

In the case of an ASP .NET Silverlight web control:

```
<asp:Silverlight ID="Silverlight1" runat="server"
    Source="~/ClientBin/chapter6.xap" MinimumVersion="3.0.40307.0" ➡
    Width="100%" Height="100%" EnableCacheVisualization="True" />
```

When cache visualization is enabled, objects that are cached (i.e., handled by the GPU) are displayed in their normal colors, while others are tinted. This features works in full-screen mode only on Mac machines.

Some care should be taken when choosing user interface elements for bitmap caching. Choose elements in the user interface that are mostly static, like scrolling backgrounds. Items that animate, rotate, or scale can be accelerated, but if an element changes, such as through `StoryBoard` animation, the element will need to be re-rendered frequently and the cache will be invalidated, reducing performance.

Multiscale Images (Deep Zoom)

Deep Zoom first debuted as SeaDragon at the TechEd technology conference. The various Silverlight announcements at MIX08 included the revelation that SeaDragon is now called Deep Zoom and is a standard feature in Silverlight 2 and 3. The MultiScaleImage control is used to provide the deep zoom functionality in a Silverlight user interface.

Just what is Deep Zoom? It is technology that makes it easy to develop applications that can display a set of high-quality images (imagine 20MB per image or more) in a grid-style layout, allowing a user to explore the images at different zoom levels. When the user is zoomed out, the quality is not as high as when they are zoomed in. Because of this, the full source images don't need to be downloaded by the client; instead, lower-quality images are sent. As the user zooms in, images closer to the quality level of the original are sent, but only pieces of the images the user can see. This provides a highly optimized way to explore a collection of high-quality images. Since the images are laid out in a grid, the MultiScaleImage control also provides the ability to pan around the image collection.

You can get the gist of what Deep Zoom does to an image by consulting Figure 6-4.

Figure 6-4. *The bull's-eye graphic at different zoom levels*

In this figure, we revisit the image of a bull's-eye used earlier. The image stored at 100% has full detail. When we zoom out, we lose detail, but this also gains us an important advantage—less data has to be sent from the server to the client. This means that if we have a large collection of images and we're zoomed out, Silverlight won't immediately request a 100% zoom level for all the images. Instead, it will request a 50% zoom level, or 25%, or something even lower. As the user zooms into specific images, most of the images around it disappear from view, so these don't need to be downloaded. The images still in view, however, are sent to the client—but now Silverlight requests a 50% zoom, or perhaps a 100% zoom when the user zooms all the way in. Feel free to use images with the highest resolutions you can get—the higher the resolution, the more detail there is for users to zoom in to.

The Deep Zoom Composer tool is used to create a package that Silverlight's MultiScaleImage control can use. You can obtain this tool at `http://silverlight.net/GetStarted`. This generated package contains versions of the images (stored at a possibly large number of different zoom levels, along with certain slices of images used to optimize partial image display) and information describing the layout as designed in the composing tool. The MultiScaleImage control is pointed to this package and then handles all the logic on the client side, such as displaying the images and downloading the right images at the right time to maintain a smooth user experience.

The MultiScaleImage control exposes some useful properties, methods, and events; these are shown respectively in Tables 6-6, 6-7, and 6-8.

Table 6-6. *Properties of MultiScaleImage*

Property	Type	Description
AllowDownloading	bool	Gets or sets whether downloading is permitted by this MultiScaleImage, enabling developers to control which MultiScaleImage objects are downloading data at any point in time.
AspectRatio	double	Current aspect ratio of the images; read-only.
BlurFactor	double	Gets or sets the extent to which data is blurred while rendering. A value of 2 means to use data that is twice as blurry (one level lower), while a value of 0.5 means to try to use data that is extra sharp (one level higher). The default value is 1.
IsIdle	bool	Gets whether Deep Zoom is done downloading, decoding, blending images, and animating if springs are used. Even if AllowDownloading is false, IsIdle will be false if any images are pending.
IsDownloading	bool	Gets whether the image is still downloading. If true, requests are still outstanding. If false, then all needed tiles have been downloaded. If the image is moved, IsDownloading may become true again.

Table 6-6. *Properties of MultiScaleImage*

Property	Type	Description
Source	Uri	The URI to the Deep Zoom package containing the images, metadata, and so forth.
SubImages	ReadOnlyCollection<MultiScaleSubImage>	Read-only collection of the subimages used by the control. A MultiScaleSubImage exposes a read-only AspectRatio property along with Opacity, ViewportOrigin, ViewportWidth, and ZIndex properties that can be used to set or discover which set of images and which layer of images is currently exposed.
UseSprings	bool	Controls spring motion of the control. Can be set to false and later reset to true to block initial animation when the control loads.
ViewportOrigin	Point	The top-left corner of the current view as an (x,y) coordinate.
ViewportWidth	double	The width of the current viewport.

Table 6-7. *Methods of MultiScaleImage*

Method	Description
ElementToLogicalPoint	Translates a physical point (the screen) to a point located within the image currently visible beneath the physical point.
LogicalToElementPoint	Translates a point within a currently visible image to a physical point (the screen).
ZoomAboutLogicalPoint	Accepts a zoom increment factor and a center (x,y) point about which to zoom. All parameters are of type double.

Table 6-8. *Events of MultiScaleImage*

Events	Description
ImageFailed	Fires when the image cannot be downloaded or the image format is invalid. The event handler method is passed ExceptionRoutedEventArgs, which provides ErrorException (the thrown Exception) and ErrorMessage properties.
ImageOpenFailed	Fires when an image cannot be opened.
ImageOpenSucceeded	Fires when an image is successfully opened.
MotionFinished	Fires when the currently ongoing motion is complete.
ViewportChanged	Fires when the viewport (the area of the image displayed) changes.

The Deep Zoom Composer is a development tool that allows you to aggregate and package images for a Deep Zoom implementation.

When you start the Deep Zoom Composer, you'll see a screen similar to the Expression products (Figure 6-5). Unsurprisingly, this tool is part of the Microsoft Expression family, which supports WPF and Silverlight applications.

Figure 6-5. *The Deep Zoom Composer's start screen*

There are three steps to creating a new Deep Zoom package, and these are clearly defined at the top of the Deep Zoom Composer interface after you create a new project. These steps are also listed at the top of the Deep Zoom Composer interface, clearly showing the workflow in this tool.

1. Import: This is where you add the images you want to include in the project. Information about the type, dimensions, and file size of each image appear in the lower left, and the full list of added images appears to the right. You can right-click an image to remove it from the project.

2. Compose: The second step is where you define how the images are oriented for display, including setting their initial size and position relative to each other.

3. Export: The final step allows you to create a package suitable for use by the MultiScaleImage control. You can export in one of two formats: as a composition or as a collection. Optionally, you can create a new Silverlight application as a wrapper.

The example code with this chapter features a Deep Zoom example with several Space Shuttle pictures. Two of the pictures have other pictures, initially tiny (they're zoomed way out), but increasing in detail as you zoom into them. Figure 6-6 shows what the Shuttle images look like zoomed out.

Figure 6-6. *Zoomed-out views of the Space Shuttle*

By zooming in to the image on the bottom right, four other images in the sky become visible, as shown in Figure 6-7.

Figure 6-7. *Zooming in to the sky of one of the Shuttle pictures*

After zooming in to the tiny image on the left (in the sky), you can see the detail of this new image (see Figure 6-8).

Figure 6-8. *Zooming in to one of the initially tiny images in the sky*

This entire Deep Zoom example was built in the Deep Zoom Composer in a matter of a few minutes. After I exported it to its own Silverlight application, I brought it into this chapter's Silverlight application by first copying the GeneratedImages folder into the chapter6Web folder. This folder contains all of the images and metadata required by the MultiScaleImage control. The XAML for this example is rather bare:

```
<MultiScaleImage Height="600" x:Name="msi" Width="800"/>
```

■**Note** At the time of writing this book, the Deep Zoom Composer Preview 2 version exports the project in Silverlight 2 format. So when you open the project in a Silverlight 3 environment, the Visual Studio Conversion Wizard will convert your project to the latest.

As part of the generated Silverlight application, the MainPage.xaml.cs file contains the code to connect the MultiScaleImage control to the GeneratedImages folder stored in the web site:

```
this.msi.Source = new DeepZoomImageTileSource
    (new Uri("GeneratedImages/dzc_output.xml", UriKind.Relative));
```

The Deep Zoom Composer also includes, as part of the generation, all the code necessary to hook the MultiScaleImage control up to user input. Between the MouseWheelHelper.cs class and the event handlers in MainPage.xaml.cs (in the generated application), users can click to zoom, use the mouse wheel to zoom, and also click and drag to pan around the scene.

Media (Video and Audio)

The System.Windows.Controls.MediaElement control provides media playback capability in Silverlight 2. It can handle both audio and video in a variety of formats. These are the supported video formats:

WMV1: Windows Media Video 7

WMV2: Windows Media Video 8

WMV3: Windows Media Video 9

WMVA: Windows Media Video Advanced Profile (non-VC-1)

WMVC1: Windows Media Video Advanced Profile (VC-1)

ASX: Advanced Stream Redirector files; extension might be .asx, .wax, .wvx, .wmx, or .wpl

Silverlight 3 has enhanced media management supporting high-quality and secured multimedia streaming. The following is a brief list of media management improvements in Silverlight 3:

- Support for new media formats such as H.264/Advanced Audio Coding (AAC)/MP4 and the new RAW audio/video pipeline, which supports third-party codecs, brings opportunities to develop a broad range of media formats that support rich Internet applications (RIAs), and broadens the overall industry-wide acceptance of Silverlight as a main web-development technology platform.

- IIS Media Services (an integrated HTTP media delivery platform, see `http://www.iis.net/media` for more information) enable high-performing and smooth, live, and on-demand high-quality and HD (720p+) media streaming. Silverlight 3 also leverages GPU hardware acceleration to deliver a true HD media experience in the in-browser and full-screen modes.

- Silverlight digital rights management (DRM) for media streaming enables Advanced Encryption Standard (AES)–based encryption or Windows Media DRM of media files and allows the protected distribution of digital media. Silverlight 2 and 3 support the following audio formats:

  - *WMA 7*: Windows Media Audio 7

  - *WMA 8*: Windows Media Audio 8

  - *WMA 9*: Windows Media Audio 9

  - *MP3*: ISO/MPEG Layer-3; 8 to 320Kbps and variable bit rate; 8 to 48KHz sampling frequencies

You can reference a media file using either the HTTP or HTTPS protocol, or using MMS, RTSP, or RTSPT. The latter three will fall back to HTTP. Using the MMS protocol causes Silverlight to attempt to stream the media first; if that fails, it will attempt to download the media progressively. Other protocols work in reverse—Silverlight attempts to progressively download the media first, and if that fails, the media is streamed. The properties, methods, and events of `MediaElement` are shown in Tables 6-9, 6-10, and 6-11, respectively.

Table 6-9. *Properties of MediaElement*

Property	Type	Description
Attributes	Dictionary<string,string>	A collection of attributes; read-only.
AudioStreamCount	int	The number of audio streams in the current media file; read-only.
AudioStreamIndex	int	The index of the audio stream that is currently playing with a video.
AutoPlay	bool	If true, the media will begin playing immediately after Source is set (i.e., it will transition into the Buffering state and then into the Playing state automatically). If false, the media will start in the Stopped state.
Balance	double	The ratio of volume across stereo speakers.
BufferingProgress	double	The current buffering progress, between 0 and 1. Multiply by 100 to get a percentage value; read-only.

Table 6-9. *Properties of MediaElement (Continued)*

Property	Type	Description
BufferingTime	TimeSpan	The amount of time to buffer; the default is 5 seconds.
CanPause	bool	Returns true if the media can be paused via the Pause method; read-only.
CanSeek	bool	Returns true if the current position in the media can be set via the Seek method; read-only.
CurrentState	MediaElementState	The current state of the media. Possible states include Closed, Opening, Individualizing, AcquiringLicense, Buffering, Playing, Paused, and Stopped. It is possible for several state transitions to happen in quick succession, so you may not witness every state transition happen; read-only.
DownloadProgress	double	The current download progress, between 0 and 1. Multiply by 100 to get a percentage value; read-only.
DownloadProgressOffset	double	The offset in the media where the current download started. Used when media is progressively downloaded; read-only.
LicenseAcquirer		Gets or sets the LicenseAcquirer associated with the MediaElement. LicenseAcquirer handles acquiring licenses for DRM-encrypted content.
IsMuted	bool	Used to set or determine whether audio is currently muted.
Markers	TimelineMarkerCollection	Accesses the collection of timeline markers. Although the collection itself is read-only, it is possible to dynamically add timeline markers. These are temporary since they are not saved to the media and are reset if the Source property is changed.
NaturalDuration	Duration	Duration of the currently loaded media; read-only.
NaturalVideoHeight	int	The height of the video based on what the video file itself reports; read-only.
NaturalVideoWidth	int	The width of the video based on what the video file itself reports; read-only.
Position	TimeSpan	The current position in the media file.
RenderedFramesPerSecond	double	Gets the number of frames per second being rendered by the media.

Table 6-9. *Properties of MediaElement (Continued)*

Property	Type	Description
Source	Uri	Sets or retrieves the source of the current media file.
Stretch	Stretch	Gets or sets how the media fills its bounding rectangle. See the "Images" section of this chapter for a discussion of this property.
Volume	double	Gets or sets the volume of the media based on a linear scale. The value can be between 0 and 1; the default is 0.5.

Table 6-10. *Methods of MediaElement*

Method	Description
Pause	Pauses the media at the current position if it is possible to pause. If the media cannot be paused, this method does nothing.
Play	Plays the media from the current position if the media can be played.
RequestLog	Sends a request to generate a log, which will then be raised through the LogReady event. What this method does depends on the current state of the media. Closed: No operation. Opening: Queues the request and raises the log when the MediaOpened event is raised. Individualizing: Generates the log. AcquiringLicense: Generates the log. Buffering: Generates the log. Playing: Generates the log. Paused: Generates the log. Stopped: Generates the log.
SetSource	Used when you want to set the source of the media to a Stream object. Use the Source property to set the URI of the media file.
Stop	Stops the media from playing, and sets the current position to 0.

Table 6-11. *Events of MediaElement*

Event	Description
BufferingProgressChanged	Fires each time BufferingProgress changes by at least 0.05 or when it reaches 1.0.
CurrentStateChanged	Fires when the state of the media changes. If states transition quickly (such as bouncing between buffering and playing), some transitions can be lost.
DownloadProgressChanged	Fires when the progress of the downloading media changes. Use the DownloadProgress property to discover the current progress.

Table 6-11. *Events of MediaElement (Continued)*

Event	Description
LogReady	Occurs when the log is ready. Note that this event is only raised for progressive downloads. It can be raised either by a specific request (the RequestLog method) or by the generation of a log due to an automatic log event such as Seek, Stop, or SourceChanged.
MarkerReached	Fires when a timeline marker is reached. The event handler method is passed a TimelineMarkerRoutedEventArgs instance, which exposes a Marker property of type TimelineMarker.
MediaEnded	Fires when the media is done playing.
MediaFailed	Fires when there is a problem with the media source (e.g., when the media can't be found or when the format is incorrect).
MediaOpened	Fires after media file is opened and validated, and the headers are read.

Since a variety of state changes can happen to media, such as a video switching from playing to buffering when it needs to load more of the file, in most applications you will want to implement an event handler for CurrentStateChanged. The states and state transitions are shown in Figure 6-9. The one transition left out of this diagram is to the Opening state. This can happen any time a new source is set for MediaElement.

While it's fairly simple to specify a source for MediaElement, set AutoPlay to true, and let it just go, you probably want to build something with more control for the user. Figure 6-10 shows a simple video player.

Implementing the Start/Stop and Pause/Resume buttons is straightforward. The start/stop event handler checks the media's current state and acts accordingly. This gives you the basic play/stop functionality. Pause and resume are implemented similarly by checking for those states.

```
if (mainVideo.CurrentState == MediaElementState.Stopped ||
    mainVideo.CurrentState == MediaElementState.Paused)
{
    startStopButton.Content = "Stop";
    mainVideo.Play();
    pauseResumeButton.IsEnabled = true;
}
else
{
    startStopButton.Content = "Play";
    mainVideo.Stop();
    pauseResumeButton.IsEnabled = false;
}
```

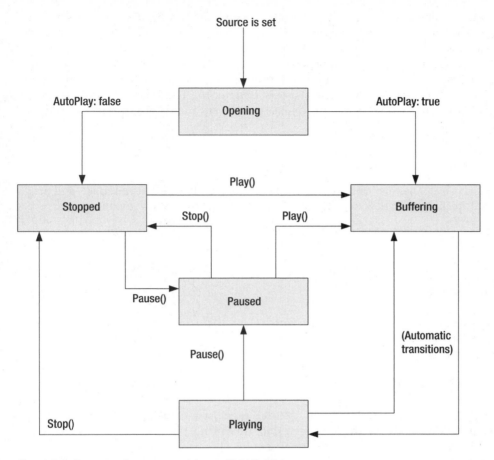

Figure 6-9. *States and state transitions of MediaElement*

Figure 6-10. *Simple video player with position indicator*

There's another aspect to media players that is common for users to see: a time signature displaying the length of the video and the current position as it plays. The best approach to add the current media position to a user interface is to use a timer to poll the Position property of MediaElement and then display it. The best timer to use is DispatcherTimer since it works on the user interface thread, allowing you to modify user interface elements directly. (We'll take a closer look at threading and DispatcherTimer in Chapter 15.) The following code creates an instance of the timer and sets it to raise the Tick event every quarter of a second:

```
timer = new DispatcherTimer();
timer.Interval = new TimeSpan(0, 0, 0, 0, 250);
timer.Tick += new EventHandler(timer_Tick);
```

The Tick event handler calls showCurrentPosition to update the user interface, and the CurrentStateChanged event of MediaElement is handled in order to start/stop the timer:

```
void timer_Tick(object sender, EventArgs e)
{
    showCurrentPosition();
}
private void showCurrentPosition()
{
    currentPositionText.Text = string.Format("{0:00}:{1:00}",
            mainVideo.Position.Minutes,
            mainVideo.Position.Seconds);
}
private void mainVideo_CurrentStateChanged(object sender, RoutedEventArgs e)
{
    MediaElementState currentState = ((MediaElement)sender).CurrentState;
    currentStateTextBlock.Text = currentState.ToString();
    if (currentState == MediaElementState.Paused ||
            currentState == MediaElementState.Stopped)
        timer.Stop();
    else
        timer.Start();
}
```

Timeline Markers

A timeline marker is a point of time in a media file that has some data associated with it. A specific timeline marker (of the System.Windows.Media.Animation.TimelineMarker class) contains three members: Text and Type, both of type String; and Time, of type TimeSpan. Both Text and Type are arbitrary, so you can configure these however you want. Timeline markers can either be embedded in the video file using an editor such as Microsoft Expression Media Encoder or dynamically during program execution. Figure 6-11 shows the Markers pane in Expression Media Encoder. I added one timeline marker to the bear.wmv video to mark when the bird starts flying away. If this were a full-length nature documentary, the timeline markers could be used to initiate different audio files in sync with events happening in the video.

If you define these dynamically, they are good only as long as a particular MediaElement exists and references the same video file. If you load a new video file into a MediaElement control, the timeline marker collection is reset.

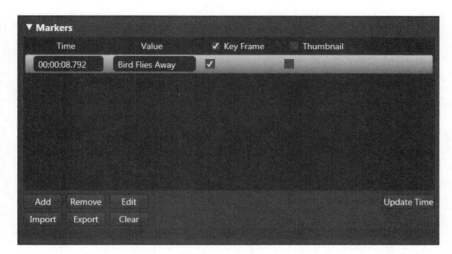

Figure 6-11. *Editing the interface for timeline markers in Expression Media Encoder*

The Markers property of MediaElement acts much like a regular collection since it implements the IList interface. Here's an example of creating a new TimelineMarker and adding it to a particular MediaElement:

```
TimelineMarker mark = new TimelineMarker();
mark.Type = "Commercial Cue";
mark.Text = "First Commercial";
mark.Time = new TimeSpan(0, 5, 11);
mainVideo.Markers.Add(mark);
```

Regardless of whether markers are defined in the media file itself or during program execution, you can use the MarkerReached event to perform custom processing when a specific marker is reached. The TimelineMarkerRoutedEventArgs class provides a Marker member to access the specific marker that was reached from the event handler.

Silverlight Streaming

Silverlight Streaming is a service Microsoft provides to host and stream videos to Silverlight applications. It is currently in beta and provides 10GB of storage space free, provided each video is no longer than 10 minutes (or 105MB) and is encoded at a bit rate of no more than 1.4Mbps. Before you can use Silverlight Streaming, you must first have a Live account and a Silverlight Streaming account.

1. Create a Live account: if you don't already have a Microsoft Live account, go to `http://login.live.com/` to create one. This account will be associated with your Silverlight Streaming account.

2. Create a Silverlight Streaming account: visit `http://silverlight.live.com/` and click Get It Free. This will lead you to a page where you can create a Silverlight Streaming account. You will need the API key in order for a Silverlight application to use this service.

Before you can use Silverlight Streaming, you must ensure source videos are in the correct format. All video formats supported by Silverlight (as listed earlier in this chapter) are suitable for use by Silverlight Streaming. We'll take a brief look at using Expression Media Encoder to prepare videos; however, you can also use Windows Media Encoder or other tools as long as the encoded format is correct.

■**Tip** If you use Windows Media Encoder, you can download a set of profiles from `http://dev.live.com/silverlight/downloads/profiles.zip`. These provide preset configurations for properly encoding videos for use with Silverlight and Silverlight Streaming.

After you have created your account, you need to generate an account key. Figure 6-12 shows the Manage Account screen with an account key already generated. The account ID is public. The account key, however, is confidential, so it is blurred out in this screenshot. It will not, however, be blurred out when you access your account through Silverlight Streaming.

Figure 6-12. *The Manage Account screen on the Silverlight Streaming site*

Preparing an Application

The Silverlight Streaming servers host the Silverlight applications that use Silverlight Streaming. This means there are cross-domain considerations, since the application is embedded in a web page on a server different from the Silverlight Streaming server. In order to upload a Silverlight application to Silverlight Streaming, it must have a manifest file, `manifest.xml`, placed in the root of the archive. Parameters passed to the `Silverlight.createObject` function should be moved to this manifest file. Most child elements are optional—the one that is mandatory is `source`, so Silverlight Streaming knows which file in the uploaded archive to use to start the application. Here's a manifest file with text describing the purpose of each element. All paths are relative to the root of the archive.

```
<SilverlightApp>
    <source>Path to main XAML or XAP file</source>
    <version>Minimum Silverlight runtime version
            (1.0 or 2.0) or latest if this is not specified</version>
    <width>percentage or value</width>
    <height>percentage or value</height>
    <background>
        Named color, 8-bit or 16-bit color value,
        optionally with alpha transparency
    </background>
    <backgroundImage>
        Path to background image to show while application is initializing
```

```
    </backgroundImage>
    <isWindowless>
        Set to "True" or "False", specifies whether
        Silverlight control is in windowless mode
    </isWindowless>
    <framerate>Maximum number of frames to render per second</framerate>
    <inPlaceInstallPrompt>
        Specifies whether to display install prompt
        in case Silverlight version is out of date
    </inPlaceInstallPrompt>
    <onLoad>
        JScript function to run when application's content is done rendering
        (not same as Silverlight's onLoad event)
    </onLoad>
    <onError>JScript function called to handle errors</onError>
    <jsOrder>
        <js>Path to first .js file to load</js>
        <js>Path to second .js file to load</js>
        <js>... etc ...</js>
    </jsOrder>
</SilverlightApp>
```

There is a limit on the file types you can place within an archive you upload to Silverlight Streaming. You can include text/XML formats (.js, .xaml, .xml, .txt, .sdx, and .bin), image files (.gif, .jpg, and .png), media files (.wma, .wmv, and .mp3), and certain binary formats (.ttf, .odttf, .dll, .zip, and .xap). If there are any unrecognized file types within the archive, the upload to Silverlight Streaming will fail.

Once you have the Silverlight application created and packaged with a manifest.xml file, it's time to upload it to the Silverlight Streaming servers. You can do this by clicking Manage Applications and then "Upload an application" on the administration site, as shown in Figure 6-13.

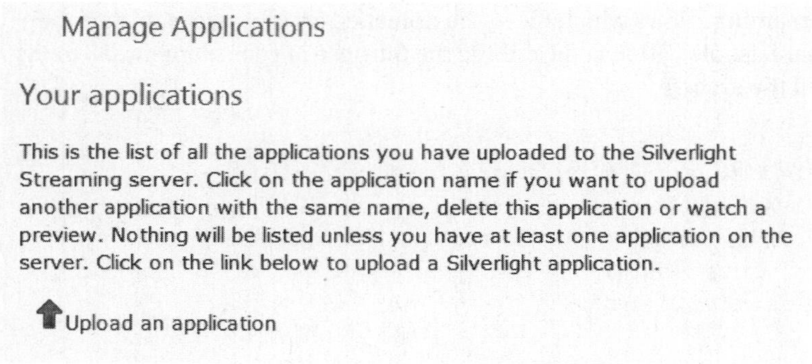

Manage Applications

Your applications

This is the list of all the applications you have uploaded to the Silverlight Streaming server. Click on the application name if you want to upload another application with the same name, delete this application or watch a preview. Nothing will be listed unless you have at least one application on the server. Click on the link below to upload a Silverlight application.

⬆ Upload an application

Figure 6-13. *Creating a new application in Silverlight Streaming*

The first step is to name the application and click Create. Next, you select an archive containing the Silverlight application and, optionally, videos to upload (although videos are typically uploaded via Manage Videos), as shown in Figure 6-14.

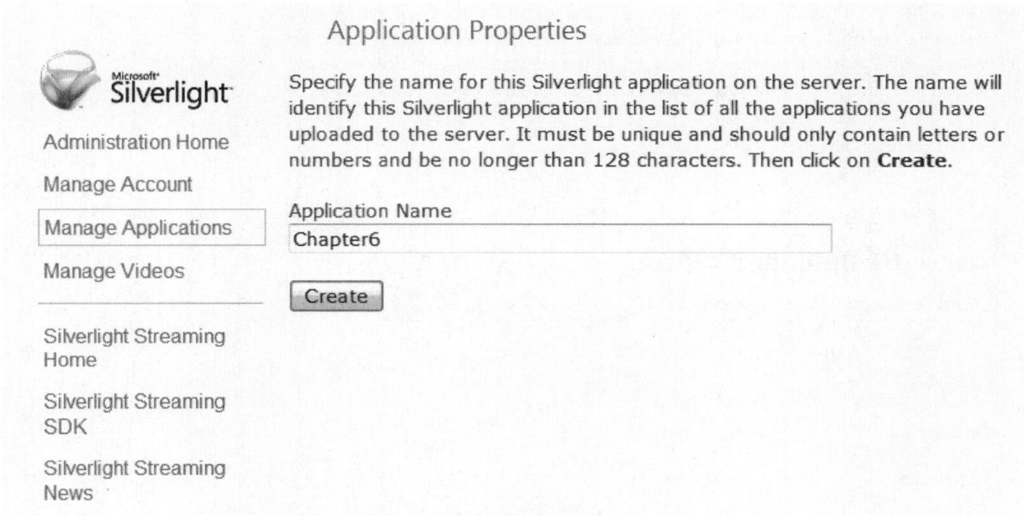

Application Properties

Microsoft Silverlight

Administration Home

Manage Account

Manage Applications

Manage Videos

Silverlight Streaming Home

Silverlight Streaming SDK

Silverlight Streaming News

Specify the name for this Silverlight application on the server. The name will identify this Silverlight application in the list of all the applications you have uploaded to the server. It must be unique and should only contain letters or numbers and be no longer than 128 characters. Then click on **Create**.

Application Name

Chapter6

Create

Figure 6-14. *Uploading a packaged archive*

Once the Silverlight application is uploaded, the easiest way to reference the Silverlight application in your own web site is by using an IFrame. You do this by using an `iframe` tag with the `src` attribute pointing to the Silverlight application you uploaded:

```
<iframe src="..." frameborder="0" width="200" height="300" scrolling="no"></iframe>
```

The value for `src` takes the following format:

```
http://silverlight.services.live.com/invoke/ [account ID] / [App. name]/iframe.html
```

The [`account ID`] is replaced with your account ID, which you see when you log in to your Silverlight Streaming account (shown earlier in Figure 6-12). The [`App. name`] is replaced with the application name you specified when creating an application.

You can include videos as part of the application upload you archive (these videos are still limited in size, bit rate, etc.), or you can upload videos directly to Silverlight Streaming using the Manage Videos link on the administration site. After the video is done uploading, the server processes it to ensure it is encoded properly and meets the restrictions. After this validation is done, an Acknowledge button will appear. Click this button and the video will be properly migrated to your account. Figure 6-15 shows the result of uploading the `bear.wmv` video that comes with Windows Vista.

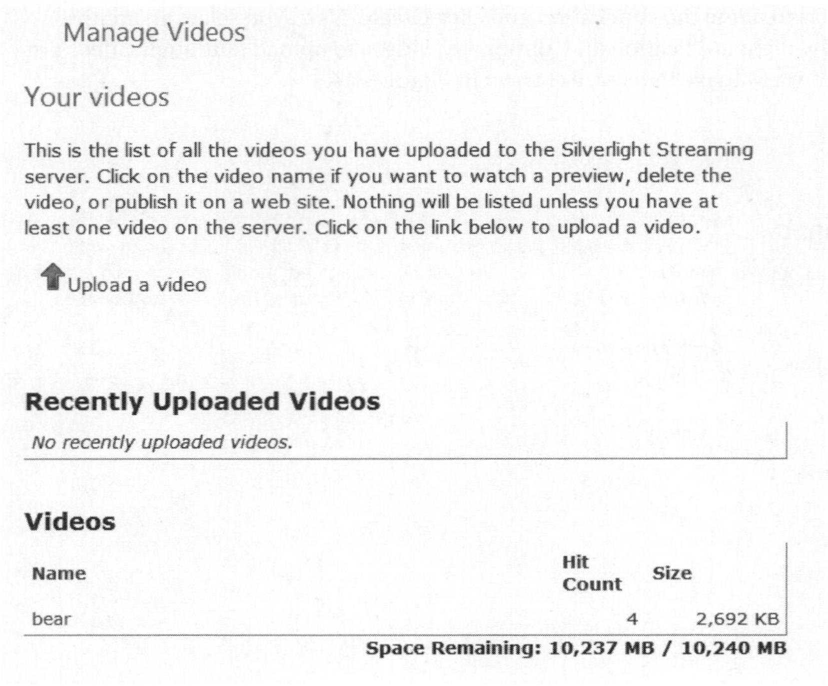

Manage Videos

Your videos

This is the list of all the videos you have uploaded to the Silverlight Streaming server. Click on the video name if you want to watch a preview, delete the video, or publish it on a web site. Nothing will be listed unless you have at least one video on the server. Click on the link below to upload a video.

⬆Upload a video

Recently Uploaded Videos

No recently uploaded videos.

Videos

Name	Hit Count	Size
bear	4	2,692 KB

Space Remaining: 10,237 MB / 10,240 MB

Figure 6-15. *Administrative interface after uploaded video is done processing*

Now that you have all the pieces, the rest is putting together an actual application. Let's take the simple video player used earlier and use it with Silverlight Streaming. The good news is that the only thing you really have to change within the application is the source URI for the video.

```
<MediaElement
    x:Name="mainVideo"
    AutoPlay="False"
    CurrentStateChanged="mainVideo_CurrentStateChanged"
    VerticalAlignment="Stretch"
    Source="http://silverlight.services.live.com/64914/bear/video.wmv"
    Stretch="Fill" />
```

When you click Manage Videos, and then click a specific video you've uploaded, the Silverlight Streaming web site will give you the exact code to drop into your web site or Silverlight application, as shown in Figure 6-16.

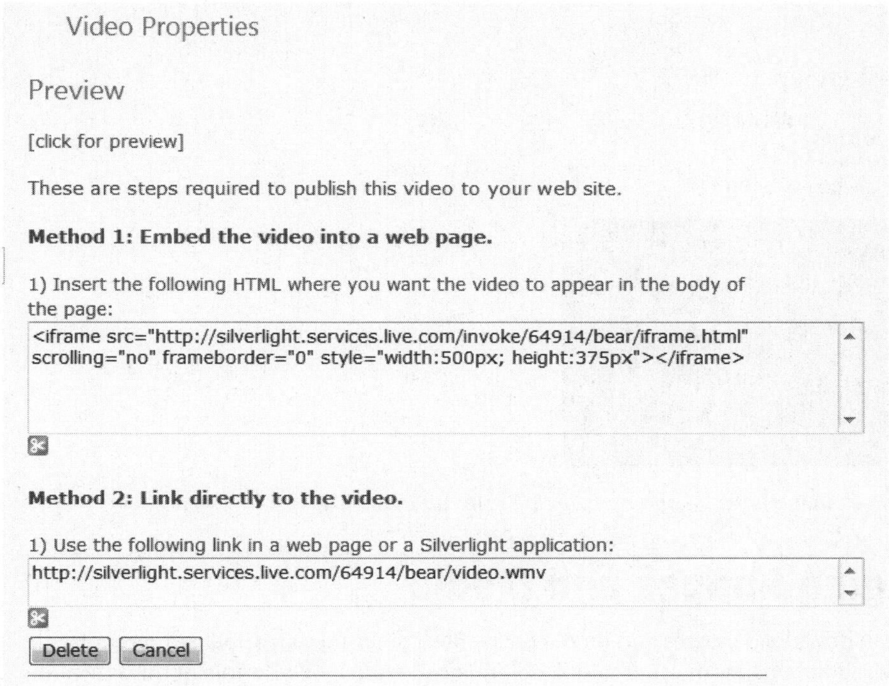

Video Properties

Preview

[click for preview]

These are steps required to publish this video to your web site.

Method 1: Embed the video into a web page.

1) Insert the following HTML where you want the video to appear in the body of the page:

```
<iframe src="http://silverlight.services.live.com/invoke/64914/bear/iframe.html"
scrolling="no" frameborder="0" style="width:500px; height:375px"></iframe>
```

Method 2: Link directly to the video.

1) Use the following link in a web page or a Silverlight application:

```
http://silverlight.services.live.com/64914/bear/video.wmv
```

Delete   Cancel

Figure 6-16. *Links to the video provided by the administrative interface*

Before the application can be uploaded to Silverlight Streaming, it must have a manifest, and the XAP file and manifest file must be packaged into a ZIP file. The manifest for this application supplies just a few parameters:

```
<SilverlightApp>
    <source>chapter6_streaming.xap</source>
    <width>400</width>
    <height>350</height>
    <background>white</background>
    <isWindowless>false</isWindowless>
</SilverlightApp>
```

The rest is a simple matter of uploading the ZIP archive and then clicking the link to preview it. The video player, as served by Silverlight Streaming, is shown in Figure 6-17.

Figure 6-17. *The video player, as shown from Silverlight Streaming*

Packaging Images and Media

While you can download images and media file by file, sometimes an application requires a collection of related images or other media before it can start. One example of this is a game that might need a number of images to display scenes, characters, and the background. You can package these resources into a single ZIP archive and download it. After downloading the ZIP file, using the WebClient class perhaps, you can save its stream. Let's revisit the image browser from earlier in the chapter and alter it to download the images stored in a ZIP file. The image-browsing interface is essentially the same, but there's a download button that initiates the download of the image archive.

```
private StreamResourceInfo imageArchiveStream;
private void downloadButton_Click(object sender, RoutedEventArgs e)
{
    WebClient wc = new WebClient();
    wc.OpenReadCompleted +=
        new OpenReadCompletedEventHandler(wc_OpenReadCompleted);
    wc.OpenReadAsync(
        new Uri("/chapter6Web/HubbleImageArchive.zip",
                UriKind.Relative));
}
```

The OpenReadCompleted event handler is where the ZIP archive is processed. First, the stream is saved, and then we get a reference to a custom XML file stored within the archive.

```
void wc_OpenReadCompleted(object sender, OpenReadCompletedEventArgs e)
{
    imageArchiveStream = new StreamResourceInfo(e.Result, null);
    StreamResourceInfo manifestStream =
                    Application.GetResourceStream(imageArchiveStream,
                            new Uri("manifest.xml", UriKind.Relative));
    // ...
}
```

The manifest.xml file exists to specify where files such as images are stored within the archive. The manifest.xml file is stored at the root of the archive and the images are stored in a directory named images. Here's the manifest. xml file:

```
<?xml version="1.0" encoding="utf-8" ?>
<contents>
    <images>
        <image label="Hubble Picture 1" path="images/gpn-2000-000876.jpg"/>
        <image label="Hubble Picture 2" path="images/gpn-2000-000877.jpg"/>
        <image label="Hubble Picture 3" path="images/gpn-2000-000880.jpg"/>
        <image label="Hubble Picture 4" path="images/gpn-2000-000891.jpg"/>
        <image label="Hubble Picture 5" path="images/gpn-2000-000938.jpg"/>
    </images>
</contents>
```

The code that fills in the ... in the OpenReadCompleted event handler processes the manifest file and adds thumbnails of the images to the ListBox:

```
XmlReaderSettings settings = new XmlReaderSettings();
settings.IgnoreWhitespace = true;
XmlReader reader = XmlReader.Create(manifestStream.Stream, settings);
reader.ReadToDescendant("image");
do
{
    string path = reader.GetAttribute("path");
    StreamResourceInfo imageStream =
                    Application.GetResourceStream(
                                    imageArchiveStream,
                                    new Uri(path, UriKind.Relative));
    ListBoxItem item = new ListBoxItem();
    Image thumb = new Image();
    BitmapImage imgSource = new BitmapImage();
    imgSource.SetSource(imageStream.Stream);
    thumb.Source = imgSource;
```

```
     item.Content = thumb;
     thumb.Width = 75;
     thumb.Height = 50;
     thumb.Tag = path;
     thumbnailList.Items.Add(item);
} while (reader.ReadToNextSibling("image"));
reader.Close();
```

You can use this approach to store references to other media files (video/audio) and even any arbitrary data you might need to download on demand.

Summary

So far, we've been laying the groundwork to build a Silverlight application. This chapter covered the pieces most popularly associated with Silverlight since its 1.0 days: displaying images and media. However, as we learned with Silverlight 3, you have more capabilities to handle images with the use of the Bitmap API and to develop high-performing applications by enabling GPU hardware acceleration and bitmap caching for Silverlight applications. You also saw how to manage and manipulate images, including exploring the MultiScaleImage control, which provides the Deep Zoom user experience. Next, we examined video and audio via the MediaElement control and explored the Silverlight Streaming technology. The media support is a rich and deep topic that cannot fully be explored in a single chapter, but you should have a good grasp of the possibilities when using Silverlight. As explained, Silverlight 3 includes enhanced media management capabilities by supporting new media formats in a secured environment.

In the next chapter we'll explore more aspects of building user interfaces, such as 2D and 3D drawing and brush support in Silverlight. We'll look at the ImageBrush and VideoBrush, which provide the ability to use images and videos in even more interesting ways than described in this chapter, along with other new controls offered by Silverlight 3.

■ ■ ■

CHAPTER 7

Extending the User Interface

We've covered a lot of ground so far, but now it's time to pull our focus back from the details of the supporting infrastructure and revisit building user interfaces in Silverlight. Silverlight provides a rich set of classes to perform 2D drawing, including lines, Bezier curves, and various geometrical figures such as ellipses and rectangles. Next, we'll take a look at the newly introduced perspective transformation for developing 3D effects, pixel shaders, and brushes, both of which provide a great deal of control in how elements are presented on an interface. Any element inheriting from `UIElement` can have a transform applied to it—you can create some interesting video presentations, for example, by skewing or growing/shrinking a video. You can use specific brushes to fill surfaces with images or video and other effects such as gradients. We will end the chapter with Silverlight 3 Save File dialog box, the Accordion control, and the Silverlight Child Window template to develop richer and simplified user interface and functionality.

2D Graphics

Silverlight provides two categories of classes for two dimensional graphics: shapes and geometries. The `System.Windows.Shapes.Shape` class forms the base for all shape-related classes. The `Shape` class inherits directly from `FrameworkElement`, so it gains all that is provided by the `UIElement` and `FrameworkElement` classes. The `System.Windows.Media.Geometry` class, however, inherits directly from `DependencyObject`, not from `UIElement` or `FrameworkElement`. There are similarities between the two categories, but the difference is what they are designed for. The `Geometry`-based classes provide more flexibility and focus more on the behavior of the geometric shapes (and are actually used by some of the `Shape`-based classes). The `Shape`-derived classes, however, are meant for easily adding 2D shapes to a Silverlight user interface. The hierarchy of 2D classes we will look at is shown in Figure 7-1.

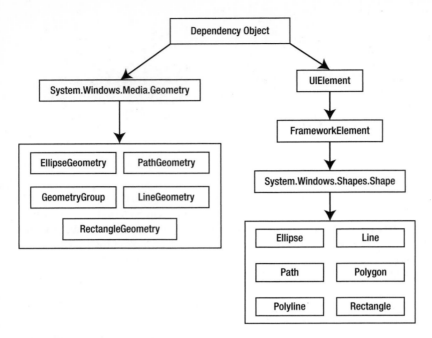

Figure 7-1. *Geometry- and Shape-based classes*

Using Geometries

We'll take a look at the Geometry-based classes first since these provide more versatility. The UIElement class uses a Geometry object to define a region used to clip what's shown, and the Path class derives from the Shape class, which uses a Geometry object to know what to draw. The Shapes.Path class is the mechanism to use if you want to draw a Geometry-derived class on a user interface, since the Geometry classes on their own can't do this.

Simple Geometries

The LineGeometry, RectangleGeometry, and EllipseGeometry classes represent basic geometrical figures. These classes cover the basic shapes, including lines, rectangles, and ellipses. These geometries are shown in Figure 7-2.

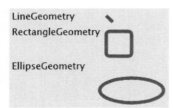

Figure 7-2. *Line, rectangle, and ellipse geometries*

LineGeometry

The LineGeometry class represents a single line with a start point and endpoint. Its two properties are shown in Table 7-1.

Table 7-1. *Properties of the System.Windows.Media.LineGeometry Class*

Property	Type	Description
StartPoint	Point	The (x,y) point of the start of the line
EndPoint	Point	The (x,y) point of the end of the line

Since the Geometry-based classes can't be shown directly, they must be shown using the Path class. Let's draw a line using the LineGeometry class in XAML:

```
<Path Stroke="Red" StrokeThickness="5">
   <Path.Data>
      <LineGeometry StartPoint="10,10" EndPoint="20,20"/>
   </Path.Data>
</Path>
```

RectangleGeometry

The RectangleGeometry class is used for representing rectangles (and squares, of course). Its properties are shown in Table 7-2. The RadiusX and RadiusY properties are used to round the corners. Combined, these properties represent an ellipse that is used to control the degree to which the corners are rounded. If you set these sufficiently high, the rectangle will not disappear but instead will render as an ellipse or a circle.

Table 7-2. *Properties of the System.Windows.Media.RectangleGeometry Class*

Property	Type	Description
RadiusX	double	Gets or sets the x radius of the ellipse used for rounding the rectangle's corners.
RadiusY	double	Gets or sets the y radius of the ellipse used for rounding the rectangle's corners.
Rect	System.Windows.Rect	Gets or sets the rectangle's dimensions. The Rect class has x, y and width, height properties, each of type double.

Let's draw a rectangle on the screen again using the Path class:

```
<Path Stroke="Red" StrokeThickness="5">
   <Path.Data>
      <RectangleGeometry Rect="10,10,40,40" RadiusX="5" RadiusY="5"/>
   </Path.Data>
</Path>
```

EllipseGeometry

The EllipseGeometry class represents an ellipse defined by a center point and two radii, one for the top and bottom of the ellipse and the other for the sides. Its properties are shown in Table 7-3.

Table 7-3. *Properties of the System.Windows.Media.EllipseGeometry Class*

Property	Type	Description
RadiusX	double	Gets or sets the x radius of the ellipse used for defining the ellipse's sides
RadiusY	double	Gets or sets the y radius of the ellipse used for defining the ellipse's top and bottom
Center	Point	Gets or sets the center point of the ellipse

Yet again, we use the Path class to display EllipseGeometry on the screen:

```
<Path Stroke="Red" StrokeThickness="5">
   <Path.Data>
      <EllipseGeometry Center="50,50" RadiusX="50" RadiusY="20"/>
   </Path.Data>
</Path>
```

Path Geometries

The PathGeometry class, inherited from the Geometry class, is where the geometries get interesting. The PathGeometry class is used to represent an arbitrary geometrical shape made up of lines and/or curves. PathGeometry contains one or more PathFigure objects. Each PathFigure object contains one or more PathSegment objects. The various segments are connected automatically within each PathFigure object by each segment's start point, starting at the previous segment's endpoint. There are seven segment classes you can use to construct figures, as shown in Table 7-4. Since using these segments to construct geometrical shapes can be unwieldy, there is a special syntax used with the Path class for drawing multiple segments. We'll take a closer look at this in the next section when we look at the various Shape-related classes.

Table 7-4. *Segment Classes Derived from PathSegment Used in a PathFigure*

Class	Description
ArcSegment	Elliptical arc between two points
BezierSegment	Cubic Bezier curve between two points
LineSegment	Straight line between two points
PolyBezierSegment	Represents a series of cubic Bezier curves
PolyLineSegment	Represents a series of lines
PolyQuadraticBezierSegment	Represents a series of quadratic Bezier curves
QuadraticBezierSegment	Quadratic Bezier curve between two points

Before we go over the specific properties of each segment, let's take a look at piecing together a rectangle. You can see what the rectangle looks like in Figure 7-3; its XAML code is shown following.

■**Caution** If you use a `StrokeThickness` larger than 1, the final segment will leave a gap. Keep this in mind when manually piecing together segments. The final segment might need an adjustment to go far enough to fill in the visual gap left by the difference between the endpoint and the stroke thickness.

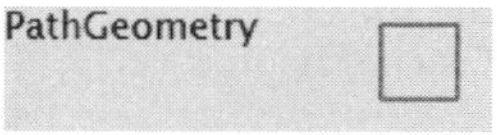

Figure 7-3. *Rectangle drawn using PathGeometry*

```
<Path Stroke="Red" StrokeThickness="1">
    <Path.Data>
        <PathGeometry>
            <PathGeometry.Figures>
                <PathFigure StartPoint="10,10">
                    <PathFigure.Segments>
                        <LineSegment Point="10,40"/>
                        <LineSegment Point="40,40"/>
                        <LineSegment Point="40,10"/>
                        <LineSegment Point="10,10"/>
                    </PathFigure.Segments>
                </PathFigure>
            </PathGeometry.Figures>
        </PathGeometry>
    </Path.Data>
</Path>
```

Let's take a look at what each segment describes and its properties.

ArcSegment

This segment draws an elliptical segment between the end of the previous segment (or the figure's start point) and the specified destination point. Since the elliptical segment has only two points, there must be a way to define how the arc is drawn since there are multiple candidate arcs. The `IsLargeArc` and `SweepDirection` properties exist for this purpose. Table 7-5 shows the properties of `ArcSegment`.

Table 7-5. *Properties of the System.Windows.Media.ArcSegment Class*

Property	Type	Description
IsLargeArc	bool	If true, the arc drawn is greater than 180 degrees. This is one of the two properties required to define how the arc is drawn.
Point	System.Windows.Point	This defines the endpoint of the arc.
RotationAngle	double	This specifies the rotation angle (in degrees) of the arc around the x-axis. It defaults to 0.
Size	System.Windows.Size	This specifies the x and y radii of the arc.
SweepDirection	System.Windows. Media.SweepDirection	This defines which direction the arc is drawn in. It can be set to Clockwise or Counterclockwise. The use of this property with IsLargeArc fully specifies the type of arc drawn.

BezierSegment

This segment represents a Bezier curve, which is a curve defined by a start point, an endpoint, and two control points. The line is bent toward each control point, so if the control points are placed on opposite sides of the line, the line appears to have a hill and a valley along its length. This class provides three properties, all of type System.Windows.Point, used to specify the Bezier segment's control points and ending point.

- Point1: Defines the first control point

- Point2: Defines the second control point

- Point3: Defines the endpoint of the curve

LineSegment

This segment represents a straight line. It has a single property, Point, which defines the endpoint of the line.

QuadraticBezierSegment

A quadratic Bezier segment is a Bezier curve with only a single control point. It defines a single control point and an endpoint.

- Point1: Defines the control point

- Point2: Defines the endpoint of the curve

PolyBezierSegment

This segment is similar to BezierSegment but provides an easy way to combine multiple Bezier curves. Each curve is defined by three points and automatically connects to the endpoint of the previous line (or previous segment if it's the first line in the series). This class contains one property, `Points`, of type `System.Windows.Media.PointCollection`.

PolyLineSegment

Similar in spirit to `PolyBezierSegment`, this segment allows you to easily combine multiple straight lines in a series. It also exposes a property, `Points`, of type `System.Windows.Media. PointCollection`. Each line is automatically connected to the endpoint of the previous line/ segment, so for each new line, all you need to do is add one new point.

PolyQuadraticBezierSegment

This segment combines multiple quadratic Bezier segments together. Each segment is defined by two points: the control point and the endpoint. These are stored in the `Points` property just like the other poly segments.

Grouping Geometries

The `GeometryGroup` class is used to group multiple geometries together. Since it is possible for multiple geometrical shapes to intersect, the `GeometryGroup` class exposes a `FillRule` property to specify how the intersections of geometries are treated to judge whether points within the intersection are in the combined geometry or not. The `FillRule` property can take on one of two possible values:

- `EvenOdd`: A point is judged within the fill region if the number of path segment rays drawn in every direction away from the point ultimately cross an odd number of segments. This is the default value.

- `Nonzero`: A point is judged within the fill region if the number of crossings of segments across rays drawn from a point is greater than zero.

    In addition to the `FillRule` property, the `GeometryGroup` class provides other properties such as `Bounds` to get a `Rect` (a structure defining the width, height, and point of origin of a rectangle) to specify the axis-aligned bounding box of the `Geometry` class, `Children` to define the `GeometryCollection` that contains the objects defining the `GeometryGroup` class, and `Transform` to define the `Transform` object applied to the `Geometry` class.

Using Shapes

The `System.Windows.Shapes.Shape` class forms the base for classes representing geometrical figures that have the ability to draw themselves on the screen. There are classes for drawing lines, rectangles, ellipses, and polygons, all deriving from `Shape`. The most interesting `Shape`-derived class is `Path`. The `Path` class is what we used in the previous section—it has the ability to draw `Geometry`-based objects on the screen, and it can also process a specialized syntax for piecing together `Path`-based geometries. Some of the most useful properties of the `Shape` class are shown in Table 7-6.

    Let's briefly look at some of the simple `Shape`-based classes before moving on to the more complicated `Path` class. The results of the XAML for each of these shapes are shown in Figure 7-4.

Table 7-6. *Properties of the System.Windows.Shapes.Shape Class*

Property	Type	Description
Fill	Brush	The brush used to fill the interior of the shape
Stretch	Stretch	The value from the Stretch enumeration; controls how the shape fills its bounding space
Stroke	Brush	The brush used to paint the outline of the shape
StrokeDashArray	DoubleCollection	Collection of double values specifying the dash pattern to use in outlining the shape
StrokeThickness	double	The thickness of the outline of the shape

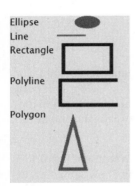

Figure 7-4. *Appearance of the Shape-based classes*

Ellipse

The Ellipse class exposes Height and Width properties that define what the ellipse looks like. Unlike the Geometry class, where you specify a center point and x and y radius values, the Ellipse class only needs to know its bounding box as defined by its Height and Width properties. This provides more flexibility in visual presentation since a Shape can have different stretch behaviors and can be affected by the width of its outline and other properties. You can specify an ellipse in XAML by using the following:

```
<Ellipse Fill="Red" Height="20" Width="40"/>
```

Line

The Line class has two properties to define the start point of the line: X1 and Y1. The X2 and Y2 properties are used to define the endpoint of the line. Drawing a line is accomplished using the following XAML:

```
<Line X1="5" Y1="10" X2="50" Y2="10" Stroke="Red" StrokeThickness="2" />
```

Rectangle

The Rectangle class defines Width and Height properties specifying the dimensions of the rectangle. The following XAML draws a rectangle:

```
<Rectangle Width="80" Height="50" Fill="White" Stroke="Black" StrokeThickness="5" />
```

Polyline

The Polyline class is used to draw multiple connected lines. The Points property contains the set of points defining the lines. The following XAML draws the letter *C*:

```
<Polyline Points="100,10 10,10 10,50 100,50" Stroke="Black" StrokeThickness="5" />
```

Polygon

A polygon is a set of two or more points that form a filled shape. If two points are specified and StrokeThickness and Stroke are defined, a line will be drawn. A set of points is specified in the Polygon's Points property. The following XAML draws a red triangle on the screen. Four points are specified in order to connect the edges back to the triangle's starting point. The shape formed must be a closed shape.

```
<Polygon Points="30,20 50,100 10,100 30,20" Stroke="Red" StrokeThickness="5" />
```

Path

The Path class is by far the most versatile Shape-based class. This class can display any Geometry object by setting its Data property to the object. While this can be used to show complex Path-based geometries using PathGeometry, there is also a special syntax supported in XAML to specify Path-based geometries in a more terse string form. This syntax is utilized by Expression Media when constructing Path-based geometries. This syntax is used when specifying the value for the Data property of the Path class.

The string starts with specifying the fill rule, which is optional. If you want to specify a FillRule enumeration, it must come first. You can use the string F0 to specify EvenOdd (the default value) or F1 to specify Nonzero for the fill rule.

After the fill rule (if you specify one) comes one or more figure descriptions. A figure description consists of a move command, a draw command, and optionally a close command. Each point in this string can take the form *x y* or *x,y*, and whitespace is ignored.

The move command is marked by either a capital M or a lowercase m and then one or more points. The capital M represents a move to an absolute position, and the lowercase m means that the point specified is relative to the previous point. Generally, only one point will be specified, since if multiple points are specified, move operations will be combined with draw operations to draw lines. If only a single point is specified, the behavior of the move command is less ambiguous.

The draw command can be used to draw eight possible shapes. Each command is either a capital letter (for absolute positioning) or a lowercase letter (for relative positioning). Table 7-7 lists the possible draw commands. For simplicity each command is shown only in its capital letter form.

The close command is optional. If specified, the current figure is automatically closed by connecting the current point to the starting point of the figure using a line. The close command is specified using a capital or lowercase Z.

Table 7-7. *Valid Draw Commands*

Command	Description
`L endPoint`	Draws a line starting at the current point and ending at `endPoint`.
`H x`	Draws a horizontal line from the current point to the specified x coordinate.
`V y`	Draws a vertical line from the current point to the specified y coordinate.
`C point1 point2 endPoint`	Draws a cubic Bezier curve, with `point1` and `point2` representing the control points and `endPoint` representing the endpoint of the curve.
`Q point1 endPoint`	Draws a quadratic Bezier curve using `point1` as the control point and ending at the point specified by `endPoint`.
`S point2 endPoint`	Draws a smooth cubic Bezier curve. The first control point is a reflection of `point2` relative to the current point. The curve ends at `endPoint`.
`T point1 endPoint`	Draws a smooth quadratic Bezier curve.
`A size rotationAngle isLargeArcFlag sweepDirectionFlag endPoint`	Draws an elliptical arc. See the "EllipseGeometry" section earlier in the chapter for a description of each parameter. You can set the flag to 0 to turn it off and 1 to turn it on.

The star shape shown in Figure 7-5 is drawn using a `Path` with a solid fill.

Figure 7-5. *Star shape drawn using a Path*

The `Path` in XAML used to make the star looks like this:

```
<Path Stretch="Fill"
        StrokeThickness="2"
        StrokeLineJoin="Round"
        Stroke="Blue"
        Data="F1 M 0,100 L 150,100 L 200,0 L 250,100 L 400,100
                    L 266, 150 L 300,300 L 200,170 L 110,300 L 133,150 Z ">
    <Path.Fill>
        <SolidColorBrush Color="#FFAACCEE"/>
    </Path.Fill>
</Path>
```

Transforms

Transforms are used to alter an element's coordinate system, so applying a transform to a root element causes it and all child content to uniformly alter in appearance. The benefit of a transform is that the underlying elements need no knowledge of the transform—they act as if the coordinate system is unaltered. Silverlight supports transforms for scaling, skewing, and rotating. Scaling makes it easy to shrink or grow an element; skewing can rotate x and y coordinates independently; and rotating causes the entire element to rotate around a center, defaulting to the element's top-left corner. Silverlight also supports a matrix transform, which provides more flexibility in transforms in case you want to do something that isn't a scale, skew, or rotation. Technically, there is one more transform, TransformGroup. This is used to group multiple transformations together and is in itself a Transform.

Many visual elements in Silverlight are eligible for transforming. The Geometry base class has a Transform property that can be set to any of the Transform inheritors. The Brush base class has both a Transform property and a RelativeTransform property. A relative transform is most useful when you don't know the size of the element being transformed—we'll briefly look at this in the next section when we discuss brushes. The UIElement base class has a RenderTransform property that can also be set to any of the Transform inheritors. Let's take a closer look at the transforms represented by classes in Silverlight.

Translation

A translation transform changes the position of an element. This is a simple operation of moving the top left of the element horizontally and/or vertically. A constant value is added to the x and/or y coordinates to reposition the entire element. These values are specified in the X and Y properties of the TranslateTransform class. The following XAML is used to translate a rectangle. Figure 7-6 shows the rectangle translated in both a positive and a negative direction. Translating an element, such as this rectangle, in XAML is a simple matter of specifying its RenderTransform.

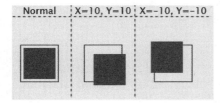

Figure 7-6. *Translating a rectangle diagonally down and up*

```
<Rectangle Stroke="Black" Width="60" Height="60"/>
    <Rectangle Stroke="Crimson" Fill="Crimson" Width="50" Height="50">
        <Rectangle.RenderTransform>
            <TranslateTransform X="10" Y="10"/>
        </Rectangle.RenderTransform>
</Rectangle>
```

Rotation

The RotateTransform class is used to rotate the entire element undergoing transformation. This transform has three important properties for specifying how the rotation is performed: Angle, CenterX, and CenterY. The CenterX and CenterY properties specify which point the rotation is done around. The top left of an element is (0,0), as illustrated in Figure 7-7, and it is around this point that rotation is done by default.

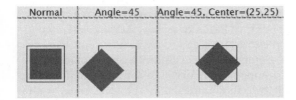

Figure 7-7. *Rotating a rectangle about its default center and true center*

You can rotate in a clockwise direction by using a positive angle (in degrees) between 0 and 360. If you want to rotate counterclockwise, you can specify a negative angle. Angles greater than 360 or less than –360 are valid, but they wrap around the circle. For example, a rotation by 405 degrees has the same result as rotating by 45 degrees, since 405 is equal to 360 (one full rotation) plus 45.

Again, we specify the rectangle's RenderTransform. We will rotate the rectangle on the screen by 45 degrees.

```
<Rectangle Height="50" Width="50" Fill="Crimson">
    <Rectangle.RenderTransform>
        <RotateTransform CenterX="0" CenterY="0" Angle="45"/>
    </Rectangle.RenderTransform>
</Rectangle>
```

Since our center point is at (0,0), the rotation is done around the top-left corner of the rectangle. If you want to rotate the rectangle around its true center, make sure you set CenterX and CenterY appropriately. In this case, we'd set the center to the point (25,25). From left to right, Figure 7-7 shows what our rectangle looks like normally, rotated by 45 degrees around its top-left corner, (0,0), and rotated 45 degrees around its true center, (25,25).

Skewing

A skew transformation stretches the coordinate space in either the x or y direction (or both). This is sometimes called a *shear* transformation. The angle controls how the corresponding coordinate plane is stretched. For example, if you specify an AngleX of 45 degrees, the x and y planes will form a 45-degree angle with each other. You can see this in Figure 7-8 (first row, second column). As the y values increase (remember, the top left of the rectangle is 0,0), the x values are shifted over until the bottom of the rectangle is reached, forming the 45-degree angle at the bottom. The third column shows a skewing transformation done using the AngleY property. Similar to rotation, you can control the center point at which skewing is performed around. The second row of Figure 7-8 shows the same skewing transformations, but with the center of the rectangle, (25,25), as the center point.

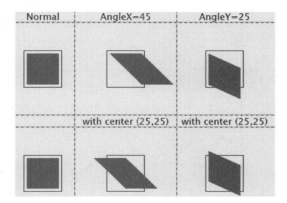

Figure 7-8. *Skewing a rectangle about its default center and true center*

```
<Rectangle Stroke="Crimson" Fill="Crimson" Width="50" Height="50">
    <Rectangle.RenderTransform>
        <SkewTransform AngleX="45"/>
    </Rectangle.RenderTransform>
</Rectangle>
```

Scaling

A scaling transformation uniformly increases or decreases the size of an element. You can zoom into an element by scaling it up, and you can zoom out (e.g., as a cheap way to show thumbnails) by scaling the element down. The ScaleX and ScaleY properties are used to specify how much to scale the element by. This transformation also has a CenterX and CenterY point. This point specifies which point will stay constant in the scaling. Figure 7-9 shows our normal rectangle again in the top left, and the first row shows a scale up and a scale down using the default, (0,0), as the center point. Notice how the top-left corner is unmoved. If we specify (25,25) as the center point, as is done in the second row, the rectangle completely overtakes its bounding box when scaled up and is centered within its bounding box when scaled down. This behavior is important to note when you utilize the scaling transformation. If you think about how some menu animation has the menu expanding while its top-left corner stays intact, you can see how using the top-left corner as the anchor point could prove useful. If this were a button, though, and you wanted its size to change when a mouse pointer hovers over it, it would be better to scale the button up with its true center as the anchor so that it would grow/shrink in a more expected manner for the user.

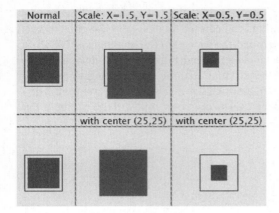

Figure 7-9. *Scaling a rectangle up and down based on its default center and true center*

Here's the XAML used for scaling the rectangle up and down in the second row of Figure 7-9:

```
<Rectangle Stroke="Crimson" Fill="Crimson" Width="50" Height="50">
   <Rectangle.RenderTransform>
      <ScaleTransform ScaleX="1.5" ScaleY="1.5"/>
   </Rectangle.RenderTransform>
</Rectangle>
```

Arbitrary Linear Transforms

The final transformation class that Silverlight provides is the matrix transformation. This can be used when the other transformations don't give you what you want or when you want to combine multiple transformations into a single transformation (although you could also use TransformGroup to group several). Each of the other transformations can be represented by a 3×3 matrix. Let's dust off our linear algebra textbooks and revisit the basics of matrix math to see how a matrix can give us the other transformations and can even combine multiple transformations into a single operation.

The 3×3 matrix that Silverlight uses looks like Figure 7-10.

$$\begin{bmatrix} M11 & M12 & 0 \\ M21 & M22 & 0 \\ offsetX & offsetY & 1 \end{bmatrix}$$

Figure 7-10. *The transformation matrix used by Silverlight*

The final column will always be (0,0,1) because Silverlight supports only affine transformations. In reality, the transformation matrix is 2×2, but it includes within its structure translation values for the x and y coordinates (in the third row). An affine transformation is essentially a linear transformation. Any three points that were on a line before the transformation continue to be on a line after the transformation. We won't trouble ourselves with proving this, since this isn't a math textbook, but if you look at a side of a rectangle in the preceding rotation and skewing figures, you'll see that three arbitrary points along this line are still on a line after the transformation (not the same line obviously, but *a* line nonetheless).

The bottom row of the 3×3 matrix contains values for the x and y offsets. These offsets are used for translation. The M11, M12, M21, and M22 properties of the MatrixTransform class are used to specify the custom transformation. Projection and reflection are two examples of affine transformations not supported directly by Silverlight with a class of their own.

The simplest transformation is the translation. By setting M11 and M22 to 1, M12 and M21 to 0, the offsetX property to 10, and the offsetY property to 0, the transformation will shift the entire element being transformed 10 units to the right. The transformed points are calculated by multiplying each point (x,y) in the element being transformed by the matrix shown in Figure 7-11.

$$\begin{bmatrix} 0 & 0 & 0 \\ 0 & 0 & 0 \\ 10 & 0 & 1 \end{bmatrix}$$

Figure 7-11. *Transformation matrix to translate 10 units to the right*

In general, the result of multiplying a point (technically a vector) by the matrix is (x * M11 + y * M12 + offsetX), (x * M21 + y * M22 + offsetY). There is a special matrix, known as the *identity matrix*, where M11 = 1, M12 = 0, M21 = 0, and M22 = 1. If you multiply any (x,y) point by the identity matrix, you'll get the same point again, provided that offsetX and offsetY are 0. (Go ahead and try this on a piece of paper.) This identity matrix is important because it is the default configuration of the matrix. It allows you to specify only offsetX and/or offsetY to perform a translation without having to worry about an unexpected transformation happening if the M values are all 0 (actually, if they are all 0, the element undergoing transformation might disappear!).

We can skew both coordinates and translate the element at the same time by specifying OffsetX and the M12 and M21 properties, as follows:

```
<Rectangle Stroke="Crimson" Fill="Crimson" Width="50" Height="50">
    <Rectangle.RenderTransform>
        <MatrixTransform>
            <MatrixTransform.Matrix>
                <Matrix OffsetX="-10" M12="0.5" M21="0.5"/>
            </MatrixTransform.Matrix>
        </MatrixTransform>
    </Rectangle.RenderTransform>
</Rectangle>
```

From left to right, Figure 7-12 shows our normal rectangle, the rectangle translated right using a matrix, and the rectangle skewed and translated at the same time.

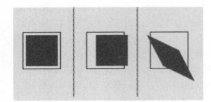

Figure 7-12. *Using MatrixTransform to translate and skew/translate*

Combining Multiple Transformations

Although you could use the MatrixTransform class to combine multiple transformations into a single transformation, if you want to combine two or more of the directly supported transformations (such as a rotation and a scale), you can use the TransformGroup transform. Figure 7-13 shows the result of combining a ScaleTransform and a RotateTransform together inside a TransformGroup.

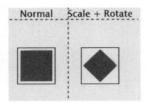

Figure 7-13. *Combining transforms using TransformGroup*

```
<Rectangle Stroke="Crimson" Fill="Crimson" Width="50" Height="50">
   <Rectangle.RenderTransform>
      <TransformGroup>
         <ScaleTransform ScaleX="0.75" ScaleY="0.75" CenterX="25" CenterY="25"/>
         <RotateTransform Angle="45" CenterX="25" CenterY="25"/>
      </TransformGroup>
   </Rectangle.RenderTransform>
</Rectangle>
```

The TransformGroup class is used in this code to apply multiple transformations simultaneously.

3D Effects Using Perspective Transforms

With Silverlight 3, you can now create 3D effects by using perspective transforms. This feature does not produce true 3D content since it does not support 3D mesh models, shading, hidden line removal, and so on; however, you can simulate live content rotation in the 3D space by applying perspective transforms to XAML elements. Another common scenario for using the perspective transforms is to arrange objects in relation to one another to create a 3D effect. You can apply perspective transforms to any XAML element such as a DataGrid or a TextBox.

To apply a perspective transform to a UIElement, you need to set the UIElement object's Projection property to PlaneProjection. The PlaneProjection class defines how the transform is rendered in space. Table 7-8 displays the key properties of the PlaneProjection class.

Table 7-8. *Common Properties of the PlaneProjection Class*

Property	Type	Description
CenterOfRotationX	Double	This gets or sets the x coordinate of the center of rotation of the object you rotate.
CenterOfRotationY	Double	This gets or sets the y coordinate of the center of rotation of the object you rotate.
CenterOfRotationZ	Double	This gets or sets the z coordinate of the center of rotation of the object you rotate.
RotationX	Double	This gets or sets the number of degrees to rotate the object around the x-axis of rotation.
RotationY	Double	This gets or sets the number of degrees to rotate the object around the y-axis of rotation.
RotationZ	Double	This gets or sets the number of degrees to rotate the object around the z-axis of rotation.
GlobalOffsetX	Double	This gets or sets the distance the object is translated along the x-axis of the screen.
GlobalOffsetY	Double	This gets or sets the distance the object is translated along the y-axis of the screen.
GlobalOffsetZ	Double	This gets or sets the distance the object is translated along the z-axis of the screen.

To achieve this functionality, you do not need to write a single line of code; you implement this feature by merely using Expression Blend. Here is a simple example of rotating an image on the y-axis with a slider by using element binding:

```
<UserControl x:Class="chapter7.MainPage"
    xmlns="http://schemas.microsoft.com/winfx/2006/xaml/presentation"
    xmlns:x="http://schemas.microsoft.com/winfx/2006/xaml"
    Width="400" Height="300">
    <Grid x:Name="LayoutRoot" Background="White">
        <StackPanel>
            <Image x:Name="image1" Source="true.png" Stretch="None">
                <Image.Projection>
                    <PlaneProjection x:Name="Rotate" RotationY="45"/>
                </Image.Projection>
            </Image>
            <Slider Value="{Binding RotationY, Mode=TwoWay,
                ElementName=Rotate}" Minimum="0" Maximum="360"/>
        </StackPanel>
    </Grid>
</UserControl>
```

Now when you run the project, you should see the check mark image set to 45 degrees by default, as shown in Figure 7-14. The image will rotate from 0 degrees on the left to 360 degrees on the right.

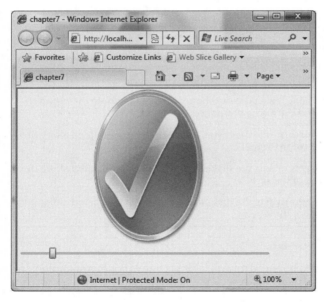

Figure 7-14. *3D effect by applying perspective transform*

▓**Note** Kit3D is a 3D graphics engine for Microsoft Silverlight. There is a JavaScript version that runs on Silverlight 1.0, but in the future, as described on the CodePlex site, the engine will be actively developed only in C#. For more details, visit `www.codeplex.com/Kit3D`.

Pixel Shaders

Pixel shader effects drive the visual behavior of the graphical content. Pixel shaders are sets of software instructions that are used to calculate the color of individual pictures onscreen, and they usually operate quickly by executing on the GPU.

Pixel shader effects are supported in Silverlight 3. By default, Silverlight 3 supports drop-down and blur effects. You can also create custom effects by using Microsoft's High-Level Shading Language (HLSL) and the DirectX SDK. However, in Silverlight 3, pixel shaders are rendered using a software-based algorithm and not on the GPU. Thus, pixel shader effects in Silverlight aren't nearly as fast as they might be using the GPU.

The `System.Windows.Media.Effects` library contains built-in pixel shaders for blurring and drop shadowing, and they can be added to an `Image` or `TextBlock` element using that element's `Effect` property in XAML or in the code-behind. In Chapter 1, we demonstrated the `DropShadowEffect` property using a TextBlock control. Here we will demonstrate the blur and drop shadow effects for an image using an Image control and will show how to set the `Effect` property of the Image control to the `BlurEffect` and `DropShadowEffect` effects:

```
<UserControl x:Class="chapter7.shadders"
    xmlns="http://schemas.microsoft.com/winfx/2006/xaml/presentation"
    xmlns:x="http://schemas.microsoft.com/winfx/2006/xaml"
    Width="600" Height="300">
<StackPanel x:Name="LayoutRoot" Background="White"
        Orientation="Horizontal" >
        <Image Source="lcd.png" Stretch="None" Margin="15,0,0,0" >
            <Image.Effect>
                <BlurEffect Radius="5" />
            </Image.Effect>
        </Image>
        <Image Source="lcd.png" Stretch="None" Margin="40,0,0,0" >
            <Image.Effect>
                <DropShadowEffect ShadowDepth="8"/>
            </Image.Effect>
        </Image>
    </StackPanel>
</UserControl>
```

Now when you run the project, you should see two images. The first image is blurred, and the second one has the drop shadow effect (see Figure 7-15).

■**Note** The Windows Presentation Foundation Pixel Shader Effects Library (WPFSLFx) with sample HLSL effects for WPF and Silverlight applications is available on the CodePlex site. You can get more details and download the sample, documentation, and library by visiting `http://wpffx.codeplex.com/`.

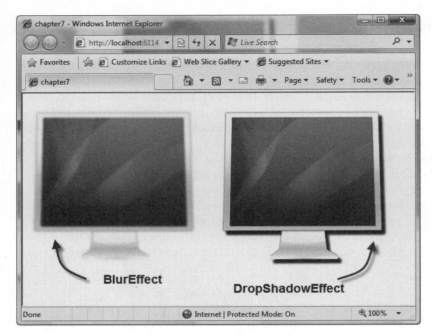

Figure 7-15. *Blur and drop shadow effects for the Image control*

Brushes

Throughout this book, brushes have been applied several times (generally, any time an element has been filled with a solid color). For filling with a solid color, the SolidColorBrush class is used. Silverlight also provides several other brushes, including an image brush, a video brush, and several gradient brushes. As you can probably surmise, combining a video brush with a geometric shape such as an ellipse or polygon (and perhaps even a transform) provides a staggering degree of flexibility in how content is presented in Silverlight. The hierarchy of brushes is shown in Figure 7-16.

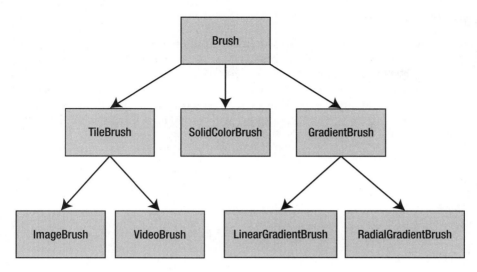

Figure 7-16. *Inheritance hierarchy of brush-related classes*

The System.Windows.Media.Brush class forms the base of all the brushes in Silverlight. This class inherits directly from DependencyObject. Its properties are listed in Table 7-9.

Table 7-9. *Properties of the System.Windows.Media.Brush Class*

Property	Type	Description
Opacity	double	Gets or sets the opacity of the brush. A value of 0 specifies a fully transparent brush, and a value of 1 specifies a fully opaque brush.
RelativeTransform	Transform	Applies a transform using relative coordinates. This is useful for applying a transform when the size of the surface being filled isn't known.
Transform	Transform	Applies a transform using absolute coordinates.

The SolidColorBrush

The simplest brush you can use is the solid color brush. This inherits directly from Brush and thus does not share functionality with other brush types. The solid color brush has a single property, Color. In XAML, this can be set to the name of a color (see the Brushes class in the MSDN documentation online for a full list of the colors, or use IntelliSense while editing the XAML in Visual Studio) or an ARGB value by using the #FFFF0000 syntax (this example sets the color to full red, no transparency). Filling a rectangle with a solid color can be accomplished with the following XAML:

```
<Rectangle Width="50" Height="50">
    <Rectangle.Fill>
        <SolidColorBrush Color="Crimson"/>
    </Rectangle.Fill>
</Rectangle>
```

The Tile Brushes

The parent of both ImageBrush and VideoBrush is TileBrush. This class cannot be instantiated on its own—it exists to provide tiling behavior to inheriting classes. There are four properties supported by the TileBrush class, listed in Table 7-10. Each is also a dependency property.

Table 7-10. *Properties of the System.Windows.Media.TileBrush Class*

Property	Type	Description
AlignmentX	AlignmentX	Horizontal alignment used for positioning. This can be set to Left, Center, or Right.
AlignmentY	AlignmentY	Vertical alignment used for positioning. This can be set to Top, Center, or Bottom.
Stretch	Stretch	Specifies how the contents of brush fill the bounding space. See Chapter 6 for a discussion of this property.

The ImageBrush

The Stretch property provides many ways to paint an image onto a surface. Figure 7-17 shows what an image brush looks like for each of the possible Stretch values.

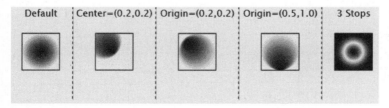

Figure 7-17. *Various stretch configurations of an image brush*

The Video Brush

The video brush works much like the image brush, but uses a video instead of an image. The VideoBrush class provides methods to play, pause, stop, and seek a different position in the video. The SourceName property of the VideoBrush class must be set to the name of a MediaElement specified in your XAML. The following XAML gives an example:

```
<MediaElement x:Name="videoMediaElement" Source="video.wmv"/>
<Rectangle Width="300" Height="250" Stroke="Red" StrokeThickness="2">
    <Rectangle.Fill>
        <VideoBrush SourceName="videoMediaElement" />
    </Rectangle.Fill>
</Rectangle>
```

The Gradient Brushes

There are two gradient brushes that are used to paint with a gradient of colors. The first is the linear gradient brush, used to paint a gradient along a straight line. The second is the radial gradient brush, used to spread colors across an elliptical surface. Both brushes utilize a gradient specified by one or more gradient stops. What a gradient looks like depends on the values of control parameters and gradient stops. *Gradient stops* specify the color at which a particular gradient ends. It's possible to paint multiple gradients within a surface by using multiple gradient stops. The GradientBrush class forms the base of both the linear and radial gradient brushes. The properties provided by GradientBrush are shown in Table 7-11.

Table 7-11. *Properties of the System.Windows.Media.GradientBrush Class*

Property	Type	Description
ColorInterpolationMode	ColorInterpolationMode	Specifies the color space to use when interpolating colors. Set it to ScRgbLinearInterpolation to use the scRGB space or SRgbLinearInterpolation to use the sRGB space.
GradientStops	GradientStopCollection	The collection of gradient stops defining how colors are spread in the surface being filled.
MappingMode	BrushMappingMode	Gets or sets the coordinate system used by the brush. Set this to Absolute for coordinates to be interpreted in local space, and set it to RelativeToBoundingBox to use coordinates relative to the bounding box (0 corresponds to 0 percent of the box, and 1 corresponds to 100 percent, so 0.5 would be interpreted as the center point). The default value is RelativeToBoundingBox. It does not affect offset values of gradient brushes.
SpreadMethod	GradientSpreadMethod	Gets or sets how the gradient is spread. Valid values are Pad (the default), Reflect, and Repeat.

The LinearGradientBrush

A linear gradient brush spreads a color gradient across a straight line. This straight line can be any straight line through the surface being painted and is described by the StartPoint and EndPoint properties of the LinearGradientBrush class. The top-left corner is (0,0), and the bottom-right corner is (1,1). Using 0 and 1 for the start point and endpoint of each coordinate plane allows you to use this brush without worrying about the actual size of the surface being painted. It is through this line that the gradient spreads by default, starting from the top left and ending at the bottom right. You can see this default behavior in the first column of Figure 7-18.

If you specify only a single gradient stop, the linear gradient brush paints a solid color. If you use two gradient stops—for example, starting at black (#FF000000) and ending in red (#FFFF0000)—the gradient starts at black, and the color spreads evenly from black to red along the length of the surface being painted, until the end of the surface is reached. Multiple gradient stops can be specified along a gradient line from 0.0 to 1.0.

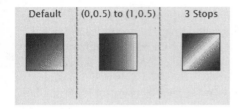

Figure 7-18. *Different configurations of the linear gradient brush*

Figure 7-18 shows the behavior of several different options for the linear gradient brush. The default behavior is shown first, spreading from black to white. Here's the XAML for this gradient:

```
<Rectangle Stroke="Black" Width="60" Height="60">
   <Rectangle.Fill>
      <LinearGradientBrush>
         <GradientStop Color="#FF000000" Offset="0.0"/>
         <GradientStop Color="#FFFFFFFF" Offset="1.0"/>
      </LinearGradientBrush>
   </Rectangle.Fill>
</Rectangle>
```

The following code shows how to spread the gradient horizontally instead of diagonally:

```
<Rectangle Stroke="Black" Width="60" Height="60">
   <Rectangle.Fill>
      <LinearGradientBrush StartPoint="0,0.5" EndPoint="1,0.5">
         <GradientStop Color="#FF000000" Offset="0.0"/>
         <GradientStop Color="#FFFFFFFF" Offset="1.0"/>
      </LinearGradientBrush>
   </Rectangle.Fill>
</Rectangle>
```

The next code block creates a gradient that spreads to the center point of the gradient line and a second gradient that spreads from the center point to fill up the other half of the surface:

```
<Rectangle Stroke="Black" Width="60" Height="60">
   <Rectangle.Fill>
      <LinearGradientBrush>
         <GradientStop Color="#FF000000" Offset="0.0"/>
         <GradientStop Color="#FFFFFFFF" Offset="0.5"/>
         <GradientStop Color="#FF000000" Offset="1.0"/>
      </LinearGradientBrush>
   </Rectangle.Fill>
</Rectangle>
```

The RadialGradientBrush

The radial gradient brush spreads a color gradient from a point outward in an elliptical pattern. The Center property specifies the center of the ellipse, and the RadiusX and RadiusY properties control how the ellipse is shaped. If RadiusX and RadiusY are equal, the resulting ellipse is a circle. The GradientOrigin property specifies the point at which the gradient starts. The gradient spreads outward from this point until it completely fills the bounding ellipse.

Figure 7-19 shows various radial gradients.

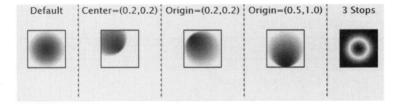

Figure 7-19. *Different configurations of the radial gradient brush*

The image on the left of Figure 7-19 shows the default radial gradient, with the center at (0.5,0.5) and the gradient going from black to white. Here's the XAML for this first radial gradient example:

```
<Rectangle Stroke="Black" Width="60" Height="60">
   <Rectangle.Fill>
      <RadialGradientBrush>
         <GradientStop Color="#FF000000" Offset="0.0"/>
         <GradientStop Color="#FFFFFFFF" Offset="1.0"/>
      </RadialGradientBrush>
   </Rectangle.Fill>
</Rectangle>
```

The first two examples use different gradient origins, and the final one uses gradient stops.

The Save File Dialog Box

The Save File dialog box is probably one of the most critical components and one of the most commonly used modal dialog boxes in desktop and web applications. Until Silverlight 2, Silverlight used only isolated storage as the primary area on the client machine for data storage. Silverlight 3 now supports a Save File dialog box to save data to the client's hard drive and is thus not limited to isolated storage.

The SaveFileDialog class is derived from the System.Windows.Controls namespace.

Table 7-12 and Table 7-13 show the key methods and properties of the SaveFileDialog class, respectively.

Table 7-12. *Key Methods of the SaveFileDialog Class*

Property	Type	Description
OpenFile	Stream	This method opens the file specified by the File property.
ShowDialog	Nullable (Boolean)	This method shows the SaveFileDialog on the screen. It returns true if the user clicks Save and false if the user clicks Cancel or closes the dialog box. You can use the return value of the ShowDialog method to determine whether the user has selected a file.

Table 7-13. *Key Properties of the SaveFileDialog Class*

Property	Type	Description
DefaultExt	String	This property gets or sets the default file name extension applied to files saved with the dialog box.
File	FileInfo	This property gets or sets the file information for the file associated with the dialog box.
Filter	String	This property gets or sets the filter string that specifies which file types and descriptions to show in the dialog box.
FilterIndex	int	This property gets the index associated with the first filter shown in the dialog box.

An Example

We'll show you a quick example that saves a file to your local drive using the Save File dialog box. First add a text box and a button to your newly created Silverlight project. The text entered in the text box will be saved as a file to a defined location through the SaveFileDialog box upon clicking the button. The following is the self-explanatory XAML code:

```
<StackPanel x:Name="LayoutRoot" Background="White">
   <TextBlock Text="Enter Text to Save" Margin="4"/>
   <TextBox x:Name="SaveText" Margin="4"/>
   <Button Content="Click to Save Text to Your Local Machine"
      Click="SaveFileButton_Click" Margin="5"/>
</StackPanel>
```

Now in the Button control's Click event, with the use of SaveFileDialog's Show method, the user can define the file name and location to save the file. In the following example, we have set the Filter property to the text file (.txt) type to save the entered text as a file:

```
private void SaveFileButton_Click(object sender,
   RoutedEventArgs e)
{
   string texttosave = SaveText.Text;

   SaveFileDialog filesavedialog = new SaveFileDialog();
   //Set Save File Dialog box FileType Filter
   filesavedialog.Filter = "TextFile (*.txt)|.txt";
   //Show standard Save File Dialog
   bool? result = filesavedialog.ShowDialog();
   //Save entered text as a text file
   if (result == true)
   {
      using (StreamWriter filestream = new
        StreamWriter(filesavedialog.OpenFile()))
      {
         filestream.Write(texttosave);
         filestream.Close();
      }
   }
}
```

The syntax of the Filter property of SaveFileDialog is a vertical bar–separated list that contains the file types and descriptions. That is, it looks like <LABEL>|<filter>| <LABEL>|<filter>|.., where <LABEL> is the description that appears in the drop-down list and <filter> is the file type filter. In our case, we set it to Text File (*.txt) |.txt. You can set multiple file types as a filter; in that case, you can use the FilterIndex property (which is 1-based) to set the default file type.

Now if you run the project, you can save the entered text as a text file, as shown in Figure 7-20.

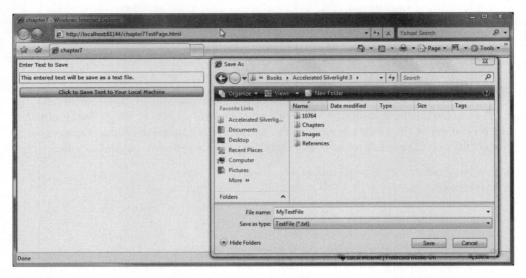

Figure 7-20. *Using SaveFileDialog to enable file save functionality to a user's local drive*

Accordion

The Accordion control is part of the Silverlight Toolkit, and in order to use this control you need to add a reference to the assembly System.Windows.Controls.Layout.Toolkit, which resides in the namespace System.Windows.Controls.

Silverlight Toolkit

The Silverlight Toolkit is a way for the community to develop different Silverlight controls, components, and utilities to be delivered as extensions to the regular Silverlight release. For Silverlight 3, the Silverlight Toolkit includes more than a dozen new controls with full source code, unit tests, samples, and documentation. These controls include an accordion control, chart controls, styling controls, and user input controls that provide enhanced key features.

You can get more details on Silverlight Toolkit and download it by visiting www.codeplex.com/ Silverlight. You will have the option to download Silverlight 2 or Silverlight 3. Once you download the toolkit, it will be installed under the C:\Program Files (x86)\Microsoft SDKs\Silverlight\ v3.0\Toolkit folder (a 32-bit Program Files folder) if your operating system is 64-bit, and it will be installed under the C:\Program Files\Microsoft SDKs\Silverlight\v3.0\Toolkit folder if your operating system is 32-bit.

The Accordion Control

The Silverlight Accordion control displays a list of expandable/collapsible AccordionItems. Select an AccordionItem control to expand it, and collapse all others. This control is helpful in optimizing the use of screen real estate by organizing the user interface effectively. The Accordion control is actually a collection of expanders that work in conjunction with each other. It can expand to any direction—up, down, left, or right. The default is down, which causes content to be displayed below each header. Expander is one of the controls of the Silverlight Toolkit.

Just like the ListBox control manages ListBoxItems, the Accordion control manages AccordionItems. The following is a summary of the key features of the Accordion control:

- The AccordionItem control allows different levels of selection (including single-selection and multiselection) based on the SelectionMode property.

- The AccordionItem control's open/close animation is a VSM state so it can easily be configured in Expression Blend.

- The AccordionItem control allows sequential animations. For example, when the user selects an item, you can first close the old one and then open the selected item.

Table 7-14 and Table 7-15 define the key properties and events of the Accordion control, respectively. You will notice that they are very similar to the ListBox control.

Table 7-14. *Key Properties of the Accordion Control*

Property	Type	Description
ContentTemplate	DataTemplate	This property gets or sets the DataTemplate used to display the content of each generated AccordionItem.
ExpandDirection	ExpandDirection	This property gets or sets the ExpandDirection property of each AccordionItem in the Accordion control and the direction in which the Accordion control does layout. The supported directions are Right, Left, Up, and Down.
HeaderTemplate	DataTemplate	This property gets or sets the DataTemplate used to display the header of each generated AccordionItem.
SelectedIndex	Int	This property gets or sets the index of the currently selected AccordionItem.
SelectedItem	Object	This property gets or sets the selected item. The default value is null. When multiple items are allowed, return the first of the SelectedItem properties.

Table 7-14. *Key Properties of the Accordion Control (Continued)*

Property	Type	Description
SelectionMode	SelectionMode	This property is used to determine the minimum and maximum selected AccordionItems allowed in the Accordion. The enumerations for SelectionMode are as follows: One: Exactly one item must be selected in the Accordion. OneOrMore: At least one item must be selected in the Accordion. ZeroOrOne: No more than one item can be selected in the Accordion. ZeroOrMore: Any number of items can be selected in the Accordion.
SelectionSequence	SelectionSequence	This property gets or sets the SelectionSequence used to determine the order of AccordionItem selections. The enumerations for SelectionSequence are as follows: CollapseBeforeExpand: This collapses the set before expansion. Simultaneous: This causes no delays; all states are set immediately.

Table 7-15. *Key Events of the Accordion Control*

Event	Type	Description
SelectedItemsChanged	NotifyCollectionChangedEventHandler	This event occurs when the SelectedItems collection changes.
SelectionChanged	SelectionChangedEventHandler	This event occurs when the SelectedItem or SelectedItems property value changes.

The AccordionItem Control

The AccordionItem control displays a header and has a collapsible content window. So, each item in the Accordion control is actually an AccordionItem. Just like the ListBoxItem control works with the ListBox control, the AccordionItem control can work only with the Accordion control. You can also add AccordionItems at design time using Expression Blend to create static Accordion controls with predefined items to your application. You can also apply styles on dynamically created AccordionItems by setting the property ItemTemplate for the Accordion control.

The Header property for the AccordionItem control defines the header of each control. Whereas the Content property defines the content of the control, you can have one or more Content properties at design time using XAML or dynamically set at runtime by using a code-behind.

Figure 7-21 shows how to add AccordionItem to the Accordion control by right-clicking the Accordion control at design time using Blend.

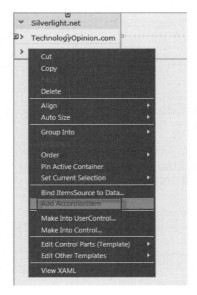

Figure 7-21. *Adding AccordionItem at design time in Blend*

Table 7-16 defines some of the key properties of the AccordionItem control.

Table 7-16. *Key Properties of the AccordionItem Control*

Property	Type	Description
AccordionButtonStyle	Style	This property gets or sets the style used by AccordionButton. This holds the header and an icon.
ExpandDirection	ExpandDirection	This property gets the direction in which the AccordionItem content window opens.
IsLocked	bool	This property gets a value indicating whether the AccordionItem can be selected by the user.
IsSelected	bool	This property gets or sets a value indicating whether the AccordionItem is selected and its content window is visible.

An Example

Now it's time to create an example on how to use the Accordion control. The following are the prerequisites before you can utilize the Accordion control in your Silverlight project:

1. Install the Silverlight Toolkit to your development machine as described in the section "Silverlight Toolkit."

2. Add at least the `Systems.Windows.Controls` and `Systems.Windows.Controls.Layout. Toolkit` assemblies as references to your project. These assemblies are available on the .NET tab of the Add Reference window.

3. Add a reference namespace to your XAML page of the `Systems.Windows.Controls. Layout.Toolkit`, as shown here:

```
xmlns:layoutToolkit="clr-namespace:System.Windows.Controls;
  assembly=System.Windows.Controls.Layout.Toolkit"
```

Now you are all set to add the Accordion control to your project. As part of the content of each AccordionItem, you can add simple text as the `Content` attribute of the AccordionItem control, or you can add other user controls such as Image or TextBlock to display single or multiple items as content. In the following example, we have used the TextBlock control to display the text. We have used the StackPanel layout control and set its `Orientation` property to `Vertical` to display multiple `Content` properties in a single AccordionItem control. The following is the complete code snippet:

```
<UserControl x:Class="chapter7.Accordion"
    xmlns="http://schemas.microsoft.com/winfx/2006/xaml/presentation"
    xmlns:x="http://schemas.microsoft.com/winfx/2006/xaml"
    xmlns:layoutToolkit="clr-namespace:System.Windows.Controls;
     assembly=System.Windows.Controls.Layout.Toolkit"
    Width="400" Height="300">
    <Grid x:Name="LayoutRoot" Background="White">
        <layoutToolkit:Accordion x:Name="Accordion1"
            HorizontalAlignment="Stretch"
            Margin="2,2,2,2"
            FontFamily="Georgia"
            FontSize="18">
            <layoutToolkit:AccordionItem Content="H.264 Support"
                Header="Media"/>
             <layoutToolkit:AccordionItem Header="Graphics" >
                <layoutToolkit:AccordionItem.Content>
                    <StackPanel Orientation="Vertical" >
                        <TextBlock Text="3D Perspective"/>
                        <TextBlock Text="Shadders"/>
                    </StackPanel>
                </layoutToolkit:AccordionItem.Content>
```

```
            </layoutToolkit:AccordionItem>
            <layoutToolkit:AccordionItem Content="Animation easing"
                Header="Animation" />
            <layoutToolkit:AccordionItem Content="Blend 3"
                Header="Design tool" />
        </layoutToolkit:Accordion>
    </Grid>
</UserControl>
```

Now if you run the project, you'll get the output shown in Figure 7-22.

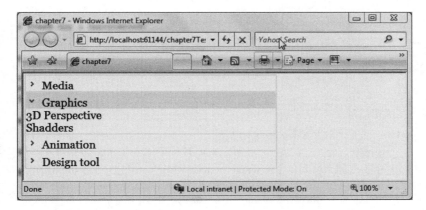

Figure 7-22. *Example of the Accordion control*

Silverlight Child Window Template

Silverlight 3 introduces a new Silverlight Child Window template as part of the default installer. By introducing this template, Silverlight makes it easy for developers to implement modal windows in Silverlight-based RIAs. For example, you can use the Silverlight Child Window template to get the user's attention by providing a modal window and pausing the application flow for user interaction until the child window is closed. You can also use this feature as a pop-up window to display a data-driven report or data entry form. The child window blocks the workflow until the window is closed. The stored result in `DialogResult` informs the application of its status upon closing. Silverlight renders the child window with an animation sequence and renders an overlay background to ensure the user focuses on the window.

You can add the Silverlight Child Window template by right-clicking the Silverlight application project and choosing Add New Item and then Silverlight Child Window, as shown in Figure 7-23.

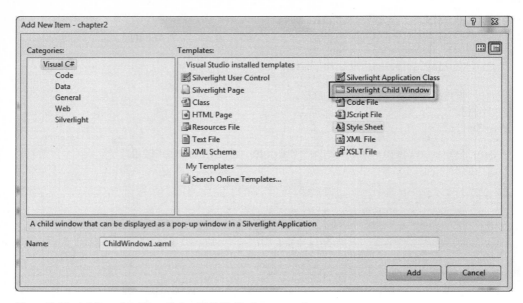

Figure 7-23. *Adding the Silverlight Child Window template*

After successful adding a child window, you'll see the following XAML code in the XAML view of Visual Studio. As you can see, the XAML code includes two buttons (OK and Cancel) along with related `Click` events. The following code snippet shows the XAML code and related code-behind. We just added a TextBlock to display the static text.

```
<controls:ChildWindow x:Class="chapter7.ChildWindow1"
    xmlns="http://schemas.microsoft.com/winfx/2006/xaml/presentation"
    xmlns:x="http://schemas.microsoft.com/winfx/2006/xaml"
    xmlns:controls="clr-namespace:System.Windows.Controls;
     assembly=System.Windows.Controls"
    Width="400" Height="300" Title="ChildWindow1">
    <Grid x:Name="LayoutRoot" Margin="2">
      <Grid.RowDefinitions>
        <RowDefinition />
        <RowDefinition Height="Auto" />
      </Grid.RowDefinitions>
      <TextBlock Text="This is a Modal Child Window" FontSize="24"/>
        <Button x:Name="CancelButton" Content="Cancel"
          Click="CancelButton_Click" Width="75" Height="23"
          HorizontalAlignment="Right" Margin="0,12,0,0"
          Grid.Row="1" />
        <Button x:Name="OKButton" Content="OK" Click="OKButton_Click"
          Width="75" Height="23" HorizontalAlignment="Right"
          Margin="0,12,79,0" Grid.Row="1" />
    </Grid>
</controls:ChildWindow>
```

The following is the code-behind. Here the DialogResult property of type Nullable<bool> gets or sets the dialog result value. It returns true if the child window was accepted, and it returns false if the child window was canceled.

```
namespace chapter7
{
    public partial class ChildWindow1 : ChildWindow
    {
        public ChildWindow1()
        {
            InitializeComponent();
        }

        private void OKButton_Click(object sender, RoutedEventArgs e)
        {
            this.DialogResult = true;
        }

        private void CancelButton_Click(object sender,
            RoutedEventArgs e)
        {
            this.DialogResult = false;
        }
    }
}
```

The next question is, how will we show this child window? As you probably predicted, we will use the Show method. Thus, the Show method of the child window causes the child window to be opened. While the child window is open, the underlying user interface is disabled by default.

So, we will add a Button control to the page, and in the Click event, we will use the Show method to open the previously created child window, as shown here:

```
private void ShowChildWindowButton_Click(object sender,
    RoutedEventArgs e)
{
    var newchildwindow = new ChildWindow1();
    newchildwindow.Show();
}
```

Now if you build the project and run it, you'll see a Click to Show Child Window button. Click the button, and the child window will open with the main application window disabled, as shown in Figure 7-24.

■**Note** Microsoft Visual Studio 2008 does not support the design preview functionality for the child window. As a result, it might be a good practice to develop it using Expression Blend.

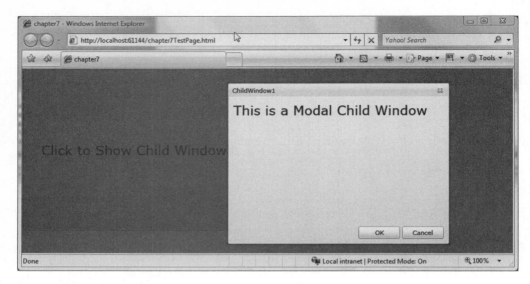

Figure 7-24. *The child window*

Summary

This chapter has covered much more of the support Silverlight provides for building user interfaces. First, it covered the support Silverlight provides for 2D drawing, including the Geometry- and Shape-based classes. Then it covered the various transformations used to alter how elements are rendered, such as applying a rotation.

You also learned about the new features introduced by Silverlight 3 such as creating 3D effects using perspective transforms, pixel shaders, and the existing brush capability in Silverlight that provides flexibility in how content is drawn within bounding elements. You can achieve some interesting effects when you animate the properties of a brush.

In the coming chapters, we will cover animation, and by combining transformations with animation, you can perform interesting effects such as setting something spinning by continually altering its rotational angle.

Finally, we covered new Silverlight 3 features: the Save File dialog box, the Accordion control, and the Silverlight Child Window template. These extend the Silverlight technology platform so you can develop highly interactive and data-driven RIAs.

In the next chapter, we'll cover the enhanced support Silverlight 3 provides for styling applications and modifying the visual appearance of controls.

CHAPTER 8

■ ■ ■

Styling and Templating

Silverlight provides the capability to easily style elements of user interfaces and alter the appearance (separate from the behavior) of controls. Styling is similar in spirit to how CSS properties work: user interface elements can reuse fonts, colors, and sizes that are specified as a style by applying a specific style to a `FrameworkElement`. Templating, however, is limited to `Control`-based classes and is used to completely change how controls are rendered visually. This mechanism works because what the control does (its behavior) is separate from how it looks. These two capabilities provide a significant amount of user interface customization to designers and developers when working with Silverlight.

Using Styles

If you're building a simple application that has just a few user interface screens, it probably makes sense to set properties such as `FontSize` and colors on user interface elements themselves. If you're building a larger application, though, you can quickly find yourself replicating the same property values on page after page. A *style*, in Silverlight, is a group of properties and specific values that you can reuse within a page or even across the whole application. A specific style is given a name and stored within a resource dictionary, so a style can be scoped to the page or application level. It's possible to place a style within any resource dictionary, but in practice, styles are rarely seen outside the page or application level since the benefit of a style is in the reuse of sets of attribute values. Figure 8-1 shows a layout that many web sites follow.

The main title and the navigation menu are omnipresent as the user navigates from one page to another. The part of the interface that changes, however, features the content from an individual page. In ASP.NET, the navigation menu and main title go into something called a *master page*, which separates the common parts of the site from the page-specific parts. Figure 8-1 shows a section title and some example text that might appear in a specific page of a Silverlight application. The section title and page text will change from one page to the next. In fact, there might be many elements used by different pages, such as hyperlinks and other text. Before you can effectively use styles, you must understand the different user interface elements used throughout your application.

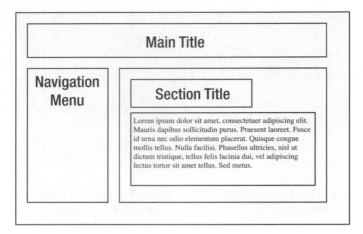

Figure 8-1. *Design layout for a web site*

Two of these elements are visible in Figure 8-1: the section title and the page-specific text. Some other possible elements are bylines (for blogs or news articles), image captions, and hyperlinks. Once you have a list of the common user interface elements, though, you have to determine exactly which properties you want applied across your application. The properties you choose to group into styles correspond to the properties from various Silverlight controls. Both the section header and the page text from Figure 8-1 could be displayed using a TextBlock. Some useful properties of TextBlock that are great for use in a style are `FontSize`, `Foreground`, `FontWeight`, `FontFamily`, `Margin`, and `TextWrapping`. All of these properties control how the text is presented.

Figure 8-2 shows this master page/content page relationship in a theoretical online bookstore. The navigation menu at the left and the title at the top are present regardless of which section of the site a user visits.

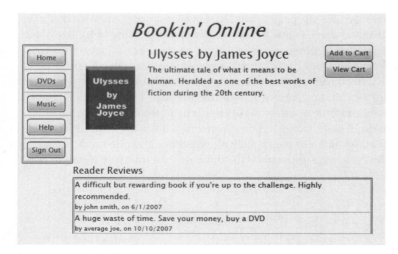

Figure 8-2. *User interface for an online bookstore*

Here's the XAML used for the section title (book name), page content (book description), and the navigation menu without using styles:

```
<StackPanel Grid.Row="1" Grid.Column="0">
    <ListBox>
        <ListBoxItem>
            <Button Content="Home" Width="60" Margin="5"/>
        </ListBoxItem>
        <ListBoxItem>
            <Button Content="DVDs" Width="60" Margin="5"/>
        </ListBoxItem>
        <ListBoxItem>
            <Button Content="Music" Width="60" Margin="5"/>
        </ListBoxItem>
        <ListBoxItem>
            <Button Content="Help" Width="60" Margin="5"/>
        </ListBoxItem>
        <ListBoxItem>
            <Button Content="Sign Out" Width="60" Margin="5"/>
        </ListBoxItem>
    </ListBox>
</StackPanel>
<StackPanel Grid.Row="1" Grid.Column="2" VerticalAlignment="Top">
    <TextBlock FontSize="20">Ulysses by James Joyce</TextBlock>
    <TextBlock FontSize="12" TextWrapping="Wrap">
    The ultimate tale of what it means to be human. Heralded as one
    of the best works of fiction during the 20th century.
    </TextBlock>
</StackPanel>
```

You can see the duplication of the Width and Margin properties in the navigation buttons. Also, the properties used for the content of a page wouldn't necessarily be the same as other content pages (e.g., DVDs and music), since the values must manually be kept consistent. These are two of the biggest issues that styles solve. These properties will be pulled out and grouped into three styles: one for the navigation buttons, one for the page header, and one for the page content.

The System.Windows namespace provides framework classes for the Silverlight client and provides many Silverlight base classes that have different presentation features. The Style class is derived from System.Windows and contains different property setters that can be applied to instances of similar types of UI elements. Table 8-1 defines key properties of the Style class.

There are two components to a style: where it is applied and what it does. In order to specify where a style is applied, you must give it a name and a target type. This target type is the name of a class that will use the style. This target type must match directly—the style will not automatically apply to descendents of the specified class. This makes styling a user interface predictable since a derived type won't take on a specific style set for its parent class. Since these user interface elements apply to the entire Silverlight application, the styles will go into the application's resource dictionary in the App.xaml file.

Table 8-1. *Properties of the Style Class*

Property	Type	Description
IsSealed	bool	This property gets a value that indicates whether the style is read-only and cannot be changed.
Setters	SetterBaseCollection	This property gets a collection of Setter objects.
TargetType	Type	This property gets or sets the type for which the style is intended.
BasedOn	Style	This property gets or sets a defined style that is the basis of the current style. Each style supports only one BasedOn style. The BasedOn style cannot be changed when a style is sealed. The TargetType property of a BasedOn style must match or be derived from the TargetType of a style.

```
<Application xmlns="http://schemas.microsoft.com/winfx/2006/xaml/presentation"
             xmlns:x="http://schemas.microsoft.com/winfx/2006/xaml"
             x:Class="chapter8.App">
    <Application.Resources>
        <Style x:Key="ContentHeader" TargetType="TextBlock">
            <Setter Property="FontSize" Value="20"/>
        </Style>
        <Style x:Key="ContentDescription" TargetType="TextBlock">
            <Setter Property="FontSize" Value="12"/>
            <Setter Property="TextWrapping" Value="Wrap"/>
        </Style>
        <Style x:Key="NavigationButton" TargetType="Button">
            <Setter Property="Width" Value="60"/>
            <Setter Property="Margin" Value="5"/>
        </Style>
    </Application.Resources>
</Application>
```

You can set Style on any UI element that is derived from the FrameworkElement. Each style is given an x:Key that serves as the key for the resource dictionary and also the key used when applying a style to a user interface element. The TargetType is set to TextBlock for the page content header and page content and to Button for the navigation buttons. These properties, grouped in styles and then placed in the application's resource dictionary, provide the consistency and ease of maintenance for your application's look and feel.

Applying the styles is a simple matter of using the StaticResouce markup extension in the Style attribute of a user interface element of the corresponding type. Here's the XAML that makes up the navigation menu and the page content using styles:

```
<StackPanel Grid.Row="1" Grid.Column="0">
    <ListBox>
        <ListBoxItem>
            <Button Content="Home" Style="{StaticResource NavigationButton}"/>
        </ListBoxItem>
```

```
        <ListBoxItem>
            <Button Content="DVDs" Style="{StaticResource NavigationButton}"/>
        </ListBoxItem>
        <ListBoxItem>
            <Button Content="Music" Style="{StaticResource NavigationButton}"/>
        </ListBoxItem>
        <ListBoxItem>
            <Button Content="Help" Style="{StaticResource NavigationButton}"/>
        </ListBoxItem>
        <ListBoxItem>
            <Button Content="Sign Out" Style="{StaticResource NavigationButton}"/>
        </ListBoxItem>
    </ListBox>
</StackPanel>
<StackPanel Grid.Row="1" Grid.Column="2" VerticalAlignment="Top">
  <TextBlock Style="{StaticResource ContentHeader}">
      Ulysses by James Joyce
  </TextBlock>
  <TextBlock Style="{StaticResource ContentDescription}">
    The ultimate tale of what it means to be human. Heralded
    as one of the best works of fiction during the 20th century.
  </TextBlock>
</StackPanel>
```

In the style, the setter is used to set a property to a specific value. Property element syntax is also supported when setting the value of a property. One example of using property element syntax is to set a control template, which can completely change the look and feel of a control. We'll examine control templates in more detail in the next section. Setting a control template in a style looks like this:

```
<Style ...>
    <Setter Property="Template">
        <Setter.Value>
            <ControlTemplate ...>
        </Setter.Value>
    </Setter>
</Style>
```

What if a property is defined in a style and also defined locally? If you consult the value precedence diagram shown in Chapter 2 again (see Figure 8-3), you'll see that the style setter actually has rather low precedence. The property values from style setters can be overridden by values from many sources, and as you can see, the local value has a relatively high precedence. If you use a style setter and it doesn't appear to work, look at these other sources for property values since something is most likely overriding the property value.

There is one significant drawback to using styles: conditional styling (also known as *property triggers*) is supported in WPF but not in Silverlight. Conditional styling is useful for applying styles to framework elements based on conditions such as a user's mouse pointer hovering over the element. Although it would be nice to have this directly supported in the styling system, you can accomplish this behavior using control templates, which we'll look at next.

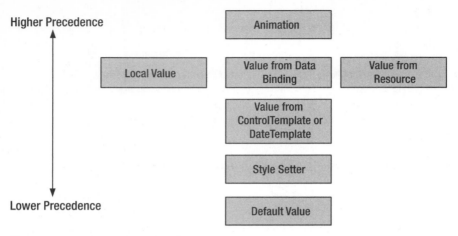

Figure 8-3. *Property value precedence chart*

Using the Enhanced Style Features in Silverlight 3

Silverlight 3 includes enhanced styling features such as style inheritance (which means you can create cascading styles by basing them on each other), style override and style resetting (for dynamic styling and skinning), and merged resource dictionaries. We'll discuss them one by one.

Style Inheritance/Style Cascading

Style inheritance, also known as *style cascading* or *based-on styles*, is one of the most widely used features in WPF-based applications. Most developers have used Cascading Style Sheets (CSS) when working with HTML pages, and style inheritance in Silverlight is the same. Having this feature incorporated in Silverlight 3 makes Silverlight application development more versatile. For example, say you need to create several different buttons that share the same control template and several style properties, but then you want to change a minor detail like the background and foreground colors. Broadly speaking, you can use style inheritance to standardize the fonts and colors throughout an application. The style inheritance is accomplished by using the new BasedOn attribute of the Style class.

Consider the following XAML code:

```
<Grid x:Name="LayoutRoot" Background="White">
    <Grid.Resources>
      <ResourceDictionary>
        <Style x:Name="Title" TargetType="TextBlock">
            <Setter Property="FontFamily" Value="Calibri" />
            <Setter Property="FontSize" Value="15" />
            <Setter Property="FontWeight" Value="Bold"/>
        </Style>
```

```xml
    <Style x:Name="MainTitle" TargetType="TextBlock"
      BasedOn="{StaticResource Title}">
      <Setter Property="Foreground" Value="Blue" />
    </Style>

    <Style x:Name="SubTitle" TargetType="TextBlock"
      BasedOn="{StaticResource Title}">
      <Setter Property="FontSize" Value="12" />
    </Style>
  </ResourceDictionary>
</Grid.Resources>
<StackPanel>
  <TextBlock Text="Title" Style="{StaticResource Title}" Margin="5"/>
  <TextBlock Text="Main Title" Style="{StaticResource MainTitle}" Margin="5"/>
  <TextBlock Text="Sub Title" Style="{StaticResource SubTitle}" Margin="5"/>
</StackPanel>
</Grid>
```

The previous code snippet has the base style `Title` that targets `TextBlock` elements and defines the values for the `FontFamily`, `FontSize`, and `FontWeight` properties. The code also contains another style, called `MainTitle`, that again targets `TextBlock` elements. Note the additional attribute `BasedOn`. By using it, we are basing this style on the style defined by its value—`Title`—in this example. Here we set the `Foreground` property of the `TextBlock` element to `Blue`.

When we use the `MainTitle` style on a `TextBlock`, we are going to have both of the values set in the `Title` style (`FontFamily`, `FontSize`, and `FontWeight`) and those set in `MainTitle`(`Foreground`).

Another style, `SubTitle`, is also based on the `Title` style, but this time it overrides the base value set for `FontSize`. Now when we use the `SubTitle` style on a `TextBlock`, we can see that it appears with font family Calibri but at the font size 12.

Figure 8-4 shows the outcome of the previous XAML code.

Figure 8-4. *Style inheritance using BasedOn style*

Style Override/Style Resetting

Silverlight 3 eliminates the limitation of the `Style` property's write-once quality. You can now override the default style multiple times by setting the `Style` property at runtime. This feature makes it easy to implement skinning in your application. As an example, with the style override capabilities, you can style your application using a set of different styles for different color schemes by basing all of your graphics' and controls' skin colors on style values. They will then automatically update when you change the style.

To demonstrate style resetting, we will add one more style with the name `DynamicTitle` to our previous style inheritance example. With the click of a button, it will allow us to show that we can reset a style easily multiple times. So, first we define the style as follows:

```
<Style x:Name="DynamicTitle" TargetType="TextBlock"
  BasedOn="{StaticResource Title}">
    <Setter Property="FontSize" Value="20" />
    <Setter Property="Foreground" Value="Green"/>
</Style>
```

Now to dynamically change the styles of UI elements at runtime, we add a Button control with the `Click` event in the existing StackPanel. To identify one of the existing TextBlock controls in the code-behind, we name the second TextBlock control `textBlock1`, as shown here:

```
<Button x:Name="button1" Click="button1_Click"
  Content="Toggle Style" Width="150"/>
<TextBlock x:Name="textBlock1" Text="Main Title"
  Style="{StaticResource MainTitle}" Margin="5"/>
```

The following is the corresponding code-behind that toggles the style of the `textBlock1` control between the `DynamicTitle` and `MainTitle` style definitions:

```
private void button1_Click(object sender, RoutedEventArgs e)
{
  if (isToggle==false)
  {
    textBlock1.Style = LayoutRoot.Resources["DynamicTitle"] as Style;
  }
  else
  {
    textBlock1.Style = LayoutRoot.
      Resources["MainTitle"] as Style;
  }

  isToggle =! isToggle;
}
```

Once you run this sample, you can toggle styles by clicking the button. Note that in the previous code snippet the `isToggle` variable needs to be defined at the class level as `boolean`.

In this example, we defined styles in `Grid.Resources`. However, it is best practice to define global styles at the application level by defining them in `App.xaml`. In that case, the code to reference such styles would be something like this:

```
textBlock1.Style = Application.Current.Resources["DynamicTitle"] as Style;
```

Merged Resource Dictionaries

In Chapter 2, we covered merged resource dictionaries, a new feature in Silverlight 3. However, it is worth revisiting these dictionaries in this chapter in the context of styles.

Merged resource dictionaries allow you to use externally defined resources. A widely used scenario is to share the same resources between different applications. The merged resource dictionaries provide a way to define and split resources into separate files. This feature can be helpful in custom control development.

In Silverlight 2, resources could not be divided into separate files, and that led to large App.xaml files having application shared resources. The same problem exists while developing custom controls. All default style keys must be specified in Themes/Generic.xaml, which again tends to create a very large file. Merged resource dictionaries resolve these issues. They enable you to split style definitions and other resources into manageable pieces, making them easy to localize and revise.

To demonstrate this feature, we'll extend the previous example and add one more resource to Grid.Resources under ResourceDictionary:

```
<ResourceDictionary.MergedDictionaries>
    <ResourceDictionary Source="external.xaml" />
</ResourceDictionary.MergedDictionaries>
```

In the previous code, a style used in the resource dictionary is defined in the external external.xaml file. Note that the Source attribute of the ResourceDictionary element is set to the external.xaml file. You also need to add a new file named external.xaml to your Silverlight project to achieve this functionality successfully. Set its Build Action property to Resource, and define an external style with the name LargeTitle, as shown in the following XAML code:

```
<ResourceDictionary
  xmlns="http://schemas.microsoft.com/winfx/2006/xaml/presentation"
  xmlns:x="http://schemas.microsoft.com/winfx/2006/xaml">
    <Style x:Key="LargeTitle" TargetType="TextBlock">
            <Setter Property="FontFamily" Value="Verdana" />
            <Setter Property="FontSize" Value="20" />
    </Style>
</ResourceDictionary>
```

You can use the same markup to apply the externally defined style that we used to apply local styles, as shown here:

```
<TextBlock Text="Sub Title" Style="{StaticResource LargeTitle}" Margin="5"/>
```

Upon running this, the subtitle text is populated with the LargeTitle style definition, as shown in Figure 8-5.

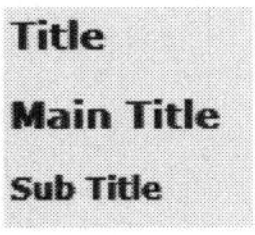

Title

Main Title

Sub Title

Figure 8-5. *Applying styles defined in merged resource dictionaries*

Using Control Templates

One of the biggest advantages to the control architecture in Silverlight is that the behavior of the standard controls is separated from their visual appearance. A control template is a mechanism used to specify how a control looks but not how it behaves. This core behavior can most simply be viewed as what makes a particular control the control that it is. For example, what is a button? Loosely defined, it is a control that can be clicked. There are specializations of buttons such as repeat buttons—but these specializations provide a different core behavior.

Each control can exist in a number of possible states, such as disabled, having input focus, mouse is hovering over it, and so on. A control template provides the ability to define what the control looks like in each of these states. Sometimes this is referred to as changing the "look and feel" of the control, since changing the visual appearance of each state can alter how a user sees and interacts with a control.

Creating a Control Template

The simplest control template contains a root layout control with a visual representation. Let's take a look at a diamond-shaped button with a gradient to color the top and bottom. You can see the result in Figure 8-6.

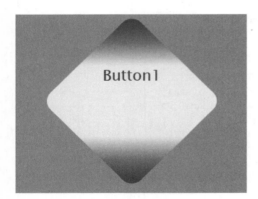

Figure 8-6. *A fancy button using a rotate transform and gradient brush*

The control template is defined as the property value for the `Template` property of the `Control` class. For ease of illustration, the style that contains the control template is stored in the StackPanel's resource dictionary. The button control sets its style and automatically picks up the control template, completely changing its appearance.

```
<StackPanel Background="#FFAAAAAA">
  <StackPanel.Resources>
    <Style  x:Key="buttonStyle" TargetType="Button">
      <Setter Property="Template">
        <Setter.Value>
          <ControlTemplate TargetType="Button">
            <Grid>
```

```xaml
                <Rectangle Width="200" Height="200" RadiusX="20" RadiusY="20">
                    <Rectangle.Fill>
                        <LinearGradientBrush>
                            <GradientStop Color="Blue" Offset="0"/>
                            <GradientStop Color="White" Offset="0.3"/>
                            <GradientStop Color="White" Offset="0.7"/>
                            <GradientStop Color="Blue" Offset="1"/>
                        </LinearGradientBrush>
                    </Rectangle.Fill>
                    <Rectangle.RenderTransform>
                        <TransformGroup>
                            <RotateTransform Angle="45"/>
                            <TranslateTransform X="100"/>
                        </TransformGroup>
                    </Rectangle.RenderTransform>
                </Rectangle>
                <TextBlock HorizontalAlignment="Center"
                           VerticalAlignment="Center"
                           FontSize="20" Text="BUTTON TEXT"/>
            </Grid>
        </ControlTemplate>
    </Setter.Value>
   </Setter>
  </Style>
 </StackPanel.Resources>
 <Button Content="Button1" FontSize="24" Style="{StaticResource buttonStyle}"/>
</StackPanel>
```

A button that uses this style takes on the diamond shape, but the button's text is forced to display the text "BUTTON TEXT." This isn't useful as a general control template since using this approach requires a new control template defined for each text you would want to display. This problem is solved by the TemplateBinding markup extension. This markup extension exists to connect properties used by a control template to properties defined on a specific control and therefore can be used only in conjunction with control templates. The first revision we will make to the preceding control template is to make TemplateBinding use the same content as that specified on a particular button.

■**Note** The TemplateBinding markup extension is one of the few cases where an aspect of XAML does not have a backing class. Since this is a XAML-only construct, there is no way to utilize a TemplateBinding in the code-behind. This also means that control templates are XAML-only, since their purpose is to replace the visual appearance of controls. Fortunately, there are tools such as Expression Blend to make working with control templates quite easy.

In order to use the `TemplateBinding` markup extension with a button, a special class called `ContentPresenter` must be used. This class provides the capability to display the wide range of content options possible with Button and other controls' `Content` property. We can revisit the control template included in the preceding style and change the TextBlock that displays "BUTTON TEXT" to the following `ContentPresenter`:

```
<ContentPresenter HorizontalAlignment="Center"
                  VerticalAlignment="Center"
                  Content="{TemplateBinding Content}"/>
```

Using the `ContentPresenter` in this case carries over the `FontSize` and `Content` properties (possibly) defined on a specific Button control. If no `FontSize` property is specified, the default value is used, so while a template might reference several properties, it doesn't mandate that these properties are set in the control utilizing the template.

If you build an application using this control template and attempt to use the button, you will observe that the button doesn't do anything. Actually, it does something—the events still work on the button—but there is no visual feedback communicated to the user reflecting the various states a Button control can have.

Defining different visual appearances based on the different states a control can be in is accomplished using something called the *Visual State Manager* (VSM). Each control declaratively defines a set of visual state groups and visual states. The states within a group are mutually exclusive, but the control can exist in multiple states if multiple groups are defined. Figure 8-7 shows the two state groups and the valid states within each group for the Button control.

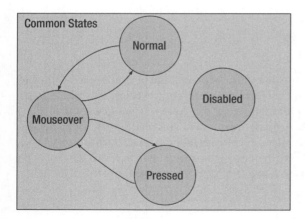

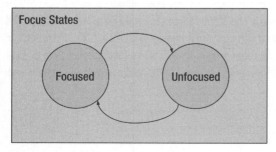

Figure 8-7. *The visual state groups and states of the Button control*

The groups and states are defined declaratively by the control's author. The states and groups shown in Figure 8-7 are defined on the Button class using attributes. We'll take a look at these attributes shortly in the context of creating a new control that supports control templates.

The control template must then specify the appearance of the control in each state. Since a control can exist in different states simultaneously (one per visual group), you must be careful to define visual appearances that can be combined. For example, the color of a button's border might change based on whether it has focus, but the contents of the rectangle change based on whether the button is pressed, disabled, moused over, or none of the above (normal). This is the approach that the default Button takes.

Fortunately, Expression Blend makes defining control templates easy. We'll first take a look at defining a new control template for the Button control and then take a closer look at the XAML generated.

Create or open a project in Expression Blend. Drag a new button onto the design surface. Right-click the button and navigate to Edit Control Parts (Template), and you'll see two options. You can edit a copy of the button's current control template or create an empty one by choosing Create Empty. If you were to click Create Empty, the visual appearance of the button would disappear from the design surface, and the generated XAML would be the minimum needed for the button's control template—specifically the list of groups and the states in each group with no state transitions (as shown in the following code). This approach creates a control template resource in the UserControl with the key you specify.

```
<UserControl.Resources>
    <Style x:Key="ButtonStyle1" TargetType="Button">
        <Setter Property="Template">
            <Setter.Value>
                <ControlTemplate TargetType="Button">
                    <Grid>
                        <vsm:VisualStateManager.VisualStateGroups>
                         <vsm:VisualStateGroup x:Name="CommonStates">
                          <vsm:VisualState x:Name="Normal"/>
                          <vsm:VisualState x:Name="MouseOver"/>
                          <vsm:VisualState x:Name="Pressed"/>
                          <vsm:VisualState x:Name="Disabled"/>
                         </vsm:VisualStateGroup>
                         <vsm:VisualStateGroup x:Name="FocusStates">
                          <vsm:VisualState x:Name="Focused"/>
                          <vsm:VisualState x:Name="Unfocused"/>
                         </vsm:VisualStateGroup>
                        </vsm:VisualStateManager.VisualStateGroups>
                    </Grid>
                </ControlTemplate>
            </Setter.Value>
        </Setter>
    </Style>
</UserControl.Resources>
<Grid x:Name="LayoutRoot" Background="White">
```

```
        <Button Height="84" Margin="257,115,256,0"
                Style="{StaticResource ButtonStyle1}"
                VerticalAlignment="Top" Content="Button"/>
    </Grid>
</UserControl>
```

When you click Edit a Copy and enter a name for the style in the dialog (as shown in Figure 8-8), the full default control template is placed into the XAML. The default control template for Silverlight's controls are part of a style because other properties of controls are also set, such as padding, content alignment, and cursor appearance. These styled properties apply to every visual state of a control.

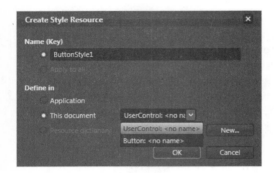

Figure 8-8. *Creating a style resource that contains a control template*

While at this point you could edit the XAML directly to change the appearance of the button in each state, Expression Blend makes it easy to modify each state and state transition without needing to drop down to the XAML. This is facilitated by the States pane in Expression Blend. Figure 8-9 shows what this looks like for the default control template for the Button class.

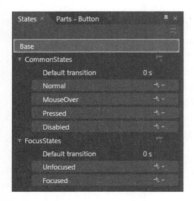

Figure 8-9. *The States pane for the Button control*

There are several important aspects to this pane. It lists all the states that are defined for the control and also provides capabilities for specifying state transitions. The star on the MouseOver and Pressed states makes it easy to handle specifying transitioning from any state to this state. The state transition duration represents the length of time it takes to transition from one state to another. If you set the MouseOver state duration (currently 0.2) to 5 seconds, the animation to reflect the moused-over state will take a lot longer.

Let's take a closer look at the copy of the default control template for the Button control before replacing it with our own. The style containing the default control template, now located in the XAML file, starts off with five simple style property setters:

```
<UserControl.Resources>
    <Style x:Key="ButtonStyle1" TargetType="Button">
        <Setter Property="Background" Value="#FF1F3B53"/>
        <Setter Property="Foreground" Value="#FF000000"/>
        <Setter Property="Padding" Value="3"/>
        <Setter Property="BorderThickness" Value="1"/>
```

The sixth style setter is the control template.

```
<Setter Property="Template">
    <Setter.Value>
        <ControlTemplate TargetType="Button">
            <Grid>
            </Grid>
        </ControlTemplate>
    </Setter.Value>
</Setter>
```

The Grid is the layout container for the various parts of the button. The Grid's resource dictionary includes a number of colors and several brushes that are used by the button. The first child element of the Grid is VisualStateManager:

```
<vsm:VisualStateManager.VisualStateGroups>
    <vsm:VisualStateGroup x:Name="CommonStates">
        <vsm:VisualStateGroup.Transitions>
            <vsm:VisualTransition GeneratedDuration="00:00:00.1" To="MouseOver"/>
            <vsm:VisualTransition GeneratedDuration="00:00:00.1" To="Pressed"/>
        </vsm:VisualStateGroup.Transitions>
        <vsm:VisualState x:Name="Normal"/>
        <vsm:VisualState x:Name="MouseOver">
            <!-- changes background gradient to reflect mouse over state -->
        </vsm:VisualState>
        <vsm:VisualState x:Name="Pressed">
            <!-- changes background gradient to reflect pressed and changes
                 opacity of the DownStroke visual element -->
        </vsm:VisualState>
        <vsm:VisualState x:Name="Disabled">
            <!-- changes opacity of DisabledVisual -->
        </vsm:VisualState>
    </vsm:VisualStateGroup>
```

```
    <vsm:VisualStateGroup x:Name="FocusStates">
      <vsm:VisualState x:Name="Focused">
         <!-- makes FocusVisual visible -->
      </vsm:VisualState>
      <vsm:VisualState x:Name="Unfocused">
         <!-- hides FocusVisual -->
      </vsm:VisualState>
    </vsm:VisualStateGroup>
</vsm:VisualStateManager.VisualStateGroups>
```

The VisualTransition class has four properties that can specify the duration and behavior of state transitions. Its properties are described in Table 8-2.

Table 8-2. *Properties of System.Windows.VisualTransition*

Property	Type	Description
GeneratedDuration	TimeSpan	Gets or sets the length of time the specified state transition takes. This duration will affect the Storyboard specified in the VisualState if none is specified here.
From	string	Gets or sets the starting state. If this property is not specified, the transition will be from any state within the state group to the state specified in the To property.
To	string	Gets or sets the name of the state to transition to.
Storyboard	string	Gets or sets the name of the storyboard that describes the behavior of the state transition. If no storyboard is specified, the Storyboard property of the VisualState class describes the behavior.

The rest of the control template consists of a number of visual elements that, when combined, create the full appearance of a default button. You can edit these visual elements directly using Expression Blend. Figure 8-10 shows each element in the Objects and Timeline pane.

Figure 8-10. *The visual elements that make up the Button control*

These various visual elements are stored next to each other. Each state contains something called a `Storyboard`, which alters the appearance of different visual elements. We'll take a closer look at what the `Storyboard` class provides and how to use it in the next chapter. For now, the important thing to note about the `Storyboard` is that it provides the capability to change the value of any dependency property over a specified length of time.

Let's now create a new button that looks like a jagged-lined bubble you might see in a comic book. This could be useful for a comic-related site, an online store or modeling program, or any site that's on the whimsical side. The outline of the button is created in Expression Design using the `PolyLine`. Figure 8-11 shows the outline of the button.

Figure 8-11. *Jagged outline for the new button skin*

The approach we will take for this button is to have separate visual elements for each state. We'll use a thin stroke for the default appearance and the mouseover, but thicken the border when the button is pressed. When the button is hovered over, the fill will change from light blue to light purple. Each visual appearance has a corresponding name that will be used in the storyboards for the state transitions. Figure 8-12 shows a default button in Silverlight, the new button as it appears normally, and the new button as it appears when pressed (from left to right).

Figure 8-12. *A default Silverlight button and the new button in two states*

Here's the corresponding XAML for the normal and pressed versions of the button:

```
<!-- Normal appearance of button -->
<Path x:Name="NormalAppearance"
        Stretch="Fill" StrokeThickness="2"
        StrokeLineJoin="Round" Data="...">
   <Path.Fill>
     <SolidColorBrush Color="#FFAACCEE"/>
   </Path.Fill>
</Path>
<!-- Pressed appearance of button -->
<Path x:Name="PressedAppearance" Visibility="Collapsed"
        Stretch="Fill" StrokeThickness="4"
        StrokeLineJoin="Round" Data="...">
```

```
      <Path.Fill>
        <SolidColorBrush Color="#FFE2CFF6"/>
      </Path.Fill>
</Path>
```

Note that PressedAppearance has its Visibility initially set to Collapsed. This is the approach used to change the appearance of the button: the versions we don't want are hidden, and the visual appearance corresponding to the state being transitioned to is shown. The disabled state of the button still works with how we set the new button up, so we can leave that part of the control template alone. The visual appearance when the button has focus features a black rectangle surrounding the button, as shown on the right in Figure 8-12. The black rectangle is illustrative of two states combined—you might want another visual indication of focus, but this usually depends on the appearance of the other controls in your application, since it's generally good to maintain a degree of consistency.

The entire control template won't be listed, but here's what the transition to the Pressed state looks like. A type of animation called *object animation* is used to modify an arbitrary property of an object, in this case the Visibility property. The visual appearance of the MouseOverAppearance and NormalAppearance states is hidden, and PressedAppearance is made visible. Again, we'll delve deeper into animation in the next chapter.

```
<vsm:VisualState x:Name="Pressed">
  <Storyboard>
    <ObjectAnimationUsingKeyFrames Duration="0"
                    Storyboard.TargetName="PressedAppearance"
                    Storyboard.TargetProperty="Visibility">
      <DiscreteObjectKeyFrame KeyTime="0">
        <DiscreteObjectKeyFrame.Value>
          <Visibility>Visible</Visibility>
        </DiscreteObjectKeyFrame.Value>
      </DiscreteObjectKeyFrame>
    </ObjectAnimationUsingKeyFrames>
    <ObjectAnimationUsingKeyFrames Duration="0"
                    Storyboard.TargetName="MouseOverAppearance"
                    Storyboard.TargetProperty="Visibility">
      <DiscreteObjectKeyFrame KeyTime="0">
        <DiscreteObjectKeyFrame.Value>
          <Visibility>Collapsed</Visibility>
        </DiscreteObjectKeyFrame.Value>
      </DiscreteObjectKeyFrame>
    </ObjectAnimationUsingKeyFrames>
    <ObjectAnimationUsingKeyFrames Duration="0"
                    Storyboard.TargetName="NormalAppearance"
                    Storyboard.TargetProperty="Visibility">
      <DiscreteObjectKeyFrame KeyTime="0">
        <DiscreteObjectKeyFrame.Value>
          <Visibility>Collapsed</Visibility>
        </DiscreteObjectKeyFrame.Value>
      </DiscreteObjectKeyFrame>
```

```
        </ObjectAnimationUsingKeyFrames>
    </Storyboard>
</vsm:VisualState>
```

Control Templates for Silverlight Controls

The following main Silverlight controls provide the ability to customize their control template:

Button: The common states are normal, pressed, moused over, and disabled. The focus states are focused and unfocused.

Calendar: The common states are normal and disabled. The Calendar uses the DayButton and MonthButton controls. The DayButton has five state groups: common (normal, disabled, moused over, and pressed); selection (selected and unselected); focus (focused and not focused); active (active and inactive); and day states (regular day and today). The Month-Button shares similar states, but only uses the common, selection, focus, and active state groups.

CheckBox: The common states are normal, moused over, pressed, and disabled. The focus states are focused and unfocused. The check states are checked, unchecked, and indeterminate.

DataGrid: The DataGrid provides normal and unfocused states. There are 11 states defined on each row (for the `DataGridRow` class), 16 states for the `DataGridRowHeader`, 3 for the `DataGridColumnHeader`, and 10 for each cell (for the `DataGridCell` class).

DataPicker: The common states are normal, disabled, moused over, and pressed.

GridSplitter: The common states are normal, moused over, and disabled. The focus states are focused and unfocused.

HyperlinkButton: The common states are normal, moused over, pressed, and disabled. The focus states are focused and unfocused.

ListBox: The ListBox control uses a ScrollViewer and the `ListBoxItem` classes. The `ListBoxItem` defines eight states: common states (normal, moused over, and disabled); focus states (focused and unfocused); and selection states (selected, unselected, and selected, but not focus).

RadioButton: The common states are normal, moused over, disabled, and pressed. The focus states are focused, unfocused, and content focused. The checked states are checked and unchecked.

RepeatButton: The common states are normal, moused over, pressed, and disabled. The focus states are focused and unfocused.

ScrollBar: The ScrollBar itself only has common states (normal, moused over, and disabled). It consists of two sets of a template, two repeat buttons, and a thumb. One set is for vertically oriented scrollbars and the other is for horizontally oriented scrollbars.

ScrollViewer: This has no states, but consists of a horizontal scrollbar, a vertical scrollbar, and a content presenter class (`ScrollContentPresenter`).

Slider: The common states are normal, moused over, and disabled. The focus states are focused and unfocused. Much like the ScrollBar, the Slider consists of two sets of templates (one set for vertical orientation and the other for horizontal). Each set consists of two repeat buttons and a thumb.

TabControl: The common states are normal and disabled. The tab control consists of TabItem instances, each of which has common states (normal, moused over, and disabled); focus states (focused and unfocused); and selection states (selected and unselected).

TextBox: The TextBox includes a normal state, a focused state, and a unfocused state.

ToggleButton: The common states are normal, moused over, pressed, and disabled. The focus states are focused and unfocused. The check states are checked, unchecked, and indeterminate.

Developing a Templated Control

If you want to create your own control, it's a good idea to also make it compatible with control templates. There are really only two things you must do: use the `TemplateVisualState` attribute to specify state groups and states, and use the `VisualStateManager` class within the control's code to handle switching from one state to the next. Since you should be quite familiar with the Button control, let's look at the definition of the `Button` class:

```
[TemplateVisualState(Name = "Normal", GroupName = "CommonStates")]
[TemplateVisualState(Name = "MouseOver", GroupName = "CommonStates")]
[TemplateVisualState(Name = "Pressed", GroupName = "CommonStates")]
[TemplateVisualState(Name = "Disabled", GroupName = "CommonStates")]
[TemplateVisualState(Name = "Unfocused", GroupName = "FocusStates")]
[TemplateVisualState(Name = "Focused", GroupName = "FocusStates")]
public class Button : Control
{
    // class implementation
}
```

The two properties of the `TemplateVisualState` attribute are used here. The groups and states you specify define the behavior of the control. Try to use as few states as possible that still completely define the behavior of your new control. Once these states are defined, the other requirement is for your new control to switch states at the right time.

Some controls consist of other controls, such as the ScrollBar using the RepeatButton control for its increasing/decreasing visual element.

```
[TemplatePartAttribute(Name = "HorizontalThumb", Type = typeof(Thumb))]
[TemplatePartAttribute(Name = "VerticalSmallIncrease", Type = typeof(RepeatButton))]
[TemplatePartAttribute(Name = "VerticalSmallDecrease", Type = typeof(RepeatButton))]
[TemplateVisualStateAttribute(Name = "Disabled", GroupName = "CommonStates")]
[TemplatePartAttribute(Name = "HorizontalLargeIncrease",
    Type = typeof(RepeatButton))]
[TemplatePartAttribute(Name = "HorizontalLargeDecrease",
    Type = typeof(RepeatButton))]
```

```
[TemplatePartAttribute(Name = "HorizontalSmallDecrease",
   Type = typeof(RepeatButton))]
[TemplatePartAttribute(Name = "HorizontalSmallIncrease",
   Type = typeof(RepeatButton))]
[TemplatePartAttribute(Name = "VerticalRoot", Type = typeof(FrameworkElement))]
[TemplatePartAttribute(Name = "VerticalLargeIncrease", Type = typeof(RepeatButton))]
[TemplatePartAttribute(Name = "VerticalLargeDecrease", Type = typeof(RepeatButton))]
[TemplatePartAttribute(Name = "HorizontalRoot", Type = typeof(FrameworkElement))]
[TemplatePartAttribute(Name = "VerticalThumb", Type = typeof(Thumb))]
[TemplateVisualStateAttribute(Name = "Normal", GroupName = "CommonStates")]
[TemplateVisualStateAttribute(Name = "MouseOver", GroupName = "CommonStates")]
public sealed class ScrollBar : RangeBase
```

When you edit the control template of a control with template parts in Expression Blend (via Edit a Copy), the control templates for each of the template parts are added as a resource to the root layout container of the main control's control template. The ScrollBar causes the following XAML to be generated (most of the details are left out for brevity). Notice the series of ControlTemplate elements added to the Grid's resource dictionary.

```xml
<ControlTemplate TargetType="ScrollBar">
   <Grid x:Name="Root">
      <Grid.Resources>
         <ControlTemplate x:Key="RepeatButtonTemplate" TargetType="RepeatButton">
            <Grid x:Name="Root" Background="Transparent">
               <vsm:VisualStateManager.VisualStateGroups>
                  <vsm:VisualStateGroup x:Name="CommonStates">
                     <vsm:VisualState x:Name="Normal"/>
                  </vsm:VisualStateGroup>
               </vsm:VisualStateManager.VisualStateGroups>
            </Grid>
         </ControlTemplate>
         <ControlTemplate x:Key="HorizontalIncrementTemplate"
                                    TargetType="RepeatButton">
         </ControlTemplate>
         <ControlTemplate x:Key="HorizontalDecrementTemplate"
                                    TargetType="RepeatButton">
         </ControlTemplate>
         <ControlTemplate x:Key="VerticalIncrementTemplate"
                                    TargetType="RepeatButton">
         </ControlTemplate>
         <ControlTemplate x:Key="VerticalDecrementTemplate"
                                    TargetType="RepeatButton">
         </ControlTemplate>
         <ControlTemplate x:Key="VerticalThumbTemplate" TargetType="Thumb">
         </ControlTemplate>
         <ControlTemplate x:Key="HorizontalThumbTemplate" TargetType="Thumb">
         </ControlTemplate>
      </Grid.Resources>
```

```
        <vsm:VisualStateManager.VisualStateGroups>
            <vsm:VisualStateGroup x:Name="CommonStates">
                <vsm:VisualState x:Name="Normal"/>
                <vsm:VisualState x:Name="MouseOver"/>
                <vsm:VisualState x:Name="Disabled">
                    <Storyboard>
                        <DoubleAnimationUsingKeyFrames
                                   Storyboard.TargetName="Root"
                                   Storyboard.TargetProperty="(UIElement.Opacity)">
                            <SplineDoubleKeyFrame KeyTime="00:00:00" Value="0.5"/>
                        </DoubleAnimationUsingKeyFrames>
                    </Storyboard>
                </vsm:VisualState>
            </vsm:VisualStateGroup>
        </vsm:VisualStateManager.VisualStateGroups>
        <Grid x:Name="HorizontalRoot">
            <!-- Grid definition and main controls -->
            <RepeatButton x:Name="HorizontalSmallDecrease" ...>
            <RepeatButton x:Name="HorizontalLargeDecrease" ...>
            <Thumb MinWidth="10" x:Name="HorizontalThumb" ...>
            <RepeatButton x:Name="HorizontalLargeIncrease" ...>
            <RepeatButton x:Name="HorizontalSmallIncrease" ...>
        </Grid>
        <Grid x:Name="VerticalRoot" Visibility="Collapsed">
            <!-- vertical appearance of ScrollBar -->
        </Grid>
    </Grid>
</ControlTemplate>
```

When you develop a control, the state changes are accomplished using the VisualStateManager's GoToState method. This method takes three parameters: a reference to a control, the name of the state to transition to, and a boolean value specifying whether to use the visual transition specified by the Storyboard in the control template. For example, in the Button control, when the button handles the MouseOver event, it triggers a state transition, accomplished by invoking the VisualStateManager.

```
VisualStateManager.GoToState(this, "MouseOver", true);
```

By using the two attributes, TemplateVisualState and TemplatePart, and handling the state transitions within your custom control via the GoToState method of the VisualStateManager, you can easily create a control that isolates its behavior and allows designers and developers to completely change the look of your control. Of course, if you create a new control that supports control templates, you must create a default control template if you expect others to consume the control.

Summary

This chapter covered styles and control templates. Styles make reusing properties easy, throughout a single page or an entire application, depending on which resource dictionary contains the styles. It also covered the enhanced styling features of Silverlight 3. Control templates are a mechanism to completely change the visual appearance of a control. This chapter also briefly covered developing custom controls to utilize a control template, and using the Storyboard class, a vital part of animation and the topic for the next chapter.

The next chapter is focused on Silverlight's animation capabilities, including newly introduced features in Silverlight 3 such as 3D animation and animation easing.

CHAPTER 9

■ ■ ■

Animation

When it comes to making user interfaces that make people go "wow," you have many of the pieces of the puzzle: media (video/audio/images), brushes to easily create interesting surfaces, and a set of controls that can be completely re-skinned. There's one final big piece to the user interface support in Silverlight: animation. Silverlight makes it easy to make elements of user interfaces move, and when you put together the various components into a full application, you end up with great visual effect. Any dependency property can potentially be influenced by animation. If you give some thought to the various properties discussed throughout this book, such as transforms and brushes, it's possible to start coming up with a variety of creative effects to jazz up a user interface. For example, by shifting offsets in gradient stops, a gradient can appear to move from one side of the surface it is filling to the other side, creating a shimmer effect. This chapter will delve into how to use animation and also discuss the support Expression Blend provides for working with animation.

Introduction to Silverlight Animation

At its most basic, animation is the modification of a property value over time. Since we generally want animation to cause a visual effect, such as a moving object on the screen, the properties you'll animate are sizes, positions, transforms, etc. If you place a rectangle on a canvas and set its `Canvas.Left` property to the width of the canvas (so it sits just off the right side), and then decrement the `Canvas.Left` property until it reaches zero, the rectangle will seem like it is suddenly appearing and moving until it settles at the far left of the canvas. The animation is made up of one logical frame (in reality, many more actual frames are involved) per change to the `Canvas.Left` property, but because the rectangle is re-positioned and updated quickly, it seems to the human eye like the rectangle is moving smoothly from one side to the other. This is the illusion of animation that we are witness to on a daily basis when we watch television or movies, or play video games.

Silverlight provides two animation mechanisms: from/to/by animation (a.k.a. basic animation) and keyframe animation. While from/to/by is a somewhat awkward name, it also explicitly describes what it is. The "from" part specifies the initial value of a particular property, the "to" is the final value of the property, and "by" is how much that value should change for each step during the animation. With the from/to/by animation type, the property value varies smoothly and continuously over the duration of the animation. Three animation classes of Silverlight are applicable to the from/to/by animation type: `DoubleAnimation`, `PointAnimation`, and `ColorAnimation`. The keyframe animation provides far more flexibility. Instead of specifying the from/to/by type, you specify what the value of the property should be at specific times. With keyframe animation, values can jump abruptly from one value to another, or they can combine jumps and periods of linear interpolation. Silverlight animation classes—`ColorAnimation`, `DoubleAnimation`, `PointAnimation`, and `ObjectAnimation`—are applicable to keyframe animation. Since only property values and their coinciding times are specified, the property must know how to change. This is accomplished via interpolation, and there are many ways you can specify this interpolation, such as using the new animation easing functions introduced in Silverlight 3 to easily create a bouncing effect. Whether you use from/to/by animation or keyframe animation, the actual animation is controlled by a storyboard. The storyboard contains a specific animation, such as moving our rectangle from the right to the left using a from/to/by animation. Before we delve into the specifics of storyboards and animation techniques, it's important to understand how time is used by the animation system in Silverlight.

Timelines

In Silverlight, the `System.Windows.Media.Animation.Timeline` class represents a timeline and forms the base class for the various types of animations (shown in Figure 9-1). The two types of animation Silverlight provides are *from/to/by* and *keyframe*. As mentioned earlier, from/to/by animations make it easy to specify the start and end values for a property. Keyframe animations, however, provide much more control because each keyframe specifies a property's value at a specific time. All animations happen over a length of time. The base `Timeline` class provides time-related behavior to inheritors, featuring a number of properties controlling duration, repeat behavior, and the speed at which time elapses.

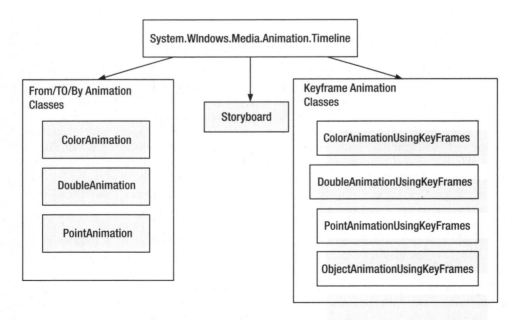

Figure 9-1. *Timeline-related animation classes*

The Timeline class defines six properties that influence how time is represented and manipulated. These properties are listed in Table 9-1.

Table 9-1. *Properties of System.Windows.Media.Animation.Timeline*

Property	Type	Description
AutoReverse	bool	If True, the animation will happen once and then repeat once in the reverse direction. For more than a single reverse, also use RepeatBehavior.
BeginTime	Nullable<TimeSpan>	If this property is null, it indicates there is no BeginTime. This property can be used to stack animations back to back, so if one animation takes 2 seconds, the BeginTime of the second animation can be set to 2s so that it starts immediately after the first.
Duration	Duration	This represents the duration of a single sequence of the animation.
FillBehavior	Animation.FillBehavior	This specifies what happens when an animation hits its end. Set this to HoldEnd to make the animation maintain its final value, or to Stop to make the animation stop when it reaches its end.
RepeatBehavior	Animation.RepeatBehavior	This specifies how many times the timeline repeats (or if it should repeat forever) and the total length of time.
SpeedRatio	double	This specifies the rate of time at which the current timeline elapses relative to its parent. The default value is 1.

Let us understand the SpeedRatio property in detail. If the SpeedRatio is set to 3, then the animation completes three times faster. If you decrease it, the animation is slowed down (for example, if SpeedRatio is set to 0.5 then the animation takes twice as long). Although the overall effect is the same as changing the Duration property of your animation, setting SpeedRatio makes it easier to control how simultaneous animations overlap.

The following snapshot describes the DoubleAnimation of the from/to/by type with the SpeedRatio property set to 2. This will cause the fade-in effect on the Image1 Image control to be completed in 0.5 seconds.

```
<Storyboard x:Name="fadeIn">
    <DoubleAnimation From="0" To="1"
        Storyboard.TargetName="Image1"
        Storyboard.TargetProperty="Opacity"
        SpeedRatio="2">
    </DoubleAnimation>
</Storyboard>
```

The Timeline class also provides a single event, Completed, that fires when the timeline has reached its end. Timeline's properties provide a wide range of capabilities in how time is managed and consequently how animation occurs. There are some subtleties in how the properties work together and how a parent timeline can affect a child timeline, so we need to dig deeper into how these properties work.

AutoReverse

The AutoReverse property causes the animation to happen in reverse after the animation reaches its end, much like rewinding a tape in a VCR while it is still playing. Figure 9-2 shows what using this property by itself does to a timeline. Note that the forward iteration happens once, the reverse iteration happens once, and then the timeline stops.

Consider the following XAML code snippet:

```
<Grid x:Name="LayoutRoot" Background="White">
   <Grid.Resources>
      <Storyboard x:Name="Grow" AutoReverse="True" >
         <DoubleAnimation Storyboard.TargetName="btnGrow"
            Storyboard.TargetProperty="Width"
            From="150" To="300" Duration="0:0:5">
         </DoubleAnimation>
      </Storyboard>
   </Grid.Resources>
   <Button x:Name="btnGrow" Width="150" Height="150"
      Content="This button grows"/>
</Grid>
```

In the previous XAML code, we defined one simple Storyboard, "Grow," as having the AutoReverse property set to True, so the animation will grow the Width of the Button "btnGrow" to 300 from 150 in 5 seconds. As AutoReverse is set to True, the reverse iteration will happen and the button will be set to its original Width after forward iteration completes. So this animation will cause the button to grow in width from 150px to 300px and then shrink from 300px to 150px.

The following code-behind will start the Grow storyboard first in the Loaded event. With the help of the SizeChanged event, when the Width of the Button control reaches 300px, the text changes to "This button now shrinks" and the button will shrink, since AutoReverse is set to True.

```
void MainPage_Loaded(object sender, RoutedEventArgs e)
{
   Grow.Begin();
}

void btnGrow_SizeChanged(object sender, SizeChangedEventArgs e)
{
   if (btnGrow.ActualWidth == 300)
   {
      btnGrow.Content = "This button now shrinks";
   }
}
```

Figure 9-2 shows the `Button` "btnGrow" in the forward and reverse iteration stages.

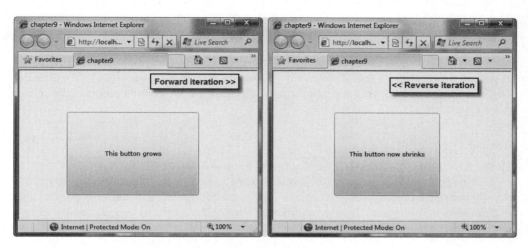

Figure 9-2. *An example of the AutoReverse property*

BeginTime

The `BeginTime` property is used to delay the start of the timeline. When the timeline is started (such as by starting an animation), the current value of this property is used, so this can be changed after a timeline is stopped but before it is restarted. Figure 9-3 illustrates the `BeginTime` property.

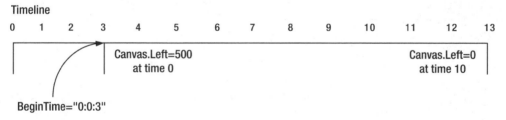

Figure 9-3. *Illustration of BeginTime's effect on a timeline*

Note The `BeginTime` property is of type `TimeSpan`. This type specifies a length of time measured in days, hours, minutes, seconds, and fractions of a second. The XAML syntax to specify a `TimeSpan` takes the form of `[days.]hours:minutes:seconds[.fractional seconds]`. The days and fractional seconds are optional and are separated from their nearest neighbor by a period instead of a colon. Hours, minutes, and seconds, however, are mandatory.

Again, we have a 10-second timeline, but there is a 3-second delay. The timeline automatically lengthens by the addition of `BeginTime` and the timeline's `Duration`. In this case, a 10-second timeline becomes a 13-second timeline. Since the timeline is used for animation, you can see the begin time as a measure of time to delay before the animation starts. This makes it possible to place timelines back to back and cause them to execute in sequence by setting the BeginTime of the next timeline to the length of time it takes for all previous timelines to complete.

It is also possible to specify a negative BeginTime. Doing this provides a way to start the animation at a specified point later in the timeline than its true beginning. For example, a 10-second timeline with a BeginTime of 0:0:-2 starts the timeline at 2 seconds, as if the timeline started at the specified time in the past. This would cause the 10-second timeline to be active only for 8 seconds.

Duration

The Duration property represents the timeline of a single iteration. This property is of the special type System.Windows.Duration. While the Duration type can represent a time span (and uses the same syntax as any property of type TimeSpan when specified in markup), you can also set a property of this type to the special value Automatic. The effects of using Automatic differ depending on whether this property is used on a Storyboard (a Storyboard contains one or more animations, and will be discussed shortly) or on a specific animation. When set on a Storyboard, Automatic causes Duration to be set to the length of time for all the animations it contains put together. For animations, Automatic causes Duration to be set to 1 second (0:0:1). The 1-second default ensures that the animation does something, despite its brevity. You'll rarely if ever use the Automatic value on animations directly. Figure 9-4 highlights the Duration section of the previous timeline.

■**Caution** The value Forever can also be specified for properties of type Duration, but this property value is deprecated; do not use it. See the "RepeatBehavior" section of this chapter for details on how to cause an animation to run continuously.

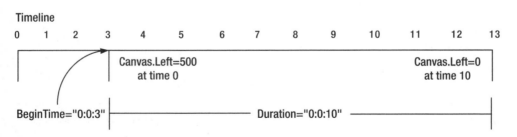

Figure 9-4. *Illustration of Duration combined with BeginTime*

FillBehavior

An animation's *active period*—also known as the animation's *fill period*—is the time during which the animation is happening. The FillBehavior property specifies what happens when the end of the fill period is reached. It can be set to two values: Stop and HoldEnd. When set to HoldEnd, the animation appears to freeze in its final state. For our original moving rectangle example, this means that the rectangle would stop at the left side of the screen, holding its final property value from the animation. The value Stop, however, causes the animation to freeze in its initial state instead of its final state. For our rectangle, this means that after the rectangle reaches the left side, it disappears (since it started completely off the right side of the canvas).

RepeatBehavior

RepeatBehavior, as its name implies, controls how the timeline repeats. It can take one of three forms: a time span, an iteration count, or the special property value Forever (which causes the repetition to happen continuously). The RepeatBehavior property is of the type Animation. RepeatBehavior, which has two properties that specify the exact repeat behavior: Count and Duration. The Count property is of type double and specifies the number of times the timeline should repeat. Since this is a double property, it's possible to repeat a fraction of the timeline by specifying a value (e.g., 1.5). To specify the Count property in XAML, the property value must be followed by x (e.g., 1.5x) to indicate that the timeline repeats a full iteration and a half. There is also a boolean property, HasCount, which is set to True if the RepeatBehavior represents a Count.

The Duration property is the other means used to specify a repeat behavior. This property is of type Duration and is used to specify the total time to run the animation. If the Duration of the repeat is longer than the Duration of the timeline, the timeline will continue for the length of the RepeatBehavior's duration. If the repeat's duration is shorter, however, the timeline will stop before reaching its end. For example, if the Duration of the RepeatBehavior property is set to 0:0:5 and the timeline's duration is 0:0:2, the timeline will repeat one and a half times.

There is also a HasDuration property that is set to true when the Duration is specified. It is also possible to set RepeatBehavior to Forever, which represents an animation that continuously repeats.

SpeedRatio

The SpeedRatio property is used to increase or decrease the rate at which time elapses within a timeline. When this value is greater than 1.0 (its default value), the time elapses faster. Likewise, values less than 1.0 cause the timeline to elongate. See Figure 9-5 for a representation of our 10-second timeline sped up and slowed down. The total length of time for a timeline with this property set (and the other properties set to their defaults) is its Duration multiplied by the SpeedRatio.

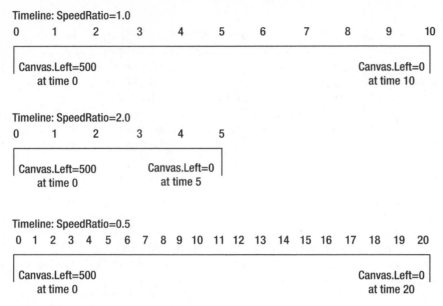

Figure 9-5. *Illustration of different SpeedRatio values*

If we put all these properties together (disregarding a RepeatBehavior set to Forever), the total time it takes for an animation is described by the formula shown in Figure 9-6.

$$\frac{\text{Total Timeline}}{\text{Duration}} = \text{BeginTime} + \frac{\text{RepeatBehavior}}{\text{(as a TimeSpan)}} + \frac{\text{Duration} \times (\text{AutoReverse ? 2 : 1})}{\text{SpeedRatio}} \times \frac{\text{RepeatBehavior}}{\text{(as a double)}}$$

Figure 9-6. *Formula describing total time span of a timeline*

Now that you're familiar with how timelines can be represented and manipulated, it's time to see exactly what the animation classes bring to the table beyond the inherited timeline support.

Storyboards and Animation

The Storyboard class also inherits from Timeline. This is a special class used as a container for other animations. Its timeline represents a length of time corresponding to the combination of all the timelines in animations stored in the storyboard (if left unspecified) or a length of time that constrains the total animation runtime. The most important aspects of this class are its methods to begin, stop, pause, and resume the animation. These, along with the other methods of the class, are described in Table 9-2.

Since the Storyboard class isn't particularly interesting by itself, you'll see it in action when we take a closer look at the animation classes.

Table 9-2. *Methods of System.Windows.Media.Animation.Storyboard*

Method	Description
Begin	Starts the animation with the first timeline in the storyboard.
GetCurrentState	Returns a ClockState enumeration value. Possible states are Active (the animation is active and is changing in direct relation to its parent timeline), Filling (the animation is active but not changing in direct relation to its parent—e.g., it might be paused), and Stopped.
GetCurrentTime	Returns a TimeSpan value corresponding to the current time in the storyboard's timeline.
Pause	Pauses the current storyboard's timeline. Call Resume to unpause the timeline.
Resume	Resumes the current storyboard's timeline.
Seek	Accepts a TimeSpan value corresponding to the time in the storyboard's timeline to move to. This can be done while an animation is active or inactive. The seek operation happens on the next clock tick.
SeekAlignedToLastTick	Same as Seek, but the seek operation happens relative to the last clock tick.
SkipToFill	Changes the frame of the animation to the end of the storyboard's active period. If AutoReverse is True, the end of the active period is the initial frame of the animation. If RepeatBehavior is Forever, using this method throws an InvalidOperation exception.
Stop	Stops the animation.

From/To/By Animations

The simplest form of animation is generally referred to as from/to/by because of its nature. As explained earlier, three animation classes of Silverlight are applicable to the from/to/by animation type—DoubleAnimation, PointAnimation, and ColorAnimation. The From and To in its name refer to the fact that these animations modify a target property's value starting at the From value and ending at the To value (not taking into account different configurations of the timeline). The By property provides a relative offset controlling where the animation ends, and is ignored if combined with the To property. Each of these properties can be used by themselves. Table 9-3 describes different configurations of these properties and how they control the timeline.

Table 9-3. *Usages of From/To/By Properties*

Property	Description
From	This specifies the starting value of the property to animate. The animation stops at the base value of the target property or at the final value of the target property from a previous animation.
To	The target property's value starts at its base value or its final value from a previous animation. It finishes at the value specified in the To property.
By	The target property's value starts at its base value or its final value from a previous animation. The final value of the target property is its initial value added to the value specified in the By property.
EasingFunction	This property gets or sets the easing function applied to this animation.

The combination of the From/To properties specifies the initial (From) and final (To) values of the target Storyboard. The combination of From/By specifies the initial value of the target Storyboard and an offset value used to calculate the target's final value (From + By). The From/To/By combination of the properties is similar to the From/To combination except To overrides By.

Since we've been using it often as an example, let's take a look at how the moving rectangle is animated using XAML. Nothing interesting is going on with the rectangle itself. We give it a name, a position, a size, and a fill.

```
<Rectangle x:Name="rect" Width="25" Height="25" Canvas.Left="370"
                       Canvas.Top="270" Fill="Black"/>
```
Then we give the Storyboard name so that it can be referenced in the code-behind:
```
<Storyboard x:Name="rectAnimation">
    <DoubleAnimation Storyboard.TargetName="rect" Duration="0:0:2"
                                 Storyboard.TargetProperty="(Canvas.Left)"
                                 From="370" To="5" />
</Storyboard>
```

DoubleAnimation is a type of animation used to modify properties of type double. The other two from/to/by animation classes exist to animate points (PointAnimation) and colors (ColorAnimation). Nothing particularly complicated is going on in this example—TargetName refers to the object to animate and TargetProperty is the property to animate. You should be familiar with Duration, From, and To.

■**Caution** If you set a Duration on a storyboard that is less than the length of time of the animations the storyboard contains, the animations will not have a chance to run to completion. While this should come as no surprise, it has repercussions when you don't specify the Duration on the animations within the story-board. Individual animations default to 1 second, so a storyboard with a Duration of less than 1 second will cause behavior that might be unexpected if you're unprepared.

■**Caution** Attempting to animate a single target property using multiple animations within a single story-board will cause the animation to fail (and possibly your application to crash if you don't handle the exception). This happens even if you stagger the animations using the BeginTime property. If you want to stagger animations of a specific property, place them in different storyboards and handle the Completed event to transition to the next storyboard automatically. For example, assume that we have created three storyboards named "SB1," "SB2," and "SB3." Now if we want to start these storyboards one after another in the order SB1, SB2, SB3, we need to wire up the Completed event as shown in the following code snippet.

```
SB1.Completed += new EventHandler(SB1_Completed);
SB2.Completed += new EventHandler(SB2_Completed);

void SB1_Completed(object sender, EventArgs e)
{
   SB2.Begin();
}
```

```
void SB2_Completed(object sender, EventArgs e)
{
   SB3.Begin();
}
```

You should take note of how the TargetProperty adheres to the property path syntax. The simplest property path is the name of a dependency property on the object specified in TargetName. Take, for example, the Width property:

```
TargetPropery = "Width"
```

If you want to specify an attached property (described in Chapter 2), it must be surrounded by parentheses. This was shown earlier with the Canvas.Left property:

```
TargetProperty = "(Canvas.Left)"
```

The object to the left of the dot can be qualified with an XML namespace prefix if the class is not located in the default XML namespace. The property to the right of the dot must be a dependency property. If you want to access a subproperty, you can use the parentheses to surround a *Type.Property* string before accessing the subproperty. For example, if you want to use a ColorAnimation to change the background of our moving rectangle, you can specify it using either of the following syntaxes for TargetProperty:

```
TargetProperty = "(Rectangle.Fill).Color"
TargetProperty = "(Rectangle.Fill).(SolidColorBrush.Color)"
```

The second syntax simply adds the extra qualification to the Color property. This syntax illustrates how to specify other subproperties if they are needed. A final syntax for property paths is required for animating elements such as gradient stops that require indexing:

```
TargetProperty = "GradientStops[0].Offset"
```

As previously shown, the three types of properties you can animate with from/to/by animations are doubles, Points, and Colors. None of these classes provide any specific properties unique to them, and having seen XAML throughout this book, you should be familiar with the property syntaxes for these types. The important thing to keep in mind is that from/to/by animations provide a linear interpolation of values, meaning that the rate at which animation happens is the difference between the initial and final property values during a single iteration, divided by the duration of a single iteration. That is, the rate of change is constant throughout the entire duration of the animation. If you want more control over the animation or the possibility of differing rates of change, Silverlight provides something called a *keyframe animation*, which is discussed in the next section.

Let's make the rectangle animation a little more complicated. In the next example, the rectangle will make a circuit around its host canvas and slowly spin as it goes around. While this implies two logical animations, it requires five actual animations (one for each side of the canvas and one for the rotation) and three storyboards (two for the circuit, since we can't animate the same property twice within a storyboard, and one for the rotation).

■**Note** Many of the animation examples use the `Canvas.Left` and `Canvas.Top` attached properties to change an object's position during animation. In more complete applications, this is a poor approach because it assumes the object being animated is within a Canvas and that the position uses absolute coordinates. A much better approach to animating the position and size of objects is to animate the `TranslateTransform` and `ScaleTransform` properties that belong to the object being animated.

```
<Storyboard x:Name="rectAnimBottomLeft"
                    Completed="rectAnimBottomLeft_Completed">
    <DoubleAnimation Storyboard.TargetName="rect"
                    Storyboard.TargetProperty="(Canvas.Left)"
                    From="370" To="5" Duration="0:0:2" />
    <DoubleAnimation Storyboard.TargetName="rect"
                    Storyboard.TargetProperty="(Canvas.Top)"
                    From="270" To="5" Duration="0:0:2" BeginTime="0:0:2"/>
</Storyboard>
<Storyboard x:Name="rectAnimTopRight" Completed="rectAnimTopRight_Completed">
    <DoubleAnimation Storyboard.TargetName="rect"
                    Storyboard.TargetProperty="(Canvas.Left)"
                    From="5" To="370" Duration="0:0:2"/>
    <DoubleAnimation Storyboard.TargetName="rect"
                    Storyboard.TargetProperty="(Canvas.Top)"
                    From="5" To="270" Duration="0:0:2" BeginTime="0:0:2" />
</Storyboard>
<Storyboard x:Name="rectRotationAnim">
    <DoubleAnimation Storyboard.TargetName="rect"
                    Storyboard.TargetProperty="(Rectangle.RenderTransform).Angle"
                    From="0" To="360" RepeatBehavior="Forever" Duration="0:0:4" />
</Storyboard>
```

Each animation is controlled by its own Start/Stop and Pause/Resume button.

```
<StackPanel Orientation="Horizontal"
            Grid.Row="0" Grid.Column="0" Background="White">
    <StackPanel Orientation="Vertical">
        <TextBlock FontSize="14">Movement Animation</TextBlock>
        <StackPanel Orientation="Horizontal" Margin="15 0 0 0">
            <Button Content="Start" x:Name="movementStartStopButton"
                    Margin="2" Width="40"
                    Click="movementStartStopButton_Click"/>
            <Button Content="Pause" x:Name="movementPauseResumeButton"
                    Margin="2" Width="60"
                    Click="movementPauseResumeButton_Click"/>
        </StackPanel>
    </StackPanel>
</StackPanel>
```

```
<StackPanel Orientation="Vertical" Margin="15 0 0 0">
    <TextBlock FontSize="14">Rotation Animation</TextBlock>
    <StackPanel Orientation="Horizontal" Margin="10 0 0 0">
        <Button Content="Start" x:Name="rotationStartStopButton"
                Margin="2" Width="40"
                Click="rotationStartStopButton_Click"/>
        <Button Content="Pause" x:Name="rotationPauseResumeButton"
                Margin="2" Width="60" Click="rotationPauseResumeButton_Click"/>
    </StackPanel>
</StackPanel>
</StackPanel>
```

We define the Completed event handlers in order to track which of the movement animations is currently executing.

■**Caution** Never invoke the Begin method in a constructor to start animation when the page is loaded. The animation will not start and you will not get any feedback detailing why. Instead, handle the Loaded event of the UserControl or a layout container, and then invoke Begin.

```
private void rectAnimBottomLeft_Completed(object sender, EventArgs e)
{
    //current is a reference of Storyboard
      //that is used for Pause/Resume
    current = rectAnimTopRight;
    rectAnimTopRight.Begin();
}
private void rectAnimTopRight_Completed(object sender, EventArgs e)
{
    current = rectAnimBottomLeft;
    rectAnimBottomLeft.Begin();
}
```

The start/stop and pause/resume functionality for each animation are similar. Here's the pause/resume button click handler. We need to check whether the animation is running and whether it's paused (in order to build the expected behavior into the buttons).

```
private void movementPauseResumeButton_Click(object sender, RoutedEventArgs e)
{
    if(current.GetCurrentState() != ClockState.Stopped && !movementPaused)
    {
        current.Pause();
        movementPauseResumeButton.Content = "Resume";
        movementPaused = true;
    }
```

```
    else
    {
        current.Resume();
        movementPauseResumeButton.Content = "Pause";
        movementPaused = false;
    }
}
```

Animation does not need to always happen in the foreground. We can create a shimmering effect in the background by changing gradient offsets in a linear gradient brush that is used as the background for a Canvas. We also handle the Loaded event of the Canvas in order to start the animation.

```
<Canvas x:Name="LayoutRoot" Loaded="LayoutRoot_Loaded">
    <Canvas.Background>
        <LinearGradientBrush x:Name="background" StartPoint="0,1" EndPoint="1,0">
            <GradientStop Color="#FF000000"/>
            <GradientStop Color="#FFAAAAAA"/>
            <GradientStop Color="#FF000000"/>
        </LinearGradientBrush>
    </Canvas.Background>
    <Rectangle Width="350" Height="250" Canvas.Left="25"
                    Canvas.Top="25" Fill="Beige"/>
</Canvas>
```

The animation changes the offsets for each gradient stop evenly over the duration of the animation (1 second). The storyboard's duration is set to 5 seconds so that the shimmering effect doesn't immediately repeat. If it did, it would make the shimmering effect far less effective.

```
<Storyboard x:Name="shimmer" Duration="0:0:5" RepeatBehavior="Forever">
    <DoubleAnimation Storyboard.TargetName="background"
                    Storyboard.TargetProperty="GradientStops[0].Offset"
                    From="-0.2" To="1.0" Duration="0:0:1" />
    <DoubleAnimation Storyboard.TargetName="background"
                    Storyboard.TargetProperty="GradientStops[1].Offset"
                    From="-0.1" To="1.1" Duration="0:0:1" />
    <DoubleAnimation Storyboard.TargetName="background"
                    Storyboard.TargetProperty="GradientStops[2].Offset"
                    From="0" To="1.2" Duration="0:0:1" />
</Storyboard>
```

Let's look at a more complicated example: the classic sliding puzzle game that is commonly given out as children's party favors. Figure 9-7 shows an example.

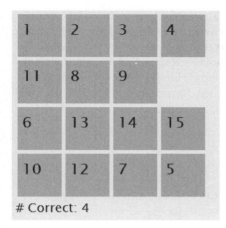

Figure 9-7. *Sliding puzzle game*

This example uses the By property of the Number Block animation to perform relative positioning on it. The XAML for the animation would look like the following:

```
<Storyboard x:Name="horizStoryboard" Completed="horizStoryboard_Completed">
    <DoubleAnimation x:Name="horizAnimation" Duration="0:0:0.5"
                                    Storyboard.TargetProperty="(Canvas.Left)"/>
</Storyboard>
<Storyboard x:Name="vertStoryboard" Completed="vertStoryboard_Completed">
    <DoubleAnimation x:Name="vertAnimation" Duration="0:0:0.5"
                                    Storyboard.TargetProperty="(Canvas.Top)"/>
</Storyboard>
```

In order to create a smooth game experience, the storyboards will not be defined in the XAML, but will instead be created on the fly programmatically. The actual XAML used for the game is minimal.

```
<navigation:Page x:Class="chapter9.SlidingGame"
         xmlns="http://schemas.microsoft.com/winfx/2006/xaml/presentation"
         xmlns:x="http://schemas.microsoft.com/winfx/2006/xaml"
         xmlns:navigation=
         "clr-namespace:System.Windows.Controls;
         assembly=System.Windows.Controls.Navigation"
         Title="SlidingGame Page"
         Width="300" Height="340" Margin="10">
    <Canvas x:Name="LayoutRoot" Background="White"
          MouseLeftButtonUp="LayoutRoot_MouseLeftButtonUp">
      <TextBlock Canvas.Top="300" x:Name="status"
                FontSize="20"></TextBlock>
    </Canvas>
</navigation:Page>
```

We have a canvas and a status line via a TextBlock. The rest is done in the code-behind, from creating the blocks to making animation happen when a user clicks a block. Each block is represented by a Canvas with a white background, a gray rectangle, and a TextBlock to display the number. The Tag property of the Canvas stores an index corresponding to the correct position on the board (the Tag property is set to null for the empty block). What we are interested in is the actual animation of the blocks. The two animations (horizontal and vertical) use code with a similar structure, so we'll just examine the vertical animation.

```
if (emptyCol == col)
{
    if (emptyRow == row - 1 || emptyRow == row + 1)
    {
        Storyboard vertStoryboard = new Storyboard();
        DoubleAnimation vertAnimation = new DoubleAnimation();

        vertAnimation.Duration = TimeSpan.FromSeconds(0.5);

        Storyboard.SetTarget(vertAnimation, currentCanvas);
        Storyboard.SetTargetProperty(vertAnimation,
                        new PropertyPath("(Canvas.Top)"));

        vertAnimation.By = boardHeight / 4;

        if (emptyRow < row)
            vertAnimation.By *= -1;

        vertStoryboard.Children.Add(vertAnimation);
        vertStoryboard.Begin();

        tempCanvas = gamePieces[row * 4 + col];
        gamePieces[row * 4 + col] = gamePieces[emptyCanvasIndex];
        gamePieces[emptyCanvasIndex] = tempCanvas;
    }
}
```

The first if ensures that the animation will be vertical (we know the empty block is above or below since it's the row that differs between the empty block and the block clicked), and the second if ensures that the block clicked is only one space away from the empty block. Once we've verified that the move is valid, we create the Storyboard and the DoubleAnimation, configure the animation, and then start it. The Storyboard.SetTarget method provides an easy way to set the target of an animation to an object. This is a convenient method when working in the code-behind. In XAML, this can only be accomplished by setting the target object's name. After setting the target, we set the By property of the animation. It starts out with a positive value, but if the empty space is above the clicked block, the property value must decrease in value, so we multiply by –1 to make the By property negative.

Since a single `Storyboard` cannot run multiple concurrent animations, creating new `Storyboard` instances programmatically gives us a smooth game. The user can click on multiple blocks and have them animating at the same time. While it's possible to replicate this using storyboards defined in the XAML, it's considerably messier since you'd need to create as many storyboards as you need to run at the same time, and then use code to select a storyboard that isn't currently active.

Keyframe Animations

Keyframe animations provide significant capabilities over the simpler from/to/by animations. Instead of specifying a starting and ending value and letting the animation smoothly change the target property's value over the animation's duration, keyframe animations instead specify the desired value at two or more points in time. Each specification of a property value is known as a *keyframe*: a moment in time when you want a property to take on a certain value. The way the value changes during each keyframe is called *interpolation*. Keyframe animation supports interpolations that are more complicated than the linear interpolations used by from/to/by animations. Keyframe animations also have another important advantage: from/to/by animations can only animate `Points`, `doubles`, and `Colors`, while keyframe animations can animate arbitrary properties using the `ObjectAnimationUsingKeyFrames` class.

A keyframe is a snapshot of a particular property at a specific moment in time. Instead of specifying the starting and ending values of a property using a single animation class, you specify each value of the property you want within a keyframe class. The specific keyframe classes correspond to the property type and interpolation method, which we will discuss shortly. Taking our rectangle from earlier, let's animate it so it moves in a straight line up and down. Figure 9-8 shows what each keyframe looks like.

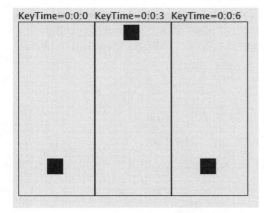

Figure 9-8. *Snapshots of the three keyframes for animating the rectangle*

The `DoubleAnimationUsingKeyFrames` class acts as a container for keyframes. There's one animation class per property type, as shown in Figure 9-2. `LinearDoubleKeyFrame` uses linear interpolation while it is active.

```
<Storyboard x:Name="rectAnimation">
    <DoubleAnimationUsingKeyFrames
            Storyboard.TargetName="rect"
            Storyboard.TargetProperty="(Canvas.Top)"
            RepeatBehavior="Forever">
        <LinearDoubleKeyFrame Value="240" KeyTime="0:0:0"/>
        <LinearDoubleKeyFrame Value="25" KeyTime="0:0:3"/>
        <LinearDoubleKeyFrame Value="240" KeyTime="0:0:6"/>
    </DoubleAnimationUsingKeyFrames>
</Storyboard>
```

Each keyframe specifies the value of the target property at the time specified in the KeyTime property. Since the KeyTime is 0:0:0 in the first keyframe, the target property is set to 240 when the animation begins. If a keyframe is not specified with a KeyTime of 0, the target property uses whatever its current value is, which might be the result of a previous animation or the property's local value.

Interpolation

Interpolation is the process of calculating the set of property values between two known values. As the timeline advances, the property changes to a value within this set. There are three types of interpolation available for use with keyframe animation: *linear*, *discrete*, and *spline*. The way interpolation works is by using a function that describes a line/curve from (0,0) to (1,1). Linear interpolation uses a diagonal line, as shown in Figure 9-9. If you think back to freshman-level calculus, you'll recall that the derivative of a function describes its rate of change. The linear interpolation function is $y = C \times f(x)$, where C is a constant and the derivative is a horizontal line, also shown in Figure 9-9. Unsurprisingly, this describes a constant rate of change. The coordinate space, although it runs from 0 to 1 in both axes, maps to any timeline/property value range. For example, if a timeline has a duration of 10 seconds, 5 seconds corresponds to x = 0.5 on the graph, and 10 seconds corresponds to 1. This coordinate space will be useful when we look at spline interpolation.

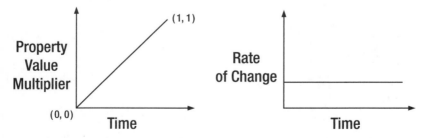

Figure 9-9. *Graph of linear interpolation and its rate of change*

You have already seen linear interpolation in action, since it is the only interpolation supported in from/to/by animations.

Discrete interpolation is even simpler than linear interpolation. The property value can have one of two values: its initial or its final value. As long as the current keyframe is active, the property has its initial value. The target property immediately changes to its final value when the end of the keyframe is reached. This might seem useless at first thought, since if a property can only assume one of two values, where's the animation? However, there are two main advantages to using discrete interpolation: it's a convenient way to hold a specific value for a length of time, and it's the only way to animate properties of types other than Point, double, and Color.

Let's use ObjectAnimationUsingKeyFrames to change an image used in an animation. This will change the Visibility property of two images to only show one image at a time. The two images are animated simultaneously to make it easy to switch between them simply by changing the Visibility.

```
<DoubleAnimationUsingKeyFrames
        Storyboard.TargetName="ballImageUp"
        Storyboard.TargetProperty="(Canvas.Top)">
    <LinearDoubleKeyFrame Value="300" KeyTime="0:0:0"/>
    <LinearDoubleKeyFrame Value="25" KeyTime="0:0:1"/>
    <LinearDoubleKeyFrame Value="300" KeyTime="0:0:2"/>
</DoubleAnimationUsingKeyFrames>
<DoubleAnimationUsingKeyFrames
        Storyboard.TargetName="ballImageDown"
        Storyboard.TargetProperty="(Canvas.Top)">
    <LinearDoubleKeyFrame Value="300" KeyTime="0:0:0"/>
    <LinearDoubleKeyFrame Value="25" KeyTime="0:0:1"/>
    <LinearDoubleKeyFrame Value="300" KeyTime="0:0:2"/>
</DoubleAnimationUsingKeyFrames>
<ObjectAnimationUsingKeyFrames
            Storyboard.TargetName="ballImageUp"
            Storyboard.TargetProperty="Visibility">
    <DiscreteObjectKeyFrame KeyTime="0:0:0">
        <DiscreteObjectKeyFrame.Value>
            <Visibility>Visible</Visibility>
        </DiscreteObjectKeyFrame.Value>
    </DiscreteObjectKeyFrame>
    <DiscreteObjectKeyFrame KeyTime="0:0:1">
        <DiscreteObjectKeyFrame.Value>
            <Visibility>Collapsed</Visibility>
        </DiscreteObjectKeyFrame.Value>
    </DiscreteObjectKeyFrame>
    <DiscreteObjectKeyFrame KeyTime="0:0:2">
        <DiscreteObjectKeyFrame.Value>
            <Visibility>Visible</Visibility>
        </DiscreteObjectKeyFrame.Value>
    </DiscreteObjectKeyFrame>
</ObjectAnimationUsingKeyFrames>
```

The animation for the other image is similar, but the Visibility values are opposite to those used in this XAML. The property element syntax for this keyframe's Value is used to animate different property types.

The final interpolation method is the most complex. Spline interpolation provides a mechanism to alter the rate at which the property value changes at different points during the time a keyframe is active. This means that Silverlight makes it easy to create some sophisticated animations, such as an object that starts out moving slowly and increases its speed over the length of the animation. Let's look at one example of modeling an object that changes its velocity over the course of its total movement. Imagine a single car in motion between two stoplights, as shown in Figure 9-10.

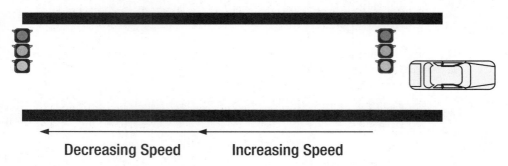

Figure 9-10. *Illustration of a car's acceleration and deceleration segments*

The car begins at a full stop and then the first light turns greens. The car's speed increases for a while, but as it approaches the second stoplight, the car must slow down before finally coming to a full stop again. The car's speed can be modeled using the Bezier curve shown in Figure 9-11.

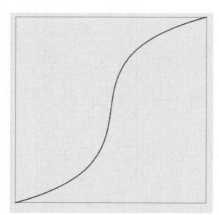

Figure 9-11. *Bezier curve describing the acceleration and deceleration of the car*

A Bezier curve is what the spline interpolation process uses to describe the varying rate of change. Keep in mind this curve describes the values of the property over time. Bezier curves were briefly mentioned in Chapter 7, but let's take a closer look at how they work so it's clear how spline interpolation can be used. The type of Bezier curve used by spline interpolation is a cubic Bezier with two control points, so the cubic Bezier curve is defined by four points, including the endpoints. If P1 and P4 are the endpoints, and P2 and P3 are the control points, the Bezier curve is a line that connects P1 to P4 but is pulled toward P2 and P3 in order to create the curve.

The control points are not necessarily touched by the curve. If you set P2 and P3 to points along the line from P1 to P4, such as setting them to (0.25,0.25) and (0.75,0.75), the Bezier curve is a straight line and the animation is effectively using linear interpolation.

The Bezier curve to model the car in Figure 9-11 used the control points (0.9,0.25) (0.1,0.75). The code in this chapter includes a plot of the Bezier curve along with our famous rectangle moving in a straight line (on top of a line that marks the full path of the rectangle). Figure 9-12 shows this curve and the rectangle in its starting position.

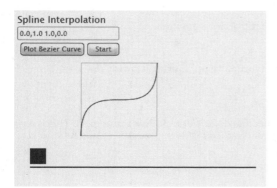

Figure 9-12. *Rectangle animated using spline interpolation, and the curve plotted*

You can divide this Bezier curve into two regions: the first curvy segment (from x = 0 to x = 0.5) and the second curvy segment (from x = 0.5 to x = 1). The first segment starts out with a subtle curve that corresponds to a slowly increasing rate of movement (it's not quite straight along a diagonal, so the rate is not constant). After the bend, the curve is quite steep up to the center point, corresponding to a fast rate of change. The second curvy segment is the mirror opposite of this: the movement continues quickly and suddenly starts slowing down before coming to a complete stop (when the final value of the property is reached).

If you want to figure out the curve that describes the animation you desire, you have several options. There are tools online that can assist, since Bezier curves are a popular approach to modeling animation. You can experiment using the code in this chapter (and possibly extending the code) by plugging in control points and using the Plot Bezier Curve button to preview the animation curve. You can also take out the trusty pen and paper and draw a curve that you think will work, roughly determine the control points, and then experiment. (The derivative for Bezier curves to show the rate of change, while interesting, is left as an exercise for the reader.)

Animation Easing

When it comes to using keyframe animations and attempting to define an interpolation function to model the effect you desire, you might spend a while getting it just right (unless you know the formula to use ahead of time). Silverlight 3 introduces a stock set of easing functions that control the change of property values over the duration of the animation. Two of these easing functions are bouncing and springing effects, and you can also define your own custom easing function with the use of the IEasingFunction interface. The full set of easing functions that come with Silverlight are shown in Table 9-4.

Table 9-4. *Stock Animation Easing Functions*

Easing Function	Description
BackEase	The property value is first "backed up" a little before animating to its end. For example, a property value animating from 10 to 90 might go from 10 to 5 first and then from 5 to 90. This function has one double property, Amplitude, that controls the animation.
BounceEase	The property bounces before stopping at its final value. The number of bounces is specified by the integer property Bounces.
CircleEase	Uses a circular function to control the animation.
CubicEase	Uses the function f(t) = t^3.
ElasticEase	Property oscillates back and forth as if on a spring, slowing down until it comes to rest.
ExponentialEase	Uses an exponential function.
PowerEase	Uses an arbitrary power (specified by the double Power property). This is a general form of the cubic, quadratic, quartic, and quintic easing functions.
QuadraticEase	Uses the function f(t) = t^2.
QuarticEase	Uses the function f(t) = t^4.
QuinticEase	Uses the function f(t) = t^5.
SineEase	Uses a sine formula.

The easing functions that come with Silverlight inherit from the base class EasingFunctionBase. This base class provides an additional property, EasingMode, that makes it easy to invert the easing function or to run it inverted for half the time and then normal for the other half. The EasingMode enums are as follows:

- EaseOut: This mode of interpolation follows 100 percent interpolation minus the output of the formula associated with the easing function.

- EaseIn: This mode of interpolation follows the mathematical formula associated with the easing function.

- EaseInOut: This mode of interpolation uses EaseIn for the first half of the animation and EaseOut for the second half.

Using an easing function in XAML starts with an Easing keyframe corresponding to the type you want to animate, such as EasingDoubleKeyFrame and EasingColorKeyFrame. Then the easing function is applied and the animation is ready to go. The following XAML animates a circle to make it appear to fall down and bounce repeatedly like a rubber ball:

```
<Storyboard x:Name="myStoryboard">
    <DoubleAnimationUsingKeyFrames x:Name="doubleAnimation"
        Storyboard.TargetProperty="(Canvas.Top)"
        Storyboard.TargetName="ball">
        <EasingDoubleKeyFrame Value="170" KeyTime="00:00:06">
            <EasingDoubleKeyFrame.EasingFunction>
```

```
            <BounceEase Bounces="5" EasingMode="EaseOut"/>
          </EasingDoubleKeyFrame.EasingFunction>
        </EasingDoubleKeyFrame>
    </DoubleAnimationUsingKeyFrames>
</Storyboard>
```

The EasingMode is set to EaseOut to cause the bounce to happen at the end of the animation. If this was set to EaseIn, the bounce would happen off the ceiling and then the ball would drop and come to rest.

Understanding Animation Easing Functions

Each animation easing function, unsurprisingly, has a mathematical function behind it. Functions for bouncing, elasticity, etc. are more complicated, so let's take a closer look at one of the mathematically simpler easing functions. The quadratic easing function uses the formula $f(t) = t^2$ where t is the time. Figure 9-13 shows what this looks like visually.

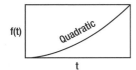

Figure 9-13. *Plot of the quadratic formula*

Easing functions use normalized time, so the beginning of the animation is always at time = 0 and the end is time = 1. The output of this function is the progress of the animation. Let's animate a Canvas.Top that starts at 0 and ends at 100 (to keep the math simple). The values for this property, sampled every 0.1 seconds, are shown in Table 9-5.

Table 9-5. *Animation Progress Every 0.1 Seconds Using Quadratic Easing*

Normalized Time	Quadratic Animation Progress	Property Value
0	0	0
0.1	0.01	1
0.2	0.04	4
0.3	0.09	9
0.4	0.16	16
0.5	0.25	25
0.6	0.36	36
0.7	0.49	49
0.8	0.64	64
0.9	0.81	81
1	1	100

The third column is arrived at using the formula shown in Figure 9-14. $V_{initial}$ is the initial value of the property and V_{final} is the final value.

$$V_{initial} + f(t) * (V_{final} - V_{initial})$$

Figure 9-14. *Formula used with easing function to get property value*

Ease-out and ease-in/out are manipulations of the core easing function and thus can be derived from the ease-in function. Easing out inverts both the domain and the range, as shown in Figure 9-15. Easing in and out is an ease-in for half the time of the animation followed by an ease-out, forming one continuous function. It is described by the function shown in Figure 9-16.

$$1.0 - f(1 - t)$$

Figure 9-15. *Formula used to modify easing function to ease out*

For t=0 to 0.5:
$$f(t*2) / 2$$

For t=0.5 to 1:
$$0.5 + (1 - f(2-2*t)) / 2$$

Figure 9-16. *Formula used to modify easing function to ease in then ease out*

If you want to create your own easing function, all you need to do is implement the IEasingFunction interface. This interface defines a single method, Ease, that takes the normalized time as a double and returns the progress of the animation as a double. This is precisely where you define your own f(t). Since the ease out and ease-in/out variants are provided by a separate class (EasingFunctionBase), implementing directly from the IEasingFunction interface allows you only a single easing. This should be fine, though, since your own easing function only needs a single implementation. If you need more capability, you can define your own properties and even your own implementation of the EasingMode property.

Animating with Expression Blend

Expression Blend makes it easy to create animation using its built-in timeline editor. You may have noticed the Timeline part of the Objects and Timeline section, and now you know exactly what it means.

In Expression Blend, let's animate another rectangle. Create a new UserControl and place a rectangle on the design surface. Next, click the plus sign next to the "(No Storyboard open)" text, as shown in Figure 9-17.

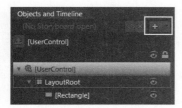

Figure 9-17. *The Objects and Timeline pane in Expression Blend*

Once you click the plus sign, a dialog appears asking for a name for the storyboard. Give it the name rectangleAnimation. The user interface will change in several ways. First, a red outline will surround the design surface and the text "Timeline recording is on" will appear. Next, the timeline editor will open, as shown in Figure 9-18.

Figure 9-18. *The timeline editor in Expression Blend*

The reason the object hierarchy and timeline editing are combined within the same pane is because each object has a corresponding line in the timeline. The control bar at the top of the timeline editor has buttons to change the current frame to the first frame, the previous frame, the next frame, or the last frame. The center button is the play button and runs the animation on the design surface. The only type of animation Expression Blend supports is keyframe, which is reflected in the organization of the timeline editor. The default interpolation used is spline, with the default control points set to effectively create linear interpolation.

Make sure the rectangle object is highlighted in gray in the object hierarchy, and then click the small green plus button next to the time signature. This creates a keyframe with the rectangle in its current position at time 0:0:0. A small white oval appears under the 0-second vertical, showing that a keyframe exists at this time for the corresponding object. Next, click the 1 on top of the timeline's 1-second vertical. This moves the yellow marker to the 1-second line. Next, after ensuring that the rectangle is currently highlighted on the design surface, hold down the Shift key and press the right arrow key to move the rectangle quickly along a straight horizontal line. Stop somewhere close to the right edge of the design surface. As soon as you start moving the rectangle, a new keyframe is created at the 1-second line, shown with another gray oval. The keyframe's target property is set to whatever value corresponds to where you complete the movement. Figure 9-19 shows what the timeline looks like after moving the rectangle to a new position at the 1-second mark.

Figure 9-19. *The timeline editor with a keyframe recorded at the 0- and 1-second marks*

Look at the XAML, and notice that the rectangle contains empty versions of the four transforms that Silverlight provides:

```
<Grid x:Name="LayoutRoot" Background="White" >
    <Rectangle Height="80" HorizontalAlignment="Left" Margin="62,0,0,82"
            VerticalAlignment="Bottom" Width="80"
            Fill="#FF000000" Stroke="#FF000000"
            x:Name="rectangle" RenderTransformOrigin="0.5,0.5">
        <Rectangle.RenderTransform>
            <TransformGroup>
                <ScaleTransform/>
                <SkewTransform/>
                <RotateTransform/>
                <TranslateTransform/>
            </TransformGroup>
        </Rectangle.RenderTransform>
    </Rectangle>
</Grid>
```

An empty transform has its default values, which effectively do nothing to the object being
transformed. This makes it easy for the animation to affect a specific transform, such as this
example does to the X property of the TranslateTransform:

```
<Storyboard x:Name="rectangleAnimation">
    <DoubleAnimationUsingKeyFrames BeginTime="00:00:00"
                                    Storyboard.TargetName="rectangle"
                                    Storyboard.TargetProperty=
                "(UIElement.RenderTransform).(TransformGroup.Children)[3].
                                            (TranslateTransform.X)">
        <EasingDoubleKeyFrame KeyTime="00:00:00" Value="0"/>
        <EasingDoubleKeyFrame KeyTime="00:00:01" Value="320"/>
    </DoubleAnimationUsingKeyFrames>
</Storyboard>
```

You can change the interpolation for a specific keyframe in two ways. The first is by right-
clicking the gray oval for a keyframe and changing the ease-in or ease-out value. The ease-in
percentage controls how the property value changes as time advances toward the selected
keyframe. The higher the ease-in value, the faster this keyframe is approached the closer time
gets to it. The ease-out functionality is similar, except it controls how the property value changes as

time advances away from the current keyframe. The ease-in and ease-out percentages alter the control points for the KeySpline, for which Expression Blend offers a full-blown editor if you click the Properties tab while a keyframe is selected. The KeySpline editor is shown in Figure 9-20.

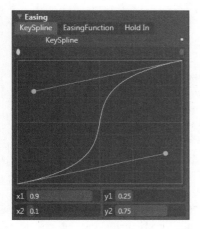

Figure 9-20. *The KeySpline editor in Expression Blend*

The yellow dots correspond to the control points, which are set to the control points used earlier in the car example. You can click and drag these yellow dots, or change the points by using the sliders or entering the numbers by hand after clicking one of the sliders. This editor is likely the best option for exploring KeySplines and discovering which control points will accomplish what you are aiming for.

If you want to change the repeat count of the animation, you need to drill down into the specific target property being animated. You can do this when in timeline recording mode by repeatedly clicking the arrow button on the left of each object until you arrive at a series of highlighted objects, as shown in Figure 9-21.

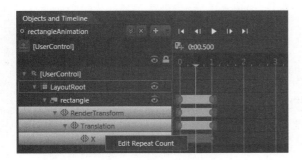

Figure 9-21. *Right-clicking the drilled-down object to modify the repeat count*

Figure 9-21 also shows the context menu when you right-click the target property (X in this case). This context menu also appears if you right-click the time span for the X property. When you select the Edit Repeat Count option, the Edit Repeat dialog appears, as shown in Figure 9-22.

Figure 9-22. *Setting the repeat count using Expression Blend*

You can set a repeat count or click the infinity sign to the right of the text entry to set the repeat count to forever. Expression Blend provides other capabilities as well, such as creating a motion path and converting it to a timeline, and manipulating keyframes in a variety of ways. This section has introduced what Expression Blend can do to make creating animations easier for you.

3D Animation

Perspective Transforms in Silverlight 3 that we just learned in Chapter 7 is the next step towards developing 3D Silverlight RIAs. In previous versions of Silverlight, transforms were processed in the X and Y axes using the UIElement's RenderTransform property. Silverlight 3 uses the PlaneProjection class to render 3D-like effects. All elements that derive from UIElement have the Projection property, which allows the element to simulate transformation in a 3D space. In the following XAML code, we have a simple example of a rotating image using PlaneProjection that simulates 3D-like animation:

```
<Grid x:Name="LayoutRoot" Background="Black">
   <Grid.Resources>
      <Storyboard x:Name="Rotate" >
         <DoubleAnimation
            From="0" To="360" Storyboard.TargetName="p1"
            Storyboard.TargetProperty="RotationY"
            RepeatBehavior="Forever" Duration="0:0:5">
         </DoubleAnimation>
      </Storyboard>
   </Grid.Resources>
   <Image x:Name="image1" Source="CD.png" Stretch="None">
      <Image.Projection>
         <PlaneProjection x:Name="p1"/>
      </Image.Projection>
   </Image>
</Grid>
```

In the previous XAML code, I have defined the Storyboard "Rotate" with DoubleAnimation having its RepeatBehavior set to Forever. The only image control image1 has is its Projection property set to PlaneProjection name p1.

In the code-behind, we need to start the storyboard in the Loaded event of the user control, as follows:

```
Rotate.Begin();
```

Run the project and you should see a continuously rotating compact disc in 3D space. The Figure 9-23 shows two positions of the rotating disc.

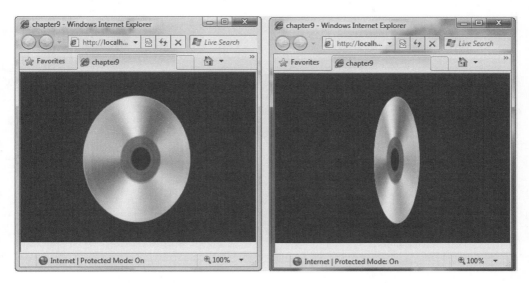

Figure 9-23. *An example of 3D animation: rotating compact disc in 3D space*

Summary

This chapter covered the animation support that comes with Silverlight. Timelines are central to the animation support, and the Timeline class provides several properties to control how time advances, possibly repeating or even reversing. The simplest form of animation is the from/to/by type, and several applications of it were demonstrated. Next, you learned about the most powerful animation support in Silverlight: keyframe animation. This provides the capability to alter how property values change by supporting different interpolation methods—specifically linear, discrete, and spline. The keyframe animation also supports modifying properties of types other than double, Point, and Color. Finally, you got a taste of the animation support built into Expression Blend, an invaluable tool for working with animation in both WPF and Silverlight, along with the newly introduced animation feature—3D animation in Silverlight 3.

In the next chapter, we will look at Silverlight support for dynamic languages such as IronRuby and IronPython.

CHAPTER 10

■■■

Dynamic Languages and the Browser

One major feature that Silverlight has that .NET doesn't is a second runtime engine designed to execute dynamic languages. A dynamic language is interpreted at runtime, meaning it is possible to add new code while a program is executing. The dynamic language you are likely most familiar with is JScript. Silverlight has direct support for both JScript and Managed JScript—which is JScript executing on the Dynamic Language Runtime (DLR). Two other dynamic languages are supported: Ruby and Python (called IronRuby and IronPython in the Silverlight/.NET world). This chapter will introduce these dynamic languages, discuss why the DLR is important in the Silverlight picture, and show how to go about using these languages. The latter part of this chapter will discuss the integration of Silverlight with the browser.

Introducing Dynamic Languages for Silverlight

One of the most technically appealing aspects of the .NET platform on Windows is that it supports a wide variety of languages due to how the Common Language Runtime (CLR) is designed. Despite the many languages .NET supports, one set of languages that aren't as well supported as they could be are dynamic languages such as Python and Ruby. This lack of support is based largely on the fact that dynamic languages are not compiled, and for a high-level language to execute on the CLR, it must be translated into Intermediate Language (IL). This is a technical hurdle that can be overcome, however. While there is an implementation of Python for .NET, known as IronPython, the most interesting work being done around dynamic languages and .NET is focused on Silverlight.

Dynamic languages are interpreted (eliminating the compilation step) and are usually dynamically typed. What this means, essentially, is you never declare variables of particular types. Everything is handled by the runtime through the context of expressions. The languages you are likely most familiar with are C# and VB .NET, which are both statically typed languages. Dynamic languages have many proponents since both development and deployment can be greatly simplified over languages such as C# that require compilation and distribution of output. A certain amount of trust is placed in the runtime that fans of statically typed languages can be resistant to granting. While you do lose type safety with dynamic languages, this can be nearly completely mitigated with a strong set of unit tests.

Both statically typed and dynamic languages have their fans. The great thing about the CLR (and now the DLR, working with the CLR) is that you have a large degree of freedom in language choice when programming on .NET and Silverlight. All the functionality exposed by the various platform assemblies in Silverlight can be accessed from dynamic languages, so you can write Silverlight applications completely in IronRuby, IronPython, or JScript (and potentially others in the future, such as Smalltalk).

One significant feature of most dynamic languages is that functions are first-class citizens. You can create a function and assign it to a variable or pass it as a parameter to another function. This makes things like closures and passing functions as parameters a lot easier. In general, two defining characteristics of closures are your ability to assign a block of code (a function) to a variable, and this block of code's ability to retain access to variables that were accessible where it was created. If you were to write a method in C# to obtain a subset of a list of words that matches a certain criterion, such as maximum length, the method might look like this:

```
public static List<string> ShortWords(List<string> wordList)
{
   List<string> shortWordList = new List<string>();
   int maximumWordLength = 3;
   foreach(string word in wordList)
   {
      if(word.Length <= maximumWordLength)
      {
         shortWordList.Add(word);
      }
   }
   return(shortWordList);
}
```

Implementing the same method in a dynamic language, such as IronRuby (an implementation of Ruby for the DLR) would be significantly shorter:

```
def ShortWords(wordList)
  maximumWordLength = 3
  return wordList.select {|w| w.Length <= maximumWordLength}
end
```

Just comparing these two implementations of the same algorithm reveals much about IronRuby (and dynamic languages in general, by extension). The IronRuby code is much more concise, and nowhere do you see a data type keyword such as string or int. However, the most interesting aspect of this block of IronRuby code is the closure, located between the curly braces. What's going on here is that the closure, essentially a function, is being passed to the select method. The select method uses a closure to extract a subset of a collection. The code that forms the closure actually executes within the select method (here, the closure extracts strings within the collection wordList that meet the criterion), but it retains access to the variables in its original scope (in this case, the maximumWordLength variable). Closures are much more powerful than this simple example illustrates. This is similar to passing a delegate to a method such as Exists or Find in C#, but closures bring the added benefit of retaining access to their original scope.

Dynamic Language Runtime (DLR) for Silverlight

Dynamic languages in Silverlight are facilitated by the DLR. The DLR is actually a set of .NET Framework libraries for Silverlight that creates a bridge between dynamic languages and the CoreCLR in Silverlight. One of the benefits of code running on a managed platform such as Silverlight is that types can typically be discovered at runtime using reflection. The DLR helps facilitate this discovery so that code written in a dynamic language can perform well.

Silverlight Dynamic Languages SDK

The Silverlight Dynamic Languages (SDL) SDK enables integration between Silverlight and dynamic languages, running on the DLR. The SDL SDK supports IronPython and IronRuby dynamic languages. The latest version of the SDL SDK, version 0.5, which supports Silverlight 2 and Silverlight 3 Beta, was released during MIX09.

The best way to get started with dynamic applications and Silverlight is by going to `www.codeplex.com/sdlsdk` and downloading the SDL SDK ZIP file (`agdlr-0.5.0` for Silverlight 2). For Silverlight 3 Beta, you also need to download the `agdlr-0.5.0.sl3b` ZIP file. After you download both, copy all the files available under the `bin` folder for the Silverlight 3 Beta package and paste them into the `bin` folder of the Silverlight 2 SDK to overwrite what's there. As described on Jimmy Schementi's blog (`http://blog.jimmy.schementi.com/2009/03/silverlight-dynamic-languages-sdk-05.html`), the binaries for Silverlight 3 are slightly different than those for Silverlight 2 (however, Silverlight 2 binaries will work fine on Silverlight 3 Beta). The key difference is that the Silverlight 3 binaries use the Silverlight Transparent Platform Extension feature to download the DLR assemblies on demand, significantly reducing the size of an IronRuby or IronPython Silverlight application. Continue to visit Jimmy's blog to get more insight on this enhancement.

Along with samples, documentation, and utilities, this SDK contains the following key components:

Scripting assemblies: Four assemblies provide the runtime scripting environment that forms the core bridge between Silverlight and dynamic languages in general. They are `Microsoft.Scripting.Core.dll`, `Microsoft.Scripting.dll`, `Microsoft.Scripting.ExtensionAttribute.dll`, and `Microsoft.Scripting.Silverlight.dll`.

Assemblies specific to a dynamic language: Each dynamic language (IronPython and IronRuby) has two assemblies that support the specific language, providing capabilities such as parsing the language and communicating with the host environment. They are `IronPython.dll` and `IronPython.Modules.dll` for IronPython, and `IronRuby.dll` and `IronRuby.Libraries.dll` for IronRuby.

`Chiron.exe`: Chiron provides a development environment using the local file system, dynamically packages applications, and executes dynamically within the development local web server.

Application templates: Each dynamic language contained in the SDK (IronPython and IronRuby) has a minimal set of files that you can copy and modify to create your own application.

The DynamicApplication Class

The `Microsoft.Scripting.Silverlight.dll` scripting assembly contains a set of classes that enable developers to develop Silverlight applications in dynamic languages. One of the key classes is the `DynamicApplication` class, which inherits directly from `System.Windows.Application`. It represents the Silverlight-based dynamic application object by providing access to visual elements from the dynamic language code and also an entry point for dynamic language applications to host on Silverlight hosts. Table 10-1 shows the properties this class provides, extending those already provided by `Application`.

Table 10-1. *Properties of Microsoft.Scripting.Silverlight.DynamicApplication*

Property	Type	Description
Current	static DynamicApplication	The `DynamicApplication` instance for the current application.
Debug	bool	`true` if debugging features are enabled. When debugging is enabled, emitted code is suitable for debugging (it's not optimized) and error reporting is enabled. You can enable debugging by specifying `debug=true` in the `initParams` parameter in the `object` tag for the application in the HTML.
EntryPoint	string	Gets the name of the code file that contains the application's entry point.
Environment	ScriptRuntime	Gets an instance of `ScriptRuntime` that represents the environment under which the application is executing.
ErrorTargetID	string	The ID of the HTML element where errors/debugging information will be displayed when `Debug=true` or `ReportUnhandledErrors=true`.
ReportUnhandledErrors	bool	When `true`, unhandled exceptions are displayed in the HTML element specified by `ErrorTargetID`. Otherwise, errors are sent to the JScript function specified in the `onerror` property of the `object` tag for the Silverlight application.

This class operates just like the `Application` class in other Silverlight applications, but provides the extra functionality that dynamic applications need.

Key Files for Silverlight Applications Using IronRuby Dynamic Language

As mentioned earlier, the SDL SDK provides application templates, a set of key files to create Silverlight applications using the dynamic languages IronRuby and IronPython. The templates are available under the `script\templates\ruby` and `script\templates\python` directories for the IronRuby and IronPython dynamic languages.

Let's take a look at the key application files for IronRuby, available as part of the SDL SDK application template. After you extract the SDL SDK, the `script\templates\ruby` directory contains the following directories and files:

```
index.html
app\app.rb
app\app.xaml
css\screen.css
js\error.js
```

The index.html File

The `index.html` file contains a large amount of comments that can help guide you (for the sake of space, the entire file won't be reproduced here). The `object` tag contains the name of the XAP file for the Silverlight application (the XAP file contains everything in the `ruby` directory from the preceding directory listing). Here's an abbreviated version of the `object` tag from this file:

```
<object data="data:application/x-silverlight,"
        type="application/x-silverlight-2 " width="100%" height="100%">
    <!--
      "source" points to the actual Silverlight application
      If using "Chiron /w", value should be the "<your app folder>.xap"
    -->
    <param name="source" value="app.xap"/>

    <!--
      "initParams" is a comma-seperated way to pass key=value pair arguments
      into your Silverlight application. Dynamic Languages use special
      arguments to configure the application:

      * start = app.(rb|py|js)
        - this is the entry-point file to the application.
        - By default, it will look for any file named "app", regardless of
          the extension. The extension will be used to figure out the language.
        - This option can be set to anything you want, but it must include
          the extension.

      * debug = [true]|false
        - Runs your code as debug-able; stack traces will be shown if an error
          occurs.
        - This lets you attach the browser to the Visual Studio
          debugger and step through the running program (only when the
          Silverlight tools are installed).
        - When omitted/set to false, all errors will be silent
          (for deployment purposes)
```

```
    * reportErrors = [HTML-element-ID]
      - In the event of an error, the error window will be written into the
        innerHTML property of the HTML element with an ID attribute matching
        the value of this field.
      - If there is no matching ID, an HTML element is created with that ID,
        and the error window inserted.
      - If this field is omitted, no errors will be shown.
        + You can define the "onerror" param, which will let you handle any
          error with JavaScript (the index.html templates do this, if you
          want sample code).
      - This just causes HTML to be generated in the HTML element; the styling
        of the error window is defined in a separate error.css file that must
        be included in the page.

    * exceptionDetail = true|[false]
      - If set to true, this will also show the entire managed stack trace
        in the error window rather than just the dynamic stack trace.
        This is useful when debugging C#/Visual Basic when called from a
        dynamic language.

    * console = true|[false]
      - If set to true, will show a read-eval-print loop (REPL) window at
        the bottom of the page, for whatever language the start script is in.
-->
<param name="initParams" value="debug=true,
    reportErrors=errorLocation, console=true" />

<!-- Handle all Silverlight errors with function defined in
    javascripts/error.js -->
<param name="onerror" value="onSilverlightError" />

<!--
  Other properties of the Silverlight plug-in. For documentation on this, see:
  http://msdn.microsoft.com/
    en-us/library/cc189089(VS.95).aspx
    #silverlight_plug_in_configuring
-->
<param name="background" value="white" />
<param name="windowless" value="true" />

<!--
  <param name="minRuntimeVersion" value="2.0.31005.0" />
<param name="autoUpgrade" value="true" />
-->
```

```
<!--
  Shows a "Install Microsoft Silverlight" link if Silverlight is
  not installed
-->
<a href="http://go.microsoft.com/fwlink/?LinkID=124807"
   style="text-decoration: none;">
  <img src="http://go.microsoft.com/fwlink/?LinkId=108181"
       alt="Get Microsoft Silverlight"
       style="border-style: none"/>
</a>
</object>
```

The `reportErrors` parameter (in the `initParams` parameter of the `object` tag) specifies the HTML element to display debugging information and errors. Creating a space for this information is as simple as creating an empty `div`. The error information will be placed into the `innerHTML` property of the HTML element.

```
<div id='errorLocation'></div>
```

If you turn debugging off and don't specify the `reportErrors` parameter, unhandled exceptions will be handled normally and will propagate to the JScript error handler specified in the `onerror` parameter. This handler is located in the `js\error.js` file that is part of the IronRuby template. This handler is essentially the same JScript that is generated when you create a new (nondynamic) Silverlight application in Visual Studio, but you're free to change this to handle errors however you want within the browser.

The app.xaml File

The two most important files that make up the application are the `app.xaml` and `app.rb` files.

The `app.xaml` file that comes with the SDL SDK just contains a TextBox.

```
<UserControl x:Class="System.Windows.Controls.UserControl"
    xmlns="http://schemas.microsoft.com/client/2007"
    xmlns:x="http://schemas.microsoft.com/winfx/2006/xaml">
  <Grid x:Name="layout_root" Background="White">
    <TextBlock x:Name="message" FontSize="30" />
  </Grid>
</UserControl>
```

The app.rb File

The `app.rb` file loads the XAML stored in `app.xaml`:

```
include System::Windows
include System::Windows::Controls
class App
```

```ruby
  def initialize
    @root = Application.current.load_root_
        visual(UserControl.new, "app.xaml")
    @root.find_name('message').text =
        "Welcome to Ruby and Silverlight!"
  end
end
$app = App.new
```

The final line of the app.rb file creates the instance of the application and thus the application itself.

Similarly, the key application files for IronPython available as part of the SDL SDK application template are available under the script\templates\python directory containing the following subdirectories and files:

```
index.html
app\app.py
app\app.xaml
css\screen.css
js\error.js
```

Creating a Starter IronRuby-based Silverlight Project

By visiting the script directory of the SDL SDK, you can execute the sl.bat file to create a starter to an IronRuby dynamic Silverlight project based on one of the available templates.

Execute the following command to create a starter IronRuby dynamic language-based Silverlight project with the name testapp:

```
C:\book\examples\agdlr-0.5.0\scriptscript>sl.bat ruby testapp
5 File(s) copied
Your ruby Silverlight application was created in testapp\.
```

The newly created testapp directory will include a folder structure and files similar to those available in the IronRuby templates:

```
index.html
app\app.rb
app\app.xaml
css\screen.css
js\error.js
```

Executing a Dynamic Language Silverlight Application Using Chiron.exe

Now that you have a starter application, you can execute it by making use of the `Chiron.exe` tool that comes with the SDL SDK. This tool provides two main functions: it dynamically packages a set of files into a XAP, and it executes dynamic language applications by providing a development environment and running within the local web server. One of the interesting features of `Chiron.exe` is that any time you modify a file within the application directory, `Chiron.exe` will repackage the application into a XAP and reload it. You must still refresh the browser if there is an active browser, though. The full list of command-line options for `Chiron.exe` is shown in Figure 10-1.

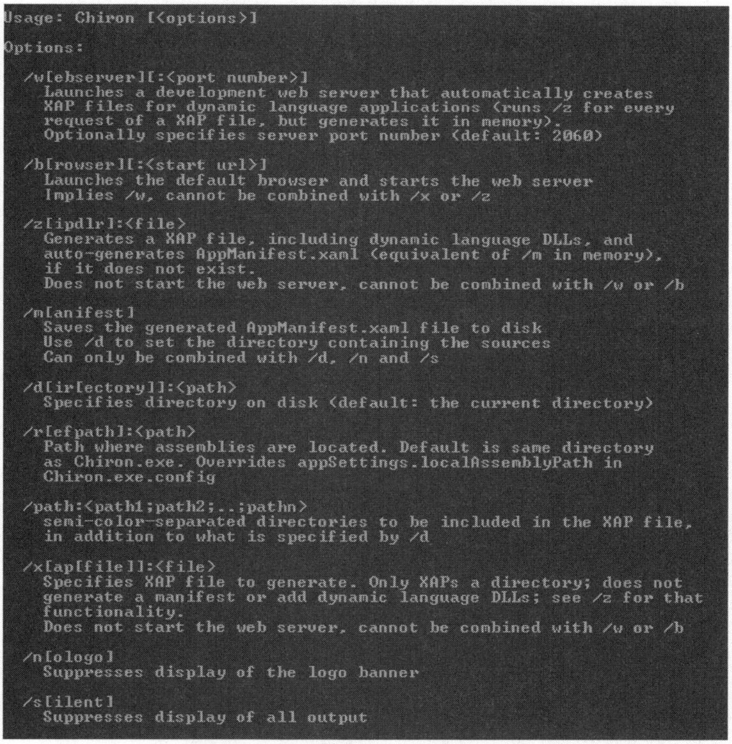

```
Usage: Chiron [<options>]

Options:

  /w[ebserver][:<port number>]
    Launches a development web server that automatically creates
    XAP files for dynamic language applications (runs /z for every
    request of a XAP file, but generates it in memory).
    Optionally specifies server port number (default: 2060)

  /b[rowser][:<start url>]
    Launches the default browser and starts the web server
    Implies /w, cannot be combined with /x or /z

  /z[ipdlr]:<file>
    Generates a XAP file, including dynamic language DLLs, and
    auto-generates AppManifest.xaml (equivalent of /m in memory),
    if it does not exist.
    Does not start the web server, cannot be combined with /w or /b

  /m[anifest]
    Saves the generated AppManifest.xaml file to disk
    Use /d to set the directory containing the sources
    Can only be combined with /d, /n and /s

  /d[ir[ectory]]:<path>
    Specifies directory on disk (default: the current directory)

  /r[efpath]:<path>
    Path where assemblies are located. Default is same directory
    as Chiron.exe. Overrides appSettings.localAssemblyPath in
    Chiron.exe.config

  /path:<path1;path2;..;pathn>
    semi-color-separated directories to be included in the XAP file,
    in addition to what is specified by /d

  /x[ap[file]]:<file>
    Specifies XAP file to generate. Only XAPs a directory; does not
    generate a manifest or add dynamic language DLLs; see /z for that
    functionality.
    Does not start the web server, cannot be combined with /w or /b

  /n[ologo]
    Suppresses display of the logo banner

  /s[ilent]
    Suppresses display of all output
```

Figure 10-1. *Command-line options for Chiron.exe*

After creating `testapp` as shown previously, you can execute it by passing the directory name to `Chiron.exe` and ensuring that a browser automatically opens by using the `/b` command-line option. The current directory's content will be listed, as shown in Figure 10-2.

```
C:\book\examples\agdlr-0.5.0\script>chiron /d:testapp /b
```

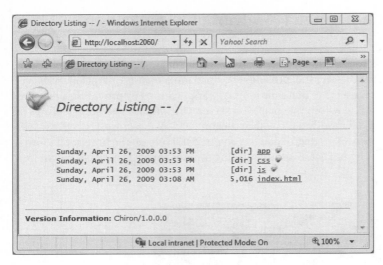

Figure 10-2. *Running the IronRuby test application using the Chiron.exe utility*

Now if you click the index.html file, notice that the app.xap file is also created and listed on the command shell, which is rather large (more than 1MB), as shown in Figure 10-3. This is because the IronRuby-specific assemblies must be included in the XAP, since they are not part of Silverlight. This is the price you pay for using a dynamic language, since the objective is to keep the Silverlight client installation as small as possible. However, you will use this package file for distribution/deployment and thus allow dynamic languages to evolve independently from the Silverlight client.

```
C:\Windows\system32\cmd.exe - chiron  /d:C:\book\examples\agdlr-0.5.0\script\testapp /b

C:\book\examples\agdlr-0.5.0\bin>chiron /d:C:\book\examples\agdlr-0.5.0\script\t
estapp /b
Microsoft(R) Silverlight(TM) Development Utility. Version 1.0.0.0
Copyright (c) Microsoft Corporation.  All rights reserved.

Chiron serving 'C:\book\examples\agdlr-0.5.0\script\testapp' as http://localhost
:2060/
23:16:09 200     1,425 /
23:16:10 200       848 /style.css↑
23:16:10 200     2,548 /sl.png↑
23:16:10 200       698 /slx.png↑
23:16:12 200     5,214 /index.html
23:16:12 200     1,305 /js/error.js
23:16:12 200       394 /css/screen.css
23:16:14 200 1,256,724 /app.xap
```

Figure 10-3. *The Silverlight XAP file package is created dynamically.*

If you look at the browser, you should see the dynamic Silverlight application in action, as shown in Figure 10-4.

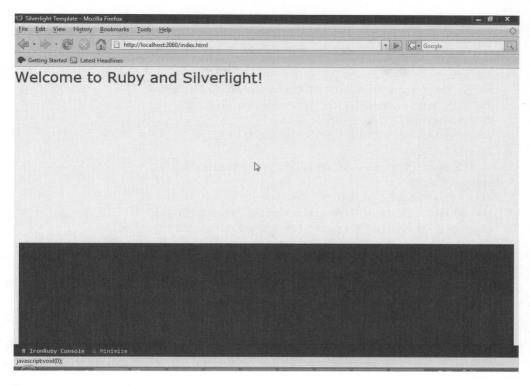

Figure 10-4. *Running the dynamic Silverlight application*

To look at the contents of the created XAP file, browse to `http://localhost:2060/app.xap`, as shown in Figure 10-5.

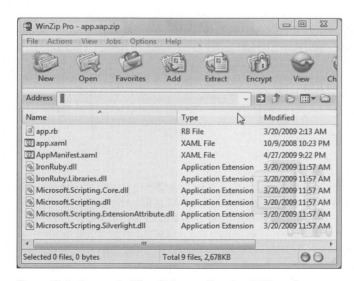

Figure 10-5. *Dynamic Silverlight application XAP package content*

You can save the ZIP file to your local disk and open the `AppMainifest.xaml` file. As you can see in the following code, the application manifest includes four Silverlight scripting library assemblies and dynamic language Ruby-specific library assemblies:

```
<Deployment
    xmlns="http://schemas.microsoft.com/client/2007/deployment"
    xmlns:x="http://schemas.microsoft.com/winfx/2006/xaml"
    RuntimeVersion="2.0.31005.0"
    EntryPointAssembly="Microsoft.Scripting.Silverlight"
    EntryPointType=
        "Microsoft.Scripting.Silverlight.DynamicApplication">
  <Deployment.Parts>
    <!-- Add additional assemblies here -->
    <AssemblyPart Source="Microsoft.Scripting.Silverlight.dll" />
    <AssemblyPart Source="Microsoft.Scripting.ExtensionAttribute.dll"
    />
    <AssemblyPart Source="Microsoft.Scripting.Core.dll" />
    <AssemblyPart Source="Microsoft.Scripting.dll" />
    <AssemblyPart Source="IronRuby.dll" />
    <AssemblyPart Source="IronRuby.Libraries.dll" />
  </Deployment.Parts>
</Deployment>
```

If you pass the `/w` instead of the `/b` switch, it will just start the server and not launch your browser.

Referencing Additional Assemblies

Each dynamic language has its own syntax. IronPython and IronRuby closely follow their parent language's syntax, and Managed JScript also is close to its parent language, JScript. Each language must support several Silverlight-specific features, such as referencing assemblies.

As mentioned earlier, the following four Silverlight Scripting assemblies are automatically available to dynamic languages (i.e., you don't need to add a reference to them). These assemblies are as follows:

- `Microsoft.Scripting.Silverlight.dll`

- `Microsoft.Scripting.ExtensionAttribute.dll`

- `Microsoft.Scripting.Core.dll`

- `Microsoft.Scripting.dll`

If you want to use classes in any assembly not listed, you must first include this assembly in the manifest file (and thus the XAP file) unless it is already part of the Silverlight runtime (in which case, you need only mimic the behavior of the `using` keyword in C#—which we'll examine next). You can use the `/m` option of `Chiron.exe` to generate the default manifest and modify it, and then use `Chiron.exe` to repackage it by regenerating the XAP file using the `/z` option. For example, if you want to add an assembly that contains a service proxy, you can invoke `Chiron.exe` as shown here, combining the /m and the /d option with the directory name testapp that contains the dynamic application:

```
C:\book\examples\agdlr-0.5.0\script>chiron /m /d:testapp
Microsoft(R) Silverlight(TM) Development Utility. Version 1.0.0.0
Copyright (c) Microsoft Corporation.  All rights reserved.
```

There is no other output to confirm that the manifest has been saved to disk, but you should now see an AppManifest.xaml file in the testapp directory, as shown in the following code, which is similar to what we mentioned in the "Executing a Dynamic Silverlight Application Using Chiron.exe" section:

```
<Deployment
    xmlns="http://schemas.microsoft.com/client/2007/deployment"
    xmlns:x="http://schemas.microsoft.com/winfx/2006/xaml"
    RuntimeVersion="2.0.31005.0"
    EntryPointAssembly="Microsoft.Scripting.Silverlight"
    EntryPointType="Microsoft.Scripting.Silverlight.DynamicApplication"
    >
  <Deployment.Parts>
    <!-- Add additional assemblies here -->
    <AssemblyPart Source="Microsoft.Scripting.Silverlight.dll" />
    <AssemblyPart
        Source="Microsoft.Scripting.ExtensionAttribute.dll"/>
    <AssemblyPart Source="Microsoft.Scripting.Core.dll" />
    <AssemblyPart Source="Microsoft.Scripting.dll" />
    <AssemblyPart Source="IronRuby.dll" />
    <AssemblyPart Source="IronRuby.Libraries.dll" />
  </Deployment.Parts>
</Deployment>
```

This manifest file also includes the reference to the DynamicApplication class, specifying the class that serves as the entry point for the dynamic application, much like Application does in the other Silverlight applications. If you add another assembly to this manifest, you then repackage the application with the /z option (to include the dynamic language assemblies in the XAP):

```
C:\book\examples\agdlr-0.5.0\script>chiron /d:testapp /z:app.xap
Microsoft(R) Silverlight(TM) Development Utility. Version 1.0.0.0
Copyright (c) Microsoft Corporation.  All rights reserved.
Generating XAP C:\book\examples\agdlr-0.5.0\script\testapp
\app.xap from C:\book\examples\agdlr-0.5.0\script\testapp
```

Once you have a new assembly in the XAP, you must add a reference to it (within a dynamic language source file, since no compilation step is involved with dynamic language applications) and import any classes/namespaces, much like the using keyword in C#. Let's take a look at how it can be achieved for the three dynamic languages that come with the SDL SDK. The following is the IronPython version:

```
import clr
clr.AddReference("Assembly Name, Version=2.0.31005.0,
        Culture=neutral, PublicKeyToken=abc012512def25a7")
import System.Windows # this makes the System.Windows namespace visible
# don't need previous line to do the following
from System.Windows.Controls import UserControl
```

Next is the IronRuby version:

```
require AssemblyName
include System.Windows.Controls
```

And finally the Managed JScript version:

```
AddReference("Assembly Name, Version=2.0.31005.0,
        Culture=neutral, PublicKeyToken=abc012512def25a7")
Import("System.Windows.Controls") // makes namespace visible
// makes the UserControl type available
Import("System.Windows.Controls.UserControl")
```

Creating a Silverlight Animation Application Using IronPython

Let's look briefly at a Silverlight animation application implementation with the use of the IronPython dynamic language (Figure 10-6).

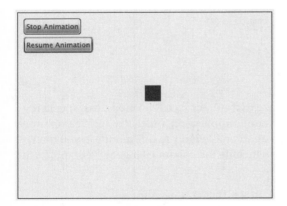

Figure 10-6. *Silverlight animation application implemented using IronPython*

To build this application, first create an `animation` folder and an `app` subfolder. Now we need to generate first the XAML file, then the IronPython as an application file, and last the `index.html` file to host the Silverlight application.

Define the app.xaml File

The XAML for the dynamic language Silverlight application (`app.xaml`) to create two buttons and a rectangle to generate the animation effect is the same as for the regular Silverlight application, as shown in the following code. The key difference is, you need to define the `x:Class` attribute with the class of the control. Here, for the UserControl it is `System.Windows.Controls.UserControl` and for Canvas it is `System.Windows.Controls.Canvas`:

```
<UserControl x:Class="System.Windows.Controls.UserControl"
    xmlns="http://schemas.microsoft.com/winfx/2006/xaml/presentation"
    xmlns:x="http://schemas.microsoft.com/winfx/2006/xaml"
    Width="400" Height="300">
    <Canvas x:class="System.Windows.Controls.Canvas"
            x:Name="layout_root" Background="White"
            Grid.Row="1" Grid.Column="0">
        <Canvas.Resources>
            <Storyboard x:Name="rectAnimation">
                <DoubleAnimationUsingKeyFrames
                Storyboard.TargetName="rect"
                Storyboard.TargetProperty="(Canvas.Top)" RepeatBehavior="Forever">
                    <LinearDoubleKeyFrame Value="240" KeyTime="0:0:0"/>
                    <LinearDoubleKeyFrame Value="25" KeyTime="0:0:3"/>
                    <LinearDoubleKeyFrame Value="240" KeyTime="0:0:6"/>
                </DoubleAnimationUsingKeyFrames>
            </Storyboard>
        </Canvas.Resources>
        <Border BorderThickness="1" BorderBrush="Black" Width="400" Height="300"/>
        <Rectangle x:Name="rect" Width="25" Height="25" Canvas.Left="200"
                    Canvas.Top="240" Fill="Black"/>

        <Button x:Name="animationButton" Canvas.Left="10" Canvas.Top="10"
                Content="Start Animation"/>
        <Button x:Name="pauseButton" Canvas.Left="10" Canvas.Top="40"
                Content="Pause Animation"/>
    </Canvas>
</UserControl>
```

Define the app.py File

Now the IronPython application file, `app.py`, connects the events in the `__init__` function (essentially a constructor) and defines the event handlers that control the animation:

```
from System.Windows import Application
from System.Windows.Controls import UserControl
from System.Windows.Media.Animation import ClockState
class App:
  def __init__(self):
    self.root = Application.Current.LoadRootVisual(UserControl(), "app.xaml")
    self.root.animationButton.Click += self.startStopAnimation
    self.root.pauseButton.Click += self.pauseAnimation
    self.isPaused = False
```

```
    def startStopAnimation(self,s,e):
      if self.root.rectAnimation.GetCurrentState() == ClockState.Stopped:
        self.root.rectAnimation.Begin()
        self.root.animationButton.Content = "Stop Animation"
      else:
        self.root.rectAnimation.Stop()
        self.root.animationButton.Content = "Start Animation"
        self.root.pauseButton.Content = "Pause Animation"
    def pauseAnimation(self,s,e):
      if self.root.rectAnimation.GetCurrentState() ==
          ClockState.Active and not self.isPaused is True:
        self.root.rectAnimation.Pause()
        self.isPaused = True
        self.root.pauseButton.Content = "Resume Animation"
      else:
        self.root.rectAnimation.Resume()
        self.isPaused = False
        self.root.pauseButton.Content = "Pause Animation"
App()
```

The App() at the bottom is what creates an instance of the App class defined in this file. There's an additional from .. import used to make ClockState visible, much like you'd use using System.Windows.Media.Animation in C#.

Put the app.xaml and app.py files in the app folder.

Define the index.html File

Last, create an index.html file, which is very similar to what we saw earlier in this chapter. The following is a snapshot of the index.html file:

```
<!DOCTYPE html PUBLIC "-//W3C//DTD XHTML 1.0 Transitional//EN"
    "http://www.w3.org/TR/xhtml1/DTD/xhtml1-transitional.dtd">
<html xmlns="http://www.w3.org/1999/xhtml" >

<head>
  <title>Silverlight Animation Sample - with Python</title>

  <style type="text/css">
    html, body {
      height: 100%;
      overflow: auto;
    }
    body {
      padding: 0;
      margin: 0;
      background-image:
      url(assets/images/silverlight_dusk1_std_1024x768.jpg);
      background-repeat: no-repeat;
```

```
      background-color: #000000;
      }
    #silverlightControlHost {
      position: absolute;
      left: 100px;
      top: 50px;
    }
  </style>

  <!-- Formatting for DLR error handling -->
  <link type="text/css" rel="stylesheet" href="assets/stylesheets/error.css" />

  <!--
    Error handling for when DLR errors are disabled (with
    reportErrors=false, or not defined at all)
  -->
  <script type="text/javascript">
    function onSilverlightError(sender, args) {
      if (args.errorType == "InitializeError")  {
        var errorDiv = document.getElementById("errorLocation");
        if (errorDiv != null)
          errorDiv.innerHTML = args.errorType + "- " + args.errorMessage;
      }
    }
  </script>
</head>

<body>
  <!--
    Syntax/Runtime errors from Silverlight will be displayed here.
    This will contain debugging information and should be removed
    or hidden when debugging is complete
  -->
  <div id='errorLocation' style="font-size: small;color: Gray;"></div>

  <div id="silverlightControlHost">

    <object data="data:application/x-silverlight,"
        type="application/x-silverlight-2" width="320" height="320">
      <param name="source" value="app.xap"/>
      <param name="onerror" value="onSilverlightError" />
      <param name="background" value="#00000000" />
      <param name="initParams" value="debug=true,
            reportErrors=errorLocation" />
      <param name="windowless" value="true" />
```

```
        <a href="http://go.microsoft.com/fwlink/?LinkID=124807"
           style="text-decoration: none;">
            <img src="http://go.microsoft.com/fwlink/?LinkId=108181"
                alt="Get Microsoft Silverlight"
                style="border-style: none"/>
        </a>
    </object>
    <iframe style='visibility:hidden;height:0;width:0;border:0px'>
    </iframe>

  </div>

</body>

</html>
```

Now if you run this application dynamically using the Chiron.exe utility and the /d and /b options, the browser should open to show the directory and files. When you click the index. html file, the Chrion.exe utility will create the app.xap package dynamically, and you will see the application window shown in Figure 10-6. If you click the Start animation button, the rectangle will move up and down continuously. If you click the Stop animation button, the rectangle resets to the original position. To pause or resume animation, click the Pause/Resume button.

This has been a rather brief overview of the dynamic language support in Silverlight, but it did show you how to go about creating real Silverlight applications using dynamic languages. Visit http://silverlight.net/learn/dynamiclanguages.aspx for resources covering dynamic languages in more detail.

Interoperating with the Browser

Along with support for dynamic languages, Silverlight provides libraries to access the properties and capabilities of its host environment. Silverlight can access the HTML Document Object Model (DOM) via the HtmlDocument class and can expose classes and data to JScript via attributes and the HtmlPage class. This functionality is also known as HTML Bridge.

The classes provided for browser interoperability are located in the System.Windows.Browser namespace. It provides seven classes related to HTML pages and elements (HtmlDocument, HtmlElement, HtmlEventArgs, HtmlObject, HtmlPage, HtmlPopupWindowOptions, and HtmlWindow), four classes related to the client script (ScriptableMemberAttribute, ScriptableTypeAttribute, ScriptObject, and ScriptObjectCollection), a BrowserInformation class to obtain properties about the browser, and an HttpUtility class that provides encoding/decoding methods for URLs and HTML.

Let's start by taking a closer look at the BrowserInformation class. Table 10-2 lists the properties of this class.

Table 10-2. *Properties of the BrowserInformation Class*

Property	Type	Description
BrowserVersion	System.Version	The version number of the browser
CookiesEnabled	bool	true if cookies are enabled; false otherwise
Name	string	String representation of the browser
Platform	string	String representation of the host platform
UserAgent	string	Contains the user agent as communicated from the browser

■**Caution** It is strongly suggested you do not make application decisions based on the UserAgent property. The UserAgent string is easy to spoof and is not a good way to determine capabilities provided by the browser, since the user may have certain options turned off, or you might block future versions of a browser.

Table 10-3 shows what the BrowserInformation class reports on Internet Explorer (IE) 7 running on Microsoft Windows Vista 64-bit.

Table 10-3. *BrowserInformation Class Properties from IE 7 on Windows Vista*

Property	Value
BrowserVersion	4.0
CookiesEnabled	True
Name	Microsoft Internet Explorer
Platform	Win32
UserAgent	Mozilla/4.0 (compatible; MSIE 7.0; Windows NT 6.0; WOW64; SLCC1; .NET CLR 2.0.50727; Media Center PC 5.0;InfoPath.2; .NET CLR 3.5. 21022; .NET CLR 3.5.30729; .NET CLR 3.5.30618)

There are ten core classes that support interoperating with the browser. The class hierarchy is shown in Figure 10-7. The HtmlPage class provides several static methods and properties for working with HtmlObject subclasses and other related bits. The methods of HtmlPage are shown in Table 10-4, and the properties are listed in Table 10-5. Note that all the methods and properties are static.

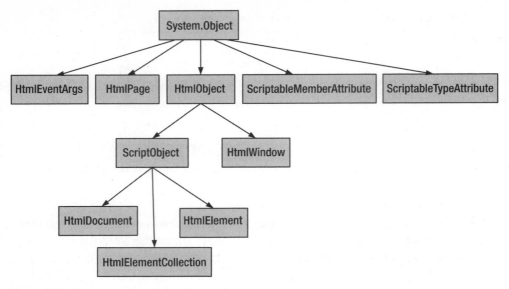

Figure 10-7. *Browser-related class hierarchy*

Table 10-4. *Methods of System.Windows.Browser.HtmlPage*

Method	Description
RegisterCreateableType	Associates a createable type with a string alias. A createable type can be created by using ManagedObject's CreateObject method.
RegisterScriptableObject	Associates an instance of a scriptable object (its class is decorated with ScriptableType) with a string alias.
UnregisterCreateableType	Unregisters a registered createable type (by passing in its alias).
PopupWindow	Opens a pop-up window.

Table 10-5. *Properties of System.Windows.Browser.HtmlPage*

Property	Type	Description
BrowserInformation	BrowserInformation	Provides information about the browser
Document	HtmlDocument	Provides a reference to the HTML document displayed in the browser
IsEnabled	bool	Returns true as long as the page is initialized, the enableHtmlAccess hosting option is false, and code isn't executing in a host such as Expression Blend
Plugin	HtmlElement	Provides a reference to the HtmlElement corresponding to the object tag that contains the Silverlight application

Table 10-5. *Properties of System.Windows.Browser.HtmlPage*

Property	Type	Description
Window	HtmlWindow	Returns an instance of the class representing the browser's window; provides access to navigating the browser, the ability to change location within the current HTML document, and shortcuts to some client script functions such as alert boxes
IsPopupWindowAllowed	Boolean	Defines whether pop-up windows are allowed

The HtmlObject class forms the base for the more interesting classes. It provides functionality to attach and detach events communicated from the browser, such as mouse-click events and keyboard events. Table 10-6 lists the key methods provided by HtmlObject.

Table 10-6. *Key Methods of System.Windows.Browser.HtmlObject*

Method	Description
AttachEvent	Overloaded. Registers an EventHandler (optionally parameterized with HtmlEventArgs) for a provided event name.
DetachEvent	Overloaded. Unregisters an EventHandler (optionally parameterized with HtmlEventArgs) for a provided event name. Note that the event handler must still be passed—this makes it possible to unregister only one of possibly many event handlers for a particular event.

The first class we'll look at that descends from HtmlObject is HtmlWindow. The HtmlWindow class provides a direct connection to the functionality of the browser, including shortcuts to display alert and confirmation dialogs, use navigation controls, execute arbitrary script code, and access bookmarks within the page. Table 10-7 displays the key methods of HtmlWindow. This class only has a single property, CurrentBookmark, which can be set or retrieved. Setting CurrentBookmark causes the browser to navigate to the specified bookmark within the current page.

Table 10-7. *Key Methods of System.Windows.Browser.HtmlWindow*

Method	Description
Alert	Displays an alert dialog containing the text passed in. It's the same as invoking alert(...) from JScript.
Confirm	Displays a confirmation dialog containing the text passed in. If the user clicks yes, this method returns true; otherwise, it returns false.
CreateInstance	Returns an instance of the specified type (can be dotted).
Eval	Directly executes client script contained in a string. It returns an object that contains the result of the executed code, if there is one.

Table 10-7. *Key Methods of System.Windows.Browser.HtmlWindow (Continued)*

Method	Description
Navigate	Overloaded. Causes the browser to navigate to the URI passed in. It can optionally specify `target` and `targetFeatures` to control navigation (such as causing a browser window to contain the content from the URI specified).
NavigateToBookmark	Currently provides the same functionality as setting the `CurrentBookmark` property directly.
Prompt	Displays a prompt dialog with the text passed in. This is a shortcut to receive user input—the text serves as a label. The input from the user is returned as a string.

The `ScriptObject` class descends directly from `HtmlObject` and introduces much useful functionality for its inheritors. It is the abstraction used to uniformly treat client objects. This class handles a lot of the communication with the browser related to the client script, such as getting and setting properties of script objects and invoking functions on script objects. Table 10-8 lists its key methods.

Table 10-8. *Key Methods of System.Windows.Browser.ScriptObject*

Method	Description
CheckAccess	Returns `true` if the thread this is called from is the user interface thread.
GetProperty	Retrieves the value of a named property.
Invoke	Invokes a named function, optionally with arguments (passed in an array of object).
InvokeSelf	Invokes a function on the browser, optionally with arguments (passed in an array of object). The browser function invoked is based on the inheriting class' type.
SetProperty	Sets the named property to an object value.

So far, we've picked up functionality for client-side script events and accessing/executing properties and functions. Beneath `ScriptObject` are the `HtmlDocument`, `HtmlElement`, and `ScriptObjectCollection` classes. These classes have a one-to-one relationship with aspects of HTML pages.

The `HtmlElement` class represents an HTML tag. It contains properties for the tag's attributes, styles, name, ID, CSS class, and of course, any children. The `ScriptObjectCollection` class represents a collection of children (it implements the generic and nongeneric `IEnumerable` interfaces). The key properties of `HtmlElement` are shown in Table 10-9, and the key methods are shown in Table 10-10.

Table 10-9. *Key Properties of System.Windows.Browser.HtmlElement*

Property	Type	Description
Children	ScriptObjectCollection	Contains a collection of HtmlElement objects, if this tag has any children. Note that this is read-only—use AppendChild and RemoveChild to manipulate this tag's children.
CssClass	string	Gets or sets the CSS class name for this tag.
Id	string	Gets or sets this tag's ID.
Parent	HtmlElement	Gets this tag's parent. This property is read-only.
TagName	string	Gets this tag's name. This property is read-only.

Table 10-10. *Key Methods of System.Windows.Browser.HtmlElement*

Method	Description
AppendChild	Appends the passed-in HtmlElement to this tag (adds it to the Children collection)
Focus	Sets focus to this tag; most useful for HTML form elements such as input boxes
GetAttribute	Returns the specified attribute's value as a string
GetStyleAttribute	Returns the value of the specified style as applied to this tag
RemoveAttribute	Removes the specified attribute from this tag
RemoveStyleAttribute	Removes the specified named style from this tag
RemoveChild	Removes the specified HtmlElement from this tag's Children collection
SetAttribute	Sets the specified attribute to the specified string value
SetStyleAttribute	Sets the specified style attribute to the specified string value

The HtmlDocument class represents an HTML document—it contains the root HtmlElement of the document, a reference to the body of the HTML document, and methods for retrieving elements on the page by ID. It also has one event, DocumentReady, that fires when the document is finished loading/initializing. If the document finishes loading before Silverlight finishes initializing, this event will *not* fire. The key properties of HtmlDocument are shown in Table 10-11, and the key methods are shown in Table 10-12.

The ScriptableMemberAttribute and ScriptableTypeAttribute classes are used to expose classes and class members in the code-behind to client-side script. The ScriptableTypeAttribute class is required in order for JScript to access classes, including granting the ability for managed code in Silverlight to handle DOM events.

Table 10-11. *Key Properties of System.Windows.Browser.HtmlDocument*

Property	Type	Description
Body	HtmlElement	A reference directly to the body of the HTML document; read-only.
Cookies	string	A string containing the cookies associated with this document.
DocumentElement	HtmlElement	A reference to the root of the document; read-only.
DocumentUri	Uri	The URI to this document; read-only.
IsReady	bool	true if the document is done downloading/initializing; read-only.
QueryString	IDictionary<string,string>	A dictionary instance containing name/value pairs corresponding to variables passed in the query string.

Table 10-12. *Key Methods of System.Windows.Browser.HtmlDocument*

Method	Description
CreateElement	Returns an HtmlElement instance corresponding to the specified tag name.
GetElementById	Returns an HtmlElement corresponding to the specified tag ID, or null if no element was found.
GetElementsByTagName	Returns a ScriptObjectCollection containing all tags that match the specified tag name.
Submit	Causes a postback to the server using the first (or only) form to submit. Via an overload, this can also submit a specific form based on its ID in case there are multiple forms in the document.

Let's create a Silverlight application project to develop a simple application that shows a drop-down list (the select element) in HTML. This list will be populated by the Silverlight application, and when the user changes the selected value, the background of the Silverlight application will change. You can see what this looks like in Figure 10-8.

The HTML for the list is put into the ASPX page (or HTML page, if you use that instead).

```
<div id="menu" style="border:solid 2px black">
   Choose color:
   <select id="colorMenu">
   </select>
</div>
```

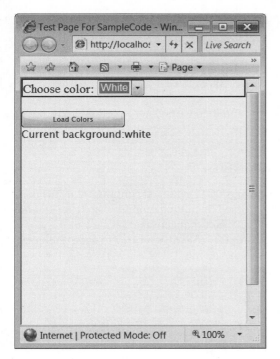

Figure 10-8. *Demonstration of Silverlight influencing and responding to the browser*

Before we move forward, ensure that the MainPage.xaml.cs class containing the managed code for script consumption has the ScriptableType attribute:

```
[ScriptableType]
public partial class MainPage : UserControl
{
    // code for class here
}
```

On page load, we can get a reference to the colorMenu element by using GetElementById from the HtmlDocument class:

```
HtmlElement menu = HtmlPage.Document.GetElementById("colorMenu");
```

We need to add option tags beneath the select element, so we use HtmlDocument. CreateElement to create new option elements. All HTML tags are treated the same in Silverlight— the HtmlElement class provides the functionality needed to work with all the various tags in HTML:

```
HtmlElement option = HtmlPage.Document.CreateElement("option");
```

We now set attributes on the new tag appropriate to the `option` tag and append it to the child collection of the `select` tag:

```
option.SetAttribute("value", "blue");
option.SetAttribute("innerHTML", "Blue");
menu.AppendChild(option);
```

We repeat this sequence for a few more colors, and then we register a method in the code-behind to handle the `onchange` event of the `select` tag:

```
menu.AttachEvent("onchange", new
    EventHandler<HtmlEventArgs>(this.onColorChanged));
```

You will always use `HtmlEventArgs` when handling DOM events. It contains many properties, including the event name, which keys were pressed (including modifiers such as Ctrl and Alt), mouse information, and a reference to the `HtmlObject` that generated the event.

The `onColorChanged` method uses the `Source` property of `HtmlEventArgs` to get a reference to the original `select` tag:

```
public void onColorChanged(object sender, HtmlEventArgs e)
{
    HtmlElement menu = (HtmlElement)e.Source;
    string color = (string)menu.GetProperty("value");
    Color c;
    if (color == "blue")
        c = Color.FromArgb(255, 0, 0, 255);
    else if (color == "red")
        c = Color.FromArgb(255, 255, 0, 0);
    else if (color == "green")
        c = Color.FromArgb(255, 0, 255, 0);
    else
        c = Color.FromArgb(255, 255, 255, 255);
    choiceTB.Text = color;
    LayoutRoot.Background = new SolidColorBrush(c);
}
```

We don't need to wait for the user to click the button to populate the drop-down list if we don't want to. However, if the HTML page is big, and the Silverlight application might finish initializing before the entire HTML document is ready, we want to avoid accessing the DOM prematurely. We can account for this case using the `DocumentReady` event of the `HtmlDocument` class:

```
HtmlPage.Document.DocumentReady += new
    EventHandler(Document_DocumentReady);
```

The code from our `onClick` handler goes into the new `Document_DocumentReady` method. Remember that if the document finishes loading before the Silverlight application is initialized, this event will not fire.

```
void Document_DocumentReady(object sender, EventArgs e)
{
    // code to manipulate DOM after HTML page is initialized
}
```

The HtmlWindow object provides an optimized method to invoke several JScript functions, including alert, confirm, eval, and prompt. When working in managed code, it is better to call these JScript functions via the HtmlWindow class instead of through the Eval method. The Eval method is quite useful, as it can call arbitrary JScript code, including functions in JScript. It returns object, but the types you can expect back are bool, string, double (for numbers), and ScriptObject (for JScript objects).

Let's take a look at calling managed code from JScript. This can be useful for leveraging the speed of managed code from interpreted JScript or for using libraries already written in Silverlight (that hopefully have the correct attributes—but if not, you can write a proxy class that exposes methods to script). To provide an interesting example, we'll use Silverlight to give Windows Communication Foundation (WCF) support to the browser. We'll invoke a service from client-side JScript. Since the generated WCF client is not visible to script by default, we have to build a layer between the JScript and the WCF client in order to expose the latter to the former. You can see what this application looks like in Figure 10-9.

Figure 10-9. *Using Silverlight as a web service proxy to retrieve image data*

This will be a different type of Silverlight application, as we aren't leveraging any of its display capabilities. To ensure the Silverlight application is on the page and doesn't unload at an inopportune time, we'll simply set its width and height to 1:

```
<asp:Silverlight ID="Silverlight1" runat="server"
                 Source="~/ClientBin/WebServiceProxy.xap"
                 Version="3.0.40307.0" Width="1" Height="1" />
```

Since the generated web service client isn't exposed to the script by default, we'll create an intermediary type and decorate it with the required attributes:

```
[ScriptableType]
public class ScriptableImageInfo
{
    [ScriptableMember]
    public string name { get; set; }
    [ScriptableMember]
    public string uri { get; set; }
}
```

The ScriptableMember attribute also has a ScriptAlias property that allows you to expose this class member via a different name to the client script.

The Silverlight application contains a class decorated with ScriptableType so we can access it from the script. This class contains methods for the script to invoke the web service. We will maintain the asynchronous approach, so when we create a method to invoke the web service, it will include a string parameter containing a callback function name.

```
[ScriptableMember]
public void getAllImages(string callbackFunc)
{
    // We should move this handler to the class constructor,
      //however it is placed here for demonstration purposes
    _serviceClient.GetAllImagesInformationCompleted += new
        EventHandler<GetAllImagesInformationCompletedEventArgs>
        (_serviceClient_GetAllImagesInformationCompleted);
    _serviceClient.GetAllImagesInformationAsync(callbackFunc);
}
```

This callback function will be invoked via HtmlPage.Eval in the GetAllImagesInformationCompleted event handler:

```
void _serviceClient_GetAllImagesInformationCompleted(object sender,
                   GetAllImagesInformationCompletedEventArgs e)
{
    string callbackFunc = (string)e.UserState;
    imageList = new ScriptableImageInfo[e.Result.Length];
```

```
    for (int i = 0; i < e.Result.Length; i++)
    {
        ScriptableImageInfo scInfo = new ScriptableImageInfo();
        scInfo.name = e.Result[i].Name;
        scInfo.uri = e.Result[i].Uri;
        imageList[i] = scInfo;
    }
    HtmlPage.Window.Eval(callbackFunc + "()");
}
```

The callback function, in this case, is used as a signaling mechanism. To get the results of the service call, we need to expose another method for the client script:

```
[ScriptableMember]
public ScriptableImageInfo[] getAllImagesResult()
{
    return (imageList);
}
```

Now let's take a look at the JScript side. We'll create a button and a table in the HTML. When the button is clicked, the Silverlight application is invoked and the results are shown in the table.

```
<input type="button" onclick="loadImages()" value="Load Images"/>
<table border="1" id="outputTable">
   <tr>
      <th>Image Name</th>
      <th>Image</th>
   </tr>
</table>
```

The loadImages function caches a reference to the web service class in our Silverlight application and invokes the getAllImages method to retrieve the image data:

```
var imageWebService;
function loadImages()
{
   slPlugin = document.getElementById('Xaml1');
   imageWebService = slPlugin.Content.imageWebService;
   imageWebService.getAllImages("GetAllImagesCompleted");
}
```

The GetAllImagesCompleted function is implemented in JScript. The array from managed code becomes a standard JScript array, so you can use the length property and iterate over it in the expected manner:

```
function GetAllImagesCompleted()
{
    var results = imageWebService.getAllImagesResult();
    for(var i=0; i<results.length; i++)
    {
        var tr = outputTable.insertRow(outputTable.rows.length);
        var td = tr.insertCell(0);
        var text = document.createTextNode(results[i].name);
        td.appendChild(text);
        td = tr.insertCell(1);
        var img = document.createElement('img');
        img.setAttribute('src',results[i].uri);
        img.setAttribute('width','100');
        img.setAttribute('height','100');
        td.appendChild(img);
    }
}
```

The previous method creates the table dynamically and populates the first cell with the image name and the related image in the second cell.

Summary

This chapter introduced the support for dynamic languages that Silverlight provides and showed how to create and deploy dynamic applications. The features of the three supported languages—IronRuby, IronPython, and Managed JScript—were briefly discussed. We also discussed how Silverlight supports interoperating with the host browser, which can be used to greatly expand the capabilities of the browser by using Silverlight as a service provider, and for enabling scenarios where Silverlight and the client script communicate. The next chapter details the security model of Silverlight.

CHAPTER 11

■■■

Security

The growth of the Internet and the World Wide Web has forever changed the way we use computers. As software engineers, we can no longer ignore security as we did when the average computer wasn't directly connected to a slew of other computers. Silverlight lives online, in users' browsers and other connected devices. No exploration of Silverlight is complete without understanding both the security features it provides and generally how to ensure your Silverlight application has been developed with security in mind. This chapter will go over Silverlight's security model and general techniques for understanding how to design for and evaluate security.

.NET Security in the CoreCLR

While application code executes under the auspices of an environment (the CoreCLR) executing on top of a host operating system, careful thought must still be given to how code is executed.

In .NET, the security model for executable code is called Code Access Security (CAS). There are several important aspects to CAS, including code making requests for specific security permissions (such as asking for the ability to write to files), stack walks to determine the permission levels granted, and the ability for an administrator to control permission levels granted to applications. For example, if your .NET application wants to modify a file stored in a specific location, it must first ensure that it has the rights to access the directory and modify the file. This permission request can be done declaratively by applying a particular permission-related attribute to a method, or imperatively by invoking the Demand method for a specific permission. In C# on the .NET platform, the imperative approach might look like the following:

```
//additional references
using System.IO;
using System.Security;
using System.Security.Permissions;
public void saveDataToFile(string outputFilename)
{
    FileIOPermission perm = new
      FileIOPermission(FileIOPermission.Write,outputFilename);
```

```
  try {
    perm.Demand(); // request permission to write to file
                   // throws exception if we don't have permission
    StreamWriter sw = new StreamWriter(outputFilename);
    // write data to sw
    sw.Close();
  } catch(SecurityException ex) {
    // handle security exception
  } catch(Exception generalEx) {
    // handle other exceptions
  }
}
```

It's also possible to make security demands declaratively using a CAS-related attribute:

```
[FileIOPermission(SecurityAction.Demand, Write=@"app.config")]
public void saveDataToFile(string outputFilename)
{
    // method code
}
```

The security model within the CLR ensures that the permission being requested can be granted, or the method won't execute. Whether making permission requests imperatively or declaratively, the application code must make specific demands based on what it needs to accomplish. This is a fine-grained approach to ensuring that executable code has only the permissions it needs and works well on the .NET platform.

Silverlight Security Model

The managed execution engine that Silverlight provides is based on .NET, specifically, the CLR. The Silverlight plug-in can interact with the host operating system to communicate over the network, modify files on the file system, and display graphics on the screen. The security of the host operating system would be compromised if a Silverlight application were able to use these features directly. Therefore, some mechanism must be in place to ensure a division between application code and code that can affect the host operating system. Silverlight's security model is slightly different than regular .NET applications. Instead of the Silverlight application code asking for permission to accomplish certain tasks, all code in Silverlight is *security transparent*— that is, it is not trusted. Silverlight applications can still interact with the host operating system (e.g., to save and read files in the file system), but not directly.

■**Note** While there is no CAS available for use by your application, if you explore the online documentation or the assemblies in Reflector, you will come across a namespace related to CAS. This is a holdover from .NET in order to allow the already existing C# compiler to compile Silverlight code, since a CAS-related attribute is emitted by the compiler if the assembly is unverifiable.

Since all application code that you write is security transparent, how is it able to still utilize services offered by the host operating system, such as file system access? There are three categories of code that can execute from the perspective of the Silverlight plug-in. First, there's all the code in a Silverlight application (the code you write and any third-party libraries your application uses). The second and third categories cover code located in the platform assemblies that provide functionality for Silverlight applications, such as isolated storage and network communication. The code in these assemblies either does something high-privilege (e.g., directly modifying a file on disk or invoking a native library on the host operating system) or calls these high-privilege methods. The code in your application invokes the second category of code. This second category is needed because it serves as the middleman between application code (security-transparent code) and code that is allowed to interact with the host operating system (security-critical code). Figure 11-1 shows the relationship between these three categories of executable code.

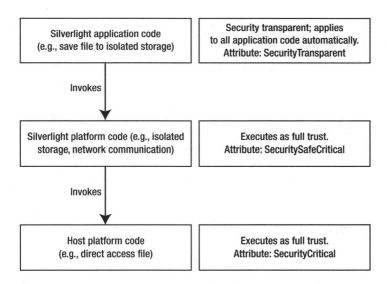

Figure 11-1. *Relationship of executable code and security categories*

Figure 11-1 also shows the attributes that correspond to each category of code. Your application's code cannot use either the SecuritySafeCritical attribute or the SecurityCritical attribute—if you attempt to use one, it will be ignored, and your code will be treated as security transparent. Any code decorated with the SecuritySafeCritical attribute can be invoked by security-transparent code. Here are several methods from the System.IO.IsolatedStorage.IsolatedStorageFile class that encompass all three categories of executable code:

```
[SecuritySafeCritical]
public void CreateDirectory(string dir);
public IsolatedStorageFileStream CreateFile(string path);
[SecurityCritical]
private string[] DirectoriesToCreate(string fullPath);
```

Both CreateFile and CreateDirectory can be called from your code. Of course, the private visibility of DirectoriesToCreate hides this method from your code regardless, but the SecurityCritical attribute helps to enforce the fact that only SecuritySafeCritical code is a valid invoker. Your code might call the CreateDirectory method, which then subsequently calls the DirectoriesToCreate method.

This brings about another question, though—why does the platform code get to use the SecuritySafeCritical and SecurityCritical attributes, but your code doesn't? This is enforced by the Silverlight plug-in only granting the ability to run as SecuritySafeCritical or SecurityCritical to code that is signed by Microsoft and downloaded from the Microsoft servers. As shown in Figure 11-1, code marked with SecuritySafeCritical acts as a proxy between code that is security transparent and code that is security critical. Without this intermediate layer, application code could make calls to the security-critical code, giving application code far more privilege than it should have. This security model firmly separates platform code (which might be security critical) from application code (which is always security transparent).

Application-Level Security

The security of executable code provided by the CoreCLR is not where the security story ends. While there are guarantees that Silverlight application code cannot gain access to the host operating system, Silverlight applications may still handle confidential information. This information might take the form of a user's credit card data, a user's login credentials, or other information that needs careful handling. This information must be secured in transit, achieved typically via HTTPS, and possibly with a further layer of encryption ensuring that only the intended recipient can decrypt the encrypted information. Secure coding practices combined with the support Silverlight provides can give you confidence that your Silverlight application is secure.

Securing Information in Transit

When a Silverlight application communicates with a server, there is the potential for a third party to listen in on or even tamper with the communication. The established way to secure communication over HTTP is by using the SSL protocol via HTTPS. Silverlight can easily make use of SSL. Both the WebClient and HttpWebRequest classes support HTTPS, and you can also configure the ServiceReferences.ClientConfig class to use SSL.

Configuring a service to communicate over HTTPS is accomplished by setting the mode attribute of the security element to Transport, as shown here. Also, make sure the endpoint's address uses the HTTPS protocol.

```
<configuration>
    <system.serviceModel>
        <bindings>
            <basicHttpBinding>
                <binding name="BasicHttpBinding_AuthenticationService"
                        maxBufferSize="65536"
                        maxReceivedMessageSize="65536">
                    <security mode="Transport" />
                </binding>
```

```
        </basicHttpBinding>
      </bindings>
      ...
   </system.serviceModel>
</configuration>
```

Securing Information with Cryptography

While communicating over an encrypted channel ensures that information stays secure in transit, the information arrives unencrypted for the application to handle. Regardless of how the application receives information, the information still might need to be decrypted; or if it will be stored locally (such as in isolated storage), it is possible that the information must be encrypted before being written to disk. This is where the System.Security.Cryptography namespace enters the picture. This namespace provides capabilities for encrypting and decrypting data, generating hashes for purposes such as message authentication codes and random number generation suitable for cryptography.

■Note Visit the Microsoft MSDN web site to get a detailed overview of cryptography (http://msdn. microsoft.com/en-us/library/92f9ye3s.aspx).

Hash Algorithms and Message Authentication Codes

A hash algorithm transforms a chunk of data into a small, fixed-length set of bytes known as a *hash* (or *hash code*). As long as the same chunk of data is processed by the same hash algorithm, the resulting hash code will always be the same. If you've heard of CRC codes or digital signatures, you've heard of the result of hash algorithms. Used as a digital signature, a hash code can prove that the data has not changed, since even a small change in the data will result in a completely different hash code.

The base class of hash classes is HashAlgorithm. This class provides the main features of a hash algorithm, including hash size and hash value properties, and methods for computing a hash value. It provides additional functionality via the KeyedHashAlgorithm—most importantly the addition of a secret password (key) as input to the hash algorithm. This added functionality is important because, otherwise, a chunk of data can be tampered with and a recomputed hash code attached to it.

Taking one more step down the hierarchy brings us to the HMAC class. *HMAC* stands for *hash-based message authentication code*. A *message authentication code* (MAC) is another name for a hash value or a digital signature. Changing the data will cause the MAC value to change, thus providing evidence of data tampering. The HMAC class is the one we're most interested in from a class interface perspective since inheritors to HMAC provide specific algorithm implementations. The direct inheritors to HMAC are HMACSHA1 and HMACSHA256, implementations of the SHA-1 and SHA-256 cryptographic algorithms for computing MACs. Table 11-1 shows the properties provided collectively by these three base classes.

Table 11-1. *Properties of System.Security.Cryptography.HMAC*

Property	Type	Description
BlockSizeValue	int	Specifies the size, in number of bits, of the block used by the algorithm
CanReuseTransform	bool	Returns true if you can reuse the current hash transform
CanTransformMultipleBlocks	bool	Returns true if the algorithm can transform multiple blocks
Hash	byte[]	Gets the computed hash value
HashName	string	Gets/sets the name of the algorithm used for hashing
HashSize	int	Specifies the size, in number of bits, of the computed hash value
InputBlockSize	int	Specifies the size, in number of bits, of input blocks
Key	byte[]	Gets/sets the secret key used in the algorithm
OutputBlockSize	int	Specifies the size of the output block

Table 11-2 describes the key methods.

Table 11-2. *Methods of System.Security.Cryptography.HMAC (et al.)*

Method	Description
Clear	Releases all resources used by the algorithm.
ComputeHash	Computes a hash for a byte array (or section thereof) or a Stream. This is the method you use to generate hashes.
Initialize	Initializes an instance of the algorithm.
TransformBlock	Generates a hash value for a section of a byte array and stores it at a specific offset in another byte array.
TransformFinalBlock	Generates a hash value for a section of a byte array.

There are two algorithms that provide the specific implementation for the hash algorithms: SHA-1 and SHA-256. Both algorithms can use a key of any length. The SHA-1 algorithm returns a hash value that is 20 bytes (160 bits), and SHA-256 returns a hash value that is 32 bytes (256 bits). As long as the same input bytes and the same key are used, the specific hash algorithm will always generate the same hash value. Here's a helper method that accepts a message (the input bytes) and the key as strings and will use any specific implementation of the HMAC class that you pass in:

```
byte[] calculateHash(string key, string message,
  HMAC hashAlgorithm)
{
    UTF8Encoding encoder = new UTF8Encoding();
    hashAlgorithm.Key = encoder.GetBytes(key);
    byte[] hash =
      hashAlgorithm.ComputeHash(encoder.GetBytes(message));
    //Convert the hash byte array to Base64 string
    string hashinbase64string =
      System.Convert.ToBase64String(hash);
    return (hash);
}
```

If we pass the string this is a secret message through the HMACSHA256 class, with the secret key p@ssw0rd, and then encode the resulting byte array as a Base64 string, we get the hash value an332+/NeHKDvNIKYiQOokci/ob1xK1eMJYS1yjtwfI=. If we capitalize the first t in the message, the hash value changes to IhbwZnSZXdw95cUbXprjSUAV9VBoFmKdOd9kYT/Et3Y=, which is a significant change. Even changing a single bit in the message or the key will cause a wildly different hash value to be generated.

> **■Note** The SHA-1 algorithm is now considered an unsecured algorithm, and SHA-2 is recommended instead. Thus, for Silverlight-based applications, it is recommended that you utilize the SHA-256 algorithm instead of SHA-1. You can get more details on the SHA algorithm by visiting http://en.wikipedia.org/wiki/SHA.

Encrypting/Decrypting Data

There are two types of encryption algorithms: *symmetric key algorithms* and *asymmetric key algorithms*. A symmetric key algorithm is an algorithm where the key used to encrypt information is the same key used for decryption. An asymmetric key algorithm uses separate keys for encryption and decryption, generally referred to as a *public key* (used for encryption; anyone can obtain the public key to encrypt data for a specific recipient) and a *private key* (this key is kept secret and used to decrypt data encrypted with the public key). Silverlight supports only one encryption algorithm, the symmetric key Advanced Encryption Standard (AES).

The simplest approach to encrypting and decrypting information is by using a single password, as shown in Figure 11-2.

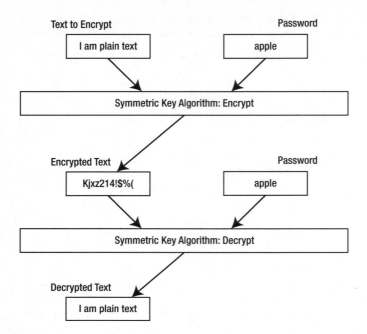

Figure 11-2. *Flow of encryption/decryption using a secret password*

Since the password is used unmodified, an attacker could conceivably launch a dictionary-based attack to find the password by brute force. For example, if an attacker has the encrypted text and has reason to believe a fruit is used for the password, he could try "banana," "orange," "pear," and finally "apple," and suddenly he'll be staring at the original message, successfully decrypted. One way to go about preventing a dictionary-based attack is to use a *salt*. Salts are random data combined with passwords that make dictionary-based attacks much more expensive, since every word in the dictionary must be combined with every possible salt. The salt is stored with the password (usually a password transformed by a hashing algorithm), so decryption is straightforward since the original salt is known and a human-readable password can pass through the same hashing function again. It's possible to make the attacker's job even harder by using a stronger algorithm to transform a password. One such algorithm is the Public-Key Cryptography Standard (PKCS) #5, defined in RFC 2898, which you can find more about at www.ietf.org/.

PKCS #5 actually defines two modes of operation used for deriving a password. The first is Password-Based Key Derivation Function #1 (PBKDF1), and the second is PBKDF2, which you can find in the cryptography namespace in Silverlight. The main advantage to using PBKDF2 is that although the more rudimentary salt-plus-hash approach makes dictionary attacks computationally infeasible, PBKDF2 requires even more computational resources to successfully crack the password. This is accomplished by applying the hash function multiple times. So, instead of an attacker having to try every possible salt with every possible password in a dictionary, he'd also have to try a variety of iteration counts for rehashing along with every possible salt and every password in the dictionary. This means that instead of storing just the salt with a hashed password, you store the salt, the hashed password (the output from the PKCS #5 algorithm), and the iteration count.

The Rfc2898DeriveBytes class provides the implementation of the PBKDF2 algorithm. You pass the password (as a string or a byte array), the salt (as a byte array), and optionally an iteration count to the constructor. Then you invoke the GetBytes member method with the number of bytes you want returned. Here's an example method that does the work of using the Rfc2898DeriveBytes class for you:

```
private byte[] deriveBytes(string input, byte[] salt, int iterations)
{
    Rfc2898DeriveBytes deriver = new
      Rfc2898DeriveBytes(input, salt, iterations);
    return deriver.GetBytes(16);
}
```

The AesManaged class provides the implementation of the AES algorithm for encrypting/decrypting data. This class inherits from SymmetricAlgorithm. Table 11-3 describes the properties of SymmetricAlgorithm.

Table 11-3. *Properties of System.Security.Cryptography.SymmetricAlgorithm*

Property	Type	Description
BlockSize	int	Size, in number of bits, of the block used by the algorithm.
IV	byte[]	Initialization vector used by the algorithm; must be BlockSize/8 bytes long.
Key	byte[]	Secret key (e.g., password) used by algorithm.
KeySize	int	Size, in number of bits, of the secret key.
LegalBlockSizes	KeySizes[]	Array of block sizes that are valid for this algorithm. Certain algorithms, such as AES, only support a few different block sizes.
LegalKeySizes	KeySizes[]	Array of key sizes valid for this algorithm.

Used in conjunction with the CryptoStream class, it's straightforward to encrypt data in a stream such as a MemoryStream or a file stream for working with files from isolated storage. Figure 11-3 shows a simple interface for encrypting and decrypting data. The salt must be at least eight characters long. The password entered, combined with the salt, is used for both encrypting and decrypting.

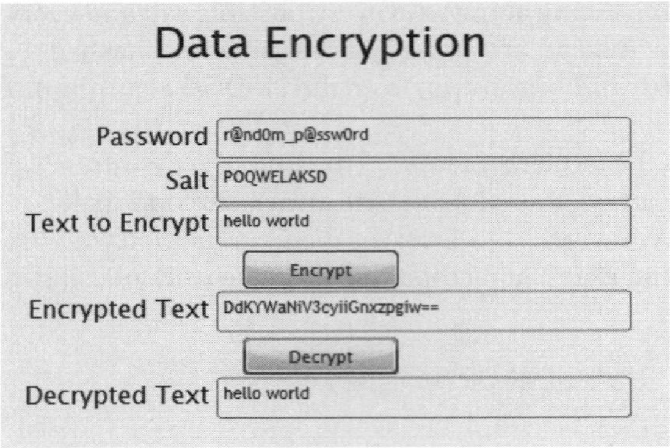

Figure 11-3. *Demonstration interface for encrypting/decrypting data*

Here's a utility encryption method that takes a key, an initialization vector, and the text to encrypt:

```
private string Encrypt(byte[] key, byte[] iv, string plaintext)
{
    AesManaged aes = new AesManaged();
    aes.Key = key;
    aes.IV = iv;
    using (MemoryStream stream = new MemoryStream())
    {
        using (CryptoStream encrypt = new CryptoStream(stream,
                                    aes.CreateEncryptor(),
                                    CryptoStreamMode.Write))
        {
            byte[] plaintextBytes =
              UTF8Encoding.UTF8.GetBytes(plaintext);
            encrypt.Write(plaintextBytes, 0, plaintextBytes.Length);
            encrypt.FlushFinalBlock();
            encrypt.Close();
            return Convert.ToBase64String(stream.ToArray());
        }
    }
}
```

The other important aspect to using the AES algorithm is using an initialization vector, as shown in the preceding code in the second parameter. By default, AES uses a 128-bit block size (a block is a fixed length of data used by certain encryption algorithms such as AES), and the initialization vector is used to initialize the block. Since the default block size is 128 bits, the default size of the initialization vector must be 16 bytes (128 bits / 8 bits per byte = 16 bytes). The initialization vector for the encryption must be the same when decrypting data, so if you send encrypted data over the wire, the other side must somehow know which initialization vector to use. This can be something agreed upon by the encryptor and decryptor in the code design phase. Here's what an example initialization vector looks like along with invoking the Encrypt method:

```
byte[] initializationVector = { 0x11, 0xAF, 0x0C, 0x07, 0x17, 0xFC, 0xAA, 0x89,
                                0x09, 0xAE, 0xDA, 0xEA, 0x83, 0x00, 0xC0, 0x90};
encryptedText.Text = Encrypt(deriveBytes(pwText.Text, saltText.Text, 10),
                                        initializationVector, plainText.Text);
```

The Decrypt method is implemented similarly, but uses the decryption functionality of the AesManaged class:

```
private string Decrypt(byte[] key, byte[] iv, string encryptedText)
{
    AesManaged aes = new AesManaged();
    byte[] encryptedBytes = Convert.FromBase64String(encryptedText);
    aes.Key = key;
    aes.IV = iv;
    using (MemoryStream stream = new MemoryStream())
    {
        using (CryptoStream decrypt =
                        new CryptoStream(stream, aes.CreateDecryptor(),
                                                CryptoStreamMode.Write))
        {
            decrypt.Write(encryptedBytes, 0, encryptedBytes.Length);
            decrypt.Flush();
            decrypt.Close();
            byte[] decryptedBytes = stream.ToArray();
            return UTF8Encoding.UTF8.GetString(
                                decryptedBytes, 0,
                                decryptedBytes.Length);
        }
    }
}
```

User Access Control

ASP.NET 2.0 introduced a membership database that combines database tables with stored procedures to provide authentication and authorization capabilities. The process of authentication is similar to a guard at a gate, checking identification cards, before allowing access. The authentication process has a binary answer: either the user has access or she doesn't. Authorization, however, controls the nature of the access once a user is inside the gate. Ushers at a concert, for example, check concertgoers' tickets to make sure they are permitted access to the concert. This is an example of authentication. Some concert attendees might have access to a VIP section or have a backstage pass. These are varying degrees of access, from a regular concert attendee who can sit and watch to someone who is allowed to go backstage and meet the performers. This is an example of authorization—what access does someone have after they get past the gate that separates insiders from outsiders?

In ASP.NET, authorization is accomplished via roles. A user can be a member of zero or more roles, and how roles define access is a detail specified in the application design. ASP.NET 3.5 introduces services to provide clients access to the authentication and authorization databases. Before these services can be used, a web application must be configured to use a membership database. If you want to install the membership capabilities into a database server, you can use the `aspnet_regsql` utility that comes with the .NET Framework.

Several services are exposed in the `System.Web.ApplicationServices` namespace. Let's take a look at the services for authentication and authorization. Exposing these services in an ASP.NET application is a simple matter of adding the services and bindings in `web.config` and enabling the services in the `system.web.extensions` configuration section. The services must also be referenced in the `ServiceHost` tag in an SVC file. Let's take a closer look at enabling these services and consuming them from Silverlight.

In `web.config`, the `authentication` and `roleManager` elements within the `system.web` section are used to configure and enable authentication for the web application:

```
<system.web>
    <authentication mode="Forms" />
    <roleManager enabled="true" />
    <!-- ... -->
</system.web>
```

These services must then be enabled in the `system.web.extensions` section. The `RoleService` provides web methods for determining whether a user is a member of a particular role:

```
<system.web.extensions>
  <scripting>
    <webServices>
        <authenticationService enabled="true" requireSSL="false"/>
        <roleService enabled="true"/>
    </webServices>
  </scripting>
</system.web.extensions>
```

It is a good idea to enable SSL for authentication. The `system.serviceModel` section contains the services, bindings, and behaviors related to these services:

```
<system.serviceModel>
  <services>
    <service name="System.Web.ApplicationServices.AuthenticationService"
            behaviorConfiguration="authServiceBehaviors">
      <endpoint contract="System.Web.ApplicationServices.AuthenticationService"
              binding="basicHttpBinding"
              bindingConfiguration="serviceBindingConfig"
              bindingNamespace="http://asp.net/ApplicationServices/v200"/>
    </service>
    <service name="System.Web.ApplicationServices.RoleService"
            behaviorConfiguration="roleServiceBehaviors">
```

```
            <endpoint contract="System.Web.ApplicationServices.RoleService"
                    binding="basicHttpBinding"
                    bindingConfiguration="serviceBindingConfig"
                    bindingNamespace="http://asp.net/ApplicationServices/v200"/>
        </service>
    </services>
    <bindings>
        <basicHttpBinding>
            <binding name="serviceBindingConfig">
                <security mode="None"/>
            </binding>
        </basicHttpBinding>
    </bindings>
    <behaviors>
        <serviceBehaviors>
            <behavior name="authServiceBehaviors">
                <serviceMetadata httpGetEnabled="true"/>
            </behavior>
            <behavior name="roleServiceBehaviors">
                <serviceMetadata httpGetEnabled="true"/>
            </behavior>
        </serviceBehaviors>
    </behaviors>
    <serviceHostingEnvironment aspNetCompatibilityEnabled="true"/>
</system.serviceModel>
```

Each service has a corresponding SVC file within the web application in order to connect a service host with the service. For the authentication service, you need to add a Silverlight-enabled WCF service to the web project with the name AuthenticationService.svc and replace existing content with the following code (you can refer to the "Creating a WCF Service Consumable by Silverlight" section of Chapter 4 for further details on adding a WCF service with Silverlight):

```
<%@ ServiceHost Language="C#"
                Service="System.Web.ApplicationServices.AuthenticationService" %>
```

Similarly, the following is for the role service, placed in RoleService.svc:

```
<%@ ServiceHost Language="C#"
                        Service="System.Web.ApplicationServices.RoleService" %>
```

Once you have this configuration done, you can attempt to access a service directly from a browser—for example, by browsing to http://localhost/AuthService.svc.

Using the Authentication Service

The authentication service provides methods to log in and log out, along with checking whether the user is logged in. When a successful login happens, a cookie is set on the client side to store this state. Let's look closer at the methods the authentication service provides:

IsLoggedIn: Returns true if the user is logged in (authentication cookie is present) and returns false otherwise.

Login: Verifies user's credentials, and if they are validated successfully, the authentication cookie is set. This method takes the username and password, a custom credentials of type string, and a boolean value specifying whether the authentication cookie persists across sessions.

Logout: Clears the authentication cookie from the browser.

ValidateUser: Verifies a user's credentials. This is similar to Login, but it does not set the authentication cookie if the user's credentials are validated successfully.

Figure 11-4 shows a sample login screen. The login and password shown (testuser/testuser!) are valid with the database distributed with this chapter's code.

Figure 11-4. *Sample login screen*

In order to transition from a login screen to a screen that represents the main user interface to the application, the XAML that houses the login screen also houses a layout panel that has the main interface. There's a login button on the login screen and a logout button that generally will appear on each screen of the application.

```xml
<UserControl x:Class="chapter11.LoginScreen"
    xmlns="http://schemas.microsoft.com/winfx/2006/xaml/presentation"
    xmlns:x="http://schemas.microsoft.com/winfx/2006/xaml"
    Width="400" Height="300">
    <Canvas x:Name="LayoutRoot">
        <Grid x:Name="loginScreen" Background="White" Width="400" Height="300">
            ...
            <Button Width="50" Content="Login" x:Name="loginButton"
                        Click="login_clicked" Margin="5"/>
            ...
        </Grid>
        <Canvas x:Name="mainCanvas" Visibility="Collapsed">
            <TextBlock Canvas.Left="25" Canvas.Top="25"
                        Text="You have successfully logged in."/>
            <Button Width="70" Height="50" Content="Logout"
                        Canvas.Left="25" Canvas.Top="75"
                        Click="logoutButton_Click" x:Name="logoutButton"/>
        </Canvas>
    </Canvas>
</UserControl>
```

After adding a service reference to the authentication service, you just need to implement the click event handlers on the buttons for logging in and out:

```
AuthenticationServiceClient client;
public LoginScreen()
{
    InitializeComponent();
    client = new AuthenticationServiceClient();
    client.LoginCompleted +=
            new EventHandler<LoginCompletedEventArgs>(client_LoginCompleted);
    client.LogoutCompleted +=
            new EventHandler<AsyncCompletedEventArgs>(client_LogoutCompleted);
}
```

The login button click handler calls LoginAsync. The third parameter can be custom authentication credentials, but in this case we just pass null. The final parameter is set to true in order to maintain the authentication cookie on the client even after the browser navigates away. This is similar to the "Remember me" check box on the ASP.NET login control.

```
private void login_clicked(object sender, RoutedEventArgs e)
{
    client.LoginAsync(username.Text, password.Password, null, true);
}
```

The LoginCompleted event checks the result of the Login call, and if it indicates that the user successfully logged in, the main user interface is shown. Otherwise, an error message is displayed to the user.

```
void client_LoginCompleted(object sender, LoginCompletedEventArgs e)
{
    if (e.Result)
    {
        loginScreen.Visibility = Visibility.Collapsed;
        mainCanvas.Visibility = Visibility.Visible;
    }
    else
    {
        resultText.Text = "Incorrect username or password";
    }
}
```

The logout button calls the Logout method on the authentication service in order to clear the authentication cookie from the user's browser, and the asynchronous callback handler hides the main user interface and shows the login screen again:

```
private void logoutButton_Click(object sender, RoutedEventArgs e)
{
    client.LogoutAsync();
}
void client_LogoutCompleted(object sender, AsyncCompletedEventArgs e)
```

```
{
    loginScreen.Visibility = Visibility.Visible;
    mainCanvas.Visibility = Visibility.Collapsed;
}
```

Since the authentication cookie might be valid when a user first visits the application, your application should call ValidateUser and react accordingly (such as displaying a message that the user is logged in; similar to how web sites display it).

If you don't want to (or can't) use the ASP.NET authentication service, the ASP.NET authentication service serves as a good model for an authentication service you could implement.

Using the RoleService

Once a user is authenticated and logged in, the RoleService is used to obtain the roles the user belongs to and to check whether he belongs to a specified role as part of the authorization process. Let's take a look at the methods the RoleService provides:

GetRolesForCurrentUser: Returns an array of strings containing the roles the currently authenticated user belongs to

IsCurrentUserInRole: Takes a role name and returns true if the user is a member of the role

Once the user is authenticated and logged in, you can retrieve the list of roles the user is in using the GetRolesForCurrentUser method. If your application will make a number of role-based decisions, it's better to cache this list of roles locally instead of repeatedly calling the IsCurrentUserInRole service method.

Again, we create an instance of the RoleService client and register the GetRolesForCurrentUser event handler:

```
roleClient = new RoleServiceClient();
roleClient.GetRolesForCurrentUserCompleted +=
    new EventHandler<GetRolesForCurrentUserCompletedEventArgs>
      (roleClient_GetRolesForCurrentUserCompleted);
```

One opportunity to cache the user's roles occurs when the user successfully logs in—although you might want to delay this, since it adds to the amount of time it takes to log the user in. You'd also have to handle loading roles for when the user is already logged in:

```
roleClient.GetRolesForCurrentUserAsync();
```

Once the callback for this web service method occurs, the roles are cached in a List<string>:

```
private List<string> cachedRoles;
private void roleClient_GetRolesForCurrentUserCompleted(object sender,
                        GetRolesForCurrentUserCompletedEventArgs e)
{
    cachedRoles = new List<string>();
    foreach (string role in e.Result)
    {
        cachedRoles.Add(role);
    }
}
public bool isUserInRole(string role)
{
    return(cachedRoles.Contains(role));
}
```

The application can now use the isUserInRole method, instead of the RoleService directly, to make role-based decisions.

Division of Responsibility

You should use a secure communication channel with a server by using HTTPS and enforce application-level access control (such as using the authentication and authorization services provided by ASP.NET 3.5). This doesn't fully ensure that your application is secure, however. There are several security-related concerns regarding your application's code getting downloaded to the client. These concerns all relate to the possibility that someone can get at the code and resources within a Silverlight application. They can be addressed by application architecture.

The XAP file is just a ZIP archive containing one or more DLL files and resource files. Assume someone wants to take a Silverlight application apart—all they need to do is obtain the XAP file (in the browser's cache or by other means), rename the file extension to zip, and open it in an application that can extract and create ZIP files. The XAP file from this chapter includes chapter11.dll and a manifest file. If you unzip this XAP, someone can now easily get at the DLL.

Once someone has a DLL expanded on disk, it can be disassembled in a utility such as Reflector. Figure 11-5 shows chapter11.dll taken apart in Reflector. It is possible to go a step further and decompile the code, as you can see in Figure 11-6, which shows a method from the LoginScreen class.

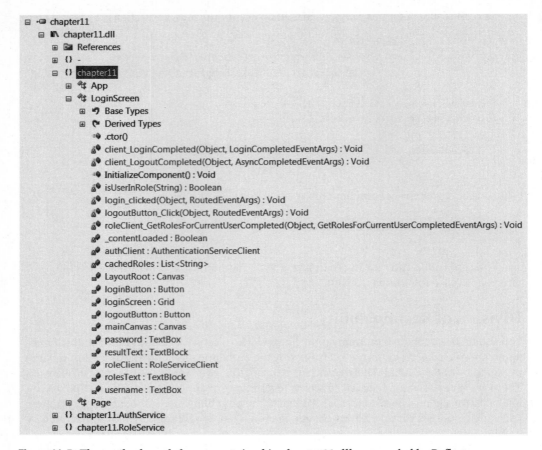

Figure 11-5. *The methods and classes contained in chapter11.dll as revealed by Reflector*

```
Disassembler

private void roleClient_GetRolesForCurrentUserCompleted(object sender, GetRolesForCurrentUserCompletedEventArgs e)
{
    this.cachedRoles = new List<string>();
    foreach (string role in e.Result)
    {
        this.cachedRoles.Add(role);
        this.rolesText.Text = this.rolesText.Text + role + " ";
    }
}
```

Figure 11-6. *The decompiled GetRolesForCurrentUser event callback*

Of course, most users won't have the skill or knowledge to disassemble and decompile a Silverlight application, but an application built with security in mind must pay attention to the people that can. The best solution to the disassembling/decompiling of code is to use an obfuscator, such as Dotfuscator, which is distributed with Visual Studio. After running the DLL for this chapter through Dotfuscator, the identifiers are garbled, and the decompiled methods are a challenge to understand unless you're the CoreCLR. Figure 11-7 shows the obfuscated DLL in Reflector.

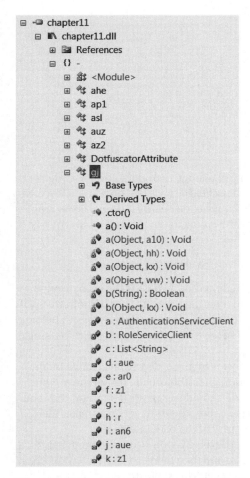

Figure 11-7. *The obfuscated chapter11.dll file*

The method to retrieve and cache roles, after obfuscation, looks like this:

```
private void a(object A_0, hh A_1)
{
    this.c = new List<string>();
    IEnumerator<string> enumerator = A_1.a().l();
    try
    {
        {
```

```
        while (enumerator.g())
        {
            string str = enumerator.f();
            this.c.d(str);
            this.k.b(zt.a(this.k.r(), str, " "));
        }
    }
    finally
    {
        if (enumerator != null)
        {
            enumerator.h();
        }
    }
}
```

As you can see, obfuscation is great at making it a challenge to understand the code. But make sure as much code related to the application is obfuscated as possible, since some revealed method names or variable names provide clues to what the code nearby is doing. For example, the decompiled constructor makes the following call, revealing that no matter what type b is, it has an event named GetRolesForCurrentUserCompleted:

```
this.b.add_GetRolesForCurrentUserCompleted(new EventHandler<hh>(this.a));
```

Between this and the previously shown obfuscated method (which is the asynchronous callback), it is obvious where code can be modified to alter the roles the user belongs to. So, if it's possible to trick a Silverlight application into believing a user is in roles he doesn't belong to, it demonstrates why you must guard against placing too much functionality within a single Silverlight application.

The simplest application design principle to follow is to place all privileged code on the server side and let the server perform an authentication check before the rest of the method executes. Role-based decisions made on the client side should not create a decision between executing normal-privileged code and high-privileged code. However, you can make role-based decisions on such benign things as the appearance of the user interface.

Another approach to separating different privilege levels of code is to place them behind a traditional web site login screen for user authentication and then deliver a completely different Silverlight application to the user based on her access level. This is illustrated in Figure 11-8.

If you take this approach, make sure any more highly privileged Silverlight applications are not cached on the client side. This helps make it tougher to augment an application to grant a regular user higher privileges. Even if you take this approach, it's wise to place as much high-privilege code on the server side as possible so you can make sure only users with the right access level are allowed to run the code.

Another valid concern is the security of resources used by a Silverlight application. As shown in Figure 11-9, even though the main application assembly has been obfuscated, not only are resources such as the embedded XAML easily viewable, but they can also be easily extracted.

Login screen
in ASP.NET
Successful login
If no elevated access
levels, redirect to ...
For privileged users (such
as administrators), redirect to ...
Silverlight application
for regular users
Silverlight application
for privileged users

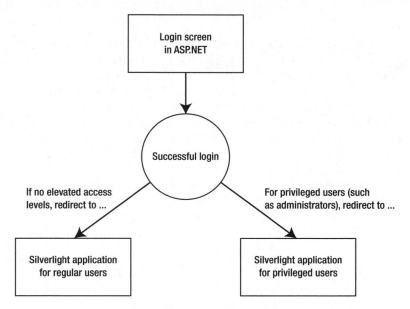

Figure 11-8. *Redirecting to a different Silverlight application based on users' roles*

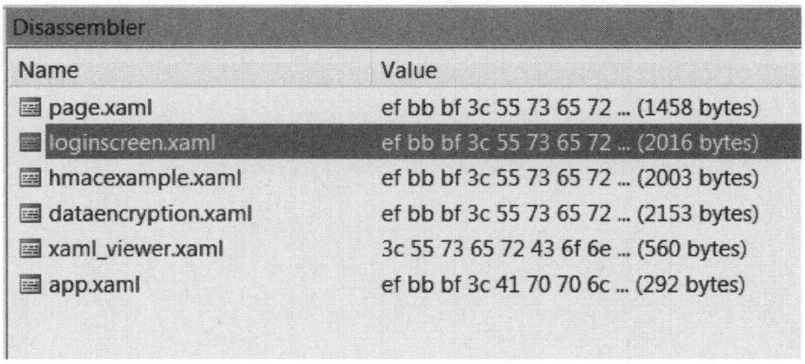

Disassembler
Name
Value
page.xaml
ef bb bf 3c 55 73 65 72 ... (1458 bytes)
loginscreen.xaml
ef bb bf 3c 55 73 65 72 ... (2016 bytes)
hmacexample.xaml
ef bb bf 3c 55 73 65 72 ... (2003 bytes)
dataencryption.xaml
ef bb bf 3c 55 73 65 72 ... (2153 bytes)
xaml_viewer.xaml
3c 55 73 65 72 43 6f 6e ... (560 bytes)
app.xaml
ef bb bf 3c 41 70 70 6c ... (292 bytes)

Figure 11-9. *The resources embedded in the application assembly*

One strategy to protect resources is to encrypt them. This is useful for any data files that you want downloaded at the same time as the Silverlight application. You can use the `AesManaged` class previously detailed with a secret key that is downloaded as part of the Silverlight application (perhaps an authenticated user's data protection password stored with his profile) to encrypt and decrypt data locally.

Another approach to protecting resources is to avoid packaging them with the Silverlight application. Once a user is authenticated, the application can download the appropriate resources on demand. This applies to both resources stored within the application's DLL and resources stored in the XAP file. Your application design must account for this anywhere a resource (such as an image) differs based on a user's access level.

Summary

Applications must be designed and developed with security in mind. This chapter started off by detailing the security model Silverlight provides for executable code, illustrating how application code cannot directly invoke any code that can interact with the host platform. The rest of this chapter detailed application-level security, such as using HTTPS as a secure channel, encrypting/decrypting information, authenticating and authorizing users, and ensuring your applications are designed well to protect code and resources. Make sure your Silverlight application and surrounding infrastructure (such as an ASP.NET application) are designed and developed with security in mind. Late in development or immediately before deployment are not the times to start thinking about security.

The next chapter is focused on how to use the Silverlight unit testing framework to implement the unit testing strategy during the Silverlight development project life cycle; it also explains key points for debugging Silverlight applications using Visual Studio.

CHAPTER 12

■■■

Testing and Debugging

Testing and debugging are vital activities in building quality software. From a developer's perspective, unit testing ensures small units of code work. By having a suite of tests, it is easy to catch a bug introduced into code that was previously shown to be bug free. Testing helps ensure software quality by catching as many bugs as possible and proactively ensuring bugs aren't introduced. Debugging, however, is generally done after a bug has been found. Debugging involves tools and an effective problem-solving process to find the root cause of a bug in order to apply a fix. You can build defenses into your application to make debugging easier, such as error logs (to capture errors) and audit logs (to reconstruct what the user of the application did to trigger the bug). This chapter aims to show you how to go about testing Silverlight applications and preparing for and conducting debugging when things do go wrong.

Testing

Testing involves both ensuring applications are error free and verifying applications work according to requirements and design. It is the software developer's job to implement tests, known as *unit tests*, to thoroughly test the code he writes. *Integration testing*, usually the next step after unit testing, is where two or more unit-tested components are integrated together as a part of the larger system or composite component. *Regression testing* features thorough system testing of the software application (usually as the last phase of testing cycle), and needs to be repeated if a software defect is identified and fixed. Regression testing confirms/validates that the fixed defect does not introduce one or more new defects. Unit testing, integration testing, and regression testing are part of the development phase of the software development project life cycle.

    Functional testing verifies the application corresponds to its specifications and requirements, and *usability testing* ensures the application is well designed from a user interface perspective. Unit testing, integration testing, and regression testing can be part of functional testing, usability testing, or both. Functional testing and usability testing generally belong to a quality assurance department.

Unit Testing

The goal of unit testing is to test the smallest possible unit of a system. If you're building an airplane, it's impractical to test the smallest pieces, such as verifying that each screw can withstand a certain degree of pressure, or that hoses that pump fluid or oxygen don't disconnect or wear out absurdly fast. These pieces still need testing, however, or the airplane likely won't work. Since the airplane manufacturer can't practically test the tiniest parts, the responsibility of testing lies with the manufacturer of these parts. The screw manufacturer must know how much pressure the screws can withstand and then verify they match the specification. These smallest parts are the units of a system, the building blocks that, when assembled, create something much larger. Just like the screw manufacturer must test his screws, the software developer must test his code at the smallest unit possible—typically methods.

Silverlight Unit Testing Framework

Microsoft provides a Silverlight unit testing framework very similar to the testing framework used by Visual Studio 2008; however, the testing output is not integrated with Visual Studio. The testing framework takes the form of a Silverlight application, but it isn't distributed as part of Silverlight or the Silverlight SDK. Visit the home page of the Microsoft Silverlight Unit Test Framework (`http://code.msdn.microsoft.com/silverlightut`) to download the unit-testing framework for Silverlight 2. As I am writing this chapter, the latest version is the December 2009 version for Silverlight 2. The Silverlight 3 version is still not available; however, the preliminary test with the December 2008 version of the unit testing framework for Silverlight 3 applications passed.

The unit testing framework is a ZIP file with the name `Unit_test_framework.zip`, and it contains the following two testing framework binaries:

- `Microsoft.Silverlight.Testing.dll`

- `Microsoft.VisualStudio.QualityTools.UnitTesting.Silverlight.dll`

Now let's look at the Silverlight unit testing framework in action. Create a new Silverlight application and add the two unit testing–related assemblies mentioned previously, as shown in Figure 12-1.

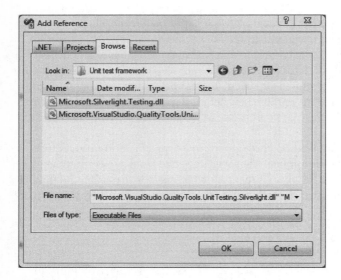

Figure 12-1. *Adding unit testing–related assemblies to the application's references*

You can remove `MainPage.xaml` and `MainPage.xaml.cs` from the project since they aren't needed in our case. Go to `App.xaml.cs` and add the following unit test library reference by placing the following `using` statement at the top:

```
using Microsoft.Silverlight.Testing;
```

The testing framework provides its own user interface that you can connect to your Silverlight testing application by invoking `UnitTestSystem.CreateTestPage`, as shown here:

```
private void Application_Startup(object sender, StartupEventArgs e)
{
    this.RootVisual = (UIElement)UnitTestSystem.CreateTestPage();
}
```

Now that you have the unit testing framework ready to go, the next step is to add a reference to the application assembly that is the subject of testing. The rest happens automatically after we apply certain test-related attributes to classes that contain tests. If you're writing a business application, user input typically must be validated to ensure it meets certain criteria. A validation class might be located in a class library assembly and used by any Silverlight applications developed by a company. Here's a `Validators` class with a single validation method that verifies a value is within a range:

```
public class Validators
{
    public static bool validateRange(int value, int lowBound, int highBound)
    {
        return (value >= lowBound && value < highBound);
    }
}
```

Even a method this simple may have a bug in it. Bugs aren't only due to poorly written code—bugs can also be due to incorrect assumptions or failure to match requirements. Or a bug can be due to a simple typo. In order to know for sure whether a piece of code contains bugs, a set of unit tests must be written. The `Validators` class is located in the `chapter12` assembly. Let's turn to the application that provides the unit testing framework and implement some tests.

Create a new class (not a UserControl) and add the following `using` statements at the top:

```
using Microsoft.Silverlight.Testing;
using Microsoft.VisualStudio.TestTools.UnitTesting;
using chapter12;
```

If you're unfamiliar with unit testing frameworks, they typically work by examining the metadata on classes and methods to get the necessary cues as to what to do. A class that contains test methods is decorated with the `TestClass` attribute, and individual test methods are decorated with `TestMethod`, as shown here. Also, the testing class must inherit from `SilverlightTest`.

```
namespace chapter12test
{
    [TestClass]
    public class ValidatorsTests : SilverlightTest
    {
        [TestMethod]
        public void TestRangeTooLow()
        {
            Assert.IsFalse(Validators.validateRange(0, 10, 20));
        }
        [TestMethod]
        public void TestRangeAtUpperBound()
        {
            Assert.IsTrue(Validators.validateRange(20, 10, 20));
        }
    }
}
```

Initially with the previous two tests, the TestRangeTooLow test will succeed and the TestRangeAtUpperBound will fail. The Assert class provides a number of methods to verify conditions to indicate test success. If the conditions are not met, an exception is thrown automatically and is caught by the unit testing framework, informing you of the test failure.

Now right-click the Chapter12TestPage.html page under the Chapter12.Web project and select the View Browser option or press Ctrl+F5 to run the project without debugging mode. All tests will execute immediately. An AssertFailedException exception will be raised if the TestRangeAtUpperBound test fails. You will see the output shown in Figure 12-2.

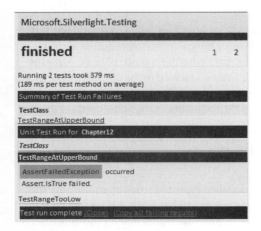

Figure 12-2. *Unit testing framework output with a failing test*

Now if you click the "Copy all failing results" link in the test output, you can see the failing results in details (as shown in Figure 12-3), which you can copy for further evaluation.

Figure 12-3. *Detailed results on the failing test*

The reason this test fails is that the requirements for the validator method specify that the lower and upper bounds must both be inclusive. This is easily fixed by changing the < to <= when testing the value against the upper bound. After making this fix, rerunning the testing application shows all tests succeeding, as shown in Figure 12-4.

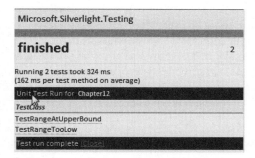

Figure 12-4. *Unit testing framework output with all tests passing*

The Assert class provides a number of useful methods for conveniently verifying test results, and also provides a way to trigger a failure in case the provided methods are not sufficient. Table 12-1 lists the static methods provided by the Assert class. Note that many methods provide a large set of overloads in order to cover a wide variety of data types. These assertion methods also give the ability to pass in a string parameter as a custom message that will be included in the test execution report.

Table 12-1. *Static Methods of Microsoft.VisualStudio.TestTools.UnitTesting.Assert*

Method	Description
AreEqual	Tests whether two values are equal.
AreNotEqual	Tests whether two values are not equal.
AreNotSame	Tests whether two object references point to different objects.
AreSame	Tests whether two object references point to the same object.
Fail	Causes a test to immediately fail. Use this to fail a test based on custom logic.
Inconclusive	Causes a test to report "inconclusive" in the report. Use this for tests not implemented or for tests where it's impossible to pass or fail the test. This is an overloaded method. Assert.Inconclusive() defines that the assertion cannot be verified. Assert.Inconclusive(String) defines that the assertion cannot be verified and displays the passed message. Assert.Inconclusive(String, Object[]) defines that the assertion cannot be verified and displays a message with the specified formatting.
IsFalse	Tests whether the specified Boolean value is false.
IsInstanceOfType	Tests whether an object is an instance of a given type.
IsNotInstanceOfType	Tests whether an object is not an instance of a given type.
IsNotNull	Tests whether a given reference is not null.
IsNull	Tests whether a given reference is null.
IsTrue	Tests whether the specified Boolean value is true.
ReplaceNullChars	Utility method to replace null characters within a string with \0 so that the null characters can be displayed.

The Assert class can throw an AssertFailedException or an AssertInconclusiveException. It is recommended not to catch these exceptions by your code since they provide the mechanism for communicating test results to the unit testing framework. There are two other Assert-related classes: StringAssert and CollectionAssert. StringAssert provides a set of methods useful for string-based conditional tests, and CollectionAssert does likewise for collections. Table 12-2 lists the methods of StringAssert, and Table 12-3 shows the methods of CollectionAssert.

Table 12-2. *Static Methods of Microsoft.VisualStudio.TestTools.UnitTesting.StringAssert*

Method	Description
Contains	Tests whether one string occurs somewhere within another string
DoesNotMatch	Tests whether two strings do not match
EndsWith	Tests whether one string ends with another string
Matches	Tests whether two strings match
StartsWith	Tests whether one string starts with another string

Table 12-3. *Static Methods of Microsoft.VisualStudio.TestTools.UnitTesting.CollectionAssert*

Method	Description
AllItemsAreInstancesOfType	Tests whether all items in a collection are instances of a specific type
AllItemsAreNotNull	Tests whether all items in a collection are not null
AllItemsAreUnique	Tests whether all items in a collection are different
AreEqual	Tests whether two collections contain the same items (object values are tested, not references) in the same order
AreEquivalent	Similar to AreEqual, but the items can be in any order as long as two collections contain the same items
AreNotEqual	Tests whether two collections contain a different number of items, a different set of items, or the same items in different orders
AreNotEquivalent	Tests whether two collections contain a different number of items or a different set of items
Contains	Tests whether a collection contains a specified item
DoesNotContain	Tests whether a collection does not contain a specified item
IsNotSubsetOf	Tests whether one collection does not contain a subset of items from another collection
IsSubsetOf	Tests whether one collection contains a subset of items from another collection

Besides TestClass and TestMethod, there are many useful attributes for controlling how tests behave. Table 12-4 lists attributes that are useful for the initialization and cleanup of resources. All attributes shown in Table 12-4 apply to methods.

Table 12-4. *Testing Framework Attributes Related to Resource Initialization and Cleanup*

Attribute	Description
AssemblyCleanup	Marks the method that executes after all tests within the assembly have completed executing; can only be used on one method within an assembly
AssemblyInitialize	Marks the method that executes before any tests within the assembly have executed; can only be used on one method within an assembly
ClassCleanup	Marks the method that contains the code to execute after all tests within a class containing tests have completed executing; can only apply to a single method within a class
ClassInitialize	Marks the method that contains the code to execute before any tests within a class execute; can only apply to a single method within a class
TestCleanup	Marks the method that contains the code to execute after each test completes executing; can only apply to a single method within a class
TestInitialize	Marks the method that contains the code to execute before each test executes; can only apply to a single method within a class

Note that both TestInitialize and TestCleanup execute once per test, ClassInitialize and ClassCleanup execute once per testing class, and AssemblyInitialize and AssemblyCleanup execute once per testing assembly. These attributes provide for a variety of resource management in a test class.

There are several other useful attributes you might encounter a need for when writing your unit tests. These are shown in Table 12-5.

Table 12-5. *Testing Framework Attributes*

Attribute	Description
Description	Used to provide a description for a test.
ExpectedException	Normally, exceptions indicate the code under test has failed. When a thrown exception indicates success (such as verifying certain methods aren't implemented yet on purpose), this attribute tells the testing framework that the specific exception is expected and avoids failing the test. You can specify this attribute multiple times.
Ignore	Indicates the test should be skipped.
Owner	Provides information on who is responsible for the test.
Priority	Specifies the integer priority of the test.
Timeout	Specifies a timeout in milliseconds for a test. If an operation takes longer than the timeout value specified, the test fails.

The TestContext class is also available for unit test classes; however, the only supported operation for Silverlight testing is the WriteLine method. Before you can use this class, however, you must provide the property in your test class. When the testing framework discovers that your test class provides the following public property, it automatically sets the test context for your class to use:

```
private TestContext testContext;
public TestContext TestContext
{
    get
    {
        return testContext;
    }
    set
    {
        testContext = value;
    }
}
```

There are also just a few properties in the `TestContext` class that are usable in Silverlight testing. These are shown in Table 12-6.

Table 12-6. *Properties of TestContext*

Name	Type	Description
CurrentTestOutcome	UnitTestOutcome	Represents the outcome of the test; possible values are Aborted, Error, Failed, Inconclusive, InProgress, Passed, Timeout, and Unknown
TestName	string	The name of the method containing the test

If you want to save your test results, you can use the properties of `TestContext` along with a method marked with `TestCleanup` that saves results to isolated storage or communicates them to a custom web service.

Since the testing application has access to your main application, you can interact with controls on different pages of the application, including calling event handler methods directly to simulate an event firing. It is also important to perform the user interface–driven test. It would be nice if it were possible to test an application's user interface from an outsider's perspective, and automate this if possible. Fortunately, Silverlight provides for this automation.

Automated User Interface Testing

Testing must be automated. Software is too complex to reliably test well manually on a consistent basis. Test automation carries over to user interfaces. Manually testing user interfaces is boring, tedious, and highly unreliable since test cases may be skipped or the order of operations for tests violated. Optimally, we want user interface testing to happen automatically, instead of a tester having to manually click every button and explore every screen. Another reason for automated user interface testing is the ability to easily capture test results. Fortunately, Silverlight does indeed provide automation capabilities in the form of a framework for programmatically controlling user interfaces. The main supporting infrastructure for user interface automation is a set of automation peer classes that closely mirror user interface classes in Silverlight.

The UI Automation Library (`System.Windows.Automation`) that works for other types of Windows applications can also be used to work with Silverlight applications. Before you can use the automation classes to interact with user interface elements, you must obtain an `AutomationElement` that serves as a parent element. You can then search for controls that are descendents of the parent. You could use the desktop as the parent, but this would make it slow when searching for controls. Instead, you want to get as close to your Silverlight application as possible.

The Microsoft .NET Framework class library also includes the `System.Diagnostics` namespace, which mainly provides a set of classes to perform interaction with system processes, event logs, and performance counters.

Once you include references to the UI Automation Library and diagnostics library, you can use the following code to search the currently running processes for a specific window title:

```
Process process = null;
foreach (Process p in Process.GetProcessesByName("iexplore"))
{
    if (p.MainWindowTitle.Contains("Silverlight (Chapter 12)"))
    {
        process = p;
        break;
    }
}
if (process != null)
{
    AutomationElement browserInstance  =
        System.Windows.Automation.AutomationElement.
          FromHandle(process.MainWindowHandle);
}
```

Once you have an AutomationElement that represents a parent to your Silverlight application, you can then search for certain controls of interest. When searching the tree of user interface elements beneath a given AutomationElement, you need to define the scope of the search and a condition used to specify what specific elements you want to find. The AutomationElement class provides two methods, FindFirst and FindAll, for finding one or more elements that match the given criteria. The first parameter to these methods is the TreeScope. Table 12-7 shows the different TreeScope values you can use.

Table 12-7. *Enumeration Values from System.Windows.Automation.TreeScope*

Enumeration Value	Description
Element	Search only within the element
Children	Search within the element and its children
Descendents	Search within the element and all its descendents (its children, its children's children, etc.)
Subtree	Search within the root of the search and all descendents

The second parameter to these methods is the condition. A *condition* is essentially a search criterion. The Condition class itself provides two shortcuts for making searching easy: Condition. TrueCondition and Condition.FalseCondition. By combining the first with a search scope, you can obtain all elements within the scope. The latter will return no elements. By combining one of these with one of the Condition class' four inheritors, you can create sophisticated search criteria. The AndCondition, OrCondition, and NotCondition classes can be continually nested to support as complicated a search condition as you need. The other inheritor, PropertyCondition, is used to find elements with certain properties set to certain values. You can use PropertyCondition to search for a value of any of the properties from `AutomationElement`, such as `ClassNameProperty`, `NameProperty`, `AcceleratorKeyProperty`, and many others.

Revisiting the preceding `browserInstance`, which now holds a reference to the Internet Explorer (IE) instance that hosts this chapter's Silverlight application, you can search for a specific XAML page with the name "Login Screen" within the application using the `FindFirst` method, as shown in the following code:

```
AutomationElement loginScreen =
    browserInstance.FindFirst(TreeScope.Descendents,
        new PropertyCondition(AutomationElement.NameProperty,
        "Login Screen"));
```

Now you can find the collection of TextBox-type controls available within the "Login Screen" XAML page by utilizing the `loginScreen` `AutomationElement` returned in the previous example and the `FindAll` method shown in the following code snippet. Here we use `ControlType.Edit` to represent the TextBox control.

```
AutomationElementCollection loginpageTextBoxes =
    loginScreen.FindAll(TreeScope.Children,
        new PropertyCondition(AutomationElement.ControlTypeProperty,
        ControlType.Edit));
```

The `AutomationProperties` class provides several useful attached properties you can use to provide cues for the automation system while leaving the rest of your object's properties intact. These attached properties are shown in Table 12-8. When developing an application, you can use the `AutomationId` property to uniquely identify elements throughout your application specifically for use by automation clients.

Table 12-8. *Attached Properties in AutomationProperties*

Name	Type	Description
AcceleratorKey	string	The accelerator key for the element
AccessKey	string	The access key for the element
AutomationId	string	A unique identifier for the element; useful as a cue for automation clients in searches
HelpText	string	Help text for the element; generally the associated tool tip text
IsColumnHeader	bool	true if the element is a column header (such as in a DataGrid)
IsRequiredForForm	bool	true if the element must be filled out for a given form
IsRowHeader	bool	true if the element is a row header (such as in a DataGrid)
ItemStatus	string	Indicates the status of the item; generally application specific
ItemType	string	Describes the type of the element
LabeledBy	UIElement	Specifies which UIElement acts as a label for this element
Name	string	The element's name

Once you have a reference to the element of the Silverlight application, you can use other aspects of the UI Automation Library to simulate keyboard and mouse input for the application under test.

Debugging

The debugging process should not begin when a bug is discovered. Instead, it should start during application design. You should include logging functionality in your application, such as error logs and audit logs. An error log is useful for tracking exceptions thrown by an application. Exceptions also come with stack traces that help in identifying the code path that lead to the exception. Audit logs can be used to reconstruct what users were doing within the application leading up to an error. These are important elements that must go into application design and development, but there are also other approaches you can use to make code easier to debug, such as including extra logging or other features in special debug mode builds of an application. Any time you go about debugging, however, you must take a structured approach to hunting bugs down.

The Debugging Process

Debugging may or may not be your favorite activity when developing software, but the same general frame of mind you use for developing code can be applied to debugging. Debugging is just another form of problem solving. Having a plan of attack to discover the source of a bug is invaluable. Here are the steps you should follow when you know of a bug and need to go about fixing it:

1. Get to know the system. If you're unfamiliar with the system you're fixing, you should get enough familiarity to do as good a job as possible at fixing the bug without introducing new bugs. Knowing how the system works, what components it uses, and what technologies are involved (e.g., IIS, ASP.NET, Windows Workflow Foundation) can also possibly give you more clues to narrowing down the bug.

2. Reproduce the bug. You must know what you're fixing in order to fix it. Sometimes you're lucky enough to have a consistent reproduction; sometimes you aren't. The goal here is to have the smallest piece of code or the shortest sequence of actions that reveals the bug.

3. Make a guess. Sometimes by making a guess you can zero-in on the bug right away. This isn't always possible, but when it works, you appear to have special powers. Raymond Chen calls this "psychic debugging." It's really just a matter of having enough experience to know the source of a bug based on symptoms. If you can't solve the bug immediately, sometimes a guess will at least get you closer to the source of it in the code.

4. Gather evidence. Solving a bug isn't the most difficult activity as long as you have a solid plan. Part of this plan is to analyze the evidence at your disposal—usually bug reports, error/audit logs, analysis tools such as file/registry activity monitors, and so on.

5. Conduct heavy debugging. If you haven't discovered the source of the bug yet, then now is likely the time to step through code in a debugger. This can be a slow process, depending on how close you can get to the bug, but it will typically give you a clear view of the system at a line-by-line level.

6. Identify the solution. By now you've found the source of the bug. Sometimes a bug fix is straightforward; other times you must be careful not to affect other parts of the system. A strong set of unit tests is invaluable at this point. If you fix the bug but introduce a new bug, or reintroduce an old bug (a regression), the unit tests can identify this and you can revisit your solution.

7. Apply the fix. You've identified the solution, implemented it, and verified it hasn't broken any existing tests. After applying the fix, you may have to update unit tests or add new unit tests. Accordingly, you will probably perform integration testing and regression testing as part of your functional and usability testing to confirm that there is no adverse effect on the overall software application/service due to the applied fix.

Let's take a closer look at some tools and techniques that can save you time when you are debugging Silverlight applications.

Conditional Compilation

Much like .NET assemblies, Silverlight assemblies can be compiled in a debug mode configuration or a release mode configuration. The main differences between debug and release mode are which conditional symbols are defined and whether symbols are generated along with the assembly. For debug mode, the preprocessor symbol DEBUG is automatically defined, and for release mode, TRACE is defined.

Sometimes implementing code only for purposes of debugging can be extremely useful. For example, an application might write a significant amount of information to a log file for debugging only. This code can't run in production applications due to performance reasons, and optimally we want to get rid of this code completely. This can be achieved with conditional compilation. The best approach to conditional compilation is to use #if...#endif to isolate blocks of code that must only appear in certain configurations. Generally, these are used to only put debug code in debug builds—for example, writing to a debug trace log.

```
private void login()
{
#if DEBUG
    traceLog.WriteLine("entered login method");
#endif
    authService.Login(usernameTB.Text, passwordTB.Text, null, null);
#if DEBUG
    traceLog.WriteLine("leaving login method");
#endif
}
```

The DEBUG symbol is automatically defined for debug mode configurations, and RELEASE is automatically defined for release mode configurations. There is one other approach to conditional compilation that is used to limit the type of code that can call a particular method. This is accomplished using the Conditional attribute on a method, as shown here:

```
[Conditional("DEBUG")]
public void debugWriteLine(string message)
{
    debugLog.WriteLine(message);
}
```

A method like this can be extremely useful when providing a public API to a class library that has its own debug log. Any time client code defines the symbol applied to the method via the Conditional attribute, the code is output with the compiled IL. If the client code does not define this symbol, the code is not included. This means a client can use the following code with the knowledge the debug writes will only happen when their code is in a debug mode configuration.

```
public void doSomething()
{
    library.debugWriteLine("calling doLongOperation");
    library.doLongOperation();
    library.debugWriteLine("doLongOperation finished");
}
```

When you use the Conditional attribute, the method it applies to is always compiled and included in the finished assembly. This is an important difference between the Conditional attribute and preprocessor symbol testing via the #if command. If you're using Conditional to control code within the same assembly (such as making decisions based on symbols other than DEBUG/RELEASE), you can prevent the body of the method from being included in the compilation by combining Conditional with #if:

```
[Conditional("DEBUG")]
public void debugWriteLine(string message)
{
#if DEBUG
    debugLog.WriteLine(message);
#endif
}
```

Debugging Silverlight Applications with Visual Studio

The Visual Studio debugger is an invaluable tool for tracing through code. You need to install Silverlight 3 Beta Tools for Visual Studio 2008 (which you did in Chapter 1 while enabling Silverlight applications development) to enable Silverlight application debugging with Visual Studio.

There's little difference between debugging .NET code on Windows and debugging a Silverlight application. The important differences are that the Silverlight plug-in is hosted within a browser (which acts as the host process you debug) and the code on the Silverlight platform runs on the CoreCLR, a runtime completely separate from any other instance of the CLR you have on your system. Silverlight Tools does not support edit-and-continue, just-in-time, or mixed-mode debugging.

Controlling the Debugger

`System.Attribute` is a base class for custom attributes including attributes for the `System.Diagnostics` namespace. Application diagnostic attributes provide cues (such as preventing stepping into certain methods) and more information to the debugger. These attributes are shown in Table 12-9.

Table 12-9. *Attributes in System.Diagnostics Derived from System.Atribute That Interact with the Debugger*

Attribute	Description
DebuggableAttribute	Used to provide configuration-related cues to the JIT compiler and debugger, such as disabling optimizations.
DebuggerBrowsableAttribute	Controls the display of a member within the debugger. Valid values are Collapsed, Never (member is never shown), and RootHidden (useful for collections; shows individual items without showing the root).
DebuggerDisplayAttribute	Specifies what should be shown in the value column in the debugger for the member this decorates.
DebuggerHiddenAttribute	Used to hide the member from the debugger.
DebuggerNonUserCodeAttribute	Indicates that a type/member is not part of the user code and should be hidden from the debugger, not stepped into. This is effectively a combination of DebuggerHiddenAttribute and DebuggerStepThroughAttribute.
DebuggerStepThroughAttribute	When applied to a method, the debugger steps through the method without stopping in a method; however, it does allow a break point (if set) in the method.

If you have long (or long-running) methods that you don't want to consciously step over in the debugger, using the `DebuggerStepThroughAttribute` attribute can save significant time. It is used to avoid stepping through code since it prevents the method from being stepped into. Here's an example usage to mark a validation function that is called often. Make sure you use it in a situation like this when you're sure the method isn't the source of any bugs.

```
[DebuggerStepThrough]
private bool validateIpAddress(string ipAddress)
{
   // parse ipAddress and validate that it's a correct IPv4 address
}
```

The System.Diagnostics.Debug class provides two useful static methods: WriteLine, for sending information to the debugger output, and Assert, for testing assumptions. The WriteLine method uses the Windows OutputDebugString under the covers, so unfortunately this only works when the debugger is on Windows. There are no debug listeners/trace listeners in Silverlight as there are in .NET on Windows, so the Debug.WriteLine method is all there really is to writing debug output. Since OutputDebugString is used at its core, you can attach a debugger and see the output in the Output window (in Visual Studio) or through another debug viewer.

The other method, Assert, is used to test certain assumptions in your code. The Assert method (and its overloads) takes a Boolean parameter as a condition to test. When the condition is false, you see a message box when running in release mode as a default behavior and outputs the message to the default trace output.

Configuring Startup for Debugging

When you're developing a Silverlight application, you can debug the application either by using the development web server or another web server such as IIS or Apache. By including a web site or a web application in your solution when you create a Silverlight project, you can point IIS to this and debug a Silverlight application similar to how it will be deployed on a real server. This can help ensure your configuration is correct on the server side, which will mainly consist of ensuring the web server can serve XAP files and possibly PDB files for debugging purposes. Figure 12-5 shows configuring the web project to start up using an external server. You can separate the base URL from specific pages to make it easier to change from one startup page to the next (such as with the switching of the startup to the second Silverlight application in this chapter).

If you create a Silverlight application with no accompanying web site/web application, you can still debug a Silverlight application from Visual Studio. You can accomplish this by going to the property pages for the Silverlight application itself and ensuring "Dynamically generate a test page" is set (or set to a specific page). This page, and the Silverlight application, will then be hosted in the development web server, and you can debug your application. You can see this property page in Figure 12-6.

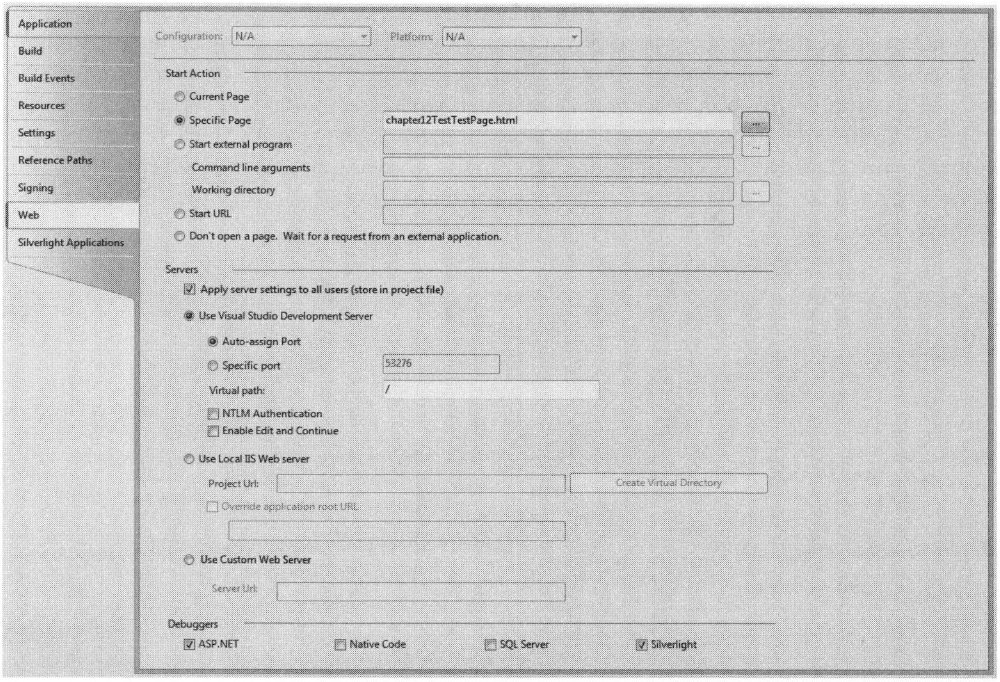

Figure 12-5. *Web site startup properties*

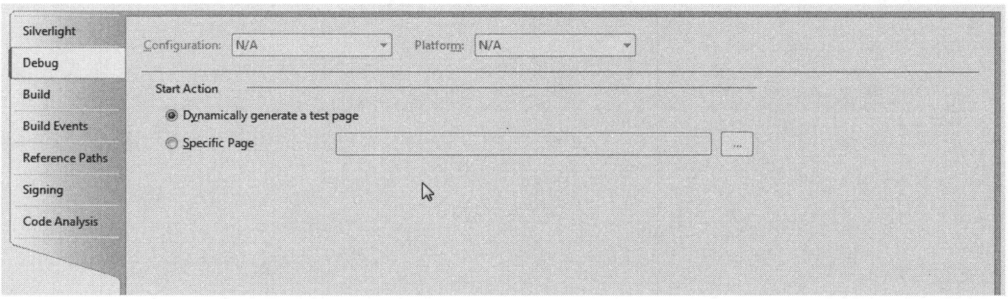

Figure 12-6. *Silverlight application startup properties*

Once you have your startup properly configured, you can set break points and debug your Silverlight application like any other. If you already have a browser running your Silverlight application outside of Visual Studio, you can attach the debugger to the host process (the browser). You can accomplish this by going to the Debug menu in Visual Studio and choosing "Attach to process." If you're debugging ASP.NET, you attach the debugger to the ASP.NET worker process. Similarly, you attach the Visual Studio debugger to the process that hosts the Silverlight plug-in: the browser. On the Attach to Process dialog (shown in Figure 12-7), you can click Select to limit the type of code the debugger focuses on.

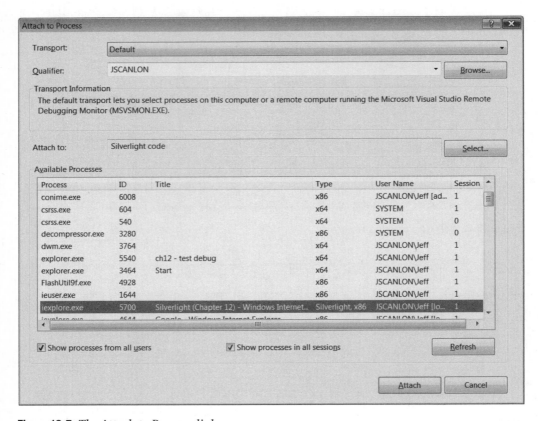

Figure 12-7. *The Attach to Process dialog*

Figure 12-8 shows the Select Code Type dialog. You can leave this on the default to let the debugger automatically determine the code type, or manually override and focus on Silverlight, as shown in the figure.

The easiest way to find the process you want to debug is by the window title. An instance of `iexplore.exe` running this chapter's Silverlight application is highlighted in Figure 12-7. Once you've successfully attached to the correct process, using the debugger is no different from starting the browser within the IDE under the debugger. You can set break points, break into the application, and so on.

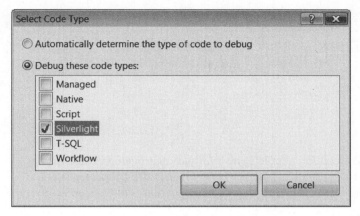

Figure 12-8. *Narrowing the type of code to debug via the Select Code Type dialog*

Handling Unhandled Exceptions

Exceptions happen. It's your mission as a software developer to handle exceptions, such as using isolated storage and reading from a file that doesn't exist. You must handle these in order to build an application that works well and is resistant to expected problems. Sometimes conditions outside your control or conditions you haven't considered will cause an exception, and the Application class provides an unhandled exception handler just for this eventuality. By default (i.e., the default Silverlight application template in Visual Studio), a Silverlight application passes unhandled exceptions on to the browser via the following unhandled exception handler:

```
private void Application_UnhandledException(object sender,
                                            ApplicationUnhandledExceptionEventArgs e)
{
    // If the app is running outside of the debugger then report the exception using
    // the browser's exception mechanism. On IE this will display a yellow alert
    // icon in the status bar and Firefox will display a script error.
    if (!System.Diagnostics.Debugger.IsAttached)
    {
        // NOTE: This will allow the application to continue running after
        //an exception has been thrown but not handled.
        //For production applications this error handling should be
        //replaced with something that will report the error to the
        //web site and stop the application.
        e.Handled = true;
        try
        {
            string errorMsg = e.ExceptionObject.Message +
                e.ExceptionObject.StackTrace;
            //Format error message
            errorMsg = errorMsg.Replace('"', '\'').
                Replace("\r\n", @"\n");
```

```
            System.Windows.Browser.HtmlPage.Window.Eval
                ("throw new Error(\"Unhandled Error in
                Silverlight 2 Application " + errorMsg + "\");");
        }
        catch (Exception)
        {
        }
    }
}
```

This is a basic unhandled exception handler. The information provided in the browser's error dialog isn't always especially useful, as you can see in Figure 12-9. The dialog isn't too friendly to users, and you won't know your Silverlight application has problems unless users manually report them.

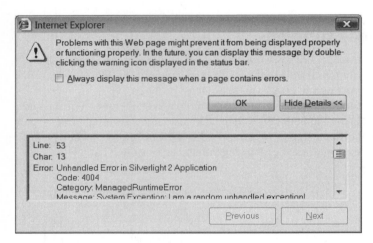

Figure 12-9. *The alert dialog in IE displaying the Silverlight exception*

This chapter's code includes a XAML page named `ErrorFrame` that provides improved handling and display of exceptions. When an exception is thrown and goes unhandled, it gets sent to the unhandled exception handler and then passed to the `ErrorFrame`. The `ErrorFrame` then displays a red bar at the top, similar to the information bar in IE. This red bar displays the simple feedback to users, "The application has caused an error. Click for details." Clicking this red bar causes a Popup control to appear that contains the exception's message and stack trace, and two buttons: one to report the exception and the other to close the pop-up. You might want to automatically send exception feedback to the server instead of waiting for the user to do so manually, but there are cases where you'll want the user to have a say. Figure 12-10 shows what this exception pop-up looks like.

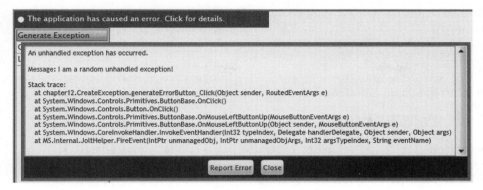

Figure 12-10. *The exception dialog as implemented within Silverlight*

The ErrorFrame page is made up of three main elements: the red error bar, the pop-up, and an empty canvas that contains your main user interface. The red error bar is a Border control that contains several elements, including a Hyperlink button to give it clickability.

```
<Border Background="#FFAA0000" Grid.Row="0"
            x:Name="errorBar" Visibility="Collapsed">
    <StackPanel Orientation="Horizontal">
        <Ellipse Fill="White" Margin="5 0 0 0" Width="10" Height="10"/>
        <HyperlinkButton x:Name="errorDetailsButton"
                                    Click="errorDetailsButton_Click">
            <HyperlinkButton.Content>
                <TextBlock Margin="5" Foreground="White" FontSize="12"
                        Text="The application has caused an error. Click for details."
                        x:Name="errorMesageTB"/>
            </HyperlinkButton.Content>
        </HyperlinkButton>
    </StackPanel>
</Border>
```

The important part of the exception pop-up is the TextBox inside the ScrollViewer:

```
<Popup x:Name="errorPopup" HorizontalOffset="10" VerticalOffset="50">
    <Border>
        ...
        <ScrollViewer Background="LightGray" Grid.Row="0"
                    HorizontalScrollBarVisibility="Auto">
            <TextBox x:Name="exceptionTB" AcceptsReturn="True"/>
        </ScrollViewer>
        ...
    </Border>
</Popup>
```

The final element is simply an empty canvas. This is where your application's user interface will appear.

```
<Canvas x:Name="FrameLayoutRoot" Grid.Row="1">
</Canvas>
```

The most important aspect to the ErrorFrame is a method used to set the exception:

```
public void setException(Exception ex)
{
    exceptionTB.Text = "An unhandled exception has occurred.\n\nMessage: " +
                          ex.Message + "\n\nStack trace:\n" + ex.StackTrace;
    errorBar.Visibility = Visibility.Visible;
}
```

Inside the App.xaml.cs file, the ErrorFrame becomes the root container, instead of the XAML_Viewer, which has been the root throughout this book. The ErrorFrame instance is stored so the unhandled exception handler can communicate the exception to the ErrorFrame.

```
private ErrorFrame errorFrame;
private void Application_Startup(object sender, StartupEventArgs e)
{
    XAML_Viewer viewer = new XAML_Viewer();
    viewer.addXamlPage("Generate Exception", new CreateException());
    errorFrame = new ErrorFrame();
    errorFrame.setLayoutRoot(viewer);
    this.RootVisual = errorFrame;
}
```

The rest is as simple as invoking the setException method of the ErrorFrame class in the unhandled exception handler.

```
errorFrame.setException(e.ExceptionObject);
```

Now any time your application encounters an exception it can't recover from (otherwise you'd be handling the exception), the user will get immediate feedback and can optionally choose to report the error (if you don't do this automatically or remove this button in case of the automatic notification to the server).

Summary

Testing and debugging are vital activities to develop software effectively. When combined, testing and debugging help form proactive and reactive strategies to reduce the number of defects in software. In this chapter you learned how to leverage the unit testing framework libraries and the test harness that you can obtain from Microsoft in order to construct and execute unit tests for Silverlight applications. You also briefly saw how user interface automation is used to interact with Silverlight, and the attached properties you can use to instrument your Silverlight application for user interface automation clients. When it comes to debugging, the class library that comes with Silverlight provides some useful features, such as attributes to control the debugger, and a Debug class useful for sending output to the debugger and testing assumptions within debug mode builds of your application. Finally, you saw an approach to catching unhandled exceptions and displaying them to a user within the Silverlight application itself, providing a prime place to also report unhandled exceptions back to your server.

In the next chapter, we will see how you can package and deploy Silverlight applications.

CHAPTER 13

∎∎∎

Packaging and Deploying Silverlight Applications

Silverlight is a client-side technology. This means any server can host a Silverlight application since there is no dependence on IIS or ASP.NET. For many applications, the only configuration that must be done on the server for the Silverlight application itself is configuring the MIME type. While server configuration is straightforward, there remain many aspects to creating and deploying Silverlight applications. This chapter will explore in detail the parts of Silverlight applications and will discuss Silverlight class assemblies, as well as issues such as versioning and caching.

Client Considerations

Since the Silverlight plug-in is a self-contained managed environment based on .NET, the plug-in itself must be developed (by Microsoft or a third party, such as Novell collaborating with Microsoft for the project Moonlight, `http://mono-project.com/Moonlight`, a Silverlight implementation for Linux) for each environment that will host it. The two major aspects of supported platforms are the host operating system and the host browser. The minimum memory requirement for all operating systems is 128 MB, though naturally, the more memory you have, the better Silverlight can perform. The supported operating systems are as follows:

- Windows XP with SP2 or later

- Windows Server 2003

- Windows Vista

- Mac OS X 10.4.8 or higher

  The supported browsers on Windows operating systems are as follows:

- Internet Explorer 6 or later

- Mozilla Firefox 1.5.0.8 or later

- Mozilla Firefox 2.0 or later

The supported browsers on OS X are as follows:

- Firefox 1.5.0.8 or later

- Firefox 2.0 or later

- Safari 2.0.4 or later

- Google Chrome Build 1251 and higher

■**Note** Google's release notes on Build 1251 mention the Silverlight Plug-in fix. You can get details by visiting `http://sites.google.com/a/chromium.org/dev/getting-involved/dev-channel/release-notes?offset=30`.

Once Silverlight is installed, it is possible to temporarily disable the add-on (this is a helpful approach for testing and diagnostic purposes). In Microsoft Internet Explorer 7, disabling add-ons is accomplished by going to Tools ➤ Manage Add-Ons ➤ Enable or Disable Add-Ons. You can then disable the add-on by highlighting Microsoft Silverlight and changing the selected radio button, as shown in Figure 13-1.

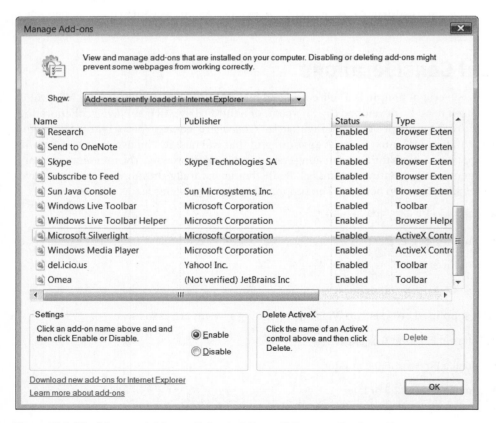

Figure 13-1. *The Manage Add-ons dialog in Microsoft Internet Explorer 7*

Every computer that has the Silverlight plug-in also has a configuration utility (named `Silverlight.Configuration.exe` and located in the Silverlight installation directory) to change options related to the Silverlight plug-in, such as automatic updating. Figure 13-2 shows the configuration utility when it first starts. This is a great place to tell your users to look for the full version number of their Silverlight plug-in if you ever need this information.

Figure 13-2. *The About tab in the Silverlight configuration utility*

The second tab, Updates (shown in Figure 13-3), provides options to let the user specify how updates to the Silverlight plug-in are handled.

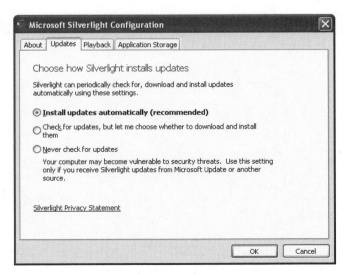

Figure 13-3. *The Updates tab in the Silverlight configuration utility*

The first option, "Install updates automatically," will be disabled on Windows Vista systems that have User Account Control (UAC) enabled. This is because explicit permission from the user is required before an installation can occur, thus making automatic installation of a Silverlight update impossible. If Silverlight is not running on Vista (or UAC is disabled), and this option is still unavailable (or "Check for updates" is unavailable), it's likely that Windows components needed to enable this functionality are not present or are outdated. Visiting Windows Update should fix this problem.

The next tab, shown in Figure 13-4, relates to Playback.

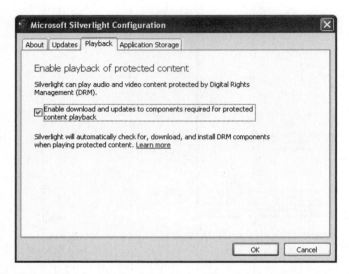

Figure 13-4. *The Playback tab in the Silverlight configuration utility*

Silverlight has the capability of playing media that is protected with digital rights management (DRM), and this provides the user with a mechanism to explicitly forbid the playing of DRM content. The final tab, shown in Figure 13-5, is Application Storage.

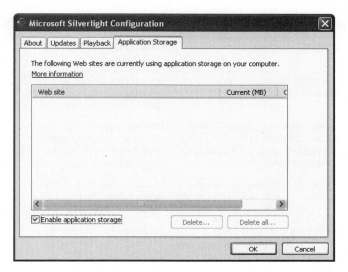

Figure 13-5. *The Application Storage tab in the Silverlight configuration utility*

This tab shows the list of Silverlight applications that utilize isolated storage, as discussed in Chapter 5. This tab provides a way for a user to see how much space is used and by which applications. The user can also selectively delete (by application) or completely delete the contents of isolated storage. Something important to note, however, is the check box at the bottom. A user can completely turn off isolated storage. If you develop a Silverlight application that has issues using isolated storage that you can't track down, this configuration option is a possible cause.

After looking at the client-side Silverlight plug-in in detail, let's look at the Silverlight application package and the different packaging options.

Silverlight Deployment Package Definition

Table 13-1 summarizes the mandatory and optional components necessary to run any Silverlight 2 and 3 application on the browser successfully.

Table 13-1. *Silverlight Components for Running Any Silverlight Application Successfully*

Mandatory/ Optional	Silverlight Component	When Is It Installed/ Downloaded?
Mandatory	Silverlight core runtime library (such as `System.dll`, `System.core.dll`)	Installed as a Silverlight 2 and 3 runtime browser plug-in (not application specific)
Mandatory	Silverlight main application package (XAP file), including in-package files such as `AppManifest.xaml`, application assembly, and other optional assemblies and resource files	Downloaded as a startup package when the user accesses the Silverlight application
Optional	Silverlight SDK library files (in-package or on-demand .NET library files such as `System.Xml.Linq.dll`)	Downloaded at runtime when referenced
Optional	Application class library assembly files (in-package or on-demand custom class library files developed as part of the Silverlight project)	Downloaded at runtime when referenced
Optional	Other referenced XAP packages, which are part of a partitioned application	Downloaded at runtime when referenced

Core Runtime Library

The *Silverlight core runtime library* is a set of core .NET Framework library components that are required on the client's machine to run any rich Internet application (RIA) based on Silverlight 2 or 3. These components are installed on the client machine as part of the Silverlight 2 runtime installer or the Developer's Edition of the Silverlight 3 runtime installer. As a result, an individual application does not need to include them as part of the Silverlight deployment package file. This helps to reduce the application startup package size and thus improves the application startup performance by reducing the startup download time.

In the "Custom Error Handling for Better User Experience" section of this chapter, we will develop a user-friendly approach to acknowledge that the Silverlight runtime is not installed on the user's machine. We recommend that users install it to run Silverlight applications successfully.

Silverlight Application Package (XAP File)

The Silverlight application deployment package is a compressed file called the XAML Application Package (XAP). The Silverlight package is automatically generated as part of the project's build process in Visual Studio 2008. This file is simply a compressed ZIP archive that stores mandatory files, such as the application manifest and the main application DLL, and optional files, such as the auxiliary library DLLs and resource files.

Figure 13-6 shows the SampleSilverlightNavigationRIA Silverlight application project (which we will develop in Chapter 14) deployment profile—the deployment package file name, application manifest file name, and startup application assembly name with the namespace definition.

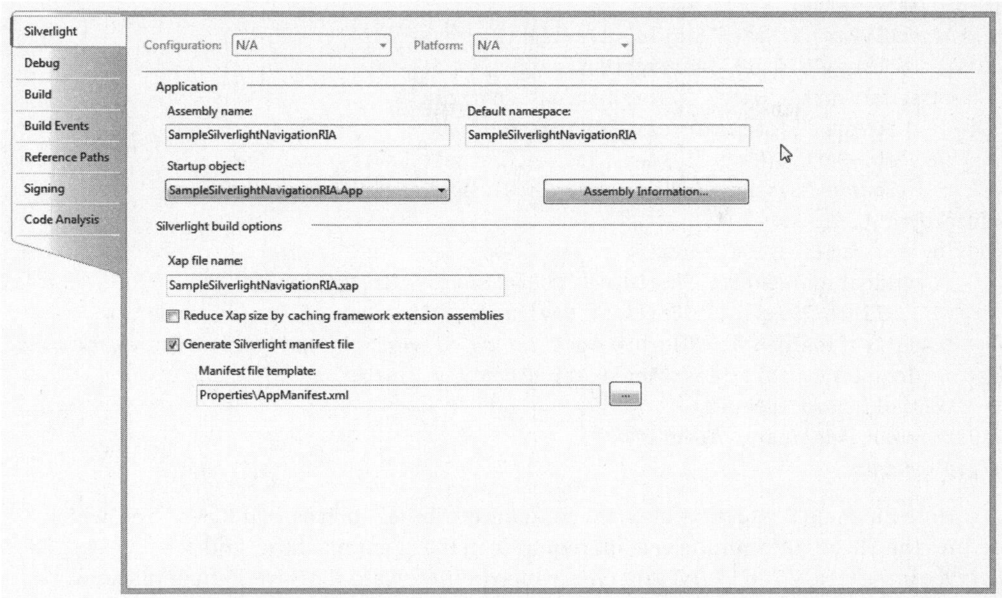

Figure 13-6. *SampleSilverlightNavigationRIA Silverlight project properties window*

As you see in Figure 13-6, a new option, *Reduce XAP size by caching framework extension assemblies*, is available with Visual Studio with Silverlight 3. If you select this option, the XAP file size will be reduced, improving overall application startup performance. In our case, the SampleSilverlightNavigationRIA Silverlight project XAP file size was reduced from 135KB to only 8KB after selecting this option.

If you open the SampleSilverlightNavigationRIA Silverlight application package file (XAP file) as a ZIP file, it contains the mandatory application manifest (AppManifest.xaml) and startup application assembly (SampleSilverlightNavigationRIA.dll) files, and the optional .NET library files (System.Windows.Controls.dll and System.Windows.Controls.Navigation.dll).

Application Manifest File

The application manifest file is a XAML file that Visual Studio creates when it creates the Silverlight project. The application manifest file mainly includes a list of assembly files that need to be downloaded upon application startup by defining the Deployment object. The application manifest file of the SampleSilverlightNavigationRIA Silverlight application we will develop in Chapter 14 is as follows:

```
<Deployment xmlns="http://schemas.microsoft.com/client/2007/deployment"
    xmlns:x="http://schemas.microsoft.com/winfx/2006/xaml"
    EntryPointAssembly="SampleSilverlightNavigationRIA"
    EntryPointType="SampleSilverlightNavigationRIA.App"
    RuntimeVersion="3.0.40307.0">
```

```
<Deployment.Parts>
    <AssemblyPart x:Name="SampleSilverlightNavigationRIA"
        Source="SampleSilverlightNavigationRIA.dll" />
    <AssemblyPart x:Name="System.Windows.Controls"
         Source="System.Windows.Controls.dll" />
    <AssemblyPart x:Name="System.Windows.Controls.Navigation"
         Source="System.Windows.Controls.Navigation.dll" />
</Deployment.Parts>
<Deployment.ApplicationIdentity>
     <ApplicationIdentity ShortName="OOB - SampleSLNavigationRIA"
         Title="Sample Silverlight Navigation RIA - Out of Browser Mode">
     <ApplicationIdentity.Blurb>Demonstrating Silverlight Navigation Framework  and
Out of Browser Capabilities</ApplicationIdentity.Blurb>
     </ApplicationIdentity>
</Deployment.ApplicationIdentity>
</Deployment>
```

Here the main `Deployment` element contains attributes such as `RuntimeVersion`, which defines the Silverlight runtime version required on the client machine, and `EntryPointAssembly` and `EntryPointType`, which point toward the Silverlight application startup assembly.

The `AssemblyPart` element can appear one or more times as a child element of `Deployment.Parts`. Each `AssemblyPart` element includes information about an assembly (with the `x:Name` and `Source` attributes) that is part of the Silverlight XAP application package. In our case, the first `AssemblyPart` element defines the startup Smart Tabs application assembly `SampleSilverlightNavigationRIA.dll`. The other two optional assemblies, `System.Windows.Controls.dll` and `System.Windows.Controls.Navigation.dll`, are Silverlight SDK component libraries, and for this project they are part of the XAP application package.

The `Deployment.ApplicationIdentity` element allows the new Silverlight Out of Browser capabilities. If this element is included in the application manifest file, the user can decide to install the Silverlight application to her machine to run the application out of the browser. This is discussed in more detail in the next chapter.

Application Startup Assembly File

Once the Silverlight application plug-in is downloaded, the startup application class assembly containing the `Startup` event initiates all initialization actions. These initialization actions include displaying the application user interface (driven by the `Page` class) and other optional application initialization processes, such as retrieving data from a data source and beginning any asynchronous downloads of other on-demand referenced assembly files and resource files.

The defining difference between an application DLL and a library DLL is that the application DLL includes a class that serves as the entry point for the application. If you suspect that this class is called `Application`, you would be correct. You've seen this as part of every application we've developed so far, but I haven't mentioned much about it since the beginning of the book. Your Silverlight application should include both a XAML file and a code-behind file that provide your application with a `System.Windows.Application`-derived class that will conduct the creation of the user interface. The default application implementation generated by Visual Studio and Expression Blend features the following XAML file:

```
<Application xmlns=http://schemas.microsoft.com/winfx/2006/xaml/presentation
    xmlns:x=http://schemas.microsoft.com/winfx/2006/xaml
    x:Class="chapter13.App">
  <Application.Resources>
  </Application.Resources>
</Application>
```

The `Application` class is a great place to put application-level resources, such as styles and control templates that you want to use throughout the application. The code-behind file that follows is also generated:

```
public partial class App : Application
{
    public App()
    {
        this.Startup += this.Application_Startup;
        this.Exit += this.Application_Exit;
        this.UnhandledException += this.Application_UnhandledException;
        InitializeComponent();
    }
    private void Application_Startup(object sender, StartupEventArgs e)
    {
        this.RootVisual = new Page();
    }
    // ...
}
```

The constructor registers default event handlers for the events defined in the `Application` class. The life cycle of a Silverlight application is shown in Figure 13-7.

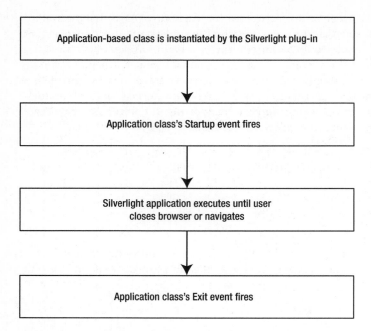

Figure 13-7. *Silverlight application life cycle*

The Startup event handler is the place to specify the UIElement-based class that provides the main user interface. This is generally a UserControl-based class, such as that generated by default and reflected in setting RootVisual to a new instance of this class (Page). The Exit event handler has no implementation, but the method body is there for you to put any code you want executed when the user exits the Silverlight application (generally by closing the browser or navigating to a different page).

The Application class also provides two useful properties. The Current property is static and returns the one (and only) instance of the Application implementation, making it easy to reference application-level resources from the code-behind. The other property is Host, of type SilverlightHost; it returns a reference to the environment hosting the Silverlight plug-in.

If you do not include an Application-based class, the compiled assembly can be used as a library, either packaged as part of a XAP file containing a Silverlight application or downloaded on demand and loaded via reflection. You can also store other resources, such as data files and media files, outside this XAP file.

Optional Files

The XAP file contains the following optional files:

- *Silverlight SDK library files*: These are additional .NET Framework library files, such as System.XML.Linq.dll, that we can package so that they will be downloaded at application startup. Alternatively, they can be downloaded when referenced. Only referenced files from the SDK library are required as part of the package or are downloaded on demand.

- *Application class library assembly files*: These are custom class libraries created to introduce reusability. If you have an application class library assembly file, it can be downloaded upon startup or will be downloaded when referenced.

- *Resource files*: The application may refer to different types of resource files such as images and videos. Usually resource files are large (especially image and video files). You can reference these as on-demand, and they will be downloaded when referenced.

- *Additional XAP packages*: In order to support enterprise-level development and maintenance and provide high-performing applications, application partitioning is one way to develop Service-Oriented Architecture (SOA)–based RIAs. Using the application partitioning approach, we can break up larger application modules into more manageable distributed and reusable application modules and deploy them individually. Silverlight enables application partitioning and supports the definition and development of different application modules as separate deployment packages (XAP files) that can be referenced on-demand dynamically. This book does not cover the application partitioning feature in detail. A good article on the subject is contained in Hanu Kommalapati's blog at http://blogs.msdn.com/hanuk/archive/2008/05/19/silverlight-for-the-enterprises-application-partitioning.aspx.

In-Package and On-Demand Files

To reduce the initial download time and improve the overall application startup performance, it is crucial to keep the size of the XAP package as small as possible. We need to consider the XAP package definition when we work with an application that has a large number of video or image files in order to provide better performance and user experience. If all the files are compiled into the XAP package, it would be a large XAP package that could take significant time to download on the client machine. Silverlight-based RIAs are usually media-rich applications, and it is important to consider different options during application and deployment design to improve overall application performance, stability, and security. Silverlight supports the in-package and on-demand file deployment options to balance initial startup performance and rich media functionality.

At minimum, the application manifest file (AppManifest.xaml), the application class, and other library assemblies and resource files that are required when initializing the application must be part of the Silverlight XAP file. These are called *in-package files*. The package needs to be uploaded on the hosting server.

All other remaining files are optional, and the design team has to decide whether to keep them as part of the application package as in-package files or deploy them on the application hosting server. These files are *on-demand files* and will be downloaded to the client machine when referenced by the application at runtime. The on-demand files can be downloaded with a direct URI reference or using the asynchronous download feature.

Copy Local Property

At design time, you can control the assembly file (.NET library file or custom application class library file) deployment behavior—in-package or on-demand—by setting the Copy Local property of each assembly. If the property value is set to True, the assembly will be part of the XAP deployment package as an in-package file and will be defined in the AppManifest.xaml file. If set to False, you need to deploy it to the hosting server, and it will be downloaded at runtime asynchronously or when referenced. Figure 13-8 demonstrates the Copy Local property for the System.XML.Linq assembly.

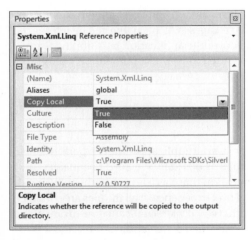

Figure 13-8. *Defining in-package/on-demand behavior using the Copy Local property of the assembly file*

Using an assembly packaged in the XAP file doesn't require anything special. You add a using reference and then use the types from the assembly:

```
using chapter13library;
// ...
private void loadButton_Click(object sender, RoutedEventArgs e)
{
    ImageUtilities iu = new ImageUtilities();
    statusText.Text = "Successfully created instance from class library";
}
```

If you choose not to package the assembly with your application, it must first be downloaded and then loaded into the application domain using the Load method of AssemblyPart. You can download the assembly using the WebClient class:

```
WebClient webClient = new WebClient();
webClient.OpenReadCompleted +=
                   new OpenReadCompletedEventHandler(webClient_OpenReadCompleted);
webClient.OpenReadAsync(new Uri("/chapter13Web/chapter13library2.dll",
                             UriKind.Relative));
```

Once the assembly is finished downloading, you pass the resulting stream to the Load method. Once the assembly is loaded, you can then create an instance of a member object, in our case an instance of the custom tree control, as shown below:

```
AssemblyPart part = new AssemblyPart();
Assembly asm = part.Load(e.Result);
Control c = (Control)asm.CreateInstance("chapter13library2.TreeControl");
```

Build Action Property

At design time, you can control the deployment behavior—in-package or on-demand—of resource files (such as image files, video files, and text files) by setting the Build Action property of each resource file. The Build Action property defines how the added file relates to the build and deployment processes. It is an extensible property, and additional options can be added very easily. For Silverlight projects, three Build Action options—None, Resource, and Content— are mainly used. Figure 13-9 shows the possible Build Action property values for the 01.jpg image file.

Figure 13-9. *Setting the Build Action property of a resource file*

■**Note** Get more information on how to add additional custom options for the Build Action property by visiting http://blogs.msdn.com/msbuild/archive/2005/10/06/477064.aspx and the Microsoft MSDN site http://msdn.microsoft.com/en-us/library/ms171468.aspx.

In the following text, we will discuss the Build Action values that are applicable within the scope of our application.

Build Action As Content

You should use the Content option when a file is large or shared among different applications. The following apply to the file with this Build Action option set:

- Added to the XAP at the application root level.

- Accessible using a URI relative to the application root. You must precede the URI with a leading slash (/)—for example, <Image Source="/SilverlightLogo.png" />.

Build Action As None with the Copy to Output Directory Property Set Relatively

The None option is a good one when you are working with video files and want to keep them out of the XAP. By default, a video file's Build Action property is set to Content with the Copy to Output Directory property set to Do not copy. As mentioned earlier for this project, we have set the Build Action property to None. So upon deployment, you must upload the referenced video files alongside the XAP package. You can also use streaming or progressive download to access them efficiently, as well as employ an absolute URI here.

In this case the file

- Is not added to the XAP, but the `Copy to Output Directory` property will ensure it gets copied to the directory where the XAP is.

- Is accessible using a URI relative to the application root. You must precede the URI with leading slash (/)—for example, `<Image Source="/SilverlightLogo.png" />`.

Build Action As Resource

By default, the XAP package is created in the `...\PrecompiledWeb\<your project name>\ClientBin` directory as the `<your Project name>.xap` file. If you set the `Resource` option, it gets embedded into the project DLL. In this case it will not be straightforward to access the resource file. You can retrieve the resource file by decompiling the DLL file using third party tools. There is no need for a leading slash (/) before the URI—for example, `<Image Source="SilverlightLogo.png" />`.

This same image can be set from the code-behind by using a relative URI:

```
Image img = new Image();
img.Source = new BitmapImage(new Uri("01.jpg", UriKind.Relative));
```

Hosting Silverlight Applications

If planned and designed properly, deploying Silverlight 2 and 3 applications in a secured enterprise environment is very straightforward compared to deploying Silverlight 1 applications. As shown in Figure 13-10, to deploy and consume a Silverlight 2 and 3 application successfully, you need to follow these steps on the server and client sides:

- *Server side*:

    1. Deploy the Silverlight application package (XAP file).

    2. Deploy additional resource files (video files, image files, other files, assembly files).

    3. Deploy additional services (with required cross-domain policy files).

    4. Deploy the required database (with required cross-domain policy files).

    5. Add the Silverlight plug-in or reference the deployed Silverlight application in your ASP.NET or HTML web page.

- Client side:

    6. Install the Silverlight 2 runtime.

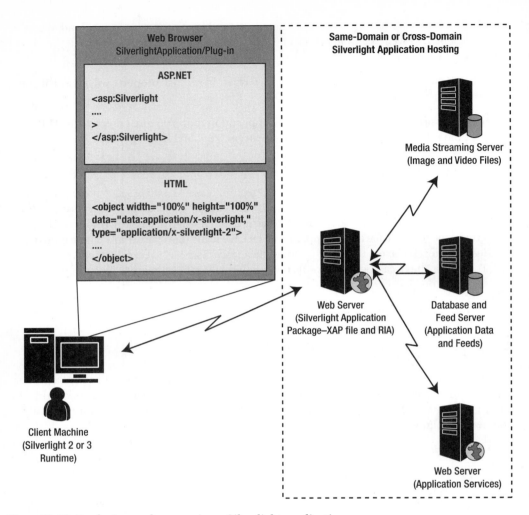

Figure 13-10. *Deploying and consuming a Silverlight application*

Server-Side Silverlight RIA Deployment

At minimum, you need to host the Silverlight XAP file on the web server. In more complex scenarios, you may have additional resource files, assembly files, databases, and web services to be deployed in the same-domain or cross-domain environment.

The simplest deployment option is to manually copy the deployment package and related resource files to the web server under the `ClientBin` directory.

Setting the IIS MIME Type

If you are using IIS 6 or earlier on the web server, you need to add the MIME type related to the Silverlight application deployment package XAP file type. You can right-click the IIS manager to open the Properties window. Click the MIME Type button to add a new MIME type for the file type XAP with the MIME type `application/x-silverlight-app`.

■**Note** If you are using IIS 7, the XAP Silverlight package file type is already related to the `application/x-silverlight-app` MIME type. No additional steps are required.

Same-Domain and Cross-Domain Deployment

It is critical to consider different security aspects as a part of your deployment strategy. RIAs and social networking are dynamic in nature and need to access different services and data across domains, which exposes you to possible computer security vulnerability such as *cross-site scripting* (XSS) and *cross-site request forgery* (CSRF or XSRF).

XSS is a type of vulnerability where, with the help of client-side scripting of web applications, hackers can gather sensitive user data by accessing stored cookies and session information.

CSRF exploits trusted web sites or services, where hackers can perform unauthorized actions to get data and information from the trusted web sites and services by gaining unauthorized control on the logged-in user's web application session. The CSRF threat enables malicious access to web-based controls of the application and executing unauthorized commands to cross-domain applications and services.

As mentioned on Wikipedia:[1]

> *"Cross-site scripting exploits the trust a user has for a particular site"* [whereas] *"cross-site request forgery exploits the trust that a site has for a particular user"*

■**Note** Get more information on XSS by visiting `http://en.wikipedia.org/wiki/Cross-site_scripting` and on CSRF by visiting `http://en.wikipedia.org/wiki/Cross-site_request_forgery`.

To provide a secure environment that prevents CSRF threats, Silverlight supports same-domain and policy-based cross-domain networking to deploy Silverlight-based enterprise RIAs. We looked at the Silverlight cross-domain policy files in Chapter 4 in the context of networking. In this chapter, we revisit the topic in the context of packaging and deploying same-domain and cross-domain Silverlight applications.

---

1. Wikipedia, `http://en.wikipedia.org/wiki/Cross-site_scripting`

Except for images and media, Silverlight allows only site-of-origin (i.e., within the same domain) communication to prevent cross-site request forgery vulnerabilities such as a malicious Silverlight control performing unauthorized actions to cross-domain applications and services. Here the term "same domain" covers the domain name, protocol, and port. As a result, the following scenarios are considered to be cross-domain deployments:

- Same protocol and domain name but different ports—as an example, `http://www.technologyopinion.com` and `http://www.technologyopinion.com:81`

- Same domain name and port but different protocol—as an example, `http://www.technologyopinion.com` and `https://www.technologyopinion.com`

- Same port and protocol but different domain names—as an example, `http://www.technologyopinion.com` and `http://www.apress.com`

Application services must explicitly opt in, detailing the scope of the cross-domain service access by a Silverlight application from all or specific domains by publishing policy files.

Note Get more information on the cross-domain concept from the Microsoft MSDN site at `http://msdn.microsoft.com/en-us/library/cc197955(VS.95).aspx`.

Silverlight enables cross-domain integration by providing two types of declaration policy methods:

- `crossdomain.xml` policy file
- `clientaccesspolicy.xml` policy file

The crossdomain.xml Policy File

As we learned in Chapter 4, this approach is very similar to the Adobe Flash policy. Silverlight supports a subset of the `crossdomain.xml` schema developed by Macromedia (now owned by Adobe). The following is a sample snapshot of the `crossdomain.xml` file:

```
<?xml version="1.0"?>
<!DOCTYPE cross-domain-policy
      SYSTEM "http://www.macromedia.com/xml/dtds/cross-domain-policy.dtd">
<cross-domain-policy>
  <allow-http-request-headers-from domain="*" headers="*"/>
</cross-domain-policy>
```

This policy file must be copied to the root of the domain where the service is hosted. As an example, if the service is hosted at `http://servicesfortechnologyopinion.com`, the `crossdomain.xml` policy file must be available at `http://servicesfortechnologyopinion.com/crossdomain.xml`. By deploying this file at the host service location, the service is publically available and can be accessed by any application from any other domain.

However, the following are two disadvantages of using crossdomain.xml as the security policy file to enable cross-domain access:

- For Silverlight, you must use the "*" value for the domain attribute and thus allow access to all external domains (<allow-http-request-headers-from domain="*" headers= "*"/>). If you would like to enable access to only specific domain(s), say, only to the technologyopinion.com domain, you cannot achieve this using the crossdomain.xml policy file. Here the headers attribute is an optional attribute.

- With the use of this method, you can decide who has access (in Silverlight's case, it is all external domains). You do not have the capability to specify what can be accessed.

The clientaccesspolicy.xml Policy File

As we learned in Chapter 4, the use of the clientaccesspolicy.xml as a security policy file is a Silverlight-specific approach. Its detailed schema supports a more selective and controlled approach, overcoming the disadvantages discussed for the crossdomain.xml file.

The following is a sample snapshot of the clientaccesspolicy.xml file:

```
<?xml version="1.0" encoding="utf-8"?>
<access-policy>
  <cross-domain-access>
    <policy>
      <allow-from http-request-headers="*">
        <domain uri="http://technologyopinion.com"/>
      </allow-from>
      <grant-to>
        <resource path="/servicesforTO/" include-subpaths="true"/>
      </grant-to>
    </policy>
  </cross-domain-access>
</access-policy>
```

This policy file must be copied to the root of the domain where the service is hosted. As an example, if the service is hosted at http://servicesfortechnologyopinion.com, the clientaccesspolicy.xml policy file must be available at http://servicesfortechnologyopinion. com/clientaccesspolicy.xml. By deploying this file at the host service location, the following rules are set:

- The service can be accessed only from the technologyopinion.com domain. We achieve this by setting the uri attribute of the domain element to http://technologyopinion.com. If you set it to the wildcard *, the services will be accessible from any cross-domain application.

- Only resources that are located at /servicesforTO/ can be accessed. We achieve this restriction by setting the path attribute of the resource element to /servicesforTO/. The default value is /, which enables full access.

Using the Policy Files

When a Silverlight application web client identifies the requirement to access the cross-domain service, it will first look at the existence of the `clientaccesspolicy.xml` file at the root of the deployed service. If it exists, it will authorize against the policy file and upon successful authorization can access and utilize the cross-domain deployed service. If the `clientaccesspolicy.xml` file does not exist at the root of the service's domain, next it will look for the `crossdomain.xml` file and authorize against it to gain access.

Custom Initialization Parameters

The `initParams` parameter is used to pass a set of delimited properties with their values to Silverlight, and thus to the Silverlight application. Each property takes the form of *Name=Value*, and the properties are separated by commas. These initialization parameters can be accessed from the Silverlight application in the `Application` class's startup handler. They are accessible via the `StartupEventArgs` parameter to the `Startup` event handler in your implementation of the `Application` class. You can cache these in your `App` class by handling the `Startup` event.

```
internal IDictionary<string, string> InitParams;
private void Application_Startup(object sender, StartupEventArgs e)
{
    this.InitParams = e.InitParams;
}
```

Once the parameters are cached in your `Application`-based class, they can be accessed via the `App` instance (though you need to cast it to your specific class type in order to access the `InitParams` member).

```
IDictionary<string,string> initParams = ((App)App.Current).InitParams;
foreach (string key in initParams.Keys)
{
    TextBlock tb = new TextBlock();
    tb.Text = key + " = " + initParams[key];
    LayoutRoot.Children.Add(tb);
}
```

Embedding Silverlight Plug-Ins to the Web Page

In the previous section, we looked at the Silverlight application security settings. Now it's time to embed the Silverlight application plug-in into your web page. Enterprises can embed the Silverlight plug-ins into web applications using the following three options:

- ASP .NET `Silverlight` server control

- HTML `object` element

- `Silverlight.js` JavaScript helper file

Upon creating a Silverlight application project using Visual Studio 2008 SP1, if the user selects "Add a new ASP.NET Web project to the solution to host Silverlight" as the hosting platform option, a separate ASP.NET web site project with two additional test web pages (`.aspx` and `.html`) are added to host the Silverlight application/user control. The naming convention of these test pages is based on the Silverlight application name—`<Name of the Silverlight Application>TestPage.aspx` for the ASPX file and `<Name of the Silverlight Application>TestPage.html` for the HTML file.

ASP .NET Silverlight Server Control

The Silverlight 3 SDK installed along with the Microsoft Silverlight Tools for Visual Studio 2008 SP1 includes the `Silverlight` server control to host Silverlight plug-ins. The following code snippet demonstrates this control, added in the `SampleSilverlightNavigationRIATestPage.aspx` file to host the SampleSilverlightNavigationRIA Silverlight application that will be developed in Chapter 14:

```
<form id="form1" runat="server" style="height:100%;">
    <asp:ScriptManager ID="ScriptManager1" runat="server"></asp:ScriptManager>
    <div   style="height:100%;">
      <asp:Silverlight
          ID="Silverlight1"
          runat="server"
          Source="~/ClientBin/SampleSilverlightNavigationRIA.xap"
          MinimumVersion="3.0.40307.0"
          Width="100%"
          Height="100%" />
    </div>
</form>
```

As shown in this code snippet, in addition to common attributes, the `Silverlight` control has a `Source` attribute containing the location of the Silverlight application XAP file (in this example, it is `ClientBin/SampleSilverlightNavigationRIA.xap`) and a `MinimumVersion` attribute, which defines the minimum Silverlight runtime version that is required on the client machine to run the Silverlight application successfully. Here you can see that it mentions the Silverlight 3 Beta version number.

You can utilize IntelliSense or MSDN if you need more information on the properties this server control supports.

HTML object Element

The HTML `object` element enables us to embed the Silverlight plug-in in the HTML web page. The following code snippet demonstrates the Silverlight control added in the `SampleSilverlightNavigationRIATestPage.html` file to host the application that will be developed in Chapter 14:

```
<div id="silverlightControlHost">
    <object data="data:application/x-silverlight-2,"
        type="application/x-silverlight-2" width="100%" height="100%">
        <param name="source"
                value="ClientBin/SampleSilverlightNavigationRIA.xap"/>
        <param name="onerror" value="onSilverlightError" />
        <param name="background" value="white" />
        <param name="minRuntimeVersion" value="3.0.40307.0" />
        <param name="autoUpgrade" value="true" />
      <a href="http://go.microsoft.com/fwlink/?LinkID=141205"
        style="text-decoration: none;">
        <img src="http://go.microsoft.com/fwlink/?LinkId=108181"
          alt="Get Microsoft Silverlight" style="border-style: none"/>
      </a>
    </object>
    <iframe style='visibility:hidden;height:0;width:0;border:0px'>
    </iframe>
</div>
```

As shown in this code snippet, you need to define the attributes of the `object` element in order to run the Silverlight plug-in in all browsers with optimal performance.

- The `data` attribute is required for some browsers to avoid performance issues. The value ends with a comma, which indicates that the second parameter is an empty value.

- The `type` attribute defines the MIME type of Silverlight to allow the browser to identify the plug-in and the required Silverlight version.

- The `width` and `height` attributes are required (with fixed pixel values or with relative percentages) to run across different types of browsers properly.

A `param` child element with its `name` attribute set to `source` is required. The `value` attribute of this element contains the location of the Silverlight XAP file (in this example, it is `ClientBin/ SampleSilverlightNavigationRIA.xap`).

The `param` child element with the `name` attribute set to `minRuntimeVersion` defines the minimum Silverlight runtime version that is required on the client machine to run the Silverlight plug-in successfully. Set the Silverlight version number as a value of the `value` attribute of this element.

This particular example of the `OBJECT` tag includes two parameters. There are actually many parameters, some of which follow, that can be specified to control and communicate with the Silverlight plug-in (get more details by visiting the Microsoft MSDN web site at `http:// msdn.microsoft.com/en-us/library/cc838259(VS.95).aspx`):

background: Defaults to white. Specifies the color used by the Silverlight plug-in to paint its background. Useful when the content of the Silverlight application does not fill up the entire space specified in the OBJECT tag. This parameter uses the same syntax for colors as in XAML.

enableFramerateCounter: Should not be used with production applications! If this is set to true, the current frame rate is displayed in the host browser's status bar. This is only supported on Internet Explorer on Windows.

enableHtmlAccess: Defaults to true. Boolean value that controls whether the Silverlight application can use the HTML Document Object Model (DOM) bridge classes.

enableRedrawRegions: Should not be used with production applications! If this is set to true, the regions that are being redrawn are specially highlighted.

initParams: Used to communicate initialization parameters to Silverlight that can be accessed from an application. Properties are comma-separated, and the property value is separated by an equal sign from the property name.

maxFrameRate: Defaults to 60. Integer value specifying an upper limit for the frame rate (the actual frame rate might be lower than what is requested).

onError: Mandatory. Specifies a JavaScript event handler to handle exceptions from the hosted Silverlight application.

onLoad: Specifies a JavaScript event handler invoked when the root XAML file has completed loading.

onResize: Specifies a JavaScript event handler that is invoked when the Silverlight plug-in's ActionWidth or ActualHeight property is changed.

onSourceDownloadComplete: Invoked when the application specified in the Source parameter has finished downloading.

onSourceDownloadProgressChanged: Invoked periodically while the Silverlight application is downloading in order to report download progress.

Source: Mandatory. Specifies the URI to the XAP file containing the Silverlight application.

splashScreenSource: Specifies the URI to a XAML file to show a splash screen while the Silverlight application is downloading.

windowless: Defaults to false. Only applies to Silverlight running on Windows. Set to true to run Silverlight as a windowless plug-in.

The other important aspects to this specific OBJECT tag are the links that provide direction to a user who does not have the Silverlight plug-in installed. The URLs corresponding to installer packages for each version of Silverlight are shown in Table 13-2.

Table 13-2. *Installer URLs for Silverlight Versions*

Silverlight Version	Installer URL
2	http://go2.microsoft.com/fwlink/?LinkId=124807
3	http://go2.microsoft.com/fwlink/?LinkId=141205[*]

[*] *Silverlight 3 is not officially released, so the Silverlight 3 link will recommend that you install the Silverlight 3 Beta Developers runtime edition. You can visit http://silverlight.net/getstarted/silverlight3/default. aspx to get more details on Silverlight 3.*

■Note The iframe tag is specified in order to prevent the Safari browser from caching the page. If the page is cached, the Silverlight plug-in will fail to reload correctly.

Several of these properties are exposed via the App.Current.Host.Settings object (of type System.Windows.Interop.Settings). These settings are shown in Table 13-3.

Table 13-3. *Properties of the System.Windows.Interop.Settings Class*

Property	Type	Description
EnableFrameRateCounter	bool	Gets or sets whether the frame rate counter is displayed (Microsoft Internet Explorer only)
EnableHTMLAccess	bool	Gets a value specifying whether HTML DOM access is permitted
EnableRedrawRegions	bool	Gets or sets a value specifying where redraw regions are shown
MaxFrameRate	int	Gets or sets the maximum frame rate per second
Windowless	bool	Gets a value specifying whether the Silverlight plug-in is windowless (only applies to Silverlight running on Windows)

Silverlight.js JavaScript Helper File

You can use the Silverlight.js JavaScript helper file and use the createObject and createObjectEx functions defined in this file to embed the Silverlight plug-in in a web page. This approach can be used if there is a need to have multiple plug-in instances in a single web page by specifying a unique identifier for each embedded Silverlight plug-in.

However, it is recommended you use the ASP.NET Silverlight server control or HTML object element approach to integrate enterprise SOA-based Silverlight 2 plug-ins in your web pages. This book does not cover this approach in detail.

■Note To get more information on the use of JavaScript to embed Silverlight plug-ins, please visit the Microsoft MSDN web site at http://msdn.microsoft.com/en-us/library/cc265155(VS.95).aspx.

Custom Error Handling for Better User Experience

Clients' machines must have the Silverlight runtime installed in order to run Silverlight plug-ins successfully. However, it is very likely that a user's machine may not have Silverlight installed or may contain the older version (i.e., the required minimum version is not installed). In this scenario, instead of providing the default Microsoft message to install Silverlight, it would be friendlier if we provided a branded explanatory message and a link to the Silverlight runtime installer.

Both recommended Silverlight plug-in integration approaches—the ASP.NET Silverlight server control and the HTML object element—support custom error handling if the Silverlight runtime is not installed on a user's machine. This section describes how to implement custom error management for Silverlight 2 RIAs.

ASP.NET Silverlight Server Control Error Management

The ASP.NET Silverlight server control exposes the PluginNotInstalledTemplate object that we can use to provide a custom branded error-handling message when the selected Silverlight version (defined by the MinimumVersion attribute of the Silverlight control) is not installed on the user's machine. The PluginNotInstalledTemplate object contains the HTML content to display the custom message. The following code snippet demonstrates the use of the PluginNotInstalledTemplate object:

```
<form id="form1" runat="server" style="height:100%;">
    <asp:ScriptManager ID="ScriptManager1" runat="server"></asp:ScriptManager>
    <div  style="height:100%;">
        <asp:Silverlight
            ID="Xaml1"
            runat="server"
            Source="~/ClientBin/SampleSilverlightNavigationRIA.xap"
            MinimumVersion="3.0.40307.0"
            Width="100%"
            Height="100%">

            <PluginNotInstalledTemplate>
                <div>
                    Write HTML markup to render in the browser providing
                        custom enterprise branded message with
                        Silverlight installation link
                </div>
```

```
                </PluginNotInstalledTemplate>

            </asp:Silverlight>

        </div>
    </form>
```

HTML object Element Error Management

You need to add the HTML markup representing the branded message with its Silverlight installation link after all param child elements of the HTML object element. If the required version of Silverlight is not installed on the user's machine, the custom message will be displayed; otherwise, the message will be skipped.

The following code snippet demonstrates the custom error handling for Silverlight when the HTML object element is used to embed the Silverlight plug-in:

```
<div id="silverlightControlHost">
    <object data="data:application/x-silverlight-2,"
        type="application/x-silverlight-2" width="100%" height="100%">
        <param name="source"
            value="ClientBin/SampleSilverlightNavigationRIA.xap"/>
        <param name="onerror" value="onSilverlightError" />
        <param name="background" value="white" />
        <param name="minRuntimeVersion" value="3.0.40307.0" />
        <param name="autoUpgrade" value="true" />
        <div id="SLNotInstalled">
            Write HTML markup to render in the browser providing
            custom enterprise branded message with Silverlight
            installation link
        </div>
    </object>
    <iframe style='visibility:hidden;height:0;width:0;border:0px'>
    </iframe>
</div>
```

Silverlight and the Build Process

An important part of an effective software development process includes a strong build and deployment process. The build process, at a minimum, should leverage scripts to make building software easy and primed for automation (either in the form of scheduled builds or continuous integration). Two of the most popular tools used for building software are NAnt and MSBuild. Both of these tools use XML configuration files that specify a series of tasks, including compiling projects, copying build output to different locations, and packaging applications (such as constructing an install package). Silverlight applications must be compiled and packaged into a XAP file for deployment to a web site. MSBuild is the official build tool from Microsoft, and the Silverlight SDK comes with MSBuild-specific tasks related to compiling and packaging Silverlight applications. You must use the version of MSBuild that comes with .NET 3.5 (this version of MSBuild also has the version number 3.5). This section will be most useful to you if you are trying to build Silverlight applications outside the IDE—for example, if you're trying to establish a build process.

One huge advantage to MSBuild is that it can use project files from Visual Studio as build scripts. A Visual Studio CSPROJ file contains a set of properties, many of which are Silverlight-specific. Let's briefly dissect one of these Visual Studio project files to see the Silverlight-specific additions:

```
<OutputType>Library</OutputType>
<AppDesignerFolder>Properties</AppDesignerFolder>
<RootNamespace>chapter13</RootNamespace>
<AssemblyName>chapter13</AssemblyName>
<TargetFrameworkVersion>v3.5</TargetFrameworkVersion>
<SilverlightApplication>true</SilverlightApplication>
<SupportedCultures>
</SupportedCultures>
<XapOutputs>true</XapOutputs>
<GenerateSilverlightManifest>true</GenerateSilverlightManifest>
<XapFilename>chapter13.xap</XapFilename>
<SilverlightManifestTemplate>
        Properties\AppManifest.xml
</SilverlightManifestTemplate>
<SilverlightAppEntry>chapter13.App</SilverlightAppEntry>
<TestPageFileName>TestPage.html</TestPageFileName>
<CreateTestPage>true</CreateTestPage>
<ValidateXaml>true</ValidateXaml>
```

You can see that this project file is configured for Silverlight applications, setting properties related to the XAP file and defining the class that inherits from the IntelliSense class, and serves as the entry point to the application. This project file also contains the directive to include the extension for building Silverlight applications. This extension controls how XAML pages are processed and how the XAP file is created. The structure of a Silverlight application as generated by Visual Studio includes the entry point for the application (the App.xaml and App.xaml.cs files), an empty UserControl (Page), an empty application manifest, the AssemblyInfo source file, and of course the project file. Let's look at using MSBuild to build this application. On disk, these files are organized as shown here:

```
chapter13\App.xaml
chapter13\App.xaml.cs
chapter13\chapter13.csproj
chapter13\Page.xaml
chapter13\Page.xaml.cs
chapter13\Properties
chapter13\Properties\AppManifest.xml
chapter13\Properties\AssemblyInfo.cs
```

Simply executing msbuild.exe with the project file specified as the command-line parameter causes MSBuild to execute, compiling and packaging this application. The output from msbuild.exe looks like this:

```
C:\book\code\chapter13>msbuild chapter13.csproj
Microsoft (R) Build Engine Version 3.5.30428.1
[Microsoft .NET Framework, Version 2.0.50727.3031]
Copyright (C) Microsoft Corporation 2007. All rights reserved.
Build started 5/6/2009 10:43:22 PM.
Project "C:\book\code\chapter13\chapter13.csproj" on node 0 (default targets).
  Processing 0 edmx files
  Finished processing 0 edmx files
PrepareForBuild:
  Creating directory "Bin\Debug\".
  Creating directory "obj\Debug\".
CopyFilesToOutputDirectory:
  Copying file from "obj\Debug\chapter13.dll" to "Bin\Debug\chapter13.dll".
  chapter13 -> C:\book\code\chapter13\Bin\Debug\chapter13.dll
  Copying file from "obj\Debug\chapter13.pdb" to "Bin\Debug\chapter13.pdb".
CreateSilverlightAppManifest:
  Begin application manifest generation
  Application manifest generation completed successfully
XapPackager:
  Begin Xap packaging
  Packaging chapter13.dll
  Packaging AppManifest.xaml
  Xap packaging completed successfully
CreateHtmlTestPage:
  Creating test page
  Test page created successfully
Done Building Project "C:\book\code\chapter13\chapter13.csproj" (default targets).
Build succeeded.
    0 Warning(s)
    0 Error(s)
Time Elapsed 00:00:01.04
```

The actual compilation and creation of the DLL and PDB files is done after the
PrepareForBuild task. After the compilation, a Silverlight-specific application manifest is
created, and the contents are packaged into a XAP file. If you examine the contents of the
obj\Debug directory, you will see the following files:

```
App.g.cs
chapter13.csproj.FileListAbsolute.txt
chapter13.dll
chapter13.g.resources
chapter13.pdb
Page.g.cs
ResolveAssemblyReference.cache
XapCacheFile.xml
```

The App.g.cs and Page.g.cs files are generated based on their corresponding XAML files
and should not be edited. These files contain the generated partial class definition for their

corresponding class. Much like with Windows Forms, these generated files include the implementation of `InitializeComponent` and objects for any XAML elements with an `x:Name` attribute defined. The DLL and PDB files are the important parts of the output, and exactly what you should be used to from .NET—the code compiled to an assembly and a symbol file for debugging purposes. The `XapCacheFile.xml` file is the Silverlight application manifest and contains instructions for the XAP packaging utility, such as the files to include in the XAP and where to place the generated XAP file.

```
<xapCache source="C:\book\code\ chapter13\Bin\Debug\chapter13.xap"
          lastWriteTime="5/6/2009 10:43:23 PM">
  <file source="C:\book\code\ chapter13\obj\Debug\chapter13.dll"
        archivePath="chapter13.dll"
        lastWriteTime="5/6/2009 10:43:22 PM" />
  <file source="C:\book\code\ chapter13\Bin\Debug\AppManifest.xaml"
        archivePath="AppManifest.xaml"
        lastWriteTime="5/6/2009 10:43:23 PM" />
</xapCache>
```

While using Visual Studio project files as the configuration files with MSBuild is a useful approach, sometimes you might need to use the native MSBuild file format. While it does share a lot with the Visual Studio project file format, there are a few differences. Let's take a look at an MSBuild file that goes a lot further than the preceding simple example. This build file is suitable for this chapter's code; therefore, it includes directives to compile library assemblies and the application, and include resources or content files. The file, `build.proj`, is annotated with line numbers and broken up for ease of discussion. Repetitive elements have been removed in the interest of space and clarity, but all line numbers match the `build.proj` included in this chapter's code. Of course, these line numbers would not appear in an actual MSBuild project file.

```
001: <Project
002:    ToolsVersion="3.5"
003:    DefaultTargets="Build"
004:    xmlns="http://schemas.microsoft.com/developer/msbuild/2003">
005:
006:    <!-- Application Configuration -->
007:    <PropertyGroup>
008:       <TargetFrameworkVersion>v3.5</TargetFrameworkVersion>
009:       <SchemaVersion>2.0</SchemaVersion>
010:       <NoStdLib>true</NoStdLib>
011:       <NoStdCfg>true</NoStdCfg>
```

`Project` is the root element for MSBuild configuration files. `TargetFrameworkVersion` is set to 3.5, but keep in mind that this has no connection to .NET 3.5 on Windows. This version number is reflective of the time when Silverlight was released (.NET 3.5 is the latest release and includes Windows Communication Foundation [WCF] and the updated MSBuild, as described here).

```
013:       <RootNamespace>chapter13</RootNamespace>
014:       <AssemblyName>chapter13</AssemblyName>
015:       <OutputType>Library</OutputType>
016:       <OutputPath>ClientBin</OutputPath>
```

The `RootNamespace`, as its name implies, specifies the root namespace used in the source code being built. The `AssemblyName` specifies the file name used for the built assembly. Since both Silverlight applications and Silverlight libraries are DLLs, the `OutputType` will always be set to `Library`. The `OutputPath` specifies the directory where the output files of tasks from this configuration file are placed.

```
018:     <SilverlightAppEntry>chapter13.App</SilverlightAppEntry>
```

This specifies the class that inherits from the `IntelliSense` class and thus serves as the entry point for the Silverlight application. Without this, the packaged XAP file won't be valid and won't successfully start in Silverlight.

```
020:     <SilverlightManifestTemplate>
                     Properties\AppManifest.xml</SilverlightManifestTemplate>
021:     <GenerateSilverlightManifest>true</GenerateSilverlightManifest>
```

These two properties are required in order to generate a Silverlight manifest file that includes the details of the XAP file. If you don't specify these, no Silverlight manifest is generated, and if you specify the next two properties, the constructed XAP file will contain only the DLL from the build process instead of all the files it should.

```
023:     <XapOutputs>true</XapOutputs>
024:     <XapFilename>chapter13.xap</XapFilename>
```

These two properties instruct MSBuild to create a XAP file with the specified name. The XAP file is placed in the directory specified in the `OutputPath` property. If these properties are not specified, no XAP file will be produced.

```
025:     </PropertyGroup>
026:
027:     <!-- Silverlight assembly references required by code -->
028:     <ItemGroup>
029:       <Reference Include="mscorlib" />
030:       <Reference Include="system" />
031:       <Reference Include="System.Windows" />
032:       <Reference Include="System.Core" />
033:       <Reference Include="System.Net" />
034:       <Reference Include="System.Windows.Browser" />
```

This `ItemGroup` section shows the set of Silverlight assemblies that are required to build a default Silverlight application that results from creating a new Silverlight project in Visual Studio. If the application being built uses assemblies other than these, this section is where they get added.

```
035:     <Reference Include=
                 "chapter13library, Version=1.0.0.0, Culture=neutral,
                                         processorArchitecture=MSIL">
036:       <SpecificVersion>False</SpecificVersion>
037:       <HintPath>libs\chapter13library.dll</HintPath>
038:     </Reference>
```

This is the first Silverlight class library. `HintPath` specifies where this library is located.

```
039:      <Reference Include=
                  "chapter13library2, Version=1.0.0.0, Culture=neutral,
                                              processorArchitecture=MSIL">
040:        <SpecificVersion>False</SpecificVersion>
041:        <HintPath>libs\chapter13library2.dll</HintPath>
042:        <Private>False</Private>
```

This is the other class library. Setting the value of the `Private` property to `False` is what prevents this assembly from being included in the XAP file.

```
043:      </Reference>
044:    </ItemGroup>
045:
046:    <!-- Files to build application class -->
047:    <ItemGroup>
048:      <Compile Include="App.xaml.cs">
049:        <DependentUpon>App.xaml</DependentUpon>
050:      </Compile>
051:      <Compile Include="Page.xaml.cs">
052:        <DependentUpon>Page.xaml</DependentUpon>
053:      </Compile>
```

This is the format used to compile the code-behind files for each XAML page. Since each XAML page is marked as a dependency, the next `ItemGroup`'s contents are built first.

```
075:      <Compile Include="Properties\AssemblyInfo.cs" />
076:    </ItemGroup>
077:    <ItemGroup>
078:      <ApplicationDefinition Include="App.xaml">
079:        <Generator>MSBuild:MarkupCompilePass1</Generator>
080:        <SubType>Designer</SubType>
081:      </ApplicationDefinition>
082:      <Page Include="Page.xaml">
083:        <Generator>MSBuild:MarkupCompilePass1</Generator>
084:        <SubType>Designer</SubType>
085:      </Page>
```

This section includes the part of the build process that turns a XAML page, such as `Page.xaml`, into its corresponding generated partial class for the code-behind, such as `Page.g.cs`. There's one entry here for each XAML file in the project.

```
114:    </ItemGroup>
115:    <ItemGroup>
116:      <Resource Include="ball_blue.png" />
117:    </ItemGroup>
```

This `Resource` element specifies that the resource file is placed into the Silverlight application assembly.

```
118:    <ItemGroup>
119:      <Content Include="ball_red.png" />
120:    </ItemGroup>
```

The Content element specifies that the resource file should be packaged in a XAP file that is created at the end of the build process.

```
122:    <!--
123:      The file that is used by MSBuild to Build C# Silverlight Applications, and
124:      which specifies the C# compiler. Note that $(MSBuildExtensionsPath) is the
125:      path to the Program Files\MSBuild folder.
126:    -->
127:    <Import Project=
                        "$(MSBuildExtensionsPath)\Microsoft\Silverlight\v2.0\
                         Microsoft.Silverlight.CSharp.targets" />
128: </Project>
```

This part is required to import the Silverlight-related tasks into the build for use by MSBuild. The Silverlight-related tasks used in this build file include compiling XAML and creating a XAP file.

Summary

This chapter covered the packaging and deployment of Silverlight applications and libraries. The XAP file is the main unit of deployment when delivering Silverlight applications to the user. A XAP file can include the application manifest file, main Silverlight application assembly, resources such as images and video, and library assemblies. We discussed in-package and on-demand files options, the importance of defining and analyzing additional components (Silverlight SDK assemblies, custom application libraries, and resource files), and making a strategic decision to define in-package and on-demand files. A balanced decision considering application needs and startup download package size helps to optimize application performance and the user experience.

Silverlight needs a client-side runtime engine. One of the key components is hosting the application with a better user experience. This chapter explained how easy it is to implement a custom message that's user friendly when the required Silverlight runtime is not installed on the user's machine.

Finally, any complete software engineering process has a build process, so you saw how to leverage MSBuild to include Silverlight in the build. You've now reached the end of the journey through how Silverlight works and learned all you need to build applications.

The next two chapters are focused on advanced Silverlight topics. The next chapter covers advanced features introduced in Silverlight 3, such as Silverlight navigation framework, Out of Browser capability, and cross-plug-in communication between Silverlight applications.

CHAPTER 14

Advanced Silverlight 3 Features

Although this book has covered a significant amount of Silverlight, there is much more to Silverlight. This chapter aims to provide information on some of the more advanced topics of Silverlight 3. Silverlight 3 introduces some very strategic features to help you develop enterprise-level rich Internet applications (RIAs). In this chapter, we will cover the Silverlight navigation framework and the new Out of Browser functionality, including deep linking and search engine optimization (SEO). We'll also cover how to implement communication across different Silverlight applications.

Silverlight Navigation Framework

Silverlight 2 did not support some basic web-based application features that would have been great additions to any RIA. Specifically, it did not support browsing from one XAML-based page to another, maintaining browser-level history, enabling the default browser's back and forward functionality, and implementing search engines. Although custom development made it possible to develop multiple-page RIAs in Silverlight 2, the implementation was pretty manual, and there were challenges when communicating between different pages. Silverlight 3 comes to the rescue and introduces the first version of the Silverlight navigation framework, which adds support for all of these features.

The initial release of the navigation framework is promising, and we're certain that more mature future versions will make architects' and developers' lives easy by allowing them to design and develop large-scale interactive RIAs based on enterprise-level and industry-level standards.

As mentioned in Chapter 1, when you create a Silverlight 3 project using Visual Studio 2008 SP1, an additional project template, the Silverlight Navigation Application template, is available. Let's walk through an example. Create a project based on the Silverlight Navigation Application template, and name it SampleSilverlightNavigationRIA. Save it in the `C:\book\ examples\SampleSilverlightNavigationRIA` folder.

You will get a sample application as a startup application with a predefined set of view pages. The `MainPage.xaml` page behaves as a central or startup page, and the pages `AboutPage.xaml`, `ErrorWindow.xaml`, and `HomePage.xaml` are available in the `View` folder, as shown in Figure 14-1.

Figure 14-1. *Master and view pages of the project based on the Silverlight Navigation Application template*

If you run the project, you will see most of the functionality available by default. The AboutPage.xaml and HomePage.xaml pages are hosted on the MainPage.xaml master page. The browser header displays the page-specific customized title defined using the Title property in the Page property. The application maintains the browser history, and you can use browser's default Back and Forward buttons. Figure 14-2 shows the default navigation framework–based Silverlight application.

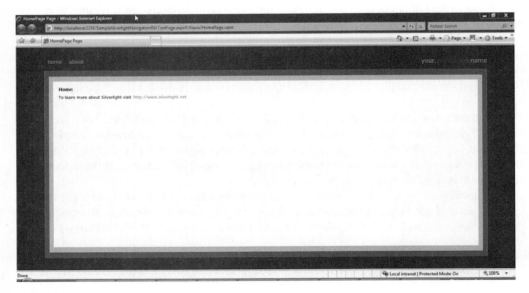

Figure 14-2. *Default view of the navigation framework–based Silverlight application viewed in Internet Explorer 7*

Understanding the Navigation Framework

Now we'll help you understand some key components of the framework, such as Frame, UserControl, and Page. Frame is the core component of the navigation framework; it mainly behaves as the master startup page/container and also performs validation. The following XAML code showing the Frame tag is added by default in the MainPage.xaml page; it declares the container for the application:

```
<navigation:Frame x:Name="Frame" Source="/Views/HomePage.xaml"
    HorizontalContentAlignment="Stretch"
    VerticalContentAlignment="Stretch"
    JournalOwnership="Automatic"
    Padding="15,10,15,10"
    Background="White"/>
```

The Source property defines the page that will be loaded as a startup page of the application. By default HomePage.xaml is the startup page of the navigation framework–based Silverlight application. You can change it appropriately to suit your requirements.

The JournalOwnership property defines the behavior of the application navigation history integration. If it is not defined specifically, by default, it is set to Automatic, which automatically records navigation history to the browser journal (if allowed). Otherwise, it will be recorded only in the Frame control journal. You can set the value of the JournalOwnership property to OwnsJournal to store history only in the Frame control journal. If set to UsesParentJournal, then the Frame control will follow the settings of the parent Frame control's JournalOwnership property. If there is no parent Frame control, then the navigation history will be stored in the browser journal.

The MainPage.xaml file's UserControl control includes a reference to System.Windows. Controls.Navigation. It also includes two default buttons, called Home and About, and the common Click event handler NavButton_Click is assigned. The Tag property of the button defines the related XAML page. In addition to two buttons, the startup page also displays the application name. The following is the complete default XAML code of the MainPage.xaml file:

```
<UserControl x:Class="SampleSilverlightNavigationRIA.MainPage"
    xmlns="http://schemas.microsoft.com/winfx/2006/xaml/presentation"
    xmlns:x="http://schemas.microsoft.com/winfx/2006/xaml"
    xmlns:navigation="clr-namespace:System.Windows.Controls;assembly=
    System.Windows.Controls.Navigation">
    <Grid x:Name="LayoutRoot" Background=
        "{StaticResource ApplicationBackgroundColorBrush}">

        <Grid Style="{StaticResource NavigationContainerStyle}">

            <Border Style="{StaticResource NavigationBorderStyle}">

                <StackPanel Style="{StaticResource NavigationPanelStyle}">
```

```
                    <Button Click="NavButton_Click"
                            Tag="/Views/HomePage.xaml" Content="home"
                            Style="{StaticResource PageLinkStyle}"/>
                    <Button Click="NavButton_Click"
                            Tag="/Views/AboutPage.xaml" Content="about"
                            Style="{StaticResource PageLinkStyle}"/>

            </StackPanel>

        </Border>

        <Border Style="{StaticResource BrandingBorderStyle}">

            <StackPanel Style="{StaticResource BrandingPanelStyle}">

                <TextBlock Text="your."
                        Style="{StaticResource BrandingTextNormalStyle}"/>
                <TextBlock Text="application."
                        Style="{StaticResource BrandingTextHighlightStyle}"/>
                <TextBlock Text="name"
                        Style="{StaticResource BrandingTextNormalStyle}"/>

            </StackPanel>

        </Border>

    </Grid>

    <Border Style="{StaticResource FrameContainerStyle}">

        <Border Style="{StaticResource FrameInnerBorderStyle}">

            <navigation:Frame x:Name="Frame" Source="/Views/HomePage.xaml"
                            JournalOwnership="Automatic"
                            HorizontalContentAlignment="Stretch"
                            VerticalContentAlignment="Stretch"
                            Padding="15,10,15,10"
                            Background="White"/>

        </Border>

    </Border>

    </Grid>
</UserControl>
```

The following code is added to the MainPage.xaml.cs code-behind file by default and defines the Click event handler for the two buttons:

```
private void NavButton_Click(object sender, RoutedEventArgs e)
{
  Button navigationButton = sender as Button;
  String goToPage = navigationButton.Tag.ToString();
  this.Frame.Navigate(new Uri(goToPage, UriKind.Relative));
}
```

In the previous code, the `Navigate` method is critical. With the use of the `Tag` property of the Button control, you retrieve the relative URI of the destination page and pass it to the `Navigate` method.

The Silverlight navigation pages are defined as follows. The `Title` attribute of the `Page` class defines the page-specific title that will be displayed as the browser heading when a user visits that particular page.

```
<navigation:Page x:Class="SampleSilverlightNavigationRIA.HomePage"
    xmlns="http://schemas.microsoft.com/winfx/2006/xaml/presentation"
    xmlns:x="http://schemas.microsoft.com/winfx/2006/xaml"
    xmlns:navigation="clr-namespace:System.Windows.Controls;
  assembly=System.Windows.Controls.Navigation"
    Title="HomePage Page">
```

The navigation framework project represents a consistent set of styles across the Silverlight application. For that, the `App.xaml` file of the project defines application resources containing styles for the main page and content pages. The styles for the main page include primary color brushes, as well as a navigation container style, navigation border style, navigation panel style, page link style, branding border style, branding panel style, branding text highlight style, branding text normal style, frame container style, and frame inner board style. The styles for the content pages include a header text style, content text style, hyperlink button style, and content text panel style. As you can see in the previous XAML code snippets, these defined styles are referenced across the project, which provides a consistent look and feel.

Deep Linking and Search Engine Optimization

If you take a closer look at Figure 14-2, you will notice that the browser address bar includes the page-specific URL, which is `http://localhost:2274/SampleSilverlightNavigationRIATestPage.aspx#/Views/HomePage.xaml`.

When you switch from one page to another page, the Frame control generates the page-specific URL and query string that can be used to go directly to that particular page. As explained earlier, with the use of the `Source` property of the `navigation:Frame` tag, you can have the default page displayed as the startup page of the application. Thus, by leveraging the navigation framework, Silverlight supports *deep linking*, which helps the user bookmark the page and supports SEO.

However, the URL exposes the real XAML page name. You can customize the page URL by using the UriMapper control. As explained in Tim Heuer's video available on Silverlight.net (`silverlight.net/learn/learnvideo.aspx?video=187319`), you can define the UriMapper control at the frame level or the application resource level. You can see the available `navigationCore` namespace containing the UriMapper control in the `App.xaml` file, as shown here:

```
xmlns:navigationCore="clr-namespace:System.Windows.Navigation;
    assembly=System.Windows.Controls.Navigation"
```

Now you can define the UriMapper control of the navigation framework. The UriMapper control can contain one or more UriMapping controls defining the mapping of specific pages. As shown in the following example, the Uri property defines the URL that is displayed by the browser, whereas the MappedUri attribute defines the actual page URL:

```
<Application.Resources>
    <navigationCore:UriMapper x:Key="uriMapper">
        <navigationCore:UriMapping Uri="Default" MappedUri="/Views/HomePage.xaml" />
    </navigationCore:UriMapper>
</Application.Resources>
```

Return to the MainPage.xaml file, and change the Tag property of the related Button control that is the same as the Uri property value; in our case, it is Home. See the following code snippet:

```
<Button Click="NavButton_Click" Tag="Default" Content="home"
    Style="{StaticResource PageLinkStyle}"/>
```

Now if you run the project, as shown in Figure 14-3, you will see the customized URL in the browser rather than the actual XAML page name. As you can see, the original URL (http://localhost:2274/SampleSilverlightNavigationRIATestPage.aspx#/Views/HomePage.xaml) is now changed to http://localhost:2274/SampleSilverlightNavigationRIATestPage.aspx#Default.

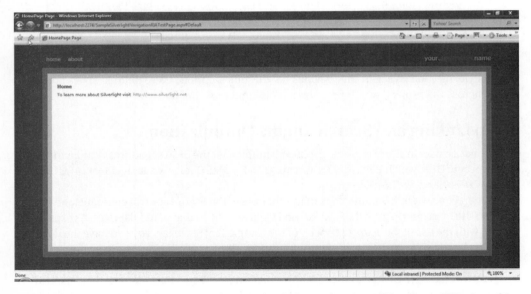

Figure 14-3. *The navigation framework–based Silverlight application with custom URL viewed in Internet Explorer 7*

Out-of-Browser Functionality

Globalization has broken the physical boundaries between organizations and end users and has introduced the concept of virtual organizations and virtual communities (as part of the social networking). As a result, enterprise mobility becomes a strategic initiative for any organization in defining next-generation RIAs that support virtual organizations and collaborative virtual community needs. Therefore, to support the mobile workforce and diversified and distributed user community, you need to consider available connectivity, signal strength, available bandwidth, and support for disconnected mode aspects of enterprise mobility while designing and developing any RIA. Support for disconnected mode (a.k.a. offline mode) makes any RIA a complete solution.

Silverlight 3 introduces Out of Browser Silverlight application capabilities, as well as offers new networking APIs (to detect the connected and disconnected modes and changes in the network connection state) and new offline APIs (to detect the application running mode and version updates). These new features mean that Silverlight applications can be installed on user machines and be running in disconnected and connected modes as rich client applications out of the browser.

The Out of Browser application is installed on the local machine, so you do not need any additional plug-ins to work offline. While running in Out of Browser mode, the application runs as a Windows application but in the sandbox environment, and you can utilize an isolated cache (25MB by default for a Silverlight application) to perform any offline operations (including file management). You can save the data in the isolated cache, and the next time you're connected, you can synchronize the updated data back to the central database system with your custom implementation.

We'll now show how easy it is to make any Silverlight 3 application capable of supporting the Out of Browser capabilities by updating the project we created earlier in this chapter.

Enabling the Out-of-Browser Functionality

Before you start anything, run the SampleSilverlightNavigationRIA application, and right-click the application displayed in the browser. You will notice that along with a Silverlight Configuration option, another option for installing is available but is disabled. This means that all Silverlight 3 applications come with the basics of Out of Browser functionality, but by default the option is not enabled. So, you'll need to enable the functionality.

To enable the Out of Browser functionality, you need to visit the Properties section of the Silverlight application and open the `AppManifest.xml` file. You will notice that the `Deployment.ApplicationIdentity` section is commented out. Go ahead and uncomment that section of the application manifest XML file, and also change the `Shortname` and `Title` properties and `ApplicationIdentity.Blurb` of `ApplicationIdentity` appropriately for your application, as shown here:

```
<Deployment.ApplicationIdentity>
    <ApplicationIdentity
        ShortName="OOB - SampleSLNavigationRIA"
        Title="Sample Silverlight Navigation RIA - Out of Browser Mode">
        <ApplicationIdentity.Blurb>Demonstrating Silverlight Navigation Framework
            and Out of Browser Capabilities</ApplicationIdentity.Blurb>
    </ApplicationIdentity>
</Deployment.ApplicationIdentity>
```

Now run the project, and right-click the application running in the browser. You should see the option enabled, just as Figure 14-4 shows the Install OOB – SampleSLNavigationRIA onto This Computer option enabled.

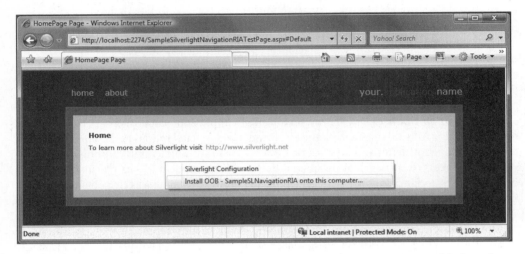

Figure 14-4. *Option to install the Silverlight application onto the computer to enable Out of Browser functionality*

Next, select the option to install the Silverlight application, and you will see a pop-up window with a default icon image with options to create shortcuts on the desktop and Start menu, as shown in Figure 14-5.

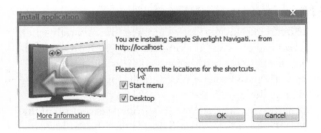

Figure 14-5. *Installing the Silverlight application with the appropriate shortcuts*

You can select or deselect the option to create shortcuts and click OK to install the application. The application will be installed onto your desktop, the appropriate shortcuts with default icons will be created based on your selections to your machine, and the application will be opened in Out of Browser mode, as shown in Figure 14-6. The application contains the default application icon as well as shows the window title with the text you populated in the Title property of the ApplicationIdentity section of the AppManifest.xml file.

If you want to remove the locally installed application, open the application in Out of Browser mode, right-click the application window, and select the Remove This Application option. The application and related shortcuts will be removed from the machine.

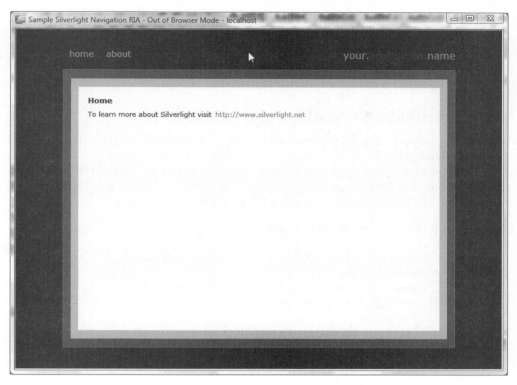

Figure 14-6. *Silverlight application running in Out of Browser mode*

Customizing Icons

You can change the default icons for the installation window, Out of Browser application window, desktop, and Start menu icons by adding <ApplicationIdentity.Icons> in the ApplicationIdentity node and adding the appropriate size of <Icon> nodes. You can use the Size attributes 16x16, 32x32, 48x48, and 128x128 to cover all the possibilities. Then you need to add the appropriate icon files in PNG format to your application and change the BuildAction property from Resource to Content for each icon image file. Then add the appropriate path for each Icon node. The following is a sample code snippet demonstrating incorporating custom icons, where required. Different sizes of images are available in the Icons folder with the following names:

```
<ApplicationIdentity.Icons>
    <Icon Size="16x16">Icons/16x16.png</Icon>
    <Icon Size="32x32">Icons/32x32.png</Icon>
    <Icon Size="48x48">Icons/48x48.png</Icon>
    <Icon Size="128x128">Icons/128x128.png</Icon>
</ApplicationIdentity.Icons>
```

If you run the application now, you should see custom-added icons for the application download window, Out of Browser application window, and shortcuts. You must consider the following three points to make sure the application installs and runs without error:

- Icon files must be of the PNG file type.

- The added icon files' BuildAction property must be set to Content.

- Icon files must be added correctly, and no icon should be missing. Otherwise, the installation process will fail.

Working with the Networking and Offline APIs

Now let's take a brief look at the new networking APIs and offline APIs by incorporating them into the sample application.

First remove the default application branding (your.application.name) XAML code, and then add the following lines of code to represent the application connectivity status (Connected/Disconnected) and application running mode (In Browser/Out of Browser):

```
<StackPanel Style="{StaticResource BrandingPanelStyle}">

    <TextBlock Text="Connectivity Status: " Style="{StaticResource
        BrandingTextNormalStyle}"/>
    <TextBlock x:Name="NWStatus"  Text=" " Style="{StaticResource
        BrandingTextNormalStyle}"/>

    <TextBlock Text=" :: " Style="{StaticResource BrandingTextNormalStyle}"/>

    <TextBlock Text="Application Mode: " Style="{StaticResource
        BrandingTextNormalStyle}"/>
    <TextBlock x:Name="AppMode"  Text=" " Style="{StaticResource
        BrandingTextNormalStyle}"/>

</StackPanel>
```

To get the application network connectivity status, add the System.Net.NetworkInformation namespace to the MainPage.xaml code-behind class:

```
using System.Net.NetworkInformation;
```

Then create a private UpdateNetworkConnectivityStatus method to get the network connection status, update the status TextBlock tag's Text property to Connected or Disconnected, and change the TextBlock tag's Foreground to Green or Red. Here you call the NetworkInterface.GetIsNetworkAvailable method to get the network connectivity status. The following code snippet demonstrates this method:

```
private void UpdateNetworkConnectivityStatus()
{
    if (NetworkInterface.GetIsNetworkAvailable())
    {
        NWStatus.Text = "Connected";
        NWStatus.Foreground = new SolidColorBrush(Colors.Green);
    }
}
```

```
    else
    {
       NWStatus.Text = "Disconnected";
       NWStatus.Foreground = new SolidColorBrush(Colors.Red);
    }
}
```

Now under the `MainPage` constructor, add the `Loaded` and `NetworkAddressChange` event handlers to raise the event when the page is loaded and to report the status of the network connection upon a change in the network connectivity state, as shown in the following code snippet:

```
Loaded += new RoutedEventHandler(MainPage_Loaded);
NetworkChange.NetworkAddressChanged += new
    NetworkAddressChangedEventHandler
      (NetworkChange_NetworkAddressChanged);
```

Next define both event handlers, and call the `UpdateNetworkConnectivityStatus` method, as shown in the following code snippet:

```
void MainPage_Loaded(object sender, RoutedEventArgs e)
{
    UpdateNetworkConnectivityStatus();
}

void NetworkChange_NetworkAddressChanged(object sender, EventArgs e)
{
    UpdateNetworkConnectivityStatus();
}
```

Save and build and then run the application. You should see the startup connected or disconnected status with green or red fonts in the browser. When you change the network connectivity state while running the application, the connectivity state will be automatically reflected in the application. If you install the application as an Out of Browser application and run it, you should see the same network connectivity status update behavior! Isn't it amazing?

Take a deep breath. Once you are ready, it's time for a small exercise. Add a new Online Purchase button to enable purchasing functionality on the `MainPage`. The button should be disabled if you are in the disconnected mode and enabled if you are in the connected mode.

■**Tip** To do this, add a Button control to the `MainPage.xaml` and then update the `UpdateNetworkConnectivityStatus` method to enable/disable the Online Purchase button as per the network connectivity condition.

Now let's update the application running status with the use of the `ApplicationServiceContext.RunningOffline` attribute. Add a new `UpdateApplicationModeStatus` method, as shown here, which will utilize the `ApplicationServiceContext.RunningOffline` attribute:

```
private void UpdateApplicationModeStatus()
{
   if (App.Current.RunningOffline)
   {
      AppMode.Text = "Out of Browser";
      AppMode.Foreground = new SolidColorBrush(Colors.Yellow);
   }
   else
   {
      AppMode.Text = "In Browser";
      AppMode.Foreground = new SolidColorBrush(Colors.Blue);
   }
}
```

Now call this method from the Loaded event of the MainPage to update the application mode.

If you run the application, you will see that the status is updated based on the network connection and application mode. Figure 14-7 shows the application running in In Browser mode with different versions for the network connection status.

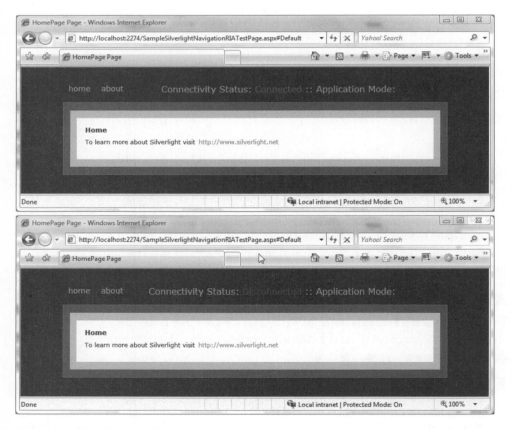

Figure 14-7. *Silverlight application running in In Browser mode with different versions for the network connectivity states*

Figure 14-8 shows the application running in Out of Browser mode with different versions for the network connection status.

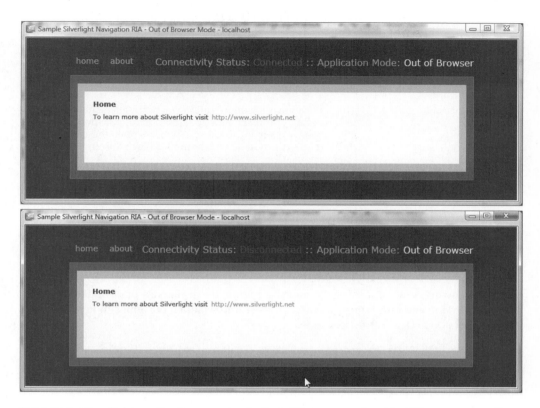

Figure 14-8. *Silverlight application running in Out of Browser mode with different versions for the network connectivity states*

Incorporating an Updated Version

The next logical question that may come to your mind is, "If the application is updated and you are running in Out of Browser mode, how would the user be notified of the availability of the new version of the application?" Here you can use Application.ExecutionState, which basically gives you a current detachment state of the application. The ExecutionStates enumeration is available as part of the core System.Windows library. ExecutionStates defines five possible constants for an application that is capable of running in offline/disconnected mode. Table 14-1 shows the possible values of the ExecutionStates enumeration.

To implement this functionality, first under the App constructor of the App class (in the App.xaml.cs file), add the ExecutionStateChanged event handlers to raise the event when the Out of Browser application is running in connected mode, and you have an updated version available on the server side, as shown here:

```
this.ExecutionStateChanged += new
    EventHandler(App_ExecutionStateChanged);
```

Table 14-1. *Possible Constants for the ExecutionStates Enumeration*

Member Name	Details
RunningOnline	The application is running in online mode hosted in the web page.
Detaching	The application is in the process of detaching from its original host web page.
Detached	The application is running in offline mode and detached from the host web page.
DetachedUpdatesAvailable	The application is running in offline mode and detached from the host web page; however, new updates to the application are available and have been downloaded. When you open the application the next time, the updates will be applicable to the application.
DetachFailed	The application fails at detaching from the host web page.

Now define the ExecutionStateChanged event handler, and check that the execution state of the application is DetachedUpdatesAvailable. If the updates are available, the Application. ExcecutionState will be DetachedUpdatesAvailable. In that case, you can perform some actions such as deactivating some key functionality until the user reopens the application with the latest version.

The following code snippet is informing users about the availability of an updated version of the application and requesting that the user close and relaunch the application to work on the latest version in Out of Browser mode:

```
void App_ExecutionStateChanged(object sender, EventArgs e)
{
   if (App.Current.ExecutionState ==
     ExecutionStates.DetachedUpdatesAvailable)
   {
       MessageBox.Show("An updated version of the application is
          available. Now the application will be closed. Please
          relaunch application to get the latest version.");
   }
}
```

Now if you update the application, the next time in connected mode when you open the Out of Browser application, you should see the message shown in Figure 14-9.

In the current version of the Out of Browser application, once the updated version is available and you are connected to the server, there is no way you can stop downloading the latest version when you access the Out of Browser application for the first time.

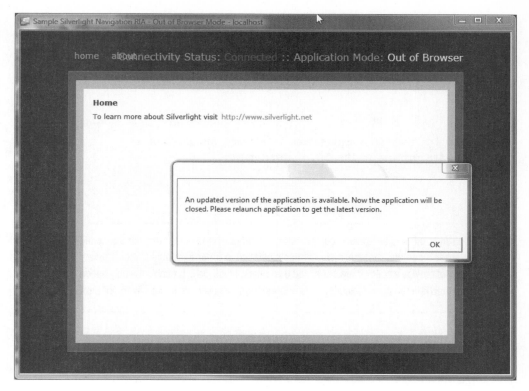

Figure 14-9. *Silverlight application running in Out of Browser mode and getting a message about the availability of the updated version on the server side*

Installing a Custom Out-of-Browser Application

Last but not least, we'll discuss how you can have a custom Out of Browser application installation option in addition to the default right-click option. For that you need to simply call `Application.Current.Detach()` to enable custom application installation to run the application in the detached Out of Browser mode.

Let's first add a new button—Install OOB—next to the existing About button. To achieve this, add a new Button control immediately after the About button code in the `MainPage.xaml` file, and set its `Click` event, as shown here:

```
<Button x:Name="InstallOOBButton" Click="InstallOOBButton_Click"
  Content="Install OOB" Style="{StaticResource PageLinkStyle}"/>
```

Now implement the `InstallOOBButton_Click` event, as shown in the following code snippet. First you check the `ExecutionState` of the application to confirm that you are not running the application in Out of Browser mode by comparing the `ExecutionState` property with the `ExecutionStates.Detached` setting. If you are not running the application in Out of Browser mode or the application is not already installed, the application will call the `Application.Current.Detach()` method to enable application installation. Otherwise, it will display an informative message.

```
private void InstallOOBButton_Click(object sender, RoutedEventArgs e)
{
    if (Application.Current.ExecutionState != ExecutionStates.Detached)
    {
        Application.Current.Detach();
    }
    else
    {
        MessageBox.Show("The application is already installed or
            you are running in the Out of Browser mode.");
    }
}
```

■**Note** Currently there is no specific custom way to distinguish the state between the application running in Out of Browser mode and the application already installed in order to enable Out of Browser mode. As a result, you cannot provide a specific message, and the generic message is probably the only option (the way we have implemented it in the previous code). This feature might be available in the Silverlight 3 released version.

Figure 14-10 shows that when you click the Install OOB button in In Browser mode, you will get the Install application window to install Silverlight application that enables Out of Browser mode.

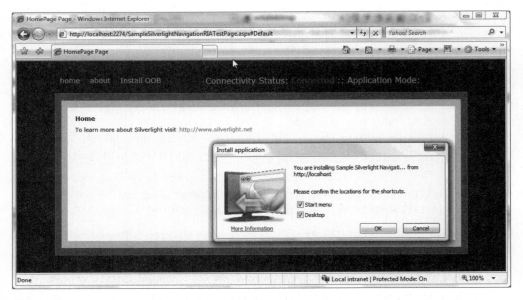

Figure 14-10. *Custom application installation option when you are in In Browser mode*

Figure 14-11 shows that when you click the Install OOB button in Out of Browser mode, you will get an informative message.

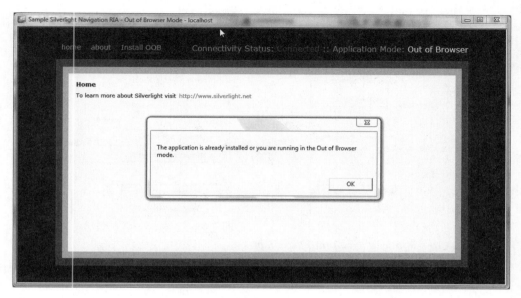

Figure 14-11. *The custom application installation option is not available when you are in Out of Browser mode.*

■**Note** An introductory video session on Out of Browser functionality by Tim Heuer is available on Silverlight.net. You can view the video by visiting `silverlight.net/learn/learnvideo.aspx?video=187318`.

Cross-Silverlight Application Communication

The Silverlight 3 local messaging feature allows Silverlight applications to communicate across different Silverlight plug-ins/applications. These Silverlight plug-ins/applications can be hosted on the same page, on different browser tabs, in different browsers, or in the Out of Browser application. To establish a local connection and perform communications between Silverlight applications executed on the client side only, no server-side round-trips are required.

Figure 14-12 explains the communication process between Silverlight applications through a flow diagram.

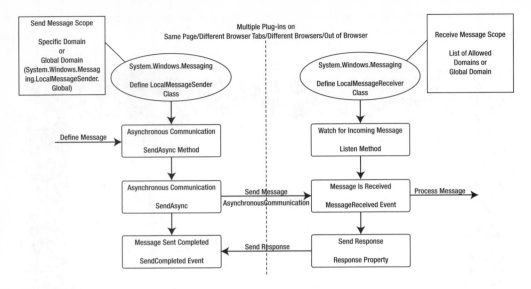

Figure 14-12. *Cross-application communication process*

Using the System.Windows.Messaging Namespace

As shown in Figure 14-12, the newly introduced System.Windows.Messaging namespace, which is a Microsoft .NET Framework library component for Silverlight, facilitates local messaging between two Silverlight applications.

The System.Windows.Messaging namespace provides the required set of classes to support local messaging between two Silverlight applications on the client side. Table 14-2 describes the key classes of this namespace.

Table 14-2. *Classes of the System.Windows.Messaging Namespace*

Class	Details
LocalMessageSender	Used on the sender Silverlight application side to send messages to the local Silverlight application receiver/listener
LocalMessageReceiver	Used on the receiver Silverlight application side to receive messages
MessageReceiveEventArgs	Provides data for the LocalMessageReceiver.MessageReceived event
SendCompletedEventArgs	Provides data for the LocalMessageSender.SendCompleted event
ListenFailedException	Occurs when a LocalMessageReceiver fails to receive a message
SendFailedException	Occurs when a LocalMessageSender fails to send a message

Table 14-3 provides details on the key members of the LocalMessageSender class.

Table 14-3. *Key Members of LocalMessageSender Class*

Member	Details
SendAsync	Method sends a message to the receiver in asynchronous mode
ReceiverDomain	Property gets the domain information of the LocalMessageReceiver for sending messages
ReceiverName	Property gets the name of the LocalMessageReceiver for sending messages
SendCompleted	Event raised when the message is successfully sent to the LocalMessageReceiver

Table 14-4 provides details on the key members of the LocalMessageReceiver class.

Table 14-4. *Key Members of LocalMessageReceiver Class*

Member	Details
AllowdSenderDomains	Property gets the domain from where receiver can receive messages
ReceiverName	Property gets the name of the LocalMessageReceiver for sending messages
MessageReceived	Event raised when the message is successfully received from the LocalMessageSender

Seeing an Example in Action

Let's develop an example demonstrating cross-communication between two Silverlight applications hosted on the same page and on the same domain. Similarly, you can establish communication between Silverlight applications that are deployed on different domains by deploying the proper cross-domain policy files.

First create a Silverlight application project named chapter14. Then delete the chapter14 Silverlight application project from the chapter14 solution, and add two new Silverlight application projects to the chapter14 solution named SenderApp and ReceiverApp. Remove the extra test pages from the chapter14.web project: chapter14TestPage.aspx, chapter14TestPage.html, ReceiverAppTestPage.aspx, and SenderAppTestPage.aspx. Figure 14-13 shows these two newly created Silverlight application projects and the related test pages in the Visual Studio Solution Explorer.

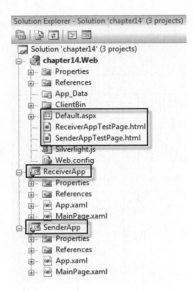

Figure 14-13. *SenderApp and ReceiverApp Silverlight applications*

Creating the Sender Silverlight Application

In this section, you'll create a very simple sender Silverlight application containing three RadioButton controls, each related to one color (red, green, and blue), and a Button control to submit the RadioButton-related color selection to the receiver application.

The following is the XAML code for the SenderApp MainPage.xaml file to achieve this simple UI:

```
<UserControl x:Class="SenderApp.MainPage"
    xmlns="http://schemas.microsoft.com/winfx/2006/xaml/presentation"
    xmlns:x="http://schemas.microsoft.com/winfx/2006/xaml"
    Width="400" Height="300">
    <StackPanel x:Name="LayoutRoot" Background="White">
        <TextBlock Text="Select Color and Press Submit"></TextBlock>
        <RadioButton Foreground="Red" IsChecked="true" Content="Red"
            Checked="Color_Checked" ></RadioButton>
        <RadioButton Foreground="Blue" Content="Blue"
            Checked="Color_Checked"></RadioButton>
        <RadioButton Foreground="Green" Content="Green"
            Checked="Color_Checked" ></RadioButton>
        <Button x:Name="btnSubmit" Width="100" Height="32"
            Content="Submit" Click="btnSubmit_Click" ></Button>
    </StackPanel>
</UserControl>
```

As you can see from the previous XAML code, by default the Red RadioButton control is selected by setting the IsChecked property to true. We also have integrated all the RadioButton controls' Checked events to the same Color_Checked event handler and the Button control's

Click event to the btnSubmit_Click event handler. Before we implement them, first include the Systems.Windows.Messaging reference, as shown here:

```
using System.Windows.Messaging;
```

Next declare the following three private string variables at the MainPage class level:

```
private const string SenderAppName = "Sender1";
private const string ReceiverAppName = "Receiver1";
private string message="Red";
```

Now define the RadioButton controls' Checked event handler. Based on the RadioButton control selection, set the message to the selected RadioButton control's Content property representing the corresponding selected color—Red, Green, or Blue—as shown here:

```
private void Color_Checked(object sender, RoutedEventArgs e)
{
   RadioButton rbtn= sender as RadioButton;
   message = rbtn.Content.ToString();
}
```

Finally, define the Submit button control's Click event handler. First you need to create a new instance of the LocalMessageSender class to establish a communication channel between two Silverlight-based applications, where the SenderApp application is representing the sending end. Then asynchronously send the message to the receiver application using the SendAsync method only if the message is not null or empty. The following is the related code snippet:

```
private void btnSubmit_Click(object sender, RoutedEventArgs e)
{
   LocalMessageSender msgSender = new
     LocalMessageSender(ReceiverAppName);

   if(message!=null || message!=string.Empty)
     msgSender.SendAsync(message);
}
```

Build the project successfully. You are all set with the sender application. Now it's time to develop the receiver application.

Creating the Receiver Silverlight Application

The receiver Silverlight application is simpler than the sender Silverlight application. Here you will have only one Rectangle control, which will be filled with the color that is received from the sender application based on the color-specific RadioButton control selection on the sending end.

The following is the XAML code for the ReceiverApp MainPage.xaml file to achieve this simple UI:

```xml
<UserControl x:Class="ReceiverApp.MainPage"
    xmlns="http://schemas.microsoft.com/winfx/2006/xaml/presentation"
    xmlns:x="http://schemas.microsoft.com/winfx/2006/xaml"
    Width="400" Height="300">
    <StackPanel x:Name="LayoutRoot" Background="White">
        <TextBlock Text="Selected Color in SenderApp..."></TextBlock>
        <Rectangle x:Name="rect" Height="25"></Rectangle>
    </StackPanel>
</UserControl>
```

Here you also need to include the Systems.Windows.Messaging reference:

```
using System.Windows.Messaging;
```

Next declare the following two private string variables at the MainPage class level:

```
private const string SenderAppName = "Sender1";
private const string ReceiverAppName = "Receiver1";
```

In the MainPage constructor, first you need to create a new instance of the LocalMessageReceiver class to establish a communication channel between two Silverlight-based applications, where the ReceiverApp application is representing the receiving end. Next, based on the MessageReceived event of the msgReceiver object, you apply the switch case on the Message parameter of MessageReceivedEventArgs e to set the Rectangle control's Fill property with the received color information. At last, call the msgReceiver.Listen() method to listen for messages from a LocalMessageSender, which is SenderApp in this case. The following is the related code snippet:

```csharp
public MainPage()
{
    InitializeComponent();

    LocalMessageReceiver msgReceiver = new
        LocalMessageReceiver(SenderAppName);
    msgReceiver.MessageReceived += (object sender,
        MessageReceivedEventArgs e) =>
    {
        switch (e.Message)
        {
            case "Red":
            {
                rect.Fill = new SolidColorBrush(Colors.Red);
                break;
            }

            case "Green":
            {
                rect.Fill = new SolidColorBrush(Colors.Green);
                break;
            }
```

```
        case "Blue":
        {
            rect.Fill = new SolidColorBrush(Colors.Blue);
            break;
        }

    }
};

msgReceiver.Listen();
}
```

Build the project successfully. You are all set with the receiver application also. Next let's host the sender and receiver applications on the same page.

Hosting the Sender and Receiver Applications on the Same Page

Because you need to host both the sender and receiver Silverlight applications on the same page, you will use the Default.aspx file in the chapter14.web ASP.NET web application project. For that, host the SenderApp and ReceiverApp Silverlight applications using the asp:Silverlight web control within the body section of the Default.aspx page:

```
<body>
    <form id="form1" runat="server">
    <table>
      <asp:ScriptManager ID="ScriptManager1" runat="server">
      </asp:ScriptManager>
      <tr>
        <td>
          <div style="float: left;">
            <h2>Sender App...</h2>
          <asp:Silverlight ID="Silverlight2" runat="server"
            Source="~/ClientBin/SenderApp.xap"
            MinimumVersion="3.0.40307.0" Width="400" Height="300" />
          </div>
        </td>
        <td>
          <div style="float: left;">
            <h2>Receiver App...</h2>
            <asp:Silverlight ID="Silverlight1" runat="server"
              Source="~/ClientBin/ReceiverApp.xap"
              MinimumVersion="3.0.40307.0" Width="400" Height="300" />
          </div>
        </td>
      </tr>
    </table>
    </form>
</body>
```

Set the `Default.aspx` page as a startup page, and you are all set to run the cross plug-in Silverlight communication sample! You should see the receiver Rectangle control is filled with the appropriate color based on the color-specific RadioButton control selected on the sending end when the user clicks the Submit button. Figure 14-14 shows the Blue RadioButton control selected on the sending end and the blue color applied to the Rectangle control on the receiving end. This black-and-white book doesn't really illustrate the point, so you should try it out to see for yourself!

Figure 14-14. *Same page hosted cross-Silverlight applications communication in action*

Summary

This chapter delved into some of the advanced aspects of Silverlight 3. You probably won't use these features in every application, but when you do need them, they will now be familiar to you. This chapter demonstrated the enterprise-level capabilities of Silverlight as an RIA development technology platform.

We started by demonstrating the newly introduced navigation framework, which can help organizations implement the reusability and standardization features along with integration with .NET RIA services to develop service-oriented applications in an agile mode. With the Out of Browser functionality, you can develop a truly rich Internet application that supports connected and disconnected modes and the integration between them. We also discussed the client-side local messaging capabilities across the Silverlight applications within the page, across browser tabs, across browsers, and in Out of Browser mode in a same-domain or cross-domain deployment scenario.

The next and last chapter of the book will cover even more advanced topics such as using multithreading and parsing XAML at runtime to build dynamic user interfaces.

■ ■ ■

CHAPTER 15

Threading in Silverlight

In the previous chapter, we covered the exciting new Silverlight 3 support for enterprise-level design concepts and features. Another advanced topic is the multithreading support that Silverlight provides, which we will cover in this final chapter of the book.

Used properly, threading is a great way to provide a smooth user experience by doing work such as lengthy calculations or downloading files while the user interface remains responsive. Another useful technique for certain applications is the use of a Timer—a way to execute some code on a certain periodic schedule (such as every 10 seconds). This chapter concludes with how to dynamically load assemblies and even dynamically add XAML to your user interface.

Using Threading

Silverlight is a *multithreaded* environment, which means multiple sequences of code can execute simultaneously. You've already encountered this in the asynchronous nature of network communication. The main application thread makes a call to the BeginGetResponse method of HttpWebRequest, and then your code doesn't need to sit around waiting for a response. The actual network communication happens on a different thread, and when a response from the server is received, the method specified as the asynchronous callback is invoked. In Silverlight, this specific callback actually happens on a thread other than the main application thread. The main application thread is usually referred to as the *user interface thread*, since this is the thread where all user interface–related code lives (for example, code that creates the user interface, code for handling events, and so on). Figure 15-1 shows an illustration of two threads of execution: the user interface thread and a worker thread that is used for the network communication. The worker thread representation is shifted down to illustrate the time when the worker thread is created.

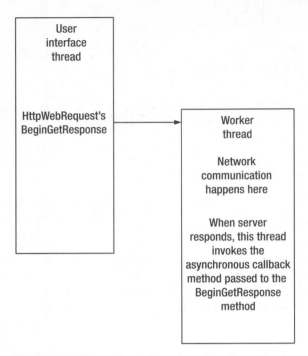

Figure 15-1. *Illustration of user interface thread and worker thread*

If you build web applications solely using technologies such as HTML, JScript, and Ajax, you can't take advantage of threading in the underlying operating system. Using multiple threads allows you to build more complex applications that have a high degree of responsiveness to users. With multiple cores and multiple processors in computers these days, it would be surprising if Silverlight did not provide support for using threads. Of course, using threads introduces new sets of problems for developers. First, you want to be careful to not overuse threads. Since ultimately each thread is backed by an operating system thread, there are a limited number of threads you can use, because each thread requires memory and costs CPU time. Another significant problem occurs any time several threads want to access the same data. If two threads want to modify a shared piece of data, such as an integer variable, it's possible to see unexpected behavior if one thread modifies the variable while the other thread is in the middle of a modification operation. This is known as a *race condition*, since both threads are in a race to access the shared data and it's unpredictable which will "win." Race conditions are only one type of potential threading issue. If you need to use threads in your Silverlight application, use them carefully. Of course, the benefit of threads can outweigh the inherent problems when used properly.

The Thread Class

The System.Threading.Thread class is the managed class that wraps a thread in the underlying operating system. This is the class you use when you manually create threads or when you want to do something like put a thread to sleep. Table 15-1 shows the properties of the Thread class.

Table 15-1. *Properties of the System.Threading. Thread Class*

Property	Type	Description
CurrentCulture	CultureInfo	Gets/sets the culture for the current thread.
CurrentThread	static Thread	Gets the currently active thread.
CurrentUICulture	CultureInfo	Gets/sets the culture used by the resource manager when accessing culture-specific resources at runtime.
IsAlive	bool	true if the thread is currently running normally and not aborted/stopped.
IsBackground	bool	true if the thread is a background thread. Background threads do not prevent the Silverlight runtime from shutting down; therefore, they may be killed abruptly without completing.
ManagedThreadId	Int32	Unique identifier assigned to the managed thread.
Name	string	Gets/sets the name of the thread.
ThreadState	System.Threading.ThreadState	Gets the current state of the thread.

Table 15-2 describes the most useful methods of the Thread class.

Table 15-2. *Methods of the System.Threading. Thread Class*

Method	Description
Abort	Causes a ThreadAbortException to occur in the thread. The thread will usually terminate. It will transition to the AbortRequested state and ultimately to the Aborted state.
Join	Blocks the calling thread until the thread that Join is invoked on is finished. This is useful when the calling thread must wait for results or other events to complete before proceeding.
Sleep	Static method. Puts the calling thread to sleep for a specified time span or number of milliseconds. While sleeping, the thread will not consume any processor time.
Start	Starts the thread. You can optionally pass an object to the Start method that the thread's work method will use.

A thread can be in one of several states, as shown in Figure 15-2. Note that the Background state is not mutually exclusive to the other states. It's possible for a thread to be a background thread and to be running, for example. Both of these states can be discovered by consulting the ThreadState property of a thread.

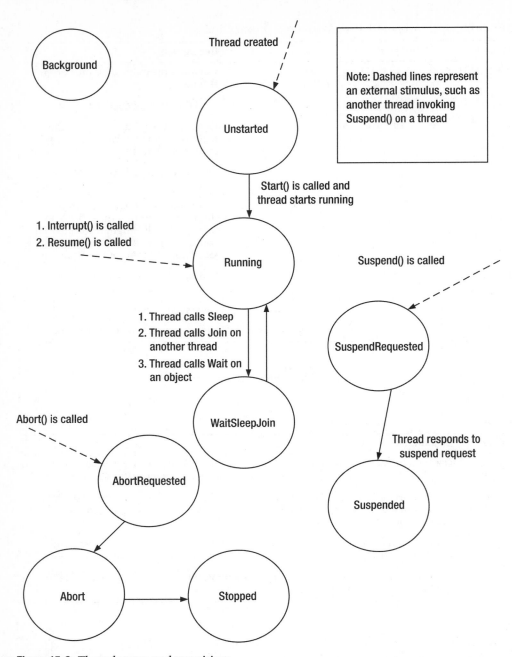

Figure 15-2. *Thread states and transitions*

Creating and Managing Threads

If you want to execute some code on an alternate thread, you can place the code to execute in its own method and then pass this method to the Thread class's constructor (by wrapping the method in a ThreadStart object). We'll use the following method to simulate some work:

```
public void doSomething()
{
    Thread.Sleep(5000); // 5 seconds
    Dispatcher.BeginInvoke(delegate() { statusText.Text = "Work done."; });
}
```

The code for this chapter contains a simple interface used to start a thread executing the doSomething method. You can repeatedly click a button to see the current state of the thread. You should see the state go from Running to WaitSleepJoin and finally to Stopped after the 5-second sleep period is over. Here's the event handler for the first button that creates and starts the thread:

```
private void startThreadButton_Click(object sender, RoutedEventArgs e)
{
    currentThread = new Thread(new ThreadStart(doSomething));
    currentThread.Start();
    statusText.Text = "Thread created and started";
    threadStateText.Text = currentThread.ThreadState.ToString();
}
```

The Thread constructor uses the ThreadStart class to wrap the method that does the work. There is an alternate class, ParameterizedThreadStart, that is used when you want to pass an object to the method that performs the work. This object gets passed to the Start method, which subsequently passes it to the method wrapped by ParameterizedThreadStart. A method suitable for use with ParameterizedThreadStart takes a single object as a parameter.

```
public void gotoSleep(object time)
{
    int timeToSleep = (int)time;
    Thread.Sleep(timeToSleep);
}
```

Starting the thread is accomplished using code similar to the nonparameterized ThreadStart class; however, the parameter is passed to the Start method:

```
currentThread = new Thread(new ParameterizedThreadStart(gotoSleep));
currentThread.Start(7500);
```

Although this is an effective way to create a thread to do some processing, it has several problems. The main problem is that creating a thread is expensive, and if you continue to create threads like this, your application's performance might be impacted, since the environment handles the creation and eventually the cleanup of threads. To address this problem, you should use something called the *thread pool*, which contains a number of already created threads ready to jump into action and do some work.

The thread pool automatically handles the allocation, creation, and cleanup of threads. If your application requires a larger number of threads than the thread pool already has, then new threads are created and added to the pool. If your application requires fewer threads than the pool has, however, your application won't incur the cost of creation of new threads, since they are already available in the pool. Another advantage to the thread pool is that if at one point your application requires a large number of threads, but later it doesn't, the unused threads will automatically clean themselves up until the pool contains a number of threads closer to what your application currently requires. You interact with the thread pool using the System.Threading.ThreadPool class. You never create an instance of the thread pool, since it is completely managed by the environment (the Silverlight plug-in), so all methods are static. The ThreadPool class provides methods to get and set the minimum and maximum number of threads, but you'll usually leave this up to the thread pool itself. The vast majority of the time the thread pool will better manage thread counts than you can. The most useful method to you is the QueueUserWorkItem method.

The simplest way to use QueueUserWorkItem is to pass it a method that does the work. This is similar to passing a method to a ThreadStart class constructor, but it requires less work and frees you from having to interact with the thread directly.

```
private void startThreadButton_Click(object sender, RoutedEventArgs e)
{
    ThreadPool.QueueUserWorkItem(doSomething);
    statusText.Text = "Work queued for a thread pool thread";
}
```

Although this code functions similarly to manually creating and using a thread, you can't get state information about the thread since there is no Thread object. The work is sent to a background thread, and then the application just carries on.

Let's say you have a user interface with a TextBox, named resultTextBox, that displays the contents of something you download using HttpWebRequest. Error handling and details of reading the response stream are left out for simplicity since they aren't needed for this illustration.

```
void responseHandler(IAsyncResult asyncResult)
{
    HttpWebResponse response = (HttpWebResponse)request.EndGetResponse(asyncResult);
    StreamReader reader = new StreamReader(response.GetResponseStream());
    string result = "";
    // read and process file
    resultTextBox.Text = result;
}
```

If you attempt to run this code, you'll get an error about cross-thread access not being allowed. This problem with modifying resultTextBox directly from the response handler is because the response handler is executing on a different thread. Only the main user interface thread can modify user interface elements. What you need, then, is a way to get the user interface thread to make the user interface modification. This happens using something called the Dispatcher.

The Dispatcher

The DependencyObject class acts as the base object for many classes in Silverlight. One important aspect of this class, however, is its single property, Dispatcher. Objects can be modified only on the thread they are created on. Each object, therefore, has a Dispatcher property that provides two important pieces of functionality. For starters, you can test whether an object can be modified from the current thread by calling the CheckAccess method. If the current thread is the same as the one the Dispatcher belongs to, CheckAccess will return true. The other important functionality is the ability to queue some code to execute on the Dispatcher's thread. This is how you go about solving the cross-thread access problem when modifying user interface objects. The method used to execute some code on the Dispatcher's thread is called BeginInvoke. Figure 15-3 shows the relationship of two threads and the Dispatcher object.

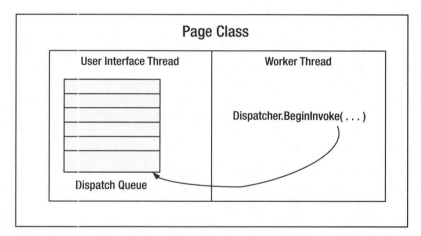

Figure 15-3. *A worker thread using the Dispatcher to queue code to execute on the main thread*

Let's rewrite the responseHandler to properly interact with the user interface by using the Dispatcher property:

```
void responseHandler(IAsyncResult asyncResult)
{
    HttpWebResponse response = (HttpWebResponse)request.EndGetResponse(asyncResult);
    StreamReader reader = new StreamReader(response.GetResponseStream());
    string result = "";
    // read and process file
    Dispatcher.BeginInvoke(delegate() { resultTextBox.Text = output; });
}
```

This usage of BeginInvoke creates an anonymous, zero-parameter method by using the delegate keyword. You can also execute a method that has parameters by using the alternate form of BeginInvoke, which takes an array of parameters as its second parameter. In this case, we call BeginInvoke directly because part of the defined behavior of HttpWebResponse is that the response handler is invoked on a thread other than the original calling thread. If you're in a situation where the invoking thread might be the user interface thread or a different thread, you can use CheckAccess combined with BeginInvoke in order to modify the user interface:

```
void modifyUserInterface()
{
    if(Dispatcher.CheckAccess())
    {
        resultTextBox.Text = "modified from UI thread";
    } else {
        Dispatcher.BeginInvoke(
            delegate() {
                outputTB.Text = "modified from non-UI thread";
            }
        );
    }
}
```

Of course, although you'll primarily use the Dispatcher to modify the user interface, it is also useful for modifying any data that is associated with a different thread. As illustrated in Figure 15-3, each thread has a dispatch queue. This is where the code you specify in a BeginInvoke method goes. Each call to BeginInvoke adds a unit of work to the dispatch queue.

The BackgroundWorker Class

If you need to perform work on a separate thread, the easiest way to do this is by using the BackgroundWorker class. This class makes it easy to do work (such as a long download) on a separate thread so your user interface stays responsive. This class also provides events for reporting progress of the work. Table 15-3 describes its properties.

Table 15-3. *Properties of the System.ComponentModel.BackgroundWorker Class*

Property	Type	Description
CancellationPending	bool	true when the application attempts to cancel the BackgroundWorker via a call to the CancelAsync method
IsBusy	bool	true when the BackgroundWorker's task is in progress (after the call to RunWorkerAsync, and as long as the task isn't complete or cancelled)
WorkerReportsProgress	bool	true when the BackgroundWorker is configured to report progress via the ProgressChanged event handler
WorkerSupportsCancellation	bool	true when the BackgroundWorker is capable of being cancelled via CancelAsync

The BackgroundWorker has three events: DoWork, ProgressChanged, and RunWorkerCompleted. Normally, a method you register with an event is invoked when the event is raised. This same mechanism, however, is used by the DoWork event. In this case, what is normally an event handler instead contains code that makes up the work that will be performed by the BackgroundWorker.

ProgressChanged is used to register a method that can handle progress change notification—most useful for displaying a status indicator on the user interface, since the method call happens on the initiating thread (most commonly the user interface thread). The RunWorkerCompleted event is raised when the work is complete.

Let's explore just how the BackgroundWorker operates. Figure 15-4 shows a demonstration with three buttons. Clicking each button will start a new BackgroundWorker configured with some information to tell it how long to execute, as well as where to send data (the TextBlock next to the button) as it executes and when it completes.

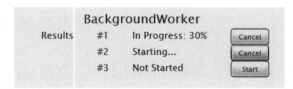

Figure 15-4. *BackgroundWorker demonstration*

Before you can use the BackgroundWorker, you must define a method that encapsulates the work that you want done on a background thread. This method supports cancellation and takes an integer argument (contained in the CustomWorkerArgs instance that is passed in via the DoWorkEventArgs object) that controls how long the method takes to execute. The long-running operation is simulated via Thread.Sleep:

```
public void performLengthyOperation(object sender, DoWorkEventArgs e)
{
    BackgroundWorker bw = (BackgroundWorker)sender;
    CustomWorkerArgs args = (CustomWorkerArgs)e.Argument;
    e.Result = args;
    for (int i = 1; i <= 10; i++)
    {
        if (bw.CancellationPending)
        {
            e.Cancel = true;
            break;
        }
        else
        {
            Thread.Sleep(args.sleepTime / 10);
            bw.ReportProgress(i * 10, args);
        }
    }
}
```

The DoWorkEventArgs object defines several useful properties: Argument, which contains an arbitrary object that was passed to RunWorkerAsync; Cancel, which you set to true to cancel the work (generally done when CancellationPending is set to true); and Result, which is used to store an object that can be processed by the RunWorkerCompleted event handler. Since this configuration of BackgroundWorker supports cancellation (something we must explicitly implement in the method that performs work), the CancellationPending property is checked, and the loop aborts prematurely if it is true. The ReportProgress method takes two parameters: an integer representing percentage completion and optionally a user state, used to communicate some form of information to the progress event handler.

The CustomWorkerArgs class simply holds an integer representing an index (so we can easily access the button/text block associated with a BackgroundWorker) and an integer for sleepTime (the total time the worker method should take to execute). Using a class like this is how you can communicate as much information as needed to the BackgroundWorker.

```
class CustomWorkerArgs
{
    public int index;
    public int sleepTime;
}
```

Since the various event handlers for BackgroundWorker include a sender (the BackgroundWorker instance), you can hold a reference to this worker at the class level and compare the instances instead of passing the index via CustomWorkerArgs. In fact, in one case (when the worker is cancelled or throws an exception), this is mandated. However, this information is included in the CustomWorkerArgs class in order to show where information can be accessed and used in the BackgroundWorker's event handlers. You can keep an array of BackgroundWorker instances at the class level, along with an array of Buttons and an array of TextBlocks. The Button, in XAML, stores the appropriate index in the Tag attribute. A single Button event handler is used to start a BackgroundWorker.

```
private void buttonTask_Click(object sender, RoutedEventArgs e)
{
    // Tag used to get index for button/text blocks
    int index = Convert.ToInt32(((Button)sender).Tag);
    if (workers[index] != null)
    {
        resultBoxes[index].Text = "Cancelling...";
        workers[index].CancelAsync();
        bwButtons[index].Content = "Start";
    }
    else
    {
        BackgroundWorker worker = new BackgroundWorker();
        worker.WorkerReportsProgress = true;
        worker.WorkerSupportsCancellation = true;
        worker.ProgressChanged +=
                new ProgressChangedEventHandler(worker_ProgressChanged);
```

```
            worker.RunWorkerCompleted +=
                    new RunWorkerCompletedEventHandler(worker_RunWorkerCompleted);
            worker.DoWork += new DoWorkEventHandler(performLengthyOperation);
            CustomWorkerArgs args = new CustomWorkerArgs();
            args.index = index;
            args.sleepTime = 25000;
            bwButtons[index].Content = "Cancel";
            resultBoxes[index].Text = "Starting...";
            workers[index] = worker;
            worker.RunWorkerAsync(args);
        }
}
```

The index is retrieved via the Tag attribute, and then the corresponding worker entry in the workers array is checked. This entry is set to null when the BackgroundWorker completes (or errors or is cancelled), so if you find it not null, then the worker is active and working. Otherwise, a new BackgroundWorker is created. This is where we set WorkReportsProgress and WorkerSupportsCancellation to true. Again, these properties should be set to true only when you construct the method that does work to explicitly handle the cancel condition and to report progress.

Next, the event handlers are registered. Let's take a closer look at these. DoWork is registered with the method that actually does the work. In this case, this is the performLengthyOperation that you already implemented. The rest of this method creates a CustomWorkerArgs instance, configures it, and passes it to the BackgroundWorker in the RunWorkerAsync method. RunWorkerAsync is what starts the actual work, provided DoWork is registered with the work method.

The progress handler is straightforward. The UserState property of ProgressChangedEventArgs contains the object originally passed to RunWorkerAsync. The source of this property, however, is the second (optional) parameter to the ReportProgress method of BackgroundWorker. If you need to pass something custom specifically to the progress report handler, you can do it using the UserState property.

```
void worker_ProgressChanged(object sender, ProgressChangedEventArgs e)
{
    int index = ((CustomWorkerArgs)e.UserState).index;
    resultBoxes[index].Text = "In progress: " + e.ProgressPercentage + "%";
}
```

The RunWorkerCompleted event handler is much more interesting. Here, you must check whether the background worker was cancelled or if it had an error. If either of these conditions is true, you can't use the Result property of the RunWorkerCompletedEventArgs, or else your code will throw an exception.

```
void worker_RunWorkerCompleted(object sender, RunWorkerCompletedEventArgs e)
{
    BackgroundWorker bw = (BackgroundWorker)sender;
    int index;
    if (e.Error != null || e.Cancelled)
    {
        // if there's an Error or this worker was cancelled,
        // we can't access Result without throwing an exception
        if (bw == workers[0])
            index = 0;
        else if (bw == workers[1])
            index = 1;
        else
            index = 2;
        if (e.Error != null)
            resultBoxes[index].Text = "Exception: " + e.Error.Message;
        else
            resultBoxes[index].Text = "Cancelled";
    }
    else
    {
        index = ((CustomWorkerArgs)e.Result).index;
        resultBoxes[index].Text = "Completed";
    }
    bwButtons[index].Content = "Start";
    workers[index] = null;
}
```

If there is no error and the worker was not cancelled, the Result property can be accessed. The else block illustrates accessing Result, providing a quick way to arrive at the right text block.

Remember that all of these event handlers happen in the thread that created the BackgroundWorker. Since these workers were created on the user interface thread, it's possible to directly access the various text blocks to set their Text property to something appropriate. There are two big advantages to using the BackgroundWorker. First, it makes it easy to do work on a background thread without needing to worry about manually creating and managing a thread. Second, the various event handlers happen on the calling thread, making modification of a user interface easy without needing to use a Dispatcher.

Working with Shared Data

One of the trickiest problems when it comes to working with multiple threads is using shared resources—typically, shared memory in the form of objects or primitive types. When it comes to shared data, one potential issue is known as a *race condition*. Figure 15-5 illustrates two threads attempting to increment a single integer variable named value. However, a simple increment is split into smaller operations behind the scenes: the value of the variable is read, incremented, and stored back into the variable.

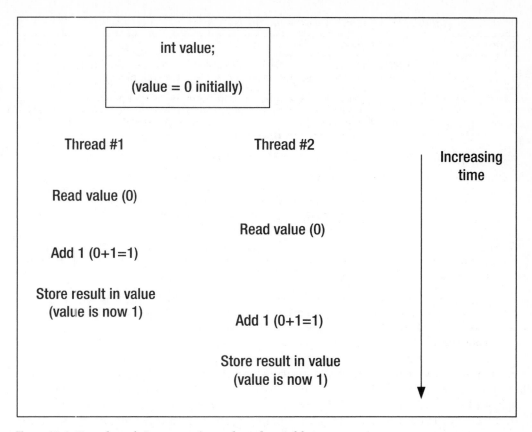

Figure 15-5. *Two threads incrementing a shared variable*

After each thread is done executing, you would expect the value of the integer variable to be 2, not 1. Unfortunately, while the second thread did read the value, the read happened before the first thread was done with its increment. This means both threads think the value was 0 and increment it to 1. The second thread clobbers the increment done by the first thread.

What you want is a way to ensure that all the tiny pieces of the increment (the read, the increment, and the write-back) work as a single unit. This increment then acts as an atomic operation—an operation (or sequence of operations) that works together and isn't preempted by another thread. This atomicity is achieved by using synchronization mechanisms. Actually, the increment and decrement are such common operations that the Silverlight base class framework provides a specialized increment and decrement that are guaranteed to happen without another thread preempting them. These convenience operations, and a few others, are provided by the System.Threading.Interlocked class. Table 15-4 describes the methods of Interlocked. All methods are static.

The Interlocked class can be extremely useful if you are performing atomic operations. You don't need to do anything other than invoke Interlocked.Increment(ref number) if you want to add 1 to an integer variable without needing to worry about other threads getting in the way. If you want to do something beyond a simple increment or add or comparison, you need a mechanism to turn an arbitrary set of operations into an atomic operation that can't be affected by other threads.

Table 15-4. *Methods of the System.Threading.Interlocked Class*

Method	Description
Add	Adds two 32-bit or two 64-bit integers and stores the result in the memory location of the first integer (pass first integer by reference).
CompareExchange	Compares two values (integers or arbitrary types via a generic version) and replaces the value in the memory location of the first parameter with the second parameter if the first parameter is equal to the third parameter (a value used in comparison with first parameter).
Decrement	Decrements a 32-bit or 64-bit integer by 1.
Exchange	Exchanges two values (32-bit or 64-bit integers, or arbitrary types via a generic version). The exchange occurs by setting the memory of the first parameter to the value of the second parameter, and then the original value stored at the memory of the first parameter is returned from the method.
Increment	Increments a 32-bit or 64-bit integer by 1.

This atomicity is achieved by using a *synchronization mechanism*. A synchronization mechanism is a way for a thread to gain exclusive access to something (possibly one or more resources), locking out all other threads. When a thread is done with its work, it sends a signal essentially saying "I'm done" and letting other threads then obtain access to the shared resources.

One of these synchronization mechanisms is known as a *monitor*. Every object instance has a monitor associated with it. You can view a monitor as a token that only a single thread can own at any given time. If there are multiple threads attempting to gain access to a monitor, only the first thread that successfully requests it gets it. Other threads then line up, waiting for the first thread to release the monitor. The C# language provides a keyword, lock, that makes it easy to obtain a lock on an object's monitor.

If you need to control access to resources within a class, it's recommended you create a private object instance to use as a lock. This solves several problems with the design of the monitors in the CLR, including ensuring that the lock cannot be obtained by an outside class. If you were to obtain a lock on the current object instance via this, an outside class could also request a lock on the same instance. In practice, this looks like the following if you attempt to write a simple list (that uses an array internally). This is a simple list without error handling to illustrate how to use this synchronization functionality.

```
class ThreadSafeList
{
    private Object m_lock = new Object();
    private int[] listItems;
    private int count;
    public ThreadSafeList()
    {
        listItems = new int[100];
        count = 0;
    }
```

```
    public void Add(int num)
    {
        lock(m_lock)
        {
            // if list is full, allocate more space
            // otherwise, just add to end...
            listItems[count] = num;
            count++;
        }
    }
    public void RemoveAt(int index)
    {
        lock(m_lock)
        {
            for(int i=index; i<count; i++)
            {
                listItems[i] = listeItems[i+1];
            }
            count--;
        }
    }
}
```

Using the lock keyword ensures that only a single thread has access to the internals of the list (the listItems array and the count variable) at any given time. If you removed the lock requests and let several threads add items to and remove items from the list, it probably won't take long for something to go wrong, such as phantom values showing up in the list or the count variable not accurately reflecting the proper size of the list.

There are other synchronization mechanisms you can use in your code, such as AutoResetEvent. This class was used in Chapter 4 to create a synchronous socket. The AutoResetEvent class works by signaling. An instance of this class can either be signaled or not signaled. When not signaled, any thread that calls the Wait method of the AutoResetEvent class will block. Conceptually, the thread is waiting for a specific event to signal. An instance of AutoResetEvent is signaled when its Set method is called. Let's look at the ReceiveAsString method from the SynchronousSocket class from Chapter 3:

```
public string ReceiveAsString()
{
    if (!this.Connected)
    {
        throw new Exception("Not connected.");
    }
    SocketAsyncEventArgs asyncEventArgs = new SocketAsyncEventArgs();
    byte[] response = new byte[1024];
    asyncEventArgs.SetBuffer(response, 0, response.Length);
    asyncEventArgs.Completed +=
            new EventHandler<SocketAsyncEventArgs>(SocketOperationCompleted);
```

```
        AutoResetEvent receiveEvent = new AutoResetEvent(false);
        asyncEventArgs.UserToken = receiveEvent;
        _socket.ReceiveAsync(asyncEventArgs);
        receiveEvent.WaitOne();
        receiveEvent.Close();
        if (asyncEventArgs.SocketError == SocketError.Success)
        {
            return (Encoding.UTF8.GetString(asyncEventArgs.Buffer,
                        asyncEventArgs.Offset, asyncEventArgs.BytesTransferred));
        }
        else
        {
            throw this.Error;
        }
    }
```

The relevant part of this code includes creating AutoResetEvent (initially in the nonsignaled state, specified by passing false to the constructor), invoking the asynchronous receive method, and then blocking by waiting for the event to signal via WaitOne. The call to Close just cleans up this particular AutoResetEvent since it isn't needed beyond this single method call. The AutoResetEvent instance is passed to the method that acts as the callback for the receive operation via the UserToken property of SocketAsyncEventArgs. The callback method, SocketOperationCompleted, gets hold of the AutoResetEvent instance and signals it.

```
protected void SocketOperationCompleted(object sender, SocketAsyncEventArgs e)
{
    if (e.SocketError != SocketError.Success)
    {
        this.Error = new SocketException((int)e.SocketError);
    }
    ((AutoResetEvent)e.UserToken).Set();
}
```

Once signaled, the ReceiveAsString method can proceed, since it now has a result from the socket receive operation completing. Although this is an effective way to impose synchronous semantics on asynchronous operations, you should in general not take this approach without considering the design of the application. A synchronous socket can be useful for quick bursts of communication, but if you're implementing a file downloader via sockets, the user interface will completely block; therefore, you should use the standard asynchronous functionality of sockets.

Using Timers

Timing can be quite useful in applications, such as to execute timecode, influence animations (such as when a certain animation starts), or perform other application-specific functions, such as using a stage timer in a game. The two most useful timer classes in Silverlight are DispatcherTimer, a timer integrated with the dispatch queue, and Timer, from the System.Threading namespace. The major difference between these two timers is where the work method that occurs periodically is executed. The Timer class executes the work method on a separate thread, leaving the user interface responsive, but requiring use of the Dispatcher to change the user interface. The DispatcherTimer, however, does not have this restriction since it executes on the same thread. This makes it much easier to use. Figure 15-6 shows an interface used to experiment with both of these timers.

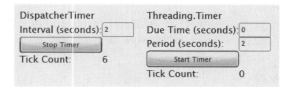

Figure 15-6. *DispatcherTimer and Timer class demonstrations*

Using the DispatcherTimer

The DispatcherTimer works by hooking its Tick event up to a method that will be called on a periodic basis. You specify how often the Tick event is raised by passing a TimeSpan to the DispatcherTimer constructor or by setting the Interval property to the TimeSpan. The timer is then started via the Start method and stopped via the Stop method. Here's code that counts to 20 in 1-second intervals, displaying each number on the user interface:

```
private int count = 0;
private void startTimer_Click(object sender, RoutedEventArgs e)
{
    DispatcherTimer timer = new DispatcherTimer();
    timer.Interval = new TimeSpan(0, 0, 1);
    timer.Tick += new EventHandler(timer_Tick);
    timer.Start();
}
void timer_Tick(object sender, EventArgs e)
{
    count++;
    outputText.Text = "Tick count: " + count;
    if (count == 20)
        ((DispatcherTimer)sender).Stop();
}
```

Using the System.Threading Timer

The Timer in the System.Threading namespace does basically the same thing, but the work (in the form of a callback method passed to Timer) is done on a thread from the thread pool. The method that does work on a periodic basis is specified as a parameter to the Timer constructor. There are five overloads of this constructor, each providing a different way to specify how often the work method is invoked. You can also optionally pass extra state information. The most important parameter to each constructor is TimerCallback, used to wrap the method that does the work. The dueTime parameter is used to specify delay before the timer starts, and the period parameter is used to specify delay between each subsequent invocation of the callback. If dueTime or period is set to infinite, each is effectively disabled (an infinite due time, for example, causes the timer to never start). A due time of zero causes the timer to start immediately, and a period of zero causes the work method to get invoked only once.

Timer(TimerCallback): Creates a timer with an infinite due time and infinite period, preventing the timer from invoking the callback. Use the Change method to set a new due time/period. The state object is the Timer itself.

Timer(TimerCallback, object state, Int32 dueTime, Int32 period): Creates a timer with a custom state object (useful for passing information to the work method), and a due time and period in milliseconds.

Timer(TimerCallback, object state, Int64 dueTime, Int64 period): Same as the Int32 version, but provides the ability to specify lengths of time that can't be represented in a 32-bit integer.

Timer(TimerCallback, object state, TimeSpan dueTime, TimeSpan period) method: Same as the Int32 version, but uses a TimeSpan to make it easier to specify lengths of time such as seconds or minutes.

Timer(TimerCallback, object state, UInt32 dueTime, UInt32 period): Same as the Int32 version, but instead uses unsigned integers to represent the due time and period.

■**Caution** Each time the Timer's period elapses, the work method passed to the TimerCallback is invoked. This work is then executed by a thread from the thread pool. If the work method takes longer to execute than the period, it is likely that the work method will be executed by two threads from the thread pool at the same time. You must ensure that the work method can tolerate this scenario. This can also happen if the threads in the pool are exhausted and the work method is queued multiple times, waiting for threads from the pool to become available.

There is only one useful method on the Timer class: Change. The Change method is used to change the due time and interval of the timer and has four overloads that match the four ways to specify due time and period in the constructor. The work method takes a single object parameter that corresponds to the state parameter passed to the constructor (or the Timer object itself if the first form of the constructor was used).

```
private void doSomething(object state)
{
    Dispatcher.BeginInvoke(
        delegate() {
            timerOutputText.Text =
                (Convert.ToInt32(timerOutputText.Text) + 1).ToString();
        });
}
```

Since the work method happens on a different thread, the `Dispatcher` must be used to make changes to the user interface. A button on the user interface is again hooked up to a method that starts/stops the timer:

```
private void timerButton_Click(object sender, RoutedEventArgs e)
{
    if (threadTimer != null)
    {
        threadTimer.Change(0, Timeout.Infinite);
        timerButton.Content = "Start Timer";
    }
    else
    {
        if (threadTimer != null)
            threadTimer.Change(Convert.ToInt32(dueTimeTextBox.Text) * 1000,
                               Convert.ToInt32(periodTextBox.Text) * 1000);
        else
            threadTimer = new Timer(new TimerCallback(doSomething), null,
                               Convert.ToInt32(dueTimeTextBox.Text) * 1000,
                               Convert.ToInt32(periodTextBox.Text) * 1000);
        timerButton.Content = "Stop Timer";
    }
}
```

You instruct the timer to stop by setting the period to `Timeout.Infinite`. The `Change` method is used to restart the timer also. This is the only way to interact with the `Timer` after it has been created, except for destroying it via `Dispose`.

Dynamically Loading Applications

Silverlight provides two mechanisms for dynamically loading applications. Assemblies can be stored outside an application's XAP file, downloaded on demand, and then loaded into the Silverlight environment via a tiny subset of the Reflection support from .NET. The other approach is to create or download XAML and add it to the visual tree. You can create fragments of XAML, stored in strings, and convert these to an object by using the `XamlReader.Load` method.

You saw the first approach in Chapter 13. You can download an assembly using `WebClient` and then pass the result stream to the `Load` method of `AssemblyPart` in order to get an `Assembly` object you can use:

```
AssemblyPart part = new AssemblyPart();
Assembly asm = part.Load(e.Result);
```

You can then use this assembly, such as for invoking `CreateInstance` to create instances of classes within the assembly. The other approach, using `XamlReader`, provides a mechanism to dynamically parse XAML at runtime and possibly add the resulting object (or tree of objects) to the user interface. Let's take a simple TextBlock stored in a XAML file in the web site (i.e., not distributed in the XAP) and then download and display it. The file contains a TextBlock by itself:

```
<TextBlock xmlns="http://schemas.microsoft.com/winfx/2006/xaml/presentation"
                  Text="Downloaded Fragment"
                  Margin="20" Foreground="Red" FontSize="16"/>
```

In order for this disembodied XAML to successfully parse via XamlReader.Load, it must meet the following criteria:

- It must be well formed. This should go without saying, but in the interest of being complete, the XAML must be well-formed XML and XAML. If an element name is misspelled or an end tag is missing, parsing will fail.

- It must have a single root element. Any XAML fragment can have only a single root element. It's easy to load a single TextBlock, but if you want to load a more complex tree of objects, they must be in a root element such as Canvas or Grid.

- The root element must specify the default XAML namescope. No matter what object you use for the root, you must add the xmlns, as shown in the preceding TextBlock. This provides the link between the XAML structure and the XAML fragment to the parser. You can specify other namescopes if there is a need.

We'll use WebClient to download this file. The DownloadStringCompleted event handler invokes XamlReader.Load to parse the downloaded file, cast it to the right class, and then add it to the user interface:

```
private void downloadFragmentButton_Click(object sender, RoutedEventArgs e)
{
    WebClient wc = new WebClient();
    wc.DownloadStringCompleted +=
        new DownloadStringCompletedEventHandler(wc_DownloadStringCompleted);
    wc.DownloadStringAsync(
        new Uri("/chapter14Web/XamlFragment.xaml", UriKind.Relative));
}
void wc_DownloadStringCompleted(object sender,
                                DownloadStringCompletedEventArgs e)
{
    TextBlock tb = (TextBlock)XamlReader.Load(e.Result);
    downloadedFragmentBorder.Child = tb;
}
```

Figure 15-7 shows what the downloaded fragment looks like after being added to the bottom Border control.

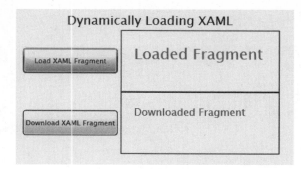

Figure 15-7. *Dynamically loaded XAML*

Summary

This chapter delved into the threading capabilities of Silverlight. Since .NET Framework is a back-end platform for Silverlight, the multithreading support is provided for the development of Silverlight-based RIAs. Although you can manually create and use threads, it's much better to either leverage the thread pool or use the BackgroundWorker class to do work on a thread other than the main application thread. You also saw two timers provided by Silverlight: the DispatcherTimer and the Timer from the System.Threading namespace. Finally, you learned how to parse XAML at runtime and even load it into the user interface.

With this chapter, you have completed your journey of getting how-to knowledge on the Silverlight technology platform. We hope that this book will be a great assistance to you as you gear up for using Silverlight 3 as a Rich Internet Application development platform.

We wish you good luck for your Silverlight journey; don't forget to send us e-mail at AskAshish@technologyopinion.com with your feedback and comments.

Index

DISCARDED
CONCORDIA UNIV. LIBRARY

You Need the Companion eBook

Your purchase of this book entitles you to buy the companion PDF-version eBook for only $10. Take the weightless companion with you anywhere.

We believe this Apress title will prove so indispensable that you'll want to carry it with you everywhere, which is why we are offering the companion eBook (in PDF format) for $10 to customers who purchase this book now. Convenient and fully searchable, the PDF version of any content-rich, page-heavy Apress book makes a valuable addition to your programming library. You can easily find and copy code—or perform examples by quickly toggling between instructions and the application. Even simultaneously tackling a donut, diet soda, and complex code becomes simplified with hands-free eBooks!

Once you purchase your book, getting the $10 companion eBook is simple:

❶ Visit **www.apress.com/promo/tendollars/**.

❷ Complete a basic registration form to receive a randomly generated question about this title.

❸ Answer the question correctly in 60 seconds, and you will receive a promotional code to redeem for the $10.00 eBook.

DISCARDED
CONCORDIA UNIV. LIBRARY
Apress®
THE EXPERT'S VOICE™

eBookshop

2855 TELEGRAPH AVENUE | SUITE 600 | BERKELEY, CA 94705

All Apress eBooks subject to copyright protection. No part may be reproduced or transmitted in any form or by any means, electronic or mechanical, including photocopying, recording, or by any information storage or retrieval system, without the prior written permission of the copyright owner and the publisher. The purchaser may print the work in full or in part for their own noncommercial use. The purchaser may place the eBook title on any of their personal computers for their own personal reading and reference.

CONCORDIA UNIVERSITY LIBRARIES
MONTREAL

Offer valid through 1/10.